A Higher Score, Guaranteed

This book is the product of hundreds of hours of test preparation and research, and represents the best system of preparation for the ACT Math and Science exams on the market. Therefore, we want to back that up with a guarantee. If you, the student, complete this book, and the preparation does not help to improve your score, we will happily refund your money. Send an email to support@theactsystem.com to make arrangements, which will require images of the completed book, the original sales receipt, ACT Math and Science scores before and after completing the book, and a written explanation.

All claims for refunds must be received within six months of original purchase.

The ACT Math and Science *System*

A step-by-step, first-things-first, systematized, secret-free, no gimmicks,

no tricks, no wasted time guide to the ACT Math and Science tests

Philip J Martin

Download Your *FREE ACT System* Cheat Sheets!

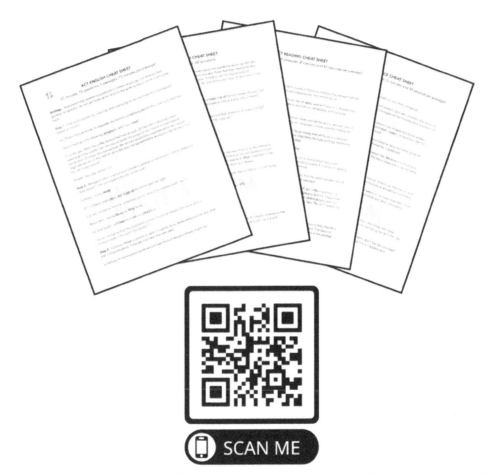

SCAN ME

Scan the QR code above to receive your free ACT System cheat sheets, yours to print and use in your ACT preparation!

ACT® is a registered trademark of ACT, Inc

Published by Test Prep by Step, LLC

For special group pricing, please email support@theactsystem.com

ISBN: 9798860416598

www.theactsystem.com

www.philipmartinact.com

Table of Contents

Introduction

Have you looked through your average ACT prep book lately? It looks and feels more like the instruction manual for running a factory than it does a test preparation book. Frankly, you don't need to memorize or read about the technical names of the various types of ACT questions, their categories, the psychology behind the questions, etc. That knowledge is good for behind the scenes, but for you, it's a waste.

Also, if I hear another book or teacher promise to give all of the "tips, tricks, and secrets" to succeed on the ACT I think I'll scream. You don't need "tips, tricks, and secrets;" phrases like that are gimmicks that, at least I think, are big on promise but short on return (mostly, they make for clickable titles of YouTube videos!). Not to mention, the ACT test makers are aware of each and every pattern and conceptions of patterns; as soon as it's circulated that "the shortest answer is almost always right," or whatever the case may be, the test makers will switch it up and defy the pattern. On the other hand, many other ACT books, instructors, and tutors are guilty of the sin of overanalyzing; this kind of instruction is so technical it borders on punishment. Teachers have to remember that they aren't training teenagers to work for the ACT one day, but rather to take the test to the best of their abilities.

My more than 1,000 hours of ACT classroom experience, on the other hand, have taught me that you, the student, need three things, especially when it comes to the ACT Math and Science tests: content knowledge (especially in ACT Math), strategy, and skills, all reinforced by guided practice. This book will get you there without overanalyzing or appealing to cheap shortcuts.

Additionally, anxiety is already high enough, so why are so many students preparing for the ACT Math test (for example) by memorizing unnecessary formulas (or learning math out of order of importance)? Think about this: here are three formulas high school students will come across: the formula of a circle, the distance formula, and the Pythagorean Theorem. Out of these three, can you tell me which of them is necessary for every ACT Math test, which is less necessary (meaning, would be needed on some, but not all, ACT Math tests), and which of them is unnecessary? That is the kind of research-based preparation that students need.

The purpose of this book is clear: to focus your attention on the content, skills, and strategies *most needed in ACT Math and Science to raise your scores*, and to do so *one at a time*. The closer a Step is to Step 1, the more important (meaning, the more likely it is to raise your score if mastered); the further a Step is away from Step 1, the less important (and by less important, I simply mean less likely to be tested on ACT day). For example, you won't find the formula for a circle or the distance formula anywhere near Step 1 of the ACT Math section! As a Step is learned, it is continually refreshed throughout the book so as not to be forgotten, but rather built upon. This preparation culminates in two full-length practice tests for both Math and Science (the final Step!).

How to Use This Book

Use of this book is simple. Review the Step, then work your way through the practice that follows. The practice contains questions that reflect the current Step as well as previous Steps when applicable. Why not simply focus on this current Step's material only? Because again, we want to treat the ACT Math and Science tests as cumulative, testing both skills (especially in ACT Science) and content (especially in ACT Math), and want to continually build upon the most important and work our way to least. This kind of guided *practice* (as opposed to blindly studying) will reveal specific problem areas, thus heightening your focus.

In addition, the vast majority of the practice offered to you in this book is within the context of full-length passages. This is to train your mind to pay attention for that span of time and to become used to the real-life length of ACT Math tests and Science passages. Following each practice section you will find a list of answers. However, the back of the book contains a written explanation for each and every question; these explanations review rules and strategy while giving the reasons behind each correct and incorrect answer.

In a time crunch? Don't have time to use this entire book from start to finish? In that case, complete as many steps as possible, then skip ahead to the two practice tests in Step 6 for both the ACT Math and Science tests.

The ACT Math *System*

Six Steps to ACT Math Perfection

How to Use This Section of the Book

Use of this section of *The ACT System* book is simple. Review the Step, then work your way through the practice that follows. The book is laid out to ensure that you put first-things-first, thus it is crucial to begin at the beginning.

In addition, most of the practice offered to you in *The ACT Math System* is within the context of full-length passages (there are 3 full-length tests of 180 problems in this format). This is to train your mind to pay attention for that span of time and to become used to the real-life length of ACT Math passages. The remaining questions follow specific content lessons, but are formatted exactly like the ACT Math test (even the practice questions are formatted like the actual ACT with the questions on the left and space on the right hand side of the page for you to use like scratch paper). Following each practice section, you will find a list of answers. However, the back of the book contains a written explanation for each and every question; these explanations review rules and strategy while explaining the proper way (or ways, if there are multiple strategies to use) to solve the problem.

The ACT Math Test - Overview and Basics

The ACT Math Test is the second of four and is preceded by English, then followed by Reading and Science, respectively. The ACT Math test is designed to test your ability to recall learned material from middle and high school, to apply learned material in a variety of situations, and to think logically and cohesively.

The ACT Math test is the longest of all four subject tests. You are given 60 minutes to answer 60 questions that test your knowledge and abilities across a wide-range of math topics. This ranges from pre-

Algebra concepts such as calculating percentages and mean, median, and mode to concepts in Trigonometry like recognizing changes in the graphs of sine and cosine….and everything in between.

As the test moves along, the questions generally increase in difficulty. This isn't linear. In other words, it isn't guaranteed that question 10 is more difficult than question 9 or 8, or that question 59 is more difficult than question 58 or 57. This means that this is a good time to talk about…

Pacing

The best way to think about the increase in difficulty is like this: questions 1-20 are the easiest block of questions on the test, questions 21-40 are of middle difficulty, and questions 41-60 are the most challenging on the test. Number 58 might be of more medium difficulty, for example, but as a whole, the final third that it is in is the most difficult group.

Your knowledge of this increase in difficulty is very important for this reason: pacing (more on this and strategy in Step 1). Though it may seem that you should allocate one minute for each question (you are given 60 minutes for 60 questions, after all), that's really not accurate. You should be spending roughly 15 minutes *total* on questions 1-20, 20 minutes *total* on questions 21-40, and 25 minutes *total* on the harder group, questions 41-60.

Mindset

The ACT Math test is an easy test to get depressed about because there are going to be math concepts that you don't remember and definitions that you've forgotten. Again, that's the purpose of this book: to increase your knowledge and familiarity of a wide range of math topics, beginning with the ACT Math that you *have to know*, followed by the math that is *good to know*.

However, just because you miss or can't remember a bunch of questions, don't sweat it during the test. Again, a 31 out of 60 in school would be a failing grade, but on the ACT that score would earn you a 22.

Question Types

In general, there are three or four types of ACT Math questions.

- First, there are questions that give you a diagram or shape or describe some kind of diagram or shape. Of course, if a diagram or shape is being described in words, *draw it out!* Failing to do so will lead to simple mistakes.

- Second, there are problems that give you a math question within some sort of story or real life example. There is a lesson in Step 3 about this kind of question since it is so common, so more on that later!

- Third, there are problems that, like in school, simply test your math abilities without either of the above. You'll find examples of this type throughout the book, but in order of importance.

- Lastly, there are some problems that I'd call concept problems in which it won't matter how much time you dedicate to them: either you know them or you don't. Again, the more important, the earlier it will appear in the book.

There are plenty of examples of all four forthcoming in this book!

Calculator Policy

The ACT is always changing its calculator policy to exclude more and more newer, very advanced kinds of calculators. Graphing calculators are allowed, including the standard TI-84; in general, if it's allowed in math class, it's allowed on the ACT. See the ACT's website for more information if you have a specific question about a particular kind of calculator. However, I do think that too many students think, "If I don't have a graphing calculator, I'm going to do terribly!" However, I can only *really* think of one possible (not even guaranteed to be on the test) ACT Math question that this could be true about (and even then, there are other, possibly simpler ways to solve it).

STEP 1

The ACT Math Two Pass Strategy

ACT Math Strategy
60 Minutes, 60 Questions

If you've taken the ACT before, there is a good chance you had the following common experience. When the proctor says, "You may begin," you start the ACT Math test at number one; then, when you're finished with that one, you move on to number two; then, when you're finished with this problem, you move on to number three, and so on.

Then, sometime around question 45 or 50, you hear the proctor shout out, "5 minutes remaining."

You now rush to answer questions that maybe you can get with time that's left and guess on a bunch and kind of go back and glance over questions that you wanted to return to if there was time. Then, during the break that follows the math test you start to question your life choices because you feel so flustered.

There is a much better, calmer, and simpler way to go through the ACT Math test. Traditionally, it is called the *Two Pass Strategy*. It is easy to implement, and I guarantee you are already familiar with the basic idea. I remember a few years ago a student who was in one of my ACT classes sought me out to say that his math score increased 4 or 5 points by simply putting the following strategy into effect (I think he would have done better if he had had a book like this one to order his content knowledge, but I digress…).

Here is the basic idea: for our purposes, there are **three types** of ACT Math questions.

First, there are questions you can probably get right in about a minute or less. For the *Two Pass Strategy*, simply answer these questions right away. My guess is that, for the average student, this is probably 30-40 of the 60 questions. For more advanced students, maybe this is 45-50 out of 60.

Second, there are questions that you *kind of* recognize; maybe you know what's being asked, but you can't quite put your finger on it. In other words, these questions would probably take you over a minute to solve or boil down to an educated guess. As you can hopefully see, questions in this category might take some time, and so you don't want to use up all of it at first. Simply circle these questions, and with spare time at the end, come back to them! My guess is that, for the average student, there are probably 15 of these kinds of questions on the ACT Math test.

Third, there are questions that test concepts in math that you have never heard or have completely left your mind. No matter how much time you spend on these questions, there is a 0% chance that you could come up with the correct answer on your own. For these questions, just *guess*, and save yourself the time. I'd say that, for the average student, there are roughly 5 of these on any given ACT Math test.

This isn't a novel concept; I would bet that you have circled and skipped questions on final exams or other important tests looking to come back to them with spare time at the end. The difference is that if you employ this strategy on ACT Math, you are likely to circle and skip a lot of them. That's OK; you aren't neglecting them. You will return to them with all of the time you have stockpiled.

But why? Why do all this circling and skipping? In the previous lesson I stressed that the first 20 math problems are the easiest third, the middle 20 of middle difficulty, and the final 20 math problems are the most difficult.

However, like I also said, that does NOT mean that number 59 is the 2nd most difficult math problem, or that number 55 is the 6th most difficult math problem, or that number 52 is the 9th most difficult problem, or that 50 is the 11th most difficult problem, or that 47 is the 14th most difficult problem. If these 5 problems are problems that you could get right in a minute or less, wouldn't it be a shame if you didn't give yourself a chance to get to them? With the Two Pass Strategy, you give yourself a chance at them.

In fact, let me break down for you what could happen if you guess on 5 questions you could get right if you simply gave yourself a chance.

If you were to guess on those 5 problems, on average you would get only 1 correct (since in ACT Math, unlike the other three ACT tests, there are 5 answer choices; more on that later). However, if you save yourself time to work them well, and if you get all 5 correct, you could raise your ACT Math score from an 18 to a 21, from a 21 to a 24, or a 27 to a 30. That bump in Math will more than likely raise your overall ACT score by 1 point.

To sum up, the best ACT Math strategy requires you to do one of three things with each math question: answer it, circle it, or guess. This will give you a chance to answer each question correctly. No more frantic guessing when the proctor shouts out "5 minutes remaining!"

You'll have 3 opportunities to apply this strategy to a full-length practice test in this book.

STEP 2

The Four ACT Math Mini-Strategies

There is no doubt that mastering your time (correct pacing on early questions, circling and skipping with the *Two Pass Strategy* as already discussed, etc.) is **THE** ACT Math strategy. However, there are what I like to call *mini-strategies* that can help you get questions correct along the way (and definitely save you time as well!). Most ACT tutors identify three of these strategies, but I add a fourth regarding the calculator that is a crucial time-saver and represents a mindset you must have about the ACT Math test.

Mini-Strategy #1: Backsolving

The first such strategy is called *Backsolving*. You may have noticed that each ACT Math question features not 4, but 5 options. This makes it unique; every question on every other test only has options A/B/C/D and F/G/H/J, but the math test adds a fifth option for each question: A/B/C/D/**E** or F/G/H/J/**K**. This isn't an accident, and it isn't arbitrary. It seems unfair; most students who I've taught think it's just another way for the ACT (and life as a whole) to make things unnecessarily harder.

The reason for the 5 answer choices, however, is not to make your life more miserable, but rather because of the math strategy that I want to teach you today. *Backsolving* simply means instead of solving the math problem in front of you forwards like you would on a typical math quiz, test, or homework assignment at school, you try out each of the answers one at a time to see which one is the correct answer.

In other words, we are taking advantage of the fact that this is a multiple choice test, and out of the 5 answer choices sitting in front of you, one of them has to work. In some situations, why not just try them out one at a time? Let's analyze the following question using the *Backsolving* strategy to show you how it's done!

ex. A restaurant wants its 5 entrees to average a price of $35.
If the first 4 meals cost $29, $55, $39, and $32, what must the price of the fifth meal be?

   A. $15
   B. $20
   C. $27
   D. $30
   E. $35

Traditionally, you would solve this problem by setting up an equation with one missing variable, x, and isolate the x on one side of the equation to solve. Doing that here would also be relatively simple. However, my purpose is simply to walk you through how *Backsolving* works. To use this mini-strategy, choose one of the answer choices and simply see if it is correct. You can begin with choice A and move down, or with choice E and move up, or even better, you can begin with choice C to determine if you need a bigger number and move down or a smaller number and move up. This works since most of the time ACT Math answers are listed in numerical (usually ascending, though sometimes descending) order.

Let's try C: $27. When I add $27 to the other 4 meal prices and divide by 5 (the total meals) I get an average of $36.40. That is too high, so I need a lower meal price. Let's now try B: $20. When I add $20 to the other 4 meal prices and divide by 5, I get an average of $35…that's it!

My purpose in creating this problem was not to make a difficult problem (it is obviously not too difficult!) but to illustrate the basics of *Backsolving*, a strategy that is beneficial in two ways: first, it can often save you precious time, and second, it can also be used in problems in which the mathematics is more difficult.

Here are three additional example questions. Give them a shot yourself first, and then see if you can figure out just how the questions can be solved backwards: trying out each answer choice one at a time. Explanations for each of these three examples can be found at the back of the book, which include detailed explanations for how *Backsolving* can be utilized for each one.

1. Sophie would like to average 30 points scored per game over the first five basketball games of her senior season. In her first four games, Sophie scored 19, 27, 34, and 27 points, respectively. How many points must Sophie score in her next game to achieve her goal of averaging 30 points per game?

   A. 30
   B. 33
   C. 34
   D. 43
   E. 44

2. Which of the following (x, y) pairs is a solution for the equation $y + \dfrac{1}{2}x = 3$?

F. $(-4, 5)$
G. $(1.5, 0)$
H. $(0, -3)$
J. $(0.5, 4)$
K. $(-2, 2)$

3. A certain manufacturing plant produces a set amount of baseball bats every year. It is found, upon inspection, that 1 out of every 60 bats produced is considered damaged. Additionally, it is found that 3 out of every 4 damaged bats is considered *permanently* damaged and cannot be repaired. If the plant's manufacturing produces 3,150 baseball bats that are *permanently* damaged every year, then how many baseball bats are produced each year?

A. 14,175
B. 25,200
C. 141,750
D. 252,000
E. 567,000

Mini-Strategy #2: Picking Numbers

The second such strategy is called *Picking Numbers*, which involves choosing numbers (such as pretending a variable like x to be equal to 5) to apply to a question and its answers, then looking for a match. Usually these kinds of questions involve variables, taking advantage of the fact that, of the 5 choices, one of them must be correct. You plug the numbers you've picked into the question, then you apply the same numbers to the answers, and if the values match up, you've found the correct answer.

Let's analyze the following question using *Picking Numbers* simply to illustrate the strategy:

2. What is the product of the expressions $(3x - 4)$ and $(2x + 0.5)$?

    F. $6x^2 - 6.5x - 2$
    G. $6x^2 - 9.5x - 2$
    H. $6x^2 - 8x + 2$
    J. $5x^2 + 10.5x - 3.5$
    K. $5x^2 + 10.5x - 4.5$

Now, let's just pretend like you don't know how to multiply these two expressions (which, if you did, would be the fastest way to solve this particular problem). What to do? Well, notice that the question and the answers both have the variable x. If I choose a value for x and plug it into both the question's expressions and its answers, I will get the same number value. Let's pretend then that $x = 4$ (in *Picking Numbers*, avoid $x = 0$, $x = 1$, and $x = -1$). When I plug $x = 4$ into both of the question's expressions, I now am looking for the product of $(3x - 4) = (3 \cdot 4 - 4) = (12 - 4) = 8$ and $(2x + 0.5) = (2 \cdot 4 + 0.5) = (8 + 0.5) = 8.5$. Well, $8 \times 8.5 = 68$. Now, apply $x = 4$ to each answer choice and find which also equals 68.

Start with F: $6x^2 - 6.5x - 2 = 6(4^2) - 6.5(4) - 2 = 96 - 26 - 2 = 68$, which matches! F is correct!

Let's take a look at a few more examples where this strategy can work so that you can understand this strategy well. Most of these involve variables (like x or y or a or b, etc.), as you can see, but one does not.

Just like the *Backsolving* examples, try them out yourself first, then see the *Picking Numbers* explanations that can be found in the back of the book for a more detailed analysis.

4. Which of the following is equivalent to
$(\dfrac{x^2 - 5x - 6}{x + 1}) + x + 1$?

   F. $x - 5$

   G. $2x - 5$

   H. $x^2 - 5x - 6$

   J. $x^2 - 4x - 5$

   K. $\dfrac{(2x - 5)}{(x + 1)}$

5. What is the average of the expressions $3a^2 - 7$, $2a^2 + 1$, $-4a^2 + 12$, and $3a^2 - 2$?

   A. $-a^2 + 1$

   B. $\dfrac{1}{2}a^2 + 1$

   C. $a^2 + \dfrac{1}{2}$

   D. $-a^2 + \dfrac{1}{2}$

   E. $a^2 + 1$

6. Between Monday and Tuesday, the number of people in line to buy ice cream at a brand new ice cream store increased by 35%. Between Tuesday and Wednesday, the number of people in line increased by an additional 40%. What was the combined percent increase of people in line to buy ice cream between Monday and Wednesday ?

   F.   40%
   G.   76%
   H.   85%
   J.   89%
   K.   99%

7. If a, b, c, and d are all positive real numbers and if $a^{-2} > b^{-2} > c^{-2} > d^{-2}$, then which of the following numbers has the least value ?

   A. a
   B. b
   C. c
   D. d
   E.   Cannot be determined from the given information

Mini-Strategy #3: Drawn to Scale

Perhaps I've said already that it is a waste of time for you to read the directions before any of the four ACT tests, and that is absolutely true. There is one line in one of the tests however, the ACT Math test, that is worth mentioning. Here is what it says: "Illustrative figures are NOT necessarily drawn to scale."

What does that mean? That means that, according to the ACT's own directions, you the student can't assume that just because one line is 5 units long, and a second line looks to be exactly twice its size, it is exactly or just about twice its size. Or, if an angle looks to be around 45 degrees, you the student can't assume that it is somewhere around 45 degrees.

The reason the ACT is saying this is not because it's true, but to cover their tracks in case something isn't drawn to scale. Thus, the third ACT Math mini-strategy worth a lesson is this: although the ACT *says* that figures are not drawn to scale, in reality *they are*. If a line *looks* to be about 7 units long, it *is* about 7 units long. If an angle *looks* to be obtuse, it *is* obtuse.

Let's say the following diagram was put on an ACT test and you were asked, based on a lot of factors, to find the length of segment $\overline{DE}$.

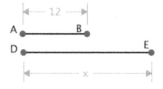

It could be that this segment is the side of a larger shape, like the leg of a triangle, or it could be that it is a piece of a larger line segment. No matter what, if you know that segment $\overline{AB}$ is 12, and can't figure out the math do determine the length of $\overline{DE}$, then you can at least remember that segments like this are actually drawn to scale. If $\overline{AB}$ is 12, you can reasonably determine that $\overline{DE}$ is somewhere between 22 and 26. If you want to be even more accurate, then use the side of your answer sheet like a ruler; put your answer sheet up against the first segment, mark it as "12," then compare it to the segment you don't know to determine an approximate length.

We can use the same kind of thinking with angles. No matter what the question stem tells you about this triangle below, let's assume that you simply can't determine the math behind how to figure out the measure of angle Θ. At a minimum, however, we *can* determine a few things about it. Although the ACT tells us that this figure is not necessarily drawn to scale, we can know for certain that *it is*. Thus, we know right off the bat that it is an obtuse angle. If we draw a 90 degree angle and a 135 degree angle on top of it, we might be able to figure out that it's somewhere between the two. It's possible that this kind of thinking can accelerate achieving of the correct answer.

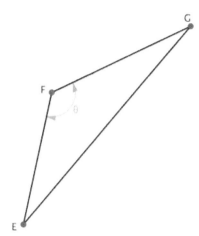

Solve the problem that follows and see if you can determine the correct answer by simply employing the *Drawn to Scale* mini-strategy; you might be surprised at just how often it can help you achieve a correct answer on the actual ACT Math test!

8. In parallelogram *ABCD* shown below, points *F*, *D*, *C*, and *E* form a straight line. Given the angle measures as shown in the figure, what is the measure of ∠*ACB* ?

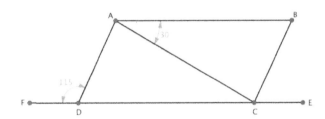

    F.   30°
    G. 45°
    H. 85°
    J.   115°
    K. 145°

Mini-Strategy #4: The Calculator

This fourth strategy is the reminder you absolutely need before the ACT Math test. It needs to be restated: use your calculator to save yourself precious time! Don't do on paper what can be done in a fraction of the time on the calculator! Think about a math problem that asks you to add a bunch of fractions, for example, like this: $\frac{2}{7} + \frac{4}{23} + \frac{5}{111} = ?$

Here's the problem: you've been trained probably since grade school that in order to solve this problem, you must first find a common denominator, then add the terms, then simplify the final result. I have no idea what such a common denominator might be, since I just made up this problem while typing, but finding it might have been your first instinct, too. Sure enough, all of the answer choices will be in fraction form as well, let's say, further making it seem like I would need to find the common denominator of 7, 23, and 111. Well I know what I am *not doing*: finding a common denominator. Why?

There is this amazing thing that can solve this problem in a matter of seconds: *the calculator!* No matter what type you have, you can type this into it: $(2 \div 7) + (4 \div 23) + (5 \div 111) =$

Sure enough, this comes out to equal to 0.505 when rounded to the nearest thousandths place. This is where a bit of *Backsolving* comes in: try out each answer choice in the calculator too until you get a decimal equivalent that matches. *Voila!* The math problem that took you 4 minutes to solve in Algebra I is now reduced to one that takes 20 seconds thanks to the calculator! No fancy calculator needed, either; you don't need to be able to demand from your calculator an answer in the form of a fraction. Just match the decimal equivalents.

Again, on the ACT, there is no partial credit for showing your work. If anything, there is *less* credit for showing your work when you don't have to, since this will cost you precious time!

Try this out on the following two examples; see if you can use the calculator straight through.

9. What is $\dfrac{4}{17} + \dfrac{1}{2} + \dfrac{1}{68}$?

   A. $\dfrac{6}{17}$

   B. $\dfrac{1}{3}$

   C. $\dfrac{25}{34}$

   D. $\dfrac{3}{4}$

   E. $\dfrac{7}{9}$

10. Which of the following inequalities orders the numbers

    $0.3, \dfrac{1}{3}$, and 0.04 from greatest to least?

   F. $0.3 > \dfrac{1}{3} > 0.04$

   G. $\dfrac{1}{3} > 0.3 > 0.04$

   H. $0.04 > \dfrac{1}{3} > 0.3$

   J. $0.04 > 0.3 > \dfrac{1}{3}$

   K. $0.3 > 0.04 > \dfrac{1}{3}$

Step 2 Correct Answers

Backsolving:
1: D
2: F
3: D

Picking Numbers:
4: G
5: E
6: J
7: A

Drawn to Scale:
8: H

The Calculator:
9: D
10: G

Mini-Strategies Practice answer explanations begin on page 272.

STEP 3

ACT Math Have to Know

ACT Math Have to Know Introduction

I recently read an article online listing something like a dozen math concepts you need to know and practice to perform well on the ACT. I noticed right away, however, that whoever wrote this article did *not* do their homework over the actual ACT test because the article prioritized a few math concepts that really aren't asked about that often on the ACT itself.

I have spent hours and hours (and hours and hours…) analyzing ACT Math tests, cataloging the types of math knowledge and abilities that are most important or asked about, and those that are least important or asked about. The lessons that follow are broken up into two categories: *Have to Know* (Steps 3 and 4) and *Good to Know* (Step 5). *Have to Know* means that, beyond a doubt, multiple ACT Math questions test this ability or knowledge, even if only as one step among a few to get a question correct. It is crucial that you understand the *Have to Know* concepts first. *Good to Know* means that it is very likely that you will have at least one ACT Math question testing this topic or ability, though it's not guaranteed.

This doesn't mean that I'll cover every basic concept in math. I'm taking it for granted that you know how to graph (that you know what the (*x, y*) coordinate plane is, that the origin is at (0, 0), that to graph point (2, 5) means you move two to the right then up 5, etc.) and that you know how to add, multiply, divide, and subtract, and that you know how to find the square root of a number (among other basics).

There's a third category that I'm not getting into with its own series of lessons, and I'm calling that category *Possibly Might Have to Know*, which consists of math concepts that you are very unlikely to see on the average ACT Math test. If you are near a 36 in ACT Math, then I'd recommend pouring over ACT Math practice tests in search of questions you do not know as one approach to bumping up that final point or two. For the rest of us, let's begin with what's most important and make our way. However, I'm ***not*** going to ignore these types of questions completely; I'll sprinkle as many of these little *Possibly Might Have to Know* topics as I can into the example questions as we go.

Have to Know #1: Writing Expressions/Equations from Word Problems

An added difficulty to the ACT Math test is that *many* of the math problems are wrapped up in little stories. It could be a story of how Roberta wanted to purchase 10 different gift cards for her 10 friends, or about how Timothy is walking at a rate of 3 MPH down the road to his aunt's house. These problems get a name; they're called *modeling* problems because they attempt to "model" a real life example (though I can't imagine it is terribly realistic to find nearly $10 in change on the ground on your walk home from school). You'll read that I'll call them either modeling problems or story problems.

One of the top two or three ACT skills is your ability to: 1) read a modeling problem, and 2) translate the story into an actual math problem, most likely an Algebra problem. If you're having difficulty with these problems, keep in mind that the actual question, aka what the question is requiring of you, is always the last sentence of the paragraph. Many students who struggle here, therefore, find it helpful to read the last sentence (the actual question) first or to reread it to make sure they get it. Here are a few examples to try:

1. Cliff wants to have a 150 foot fence installed around his pool and deck area. Baldwin Fence, Inc. charges a $600 fee, plus a set amount per foot of fence. Baldwin Fence, Inc. has given Cliff an estimate of $1,950 to install the fence around his pool and deck area. What is the set amount the company will charge per foot of fence?

    A. $4.00
    B. $9.00
    C. $12.25
    D. $13.00
    E. $17.00

2. A 4-foot-by-7-foot white board was installed on the 10-foot-by-9-foot wall of Mrs. Thomas's English classroom. What is the area, in square feet, of the part of the wall that is not covered by the white board?

    F. 28
    G. 62
    H. 72
    J. 88
    K. 90

3. Horatio reads online that, in order to make a very strong cup of coffee, he needs to drip $\frac{2}{3}$ cups of water over $1\frac{1}{4}$ tablespoons of coffee grounds. Horatio measures that his coffee mug can hold $2\frac{1}{2}$ cups of water without spilling. If Horatio uses the same ratio of water to coffee grounds as called for by the instructions he found on the internet, then how many tablespoons of coffee grounds will he need to use?

A. $2\frac{1}{12}$

B. $4\frac{11}{16}$

C. $4\frac{3}{4}$

D. $5\frac{1}{3}$

E. $5\frac{31}{32}$

4. Bernard has $1,200 invested in Stock A, and his sister Kathleen has $1,230 invested in Stock B. It is projected that Stock A will increase by $1 in value every day and that Stock B will increase by $0.50 in value every day. If projections are accurate, in about how many days will the two investments be valued at the same amount?

F. 15
G. 30
H. 40
J. 55
K. 60

Have to Know #2: Simplifying Expressions and Order of Operations

When I taught Algebra I, I remember giving my students countless problems in which they had to simplify expressions. Sometimes this involved negative exponents, and sometimes it involved going through the order of operations and then adding like terms when possible. Skills like this are extremely important for the ACT, but you have an advantage that my students didn't: *Picking Numbers*.

Many students have memorized an acronym to help them remember the order of operations: PEMDAS, which stands for: Parentheses, Exponents, Multiplication, Division, Addition, and Subtraction. For our purposes, let's just remember this rule: be really careful when you have to simplify! Careless mistakes are more likely to cost students questions than a failure to memorize PEMDAS ever would.

Before I get to a few examples, I will say that these examples feature a few ideas that are good to review in math, though in regards to the ACT itself they don't need their own separate lesson. These are: multiplying variables with exponents, what to do with negative exponents, raising exponents to an additional power, how to divide one fraction by another, and factoring trinomials.

5. Which of the following expressions is equivalent to $y(6 - y) - y(y + 9)$?

   A. $-2y^2 - 3y$
   B. $2y - 3y^2$
   C. $-y^2 + y - 45$
   D. $3y^2 + 2y$
   E. $-y^2 - 9y$

6. If x and y are positive real numbers, which of the following expressions is equivalent to $\dfrac{(3x^{-2}\sqrt{y})^4}{x^2y^{-5}}$?

F. $81y^7$

G. $\dfrac{27y^7}{x^4}$

H. $\dfrac{81}{x^7y^3}$

J. $\dfrac{3y^4}{x^6}$

K. $\dfrac{81y^7}{x^{10}}$

7. Which of the following expressions is equivalent to $\dfrac{\frac{a}{4}+\frac{1}{3}}{\frac{1}{2}-\frac{1}{3}}$?

A. $\dfrac{3a+4}{2}$

B. $\dfrac{a+6}{5}$

C. $\dfrac{2a+3}{2}$

D. $\dfrac{a-1}{2}$

E. $\dfrac{a}{2}$

8. Which of the following expressions is equivalent to $\dfrac{(x^2+5x+4)(x-8)}{(x^2-7x-8)(x+2)}$?

F. $\dfrac{x+8}{x-2}$

G. $\dfrac{2x+4}{x-8}$

H. $\dfrac{x+4}{x+2}$

J. $\dfrac{x+5}{x-2}$

K. 2

Have to Know #3: Mean, Median, Mode, and Range

Mean, median, mode, and range are math vocabulary words that you have probably heard before, but the last time you really learned them as a group together was probably a long time ago. The words have probably come up in your math class, but the memory of their definitions could have, by now, seemingly melted away.

However, in my research of ACT Math tests, I was surprised at just how often the terms are used (especially the first three: mean/median/mode). Before we get to some practice problems (which, like the last lesson, feature some small ACT Math concepts that don't deserve their own lesson), let's first review the meaning of mean, median, mode, and range.

To find any of these three values, you must have a set list of numbers (often called a number set), something like this: {2, 3, 3, 5, 6, 8, 9, 9, 9, 9, 12, 21}.

Mean - this word simply means average. It's as simple as that. In our set list of numbers here, adding all the terms together is 96, then divided by the total number of items is 96/12, which gives us an average, or mean, of 8. While there are a lot of questions that ask you for the average of a set of numbers, sometimes they may replace the word with "mean" instead.

Median - this number refers to the number that is in the middle of the number line. In our list here, the middle number would be between two numbers because we have an even number (12) of items in the list. In this case, the value would fall between the sixth term in the list and the seventh term in the list. Because the 6th term is 8 and the 7th term is 9, we average the two and find that the median of this number line is 8.5. In an odd amount of numbers, like in {1, 3, 6}, the median is simply the middle term.

Mode - the mode is the number that appears in the list most often. In our example, there are four 9's, which makes 9 the mode. If two numbers are tied, they are both the mode.

<u>Range</u> - lastly, we have the range, which is the difference between the greatest number and the least number. In our number set, the greatest number is 21 and the least is 2. Thus, the range is $21 - 2$, or 19.

Now finally for some example questions based on recent ACT's:

9. To increase the mean of 5 numbers by 5, by how much would the sum of the 5 numbers have to increase?

   A. $\dfrac{5}{3}$

   B. 1

   C. $\dfrac{3}{5}$

   D. 10

   E. 25

10. The product of the mean and the median of each factor of 12 listed in numerical order falls between which two whole numbers?

   F. 0 and 1
   G. 1 and 2
   H. 8 and 9
   J. 11 and 12
   K. 16 and 17

11. The city of Brackton holds a dinner celebrating the achievements of local artists, and a table at the front is reserved for writers. Author A is seated first and has written 1 novel. Author B is seated second and has written 3 novels. Author C is seated third and has written 2 novels. Author D is seated fourth and has written 1 novel. After dinner begins, Author E, who has written 21 novels, arrives late and is seated in the fifth seat at the authors' table. If it can be determined, which of the following statistics was *least* changed by the arrival of Author E.

   A. Mean
   B. Median
   C. Mode
   D. Range
   E. Cannot be determined from the given information

12. Dominic earns tips in the amount of $14, $15, $11, $22, and $15 in his first five nights as a waiter. Solving which of the following equations for t gives the amount of tips he needs to earn on his sixth night working to average exactly $16 in tips across the six nights?

F. $\dfrac{t + 77}{6} = \dfrac{77}{96}$

G. $\dfrac{t + 77}{5} = 96$

H. $\dfrac{77}{6} + t = 16$

J. $\dfrac{77}{5} + t = 96$

K. $\dfrac{t + 77}{6} = 16$

Have to Know #4: Higher Algebra

Don't let the title of this lesson scare you! *Higher Algebra* doesn't mean it's higher than you; it simply means that it might be a tad more difficult than finding the value of one missing variable in an equation. I spoke before about how the ACT Math test can essentially be broken up into thirds: the first 20 problems are the easiest block, the middle 20 are of medium difficulty, and the last 20 (#'s 41-60) are the most difficult on the test. These are the kinds of questions that are more likely to be found among number 30 through 60. Oftentimes, like what we've discussed before, these problems are wrapped up in modeling or story problems, other times, they are more straightforward.

Let's look through a handful of examples, all of which are important, as these kinds of questions are among the most asked in the ACT Math test. Use this as an opportunity to check those *Higher Algebra* skills:

13. Which of the following inequalities is equivalent to $-3y - 9x > 3x - 6$?

    A. $y > -4x + 2$
    B. $y < -4x + 2$
    C. $y > 4x + 2$
    D. $y < 18x - 6$
    E. $y > 18x + 6$

14. At Caffeine King, a local coffee shop, there are on average 4 bagels remaining in the display case by 11:00 AM. The probability, P, that exactly b bagels are still in the case by 11:00 AM can be modeled by the equation $P = \dfrac{4^b e^{-4}}{4!}$. Given that $e^{-4} = 0.075$, which of the following values is closest to the probability that exactly 3 bagels are in the case at 11:00 AM?

    F.   0.15
    G.   0.17
    H.   0.20
    J.   0.40
    K.   0.52

15. Given that complex numbers consist of a real and imaginary dimension, and that $i^2 = -1$, then $(i + 1)(i - 4)(i + 3) = ?$

- **A.** $14i$
- **B.** $-6i - 6$
- **C.** $6i + 6$
- **D.** $-14i - 18$
- **E.** $-14i - 12$

16. Whenever a and b are positive integers such that $16^a = (\sqrt{2})^b$, what is the value of $\frac{a}{b}$?

- **F.** $\frac{1}{8}$
- **G.** $\frac{1}{4}$
- **H.** $\frac{1}{2}$
- **J.** 4
- **K.** 8

17. The city of Cliffside is considering the purchase of a parcel of triangle-shaped land near the edge of town. The length of one side of the parcel, as shown in the image, is 9 miles. What is the perimeter of the entire parcel of land, rounded to the nearest mile?

(Note: the Law of Sines states that the sine of an angle divided by its opposite side is equal to the sine of another angle divided by its opposite side. It can be expressed in the following form: $\frac{sin(a)}{A} = \frac{sin(b)}{B}$).

- **A.** 24
- **B.** 28
- **C.** 29
- **D.** 31
- **E.** 33

18. A store displays 12 mannequin heads that can hold up to 4 items for sale (hats, scarves, sunglasses, and earmuffs). If there are 25 items displayed for sale, and none of the mannequins are empty, what is the greatest possible number of mannequins that could be displaying all 4 different products?

F. 0
G. 3
H. 4
J. 5
K. 7

Have to Know #5: Lines

There are a number of things about lines that you need to know, such as the formula for a line, finding the slope for a line, how two lines in slope-intercept formula compare to one another, the solution for two lines, and the distance and midpoint between two points when graphed. Before we get to the examples, let's summarize at least a couple of these things about lines that you need to know.

First, the formula for a line, which is $y = mx + b$, where m represents the slope, and b represents the y-intercept, meaning where the line crosses the y-axis. Putting a line in slope-intercept form involves solving the entire equation for y (or $1y$), and setting it equal to the rest of the equation. If two lines have the same slope (the same m), then they are parallel; they never *cross*, and as such they have *no solution*. Otherwise, two lines will always have 1 solution, which is the point where they cross (if you think about it, this makes sense; that means that there is only one point or value of both x and y that will satisfy each equation). If two lines are perpendicular, then their slopes will be *negative reciprocals* of one another. What does that mean? It means you make the slope negative and flip the numerator and denominator. For example, if a line has a slope of 2, and a second line is perpendicular to the first line, the slope of this second line will be $-\frac{1}{2}$ (we made it negative and moved the 2 down to the denominator).

Second, and speaking of slope, the ACT often asks students to find **the slope of a line** that is formed by 2 points (and sometimes one that is graphed). If you're given two points and asked for the slope, remember that $slope = \frac{rise}{run}$, which just means the difference in the height (or the y values) over or divided by the difference across (or the x values). For example, let's say you're asked to find the slope between these 2 points: (0, 1) and (3, 4). The difference in the y value divided by the difference in x value looks like this:

$slope = \frac{4-1}{3-0} = \frac{3}{3} = 1$. Thus, the slope is 1.

These things and more can be found in the examples below, all based on real ACT questions:

19. In the standard (x, y) coordinate plane, what is the slope of the line $5x - 2y = 7$?

A. $-\dfrac{7}{2}$

B. -2

C. $\dfrac{2}{5}$

D. $\dfrac{5}{2}$

E. 5

20. Which of the following (x, y) pairs is the solution for the system of equations $x - 2y = -3$ and $3x - 4y = -5$?

F. $(1, 2)$
G. $(-1, 1)$
H. $(3, 3)$
J. $(-2, -3)$
K. $(4, -4)$

21. In the standard (x, y) coordinate plane, the midpoint of segment $\overline{DE}$ is at $(1, 3)$, and D is at $(-4, -2)$. What are the x and y coordinates of E ?

A. $(4, 2)$
B. $(3, 5)$
C. $(-3, -1)$
D. $(6, 8)$
E. $(-9, -7)$

22. Line p passes through the point $(-3, 5)$ and crosses the y-axis at point $(0, 4)$. Line q is perpendicular to line p. What is the slope of line q ?

F. -3

G. $-\dfrac{1}{3}$

H. $-\dfrac{1}{9}$

J. $\dfrac{1}{3}$

K. 3

23. In the standard (x, y) coordinate plane, point A is at $(3, 3)$, and point B is at $(8, 15)$. What is the distance between point A and point B ?

    A. 5
    B. 12
    C. 13
    D. 15
    E. 18

24. Walker is standing at the origin. At time $t = 0$ minutes, a cloud floats directly above his head at 22,000 feet. At time $t = 2$ minutes, the cloud has maintained an elevation of 22,000 feet, but has moved across the sky 500 feet to the south. Which of the following equations represents the line along which the cloud is floating?

    F. $x = 500$
    G. $x = 22{,}000$
    H. $y = 1{,}000$
    J. $y = 22{,}000$
    K. $y = 44{,}000$

Have to Know #6: Logical Thinking with Variables

To be clear, all of mathematics is a combination of memorization and logical thinking. Usually the questions we are faced with in math class are formulaic or fall into a neat category in which there is some kind of tried and true method to resolving the problem. If you have two equations with two variables, for example, there are methods you can use to solve the problem, or if you need to find the area of a moon and see how many of them can fit into a spherical planet around which it revolves, there are formulas and methods to get you there.

However, there is a category of ACT Math question that does not fit neatly into these little methods or formula boxes, and again, in my research, I was actually surprised how often these kinds of questions are asked. There is only one way to reach true conclusions about these problems, and that is with a process that I hope you have used before: *logical thinking*. If you've ever done a Sudoku puzzle or played board or card games you have used logical thinking; it's the kind of thinking that *eliminates options that are impossible* while *testing those that are possible*.

Usually this kind of thinking is tested within little math problems that use variables, and that means that often what is needed isn't a vast library of math textbooks and formulas that you've memorized. A strategy that can be very helpful here is *Picking Numbers*. By choosing various numbers for the variables you can eliminate possibilities before narrowing in on the right answer.

Without a doubt, you will face multiple math questions on ACT day that look like the following:

25. What are the values for x that satisfy the equation
$(x - a)(x - b) = 0$?

    A. $-a$ and $-b$
    B. a and b
    C. $-a$ and b
    D. a and $-b$
    E. Cannot be determined from the information given

26. The sign of x is positive, the sign of y is positive, and the sign of z is negative. If it can be determined, what is the sign of the average of x, y, and z ?

   F. Negative
   G. Positive
   H. Both negative and positive
   J. Neither negative nor positive
   K. Cannot be determined from the given information

27. If x and y are both integers, $x > 1$, and $y < -1$, then which of the following expressions could not possibly be true?

   A. $|x| = |y|$

   B. $x^2 = y^2$

   C. $|x^2| = |y^2|$

   D. $\dfrac{1}{x^2} = \dfrac{1}{y^2}$

   E. $x^{-1} = y^{-1}$

28. For all real numbers p, q, and r, such that $r < 0 < q < 100 < p < 1000$, which of the following inequalities *must* be true ?

   F. $p + q < q + r$

   G. $\dfrac{p}{r} < \dfrac{q}{r}$

   H. $qr < pr$

   J. $p < q - r$

   K. $\dfrac{p}{r} > \dfrac{q}{r}$

Have to Know #7: Probability and Expected Outcome

Calculating probability and an expected outcome fall under the math umbrella of statistics, which is as exciting as it sounds. However, most statistics questions on the ACT are not tremendously difficult, though some may fall in that final, more difficult third. You probably know what *probability* means; it's just the likelihood that something will happen. If your weather app tells you that there is a 20% chance it will rain, then the probability that it will rain is 20%, or 0.2, or 1 in 5.

Expected outcome is a bit different. Essentially, finding an expected outcome requires that you know the probability of all possible events.

Let's say I have a strange 6-sided die. On three of the sides is a 1 (thus, the odds of rolling a 1 are 50%, or 0.5, or 1 in 2), on two of the sides is a 2 (thus, the odds of rolling a 2 are 33.3%, or 0.333, or 1 in 3), and on the last side of the die is a 3 (thus, the odds of rolling a 3 are 16.7%, or 0.167, or 1 in 6). You would think that the expected outcome would be the same thing as the most likely outcome, but it is not. To find the expected outcome, multiply each possible outcome by their probabilities and add them together. In our dice example, that would be this: $1(0.5) + 2(0.333) + 3(0.167) = 1.667$. A bit strange, I know, but the expected outcome of rolling our unique dice is 1.667, even if it isn't a real possibility.

This will all perhaps be better explained in the context of a few examples! Remember to try them yourself first before getting to the explanations.

29. A couple is deciding on a name for their baby. They put their 12 favorite names in a hat and will draw one randomly to determine the baby's name. If 4 of the names begin with the letter 'J,' 3 of the names begin with the letter 'P,' 3 of the names begin with the letter 'R,' and 2 of the names begin with the letter 'C,' then what is the probability that the name picked does NOT begin with the letter 'R'?

A. $\dfrac{1}{4}$

B. $\dfrac{1}{3}$

C. $\dfrac{1}{2}$

D. $\dfrac{3}{4}$

E. $\dfrac{5}{6}$

30. Which of the following expressions gives the number of permutations of 3 items taken and arranged from a total set of 12 items?

F. $3 + 12$

G. $(3 + 12)!$

H. $\dfrac{12!}{3!}$

J. $\dfrac{12!}{(12 - 3)!}$

K. $\dfrac{12!}{(3!)(12 - 3)!}$

31. Clement must choose one elective to fill out his university schedule, and there are 30 to choose from. Each elective will take place in one of five different locations on campus. The table below lists the frequency of locations for the 30 electives to choose from. If Clement chooses an elective at random, then what is the probability that the elective will take place either at the Intramural Fields or in the Dawson Building?

Elective location	Frequency
Intramural Fields	11
Healey Center	7
Stackle Hall	5
Dawson Building	7

A. 20%
B. 30%
C. 40%
D. 50%
E. 60%

32. A certain car dealership currently has 120 cars for sale on its lot. The owner of the dealership has prepared the following table for his salesman that shows the probability of selling different numbers of cars on any given day. Based on the probability distribution in the table, what is the expected number of cars remaining in the lot after 5 working days?

Cars sold in one day	Probability
0	0.2
1	0.4
2	0.3
3	0.1

F. 119
G. 118.7
H. 115
J. 114
K. 113.5

Have to Know #8: Percentages and Ratios

One of the most common areas of frustration on ACT Math are questions that require you to calculate and work with percentages, rates, and ratios. The reason they're frustrating is because they are the kinds of questions that seem extremely simple, but it is very easy to make a small mistake that can throw you off. And, of course, the test makers know what those simple little mistakes are, and one of the wrong answer choices is going to match up with the most likely incorrect answers.

First, let's discuss the number of ways that the ACT may expect you to work with percentages:

a) **Affecting a number by a percentage** - if the ACT asked you to find 35% of 440, here is all you need to do. Simply multiply 440 by 0.35. Do NOT divide 440 by 35 or 3.5 or .35. When you multiply, here is the result: 440(0.35) = 154. In other words, 154 is 35% of 440.

b) **Decreasing/increasing a number by a percentage (or percentages)** - if a product is decreased first by 10%, then by 50%, and the final price is $31.50, we can determine the original price. First, we need to go from the $31.50 and determine what the cost was between the two discounts (after the 10% discount but before the 50% discount). Given that it's 50%, it is rather simple to do in the head. However, the equation for determining this middle step looks like this: $0.5(x) = \$31.50$. In other words, 50% of our mystery price (x) is equal to $31.50, and when you divide both sides by 0.5 you can determine that $x = \$63.00$. Then, we need to determine still the original price because the $63 represents a price *after* an original discount of 10%. We can use this same equation as before, but let's call this time our original price y. Thus, $0.9(y) = \$63$. In other words, whatever the original price was, it was decreased by 10% (which is why we are multiplying the original price by .9, which represents a result of 90% of the original price). When we divide both sides by 0.9, we see that the original price was $63/0.9 = $70.

c) **Comparing numbers in terms of percentage** - 22 is what percent of 81? Seems fairly straightforward, but this simple question and its variations often cause students problems. Simply divide 22 by 81 and get that 22 is $(22/81) = 0.2716 = 27.16\%$ (when rounded to the nearest hundredths place) of 81. Conversely, the ACT could also ask this: 81 is what percent of 22? Students in this situation often make the mistake of doing the math we just did and divide 22 by 81, but this question calls for the opposite. 81 is (81/22) = 3.6818 = 368.18% of 22.

Let's start out with a few percentage examples to illustrate and test proper methods, then move on to an explanation of rates and ratios.

33. What is the sum of 75% of 4 and 300% of 3?

    A.   3
    B.   9
    C.   12
    D.   13
    E.   15

34. What is 1% of $\frac{1}{8}$?

    F.   0.000125
    G.   0.00125
    H.   0.0125
    J.   0.125
    K.   1.25

35. Rebecca has $10 to spend on materials to create a Christmas ornament for her grandmother. She intends to purchase popsicle sticks for $2.00, glue for $1.50, yarn for $2.30, and markers for $2.70. If purchases are subject to an 8% sales tax, how much money will Rebecca have left over after purchasing all four items?

    A. $0.82
    B. $1.12
    C. $1.44
    D. $1.50
    E. $1.61

36. The number of students who purchase ice cream increases by 30% between Monday and Tuesday. Then, because of a sale on ice cream, the number of students who purchase ice cream increases by an additional 40% between Tuesday and Wednesday. What is the combined percent increase in students purchasing ice cream between Monday and Wednesday?

    F.   40%
    G.   62%
    H.   70%
    J.   82%
    K.   91%

Now, on to rates and ratios. A **ratio** is a fixed comparison between two things. For example: for every 3 ripe blueberries in the package, there is 1 sour one. That's a ratio of 3 to 1. With that kind of knowledge, we could calculate all sorts of things. We could be told that there are 200 blueberries in the package and asked how many are sour $(200 \times \frac{1}{4})$, or we could be told that there are 45 sour blueberries, and need to find out how many total blueberries are in the package ($\frac{45}{x} = \frac{1}{4}$, then cross multiply to solve for x), which is the kind of question that overlaps ratios and percentages.

Rates often scare students, but they essentially are ratios. For example, if we were told that a car were driving at a rate of 35 miles per hour, that simply means that for every 35 miles, 1 hour has passed, or vice versa. Often, the key to using rates and ratios is this: putting a value in the numerator, another in the denominator, and then multiplying to make a value cancel out, leaving you with the correct answer.

For example: If Derek can run 12 blocks in x minutes, then how many blocks can he run in 40 minutes? Given that the rate has an unknown variable (x), the answer choices also will. If we want our answer to be in blocks, we need minutes to cancel. Thus, we would set up an equation like this:

$$\frac{x \text{ blocks}}{12 \text{ minutes}} \times 40 \text{ minutes} =$$

This equation allows minutes to cancel, giving us an answer in terms of blocks. Thus, the answer is going to end up being $\frac{40x}{12}$ blocks $= \frac{10x}{3}$ blocks . Again, remember with rates and ratios: value in numerator, value in denominator, cancel out what needs to be canceled to get answer you're looking for! Try out the following examples:

37. Chadwick is riding his skateboard at a rate of 45 inches per 2.5 seconds. At this rate, how many feet will Chadwick travel in 10 seconds?

    A. 15.00
    B. 11.25
    C. 10.75
    D. 8.00
    E. 1.50

38. From the point of view of Satellite Zephyr, $\frac{1}{4}$ centimeters represents 120 kilometers. Two images that were taken from Satellite Zephyr 12 hours apart show that a cargo ship traveled $2\frac{7}{10}$ centimeters. How many kilometers did the cargo ship travel?

    F.   81
    G.   324
    H.   342
    J.   1,296
    K.   1, 492

39. The ratio of the average height of Tree A to Tree B is 2:3. The ratio of the average height of Tree B to Tree C is 7:5. What is the ratio of the average height of Tree A to Tree C ?

    A.   10:21
    B.   11:21
    C.   14:15
    D.   15:14
    E.   21:10

Have to Know #9: Triangles, SohCahToa, & the Pythagorean Theorem

The ACT loves triangles. It loves testing your knowledge of sine, cosine, and tangent. It loves testing your knowledge of the Pythagorean Theorem. And, it loves testing your knowledge of the angles within a triangle. It also loves questions where figuring out the side of a triangle or the angle of a triangle is just one step to solving a larger problem. Hopefully some of that sounds familiar to you, even if you don't remember exactly how to use all of it like you used to. However, before we jump into any examples, we need to discuss what all of those things are.

The first thing you need to remember is this: all of these terms we're about to define all have to do with right triangles. A **right triangle** is a triangle in which the two legs form a right, or 90 degree, angle.

Let's start with the Pythagorean Theorem, which you must memorize (if you haven't already). The ACT will never give you the **Pythagorean Theorem**, which is $a^2 + b^2 = c^2$, in which a and b are the two legs of a right triangle, and c is the hypotenuse.

What this formula allows you to do is this: if you know any two sides of a right triangle, then you can always find the third. This is helpful in all sorts of problems, like we saw in our lesson on lines: the distance between two points on the (x, y) coordinate plane form the hypotenuse of a right triangle.

Sine, cosine, and tangent are relationships between the sides of a right triangle. They can most easily be remembered by the phrase **SOHCAHTOA**, or "Some Old Hippie Caught Another Hippie Tripping On Apples." The **sine** of an angle in a right triangle is equal to the length of its opposite side over the hypotenuse (thus, **SOH**). The **cosine** of an angle in a right triangle is equal to the length of the adjacent (non-opposite leg) side of the triangle over the hypotenuse (thus, **CAH**). The **tangent** is equal to the length of the opposite side of the angle over the adjacent side (thus, **TOA**).

Look at the triangle below. All we know about this triangle is the length of one side, the fact that one angle is 90 degrees, and that another angle is 36.87 degrees. But, knowing what we know now about the angles in a triangle, the Pythagorean Theorem, sine, cosine, and tangent, we can figure out the lengths of each side and the measure of the one missing angle fairly easily (*Note: you do not need to memorize the Law of Sines or the Law of Cosines*). This is the kind of math the ACT expects you to be able to do. Let's get to some examples based on real math questions from recent ACT's:

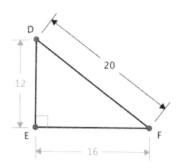

40. What is the value of tan F in right triangle △DEF below?

F. $\dfrac{3}{5}$

G. $\dfrac{3}{4}$

H. $\dfrac{4}{5}$

J. $\dfrac{5}{4}$

K. $\dfrac{5}{3}$

41. A cat is stuck at the very top of a maple tree that is 12.5 feet tall. Mr. Wilkins uses the ladder in his garage to reach the cat. If the angle between the ladder and the ground is 38.68 degrees, and if the ladder rests at the very top of the tree, then what is the length of the ladder to the nearest foot?

A. 20 feet
B. 22 feet
C. 25 feet
D. 27 feet
E. 31 feet

Numbers 42, 43, and 44 all use and refer to the following information.

The image below shows the layout for a proposed retail space. In the figure, *LMNO* is a rectangle, *LRSP* and *ROQS* are squares. Point *R* is the midpoint of $\overline{LO}$ and point *S* is the midpoint of $\overline{PQ}$. The given lengths are in meters.

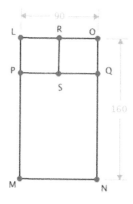

42. What is the length of *RM* to the nearest meter?

    F.   250
    G.   243
    H.   212
    J.   184
    K.   166

43. What is the measure of ∠*RMN* to the nearest degree?

    A.   89°
    B.   81°
    C.   78°
    D.   74°
    E.   66°

44. The owner of the retail space wants to run an extension cord from point *L* to point *S*. How long must the extension cord be, to the nearest meter?

    F.   45
    G.   53
    H.   64
    J.   75
    K.   90

Have to Know #10: Angles

The ACT will also test your knowledge of angles in a few different ways. The first concept that we definitely need to cover is called the **Law of Transversals**. That's a fancy name, and you don't need to remember it; it's the concept that you need to remember. Essentially, it is this: if two parallel lines are *transversed* by another line (meaning, a line goes through them), then many of the angles will have a special relationship between them. Look at this diagram:

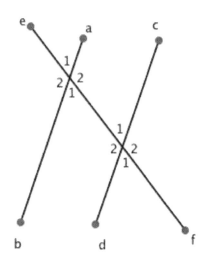

Here, lines *ab* and *cd* are parallel, and they are "cut through" or transversed by a third line, *ef*. This creates 8 angles. Let's take a closer look at where two lines cross, or where there are 4 angles. The two angles across from each other are called "opposite angles," and they are always equal. In addition, "zooming out" a bit, all four angles that are marked with a 1 are all identical; the four angles that are marked with a 2 are also identical. Without unnecessarily getting into all of the various vocabulary, this is the Law of Transversals.

The second concept that we need to know about angles is that the angles in a line add up to 180 degrees, or similarly, that the angle measure of a line is 180 degrees. When we combine those two concepts, we can do a lot with the diagram above. If we are given even just one of the 8 angles pictured, we can figure out all of the other 7 angles. For example, let's say that the topmost angle (1) is 40°. That means that every "1" is 40° and that every "2" is $180° - 40° = 140°$.

The third major concept that the above two are combined with is one we have learned about already, that being that the three angles of any triangle add up to 180 degrees. The ACT likes to combine all three of these concepts into more difficult questions, or to test one or two of them together in easier questions. Let's look at a few examples:

45. In the figure below, vertices B and D of $\triangle BCD$ lie on $\overline{AE}$, the measure of $\angle ABC$ is 155°, and the measure of $\angle CDE$ is 80°. What is the measure of $\angle BCD$?

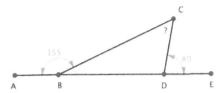

A. 25°
B. 55°
C. 70°
D. 80°
E. 100°

46. In the figure below, H and I lie on segment AB, and J and K lie on segment CD. In addition, segments $\overline{AB}$, $\overline{CD}$, and $\overline{EF}$ are all parallel and perpendicular to segment $\overline{ML}$. What is the measure of $\angle GIH$?

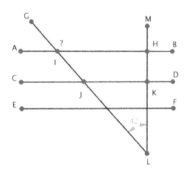

F. 21°
G. 42°
H. 48°
J. 121°
K. 132°

47. The intersection of lines c and d forms the four angles $\angle W$, $\angle X$, $\angle Y$, and $\angle Z$. The measure of $\angle Z$ is 500% larger than the measure of $\angle W$. If it can be determined, what is the value of $\angle W$?

A. 30°
B. 36°
C. 40°
D. 41°
E. Cannot be determined from the given information

48. Points *U* and *W* lie on line segment *ST*. What is the degree measure of ∠*VUW* ?

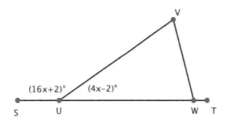

    F.   9°
    G. 19°
    H. 34°
    J.   88°
    K. 146°

Have to Know #11: Perimeter, Area, and Volume

I'm guessing that you understand that the perimeter of a shape is the length of all of its sides combined, that the area of a shape is the amount of space the shape occupies (a way to measure everything within the sides of the shape), and that the volume is the amount of space a 3-d shape occupies. Before we get into how the ACT asks problems that test your knowledge of these, which isn't as straightforwardly as you might hope, let's review the kinds of formulas you need to know, and those you don't.

Area

First, you need to know how to calculate the areas of basic shapes: squares/rectangles, triangles, and circles. We'll look into circles more in our lesson exclusively on circles. The area of a square or rectangle

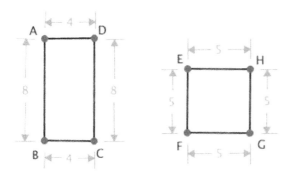

is simply the product of two sides that form a right angle. Look at these two simple examples: The area of the rectangle on the left is simply the height, 8, times the width, 4, which is 32 units squared. The area of the square on the right is the same calculation: 5 times 5 is 25 units squared.

The area of a triangle you also must know. This formula works on any triangle shape, from the funkiest shape to the simplest. The formula is simply **(½)bh**, or one half the base times the height. For example:

For both of these triangles, we apply the same formula, (½)bh. The area of the triangle on the left is (½)(4)(3.5),

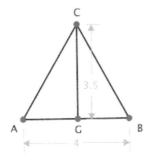
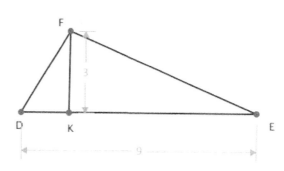

which = 7 units squared. The area of the triangle on the right is (½)(9)(3) = 13.5 units squared.

Volume

Let's talk about volume for a moment; there is a type of shape that you should know the volume of, and that is any figure that maintains the same shape uniformly up and down (a tin can as a cylinder, a block of wood for a rectangular prism, or a triangular prism of some kind). Finding the volume of these shapes is easy. You simply find the area (like we have done in plenty of example above), then multiply that area by the height. You can think of it as the same area "all of the way up".

However, there is no need to memorize the volume of more complicated shapes, like that of a cone or that of a sphere or some other 3-d shape that doesn't have uniformity along the height. I would bet that out of the last 1,000 administered ACT Math questions, not a single one requires you to know the volume of those shapes. If they want you to find the volume of shapes like those, or if finding the volume of a shape like that is required as a step to get a question right, they will give you the formula.

Draw it Out

It would be great if the ACT asked very straightforward questions about perimeter, area, and volume, but unfortunately finding any of these three things is usually one step needed in a greater problem, thus there is a greater risk for making a simple mistake. My one major piece of advice is this: if a shape or room or floor plan or anything else is described by a problem, but not given, then ***draw it out***!!!

49. Quinn wants to paint the walls of his bedroom. Each of the walls measures 12 feet wide by 10 feet tall. Two of the walls have a window that measures 3 feet wide by 5 feet tall, one of the walls has a door that measures 4 feet wide by 8 feet tall, and the final wall has no doors or windows. What is the total area that Quinn will need to paint in square feet ?

    A. 120
    B. 418
    C. 433
    D. 448
    E. 480

50. If the length of a rectangle is decreased by 30%, and the width of the same rectangle is increased by 45%, the area of the resulting rectangle is larger than the area of the original rectangle by what percent?

F. 1.50%
G. 5.00%
H. 7.15%
J. 14.30%
K. 15.00%

51. Frida has a 10 oz can of soup that she wants to share with her daughter for lunch. She decides that her daughter should receive 40% of the soup, while she receives 60%. The can has a height of 98 mm and a diameter of 65 mm. Rounded to the nearest cubic millimeter, what is the volume of the portion that Frida wants to share with her daughter ?

A. 98,065
B. 130,078
C. 195,116
D. 301,104
E. 325,194

Have to Know #12: Functions

The word "function" sometimes scares students, so does the look of a function, which is something like
this: $f(x) = 7x^2 - 2x$. However, the idea here is simple, think of it like this: the $f(x)$ part can be replaced

with y, thus $y = 7x^2 - 2x$. They are interchangeable. Another way to think about it is this: the value of y is

a *function* of x. In other words, what y is equal to depends on what x is. Typically, the ACT will ask you

(using the example above) what the value of a function is ($f(x) = 7x^2 - 2x$) when x has a certain value

(put like this: $f(4)$). In that case, simply plug in 4 for x and get a value of the function. Here, it looks like:

$f(4) = 7(4^2) - 2(4) = 112 - 8 = 104$.

Let's look at some examples to see a bit of the various ways the ACT can ask you about functions.

52. If $f(x) = 3x^2 - 12x$, then what is $f(-2)$?

    F. -24
    G. -12
    H.   0
    J.   12
    K.   36

53. A function, f , is defined by $f(a, b) = 2b^3 + 5a$. What is
the value of $f(-1, 2)$?

    A.   2
    B.   8
    C.   11
    D.   15
    E.   21

54. Given that $f(x) = x^2 + 3x$, and that $g(x) = 2x + 2$, what
is $f(g(x))$?

    F. $2(2x^2 + 7x + 5)$
    G. $4x^2 + 7x + 5$
    H. $4(x^2 + 3x + 3)$
    J. $2x^2 + 4x + 5$
    K. $x^2 + 7x + 10$

55. If $f(x) = 21$, and $g(x) = 10.5$, what is $\dfrac{f(x)}{g(x)}$?

    A.   0.5
    B.   2.0
    C.   10.5
    D.   31.5
    E.   220.5

56. If $f(x) = \dfrac{1}{(x+3)}$, and $g(x) = \dfrac{1}{(x^2 + 2x - 3)}$, then what is $\dfrac{f(x)}{g(x)}$?

    F. $x - 1$

    G. $x + 1$

    H. $\dfrac{1}{(x+3)^2}$

    J. $\dfrac{1}{(x+3)^2(x-1)}$

    K. $\dfrac{1}{(x+3)^2(x+1)}$

Have to Know #13: Circles

Although there are limitless things you could know and learn about circles, there are three things about them you MUST know for ACT Math: the formula for the area, the formula for the circumference, and what an arc is.

Area and Circumference

The formula for the area of a circle is πr^2, which is different from the formula for the perimeter or circumference of a circle, which is $2\pi r$. r, of course, represents the radius of the circle, which is half of the diameter. Look at this figure: with a simple circle like this, we can easily calculate the perimeter (circumference) and the area.

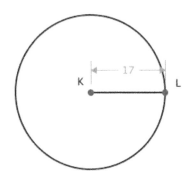

Let's start with the circumference of the circle, or the perimeter you might say, which is simply $2\pi r$. That leaves us with $2(3.14)(17)$, which is 34π or 106.8 rounded. As for area, we use πr^2, which is $3.14(172) = 289\pi$, or 907.5 rounded to the first decimal place.

Knowing and mastering these two values will get you far on most ACT Math circle questions, and many of the upcoming examples will mimic the way the ACT asks you about these two values.

Arc and Interior Angles

Another circle concept, however, that is important to know is that of an arc. An arc is simply a piece of the outside of a circle, and they have both a degree measure and a distance.

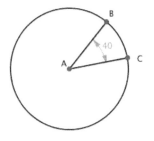

In this figure here, BC is an arc; by BC I don't mean the distance between the two that could be represented by drawing a straight line between them, but rather the length of the curve. It has a measure or angle (often called an interior angle), as you can see (40 degrees), and it also has a length or distance. Let's say that the radius of this circle is 4. That would mean that the circumference is $2\pi r$, or

$2\pi 4$, or 8π. We can find the length of arc BC by cross multiplying; this begins with realizing that there is a

ratio here: as 40 degrees is to 360 degrees (the amount of degrees in a circle), so too BC is to 8π. Thus,

$\frac{40^o}{360^o} = \frac{BC}{8\pi}$. Working this out, we learn that $BC = 0.89\pi$.

Let's look at a few examples that mimic those found on recent ACT tests. Remember, if a shape, graph, or

figure isn't drawn (as is true in all four of these), do yourself a favor and draw it out!

57. Carla purchased a round tablecloth for her outdoor table. In order to allow for the table's umbrella to be inserted into the center of the table, she must cut a circular hole out of the center of the tablecloth. If the radius of the tablecloth is 4.5 feet, and the diameter of the hole that she cuts from the center is 1 foot, then what is the total area of the tablecloth after the hole has been cut, rounded to the nearest hundredth of a foot?

  A. 55.42
  B. 60.48
  C. 62.83
  D. 63.61
  E. 72.72

58. A circle has a circumference of 22 meters. What is the area of this circle, rounded to the nearest decimal?

  F. $22.0 \ m^2$
  G. $31.6 \ m^2$
  H. $38.5 \ m^2$
  J. $153.9 \ m^2$
  K. $380.1 \ m^2$

59. The radius of one circle is 5 feet long. The radius of a second circle is 40% longer than the radius of the first circle. To the nearest square foot, how much larger is the area of the second circle than the area of the first circle?

  A. 2
  B. 22
  C. 45
  D. 58
  E. 75

60. Tommy attempts to cut a pizza with a diameter of 16 inches into 8 equal pieces. However, he accidentally cuts out the first piece with an interior angle of 55°. Rounded to the nearest hundredth of an inch, what is the length of the outside arc of the crust of this first slice of pizza?

    F. 4.29 inches
    G. 7.68 inches
    H. 8.04 inches
    J. 8.51 inches
    K. 9.42 inches

Step 3 Correct Answers

1: B	21: D	41: A
2: G	22: K	42: K
3: B	23: C	43: D
4: K	24: J	44: H
5: A	25: B	45: B
6: K	26: K	46: K
7: A	27: E	47: A
8: H	28: G	48: H
9: E	29: D	49: B
10: K	30: J	50: F
11: C	31: E	51: B
12: K	32: K	52: K
13: B	33: C	53: C
14: H	34: G	54: F
15: E	35: A	55: B
16: F	36: J	56: F
17: B	37: A	57: C
18: H	38: J	58: H
19: D	39: C	59: E
20: F	40: G	60: G

ACT Math Step 3 *Have to Know* practice answer explanations begin on page 276.

STEP 4

ACT Math Have to Know Full-Length Practice Test

<u>About This Unique Practice Test</u>

If you completed all 60 problems following the 13 *Have to Know* lessons, you have completed a practice test's worth of problems. However, before moving on to *Good to Know* ACT Math (which is the next series of lessons), it is crucial that you ensure that you have a grip on all of the *Have to Know* math presented here in this test. This isn't the end, of course, of *Have to Know* material, it is prevalent in the two complete practice tests that make up Step 6 as well.

As always, explanations for each of the following 60 problems can be found in the back of the book, beginning on page 294 (and the answers themselves are listed immediately after the test itself on page 85).

The following practice test, though it only features *Have to Know* math problems, is designed to mimic an actual ACT test. It features, for example, a gradual increase in difficulty, and is based on real-life ACT Math problems. Thus, this is a great opportunity to put into practice the *Two Pass Strategy* from Step 1 and the 4 ACT Math mini-strategies from Step 2.

Don't give up on problems, circle them and skip them, and don't use more than roughly a minute on any individual problem; circle it as well and come back if you have time; only guess if you're absolutely certain you can't get it right or give it a good guess on a second pass.

However, I have to admit something before you begin. As the creator of these questions, I was often faced with this dilemma: should I make this problem a little bit more difficult or a little bit easier? Most of the time, I leaned towards making the problems a little more difficult. This is NOT to crush your spirits or just to make me feel good for being able to make high school math questions more difficult. Instead, it's to *reinforce* what you *Have to Know* and make you *stronger* as a result.

With all of that said, remove distractions, start a 60 minute timer, and begin.

MATHEMATICS TEST

60 Minutes — 60 Questions

DIRECTIONS: Solve each problem, choose the correct answer, and then fill in the corresponding oval on your answer document.

Do not linger over problems that take too much time. Solve as many as you can; then return to the others in the time you have left for this test.

You are permitted to use a calculator on this test. You may use your calculator for any problems you choose, but some of the problems may best be done without using a calculator.

Note: Unless otherwise stated, all of the following should be assumed.

1. Illustrative figures are NOT necessarily drawn to scale.
2. Geometric figures lie in a plane.
3. The word *line* indicates a straight line.
4. The word *average* indicates arithmetic mean.

---

1. The product of $4x^2y^4 \cdot 3x^2y^2 \cdot 8x$ is equivalent to which of the following?

   A. $15x^5y^6$
   B. $15x^4y^8$
   C. $96x^5y^6$
   D. $96x^4y^8$
   E. $96(xy)^{11}$

2. Tabitha owns a craft store. A customer calls and orders 6 strips of ribbon with lengths of 10, 12, 9, 10, 11, and 12 inches, respectively. What is the mean of the lengths of the ribbon strips, rounded to the nearest tenth of an inch?

   F. 10.5
   G. 10.6
   H. 10.7
   J. 11.0
   K. 11.1

3. Three times the sum of x and -4 is equal to the addition of 8 and $-x$. What is the value of x ?

   A. -5
   B. -1
   C. 3
   D. 5
   E. 10

4. Chipper puts 7% of his $66,000 annual salary into a savings account in 12 equal monthly installments. Parker, on the other hand, deposits a flat rate of $150 a month into a savings account. Not counting for interest earned, how much more a month does Chipper put into savings than Parker?

   F. $235
   G. $250
   H. $312
   J. $322
   K. $385

DO YOUR FIGURING HERE.

5. Bus 1 and Bus 2 are 1,000 miles apart. Bus 1 travels towards Bus 2 in a straight line at 60 miles per hour, and Bus 2 travels towards Bus 1 in a straight line at 55 miles per hour. After 4 hours of continuous driving, how far apart are the two buses?

   A. 240
   B. 300
   C. 460
   D. 540
   E. 700

6. What is the median of the values of z for which $(z + 2)(z - 4)(z + 3)(z - 6) = 0$?

   F. -1
   G. -0.5
   H. 0
   J. 0.5
   K. 1

7. Square $ABCD$ is shown below. If segment $\overline{BD}$ is 10 inches long, then what is the length of any side of square $ABCD$?

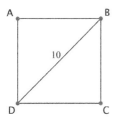

   A. 5
   B. $5\sqrt{2}$
   C. $5\sqrt{3}$
   D. 7.5
   E. 10

8. If x is an integer, and $x \neq 2$, then $(2x - 4)^4 - 1$:

   F. must be positive and odd.
   G. must be negative and odd.
   H. must be positive and even.
   J. must be negative and even.
   K. can be even, odd, positive, or negative.

9. In the figure below, $\overline{JI}$ is parallel to $\overline{HF}$ and $\overline{LK}$ is parallel to $\overline{HG}$. If $\angle JIF$ is 115° and $\angle LKG$ is 20°, then what is the measure of $\angle FHG$?

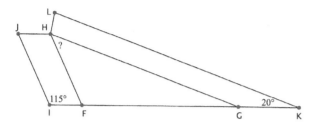

A. 45°
B. 55°
C. 65°
D. 115°
E. 120°

10. For all nonzero values of x, y, and z, $\dfrac{-15x\,y^3 z^8}{3x^3 y^2 z} = ?$

F. $\dfrac{-5x^2}{y z^7}$

G. $\dfrac{-5y z^7}{x^2}$

H. $\dfrac{5y^5 z^9}{x^4}$

J. $5x^4 y^5 z^9$

K. $-5x^2 y z^7$

11. What is the slope of any line that is parallel to $6x - 5y = 10$?

A. -2

B. $-\dfrac{6}{5}$

C. $-\dfrac{5}{6}$

D. $\dfrac{5}{6}$

E. $\dfrac{6}{5}$

DO YOUR FIGURING HERE.

12. Maggie decides that she wants to install a concrete walkway around the outside of her swimming pool. Her swimming pool is 25 feet long and 20 feet wide. If the walkway will be 3 feet wide all the way around the pool, then what will be the total area of the new walkway?

- **F.** 144 ft^2
- **G.** 162 ft^2
- **H.** 306 ft^2
- **J.** 500 ft^2
- **K.** 806 ft^2

13. Barb is trying to decide what color dress to wear to her high school dance. She has 7 red dresses, 4 black dresses, and 2 green dresses. Her sister has 3 red dresses, 6 black dresses, and 8 green dresses. If she can wear either her own dress or one of her sister's, and if she chooses a dress at random, then what is probability that the chosen dress is black?

- **A.** $\dfrac{2}{15}$
- **B.** $\dfrac{3}{15}$
- **C.** $\dfrac{3}{10}$
- **D.** $\dfrac{1}{3}$
- **E.** $\dfrac{1}{2}$

14. If $f(x) = 2x^2 - x + 1$, then what is $f(2)$?

- **F.** 3
- **G.** 7
- **H.** 9
- **J.** 15
- **K.** 17

15. Two lines intersect, creating four angles: $\angle A$, $\angle B$, $\angle C$, and $\angle D$. As a result, $\angle A \neq \angle B$ and $\angle C \neq \angle D$. If $\angle C = 40°$, then what is the value of $\angle D$?

- **A.** 160°
- **B.** 140°
- **C.** 120°
- **D.** 50°
- **E.** 40°

16. What is the diameter of a circle with an area of 36π ?

- **F.** 3
- **G.** 6
- **H.** 9
- **J.** 12
- **K.** 72

DO YOUR FIGURING HERE.

17. Timothy is a professional baseball player participating in a home run contest. For every home run, r, that he hits up to and including 5, he will receive $0. After he reaches this many home runs, he will receive $25 for each additional home run. Assuming he hits at least 5 home runs, which expression represents the total amount Timothy will earn in the home run competition?

A. $25r - 5$
B. $25(r + 5)$
C. $25(r - 5)$
D. $25r$
E. $25r + 5$

18. A car that normally sells for $38,000 is on sale for 13% off. How much does it cost during the sale, to the nearest dollar?

F. $29,100
G. $29,200
H. $32,300
J. $33,060
K. $42,940

19. If $g(x) = \dfrac{x^{\frac{1}{2}}}{x^{-1}}$, what is the value of $g(9)$?

A. $-\dfrac{1}{3}$

B. 0

C. $\dfrac{1}{3}$

D. 3

E. 27

20. Which of the following pairs of lines could have $(2, -2)$ as a solution?

F. $y = \dfrac{1}{2}x - 3 \,;\, y = 5x - 12$

G. $y = 5x - 12 \,;\, y = \dfrac{1}{3}x + 1$

H. $y = \dfrac{1}{3}x + 1 \,;\, y = 11x - 3$

J. $y = \dfrac{1}{2}x - 3 \,;\, y = 11x - 3$

K. $y = \dfrac{1}{2}x - 3 \,;\, y = \dfrac{1}{3}x + 1$

DO YOUR FIGURING HERE.

Use the following information to answer questions 21-23.

Drew is a high school track athlete who specializes in three throwing events: javelin, shot put, and discus. In order to ensure he is giving roughly equal treatment to each sport, he tracks how many practice throws he makes of each across the 5 days of the week in the chart below.

	Mon.	Tues.	Wed.	Thurs.	Fri.
Javelin	12	23	11	2	19
Shot Put	18	11	0	15	18
Discus	0	0	18	15	3

On Mondays and Tuesdays, Drew throws at full strength. At full strength, Drew averages a javelin throw of 201 feet, a shot put throw of 52 feet, and a discus throw of 179 feet. However, due to arm soreness, Drew can only throw at 90% of his strength on Wednesdays, 70% of his strength on Thursdays, and 60% of his strength on Fridays.

21. What percent of Drew's throws for the week were discus throws, rounded to the nearest percent?

   A. 22%
   B. 33%
   C. 38%
   D. 41%
   E. 78%

22. The track and field coach decided to observe a random throw of Drew's during Thursday practice. What was the expected outcome, rounded to the nearest foot, of the observed throw?

   F. 81
   G. 85
   H. 116
   J. 121
   K. 144

23. Due to arm soreness, which of the following throws is likely to travel the farthest?

   A. A shot put throw on a Wednesday
   B. A shot put throw on a Thursday
   C. A discus throw on a Thursday
   D. A javelin throw on a Friday
   E. A discus throw on a Friday

24. At her job, Gabrielle earns $\$(11h + 16.5e + 0.21s)$, where h is the number of regular time hours she worked, e is the number of overtime hours she worked, and s is the amount of her sales. What does Gabrielle earn for working 40 regular time hours and 3 overtime hours, while making $3,234 in sales?

    F. $440.00
    G. $489.50
    H. $709.50
    J. $1,119.14
    K. $1,168.64

25. In the figure below, right angles are as marked and sides are labeled in inches. What is the area of the figure in square inches?

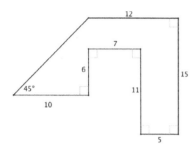

    A. 151
    B. 153
    C. 163
    D. 228
    E. 230

26. In the standard (x, y) coordinate plane, point L is at $(-3, 0)$ and point M is at $(1, 3)$. What is the distance between point L and point M?

    F. 3
    G. $3\sqrt{3}$
    H. $4\sqrt{2}$
    J. 5
    K. 7

27. At WaterTown Water Park, Bryan rides a slide that is 125 feet long into a swimming pool. If the slide meets the pool at an angle of 38°, then how many feet high off of the ground is the slide's starting point, rounded to the nearest tenth of a foot?

    A. 47.5
    B. 77.0
    C. 97.7
    D. 98.5
    E. 203.0

28. If $-5 \leq x \leq 3$ and $|y| = 2$, then what is the greatest possible value of the product of x and y?

    F. -10
    G. -6
    H. 0
    J. 6
    K. 10

29. The table below gives values for $f(x)$ and $g(x)$ for various values of x.

x	$f(x)$	$g(x)$
-2	3	10
-1	0	5
0	-2	-4
3	6	-8
5	8	-2

What is the value of $f(g(5))$?

    A. -2
    B. -1
    C. 0
    D. 3
    E. 10

30. If $i^2 = -1$, what is the value of $(i-1)(i-1)$?

    F. $-2i$
    G. -1
    H. 0
    J. i
    K. $2i$

31. Missy purchased $(12x - 41)$ dollars worth of groceries at Grocery Stop. Because Grocery Stop did not have every item on her shopping list, she then went to Fancy Foods and purchased an additional $(5x + 30)$ dollars worth of groceries. If she purchased a total of \$278 worth of groceries, how much money did she spend at Grocery Stop?

    A. \$55
    B. \$115
    C. \$163
    D. \$243
    E. \$245

DO YOUR FIGURING HERE.

32. Jeff has hit 0, 2, 4, 2, 1, 0, 0, 0, 3, and 2 home runs in Games 1 - 10 this season. How many home runs does he need in Game 11 and Game 12 so that the mode of his home runs will exceed the mean?

	Game 11	Game 12
F.	0	4
G.	4	0
H.	2	2
J.	3	3
K.	4	4

33. What is the value of tan A in right triangle $\triangle ABC$ shown below?

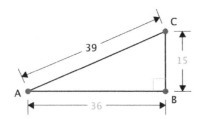

A. $\dfrac{5}{12}$

B. $\dfrac{12}{13}$

C. $\dfrac{13}{12}$

D. $\dfrac{12}{5}$

E. $\dfrac{13}{5}$

34. What is the equation of a line that is perpendicular to the line $y = -\dfrac{2}{5}x + 3$ and passes through the point (2, 3) ?

F. $y = -\dfrac{2}{5}x - 3$

G. $y = -\dfrac{2}{5}x + 5$

H. $y = \dfrac{2}{5}x - 4$

J. $y = \dfrac{5}{2}x + 3$

K. $y = \dfrac{5}{2}x - 2$

DO YOUR FIGURING HERE.

35. In the figure below, segments *JK* and *HI* are parallel and are transversed by segment *LM*. If the value of angle ∠*HNO* is 35°, then what is the value of angle ∠*LOK* ?

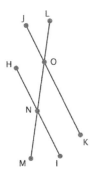

- **A.** 35°
- **B.** 55°
- **C.** 115°
- **D.** 135°
- **E.** 145°

36. The diameter of Circle *X* equals the radius of Circle *Y*. The diameter of Circle *Y* equals the radius of Circle *Z*. If the area of Circle *Z* is 225π, then what is the circumference of Circle *X*?

- **F.** 3.75π
- **G.** 7.5π
- **H.** 14.0625π
- **J.** 15π
- **K.** 56.25π

37. If $f(x) = \dfrac{2}{3}x - 14$, and $g(x) = 6x^2 + 18x + 18$, which expression represents $f(g(x))$?

- **A.** $2(2x^2 + 6x - 1)$
- **B.** $2x^2 + 6x + 1$
- **C.** $2(2x^2 + 9x + 2)$
- **D.** $9x^2 + 27x + 13$
- **E.** $9x^2 + 27x + 41$

38. For all $x \neq 2$, the expression $\dfrac{(x + 1)(x^2 + x - 6)}{(x - 2)(x^2 - 5x - 24)}$ is equivalent to which of the following?

- **F.** $\dfrac{(x - 1)(x + 2)}{(x + 8)(x - 2)}$
- **G.** $\dfrac{(x - 1)}{(x + 8)}$
- **H.** $\dfrac{(x + 1)}{(x - 8)}$
- **J.** $-\dfrac{1}{80}$
- **K.** $\dfrac{1}{8}$

39. The point $(0, 3)$ is the midpoint of the line segment in the standard (x, y) coordinate plane with endpoints $(2, -1)$ and (a, b). Which of the following is (a, b) ?

   A. $(-5, 4)$
   B. $(4, -5)$
   C. $(6, 1)$
   D. $(3, -4)$
   E. $(-2, 7)$

40. The formula for converting a Celsius temperature (C) to its equivalent Fahrenheit temperature (F) is $F = \dfrac{9}{5}C + 32$. Which of the following is the Fahrenheit equivalent of a Celsius temperature of $31°$, rounded to the nearest degree?

   F. $49°$
   G. $50°$
   H. $87°$
   J. $88°$
   K. $89°$

41. In the standard (x, y) coordinate plane, line A never crosses the y-axis. What is the slope of line A ?

   A. 1
   B. 0
   C. -1
   D. Undefined
   E. Cannot be determined from the given information.

42. In $\triangle EFG$, $\angle E$ is a right angle, $\angle F$ measures $50°$, and side EF is 14 millimeters long. What is the area of $\triangle EFG$ in square millimeters, rounded to the nearest hundredth?

   F. 76.23
   G. 116.79
   H. 152.46
   J. 196.00
   K. 233.58

43. If $(x^{3z+4})^3 = x^3$ for all x, then $z = $?

   A. $-\dfrac{4}{3}$

   B. -1

   C. $-\dfrac{3}{4}$

   D. $\dfrac{3}{4}$

   E. $\dfrac{4}{3}$

DO YOUR FIGURING HERE.

Use the following information to answer questions 44-46.

Island Spa and Resort is considering installing 8 new circular swimming pools around their large property to mimic the planets that revolve around the sun. The proposed diameters of the 8 swimming pools are listed below:

- Pool A (Mercury): 30 feet
- Pool B (Venus): 60 feet
- Pool C (Earth): 60 feet
- Pool D (Mars): 40 feet
- Pool E (Jupiter): 100 feet
- Pool F (Saturn): 90 feet
- Pool G (Uranus): 80 feet
- Pool H (Neptune): 75 feet

44. If all swimming pools have the same depth, then how much more water will Pool E (Jupiter) need compared to Pool C (Earth), rounded to the nearest percent?

- **F.** 28%
- **G.** 36%
- **H.** 167%
- **J.** 278%
- **K.** 360%

45. Island Spa and Resort is considering adding a ninth pool to represent the dwarf planet Pluto. If this pool was to have a diameter of 15 feet, then which of the following measurements of the data set of the pools' diameters would change the least?

- **A.** Mean
- **B.** Median
- **C.** Mode
- **D.** Range
- **E.** Cannot be determined from the given information.

46. Island Spa and Resort decides to allocate a section of Pool H (Neptune) for use by children only. If the interior angle of the new children's section is 120°, what is the measure of the arc of this section of Pool H (Neptune) ?

- **F.** 5π
- **G.** 25π
- **H.** 37.5π
- **J.** 75π
- **K.** 140π

47. If $4 < \dfrac{1}{x^2} < 9$, then which of the following is a possible

value of x ?

A. $\dfrac{5}{12}$

B. $\dfrac{1}{3}$

C. $\dfrac{9}{13}$

D. 4

E. 9

48. For what value of z would the following systems of equations have an infinite number of solutions?

$$2x - 7y = 4$$
$$6x - z\,y = 12$$

F. -5
G. 5
H. 7
J. 14
K. 21

49. What is the area in square units of a triangle formed by the points $(-1, \ -1), (-4, \ -1)$, and $(-4, \ -5)$?

A. 5.0
B. 5.5
C. 6.0
D. 7.5
E. 10.0

50. If $7x^3 y^4 < 0$, which of the following cannot possibly be true?

F. $x < 7$
G. $x > -7$
H. $y < 0$
J. $y > 7$
K. $x = 0$

51. When $x = -3$, $f(x) = -14$. When $x = -1$, $f(x) = 2$. When $x = 4$, $f(x) = -28$. Which of the following functions could be $f(x)$?

A. $f(x) = -2x^2 + 4$
B. $f(x) = 2x - 8$
C. $f(x) = x^3 + 3$
D. $f(x) = -2x - 20$
E. $f(x) = -x^2 - 5$

52. An elementary school decides to host a kickball tournament during P.E. For the randomization of teams, 8 marbles of 8 different colors are placed into a hat. Each student will draw a marble to indicate what team he or she is on. Joseph draws first, and he chooses a green marble. Maximilian draws second, and he also chooses a green marble, putting him on Joseph's team. If Jude is the third student to draw, what is the probability that he will also be on Joseph and Maximilian's team?

   F. $\dfrac{3}{31}$

   G. $\dfrac{7}{63}$

   H. $\dfrac{1}{8}$

   J. $\dfrac{4}{31}$

   K. $\dfrac{1}{7}$

53. What is the perimeter of a right triangle with legs 10 and 15 inches long ?

   A. 5
   B. $5\sqrt{13}$
   C. $15 + 10\sqrt{3}$
   D. 40
   E. $25 + 5\sqrt{13}$

54. $\dfrac{\frac{1}{6} + \left(\frac{5}{2}\cdot\frac{2}{3}\right)}{\left(-\frac{11}{12} + \frac{11}{4}\right) - \left(\frac{-3+14}{-3+15}\right)} = ?$

   F. 0
   G. 1
   H. 2
   J. 3
   K. 4

55. When x is squared and added to 4 times y, the result is 13. In addition, when the product of 2 and y is added to the product of negative 2 and x, the result is negative 16. Which of the following is a solution for this system of equations?

   A. $x = 8;\ y = 0$
   B. $x = 0;\ y = -8$
   C. $x = 10;\ y = 2$
   D. $x = 5;\ y = -3$
   E. $x = 3;\ y = 1$

56. Clare and MC enter a school competition to determine which student has the best handwriting. Clare writes at a pace of 22 words per minute, and MC writes at a pace of 17 words per minute. If MC starts writing at 2:00, and Clare starts writing at 2:03, then at what time will Clare pass MC in number of words written, rounded *up* to the nearest whole minute?

    F. 2:14
    G. 2:15
    H. 2:16
    J. 2:17
    K. 2:18

57. In the figure below, $\overline{AB}$ is parallel to $\overline{DF}$, and $\overline{GD}$ is parallel to $\overline{EF}$. Angle $\angle AGD$ measures 150°, and $\angle ECF$ measures 90°. If segment $\overline{FC}$ is 4 meters in length, then what is the length of $\overline{EC}$, rounded to the nearest tenth of a meter?

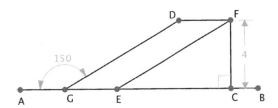

    A. 4.6
    B. 6.9
    C. 7.1
    D. 7.7
    E. 8.0

58. $\left(\sqrt{x^4} - \sqrt[4]{x^8} + \dfrac{1}{x^{-2}}\right)^{\frac{1}{2}} = ?$

    F. $-3x^2$
    G. $-x^2$
    H. $x - x^2$
    J. x
    K. x^2

59. The figure that follows shows three circles, all of which are tangent to one another. The circumference of circle L is 8π mm, the circumference of circle M is 12π mm, and the circumference of circle N is 14π mm. What is the perimeter of triangle $\triangle LMN$ in mm?

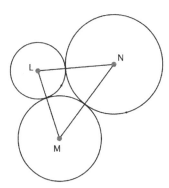

A. 8.5
B. 17
C. 25.5
D. 32
E. 34

60. Jordan decides to flip a coin 5 times in a row. What are the odds that the coin lands on heads the first, second, and third tosses, then lands on tails for both the fourth and fifth tosses?

F. $\dfrac{1}{128}$

G. $\dfrac{1}{64}$

H. $\dfrac{1}{32}$

J. $\dfrac{5}{64}$

K. $\dfrac{5}{32}$

Step 4 Correct Answers

1: C	21: A	41: D
2: H	22: G	42: G
3: D	23: C	43: B
4: F	24: K	44: J
5: D	25: B	45: C
6: K	26: J	46: G
7: B	27: B	47: A
8: F	28: K	48: K
9: A	29: D	49: C
10: G	30: F	50: K
11: E	31: C	51: A
12: H	32: H	52: F
13: D	33: A	53: E
14: G	34: K	54: H
15: B	35: E	55: D
16: J	36: G	56: F
17: C	37: A	57: B
18: J	38: H	58: J
19: E	39: E	59: E
20: F	40: J	60: H

ACT Math *Have to Know* Practice Test answer explanations begin on page 294.

STEP 5

ACT Math Good to Know

The material before this lesson represents the majority of ACT Math problems, covering the most asked about content and the most needed strategies. Here, we begin math that I'm calling *Good to Know*, a module that consists of 11 additional lessons. You may already know how to do many of these things, or maybe they are obscure to you. Nevertheless, you can expect about one question or less per ACT test on all of the math in this module. Between the 11 lessons here, and the multiple pieces of content within each, you can expect at least 10 or so questions on ACT day that require your knowledge of it all in one way or another. This is significant; correctly answering 10 more math questions on the ACT is roughly equivalent to an ACT Math score increase of 5 or 6 points!

Good to Know #1: Fundamental Counting Principle

We will begin with a simple idea with a too-long name: the **Fundamental Counting Principle**. It essentially says this: if there are p ways to do one thing, then q ways to do another, second thing, then there are p x q ways to do both of them. For example: if there are 8 types of ice cream, and 5 types of sprinkles, then there are $8 \times 5 = 40$ ways to combine one flavor of ice cream with one sprinkle topping. If you add in a third option, the number of possibilities increases. If there are 8 types of ice cream, 5 types of sprinkles, AND 6 different flavors of syrupy drizzle to go on top, then now there are $8 \times 5 \times 6 = 240$ different combinations.

Of course, the way in which the ACT will test your ability to think logically in this way differs and is rarely straightforward. Let's get into some examples.

1. Philip and Jenn desire to take a photograph of their five children together, and they decide that the photograph will look best if the children are lined up shoulder-to-shoulder. How many different ways can the couple line up their five children?

   A. 15
   B. 24
   C. 120
   D. 124
   E. 204

2. Delaney has x number of movies to choose from. Which of the following expressions gives the number of possible combinations of movies if Delaney desires to watch 3 movies in a row?

    F. $3x$

    G. x^3

    H. $x(x+1)^2$

    J. x^3x^2x

    K. $x(x-1)(x-2)$

3. The city of Doverville employs 80 police officers and 50 firefighters. The mayor will choose at random 1 police officer and 1 firefighter to represent the city during the Fourth of July Parade. How many different combinations of 1 police officer and 1 firefighter are possible?

    A. 15
    B. 50
    C. 130
    D. 131
    E. 4,000

4. McGregor County issues license plates for all of its automobiles that contain 7 digits. Due to state regulations, the first two digits of the plate are fixed and cannot be changed. Due to local law, the third digit is also fixed and cannot be changed. If the remaining digits can feature either one of the 10 numbers, 0 through 9, or one of the 26 letters of the alphabet, and if the digits *can* be repeated, how many combinations of license plates are possible in McGregor County?

    F. 108
    G. 252
    H. 1,413,720
    J. 1,679,616
    K. 60,466,176

Good to Know #2: Triangles Part II

We have talked a lot about triangles already in ACT Math *Have to Know* Lesson #9. We talked about the angles in a triangle, the trig functions sin, cosine, and tangent, and finding the area of a triangle. All of those things fall into the *Have to Know* math category. However, there are some other things about triangles that I would call *Good to Know*. First, there are *special triangles*, which is more of a helpful shortcut that we've briefly mentioned, and secondly there are the definitions of the various types of triangles.

Special Triangles

Let's start with so-called *special triangles*, which refers to the relationships between the sides of certain right triangles. Before I explain what they mean, and how to use them, let's learn what the two special triangles are that can be helpful on the ACT. There's the 3-4-5 triangle, and the 5-12-13 triangle.

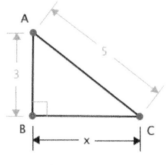

Here's what that means: when you have a right triangle with one side with a length of 3, and a hypotenuse with a length of 5, then you know automatically that the other leg is of length 4.

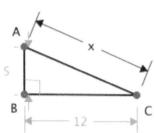

Similarly, if you have a right triangle with one leg having a length of 5, and the other leg having a length of 12, then you know for certain that the length of the hypotenuse is 13.

There is one more thing to know about these: this special relationship also works with *multiples* of each other. In other words, while there is a 3-4-5 triangle, we can multiply those numbers by 2, and learn that there is also such a thing as a 6-8-10 triangle. Like this:

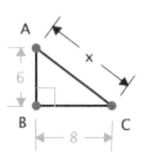

None of these special triangles fall into the *Have to Know* category, especially because you will get the same results if you use the Pythagorean Theorem, but being able to recognize these triangles can oftentimes save you precious time. Again, the ACT likes them (which just means that these kinds of triangles are used relatively often), so knowing to recognize them is only a good thing!

A second category of items that are *Good to Know* when it comes to triangles are the definitions of different triangles. The ACT occasionally likes a question that requires you to categorize a certain triangle, or a question that gives you the definition of a certain type of triangle in the question, requiring you to know what it means. Here are a few:

a) Isosceles Triangle - a triangle with exactly two sides of equal length, like these:

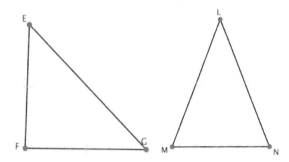

b) Equilateral triangle - a triangle with three equal sides (and also three 60° angles), like this:

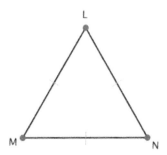

c) Scalene triangle - a triangle with three sides of unequal length. These can be right triangles, or not, like these:

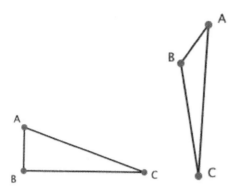

d) Acute triangle - a triangle in which all 3 angles are less than 90 degrees, like these:

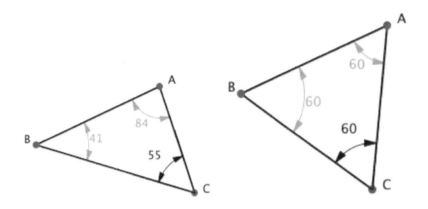

e) Obtuse triangle - a triangle in which at least one angle is greater than 90 degrees, like this:

f) Similar triangles - two triangles with the same angles and equivalent sides. The two triangles below are similar; their angles are the same. On the larger triangle, let's say that the length of side *AB* is 10 and *AC* is 14. That would mean that on the smaller triangle that if *DE* is 5 (which is half of *AB*), then we know that the length of side *DF* is half of *AC*, or 7.

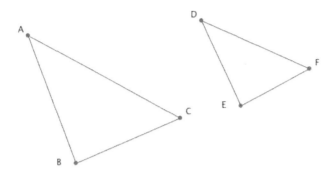

Of course, these triangle concepts overlap, and sometimes you might need to recognize that. All equilateral triangles are acute. An isosceles triangle can be obtuse. A scalene triangle can be acute or obtuse. Etc. Let's get into some examples:

5. In the standard (x, y) coordinate plane, what is the distance between the points $(-2, -2)$ and $(-7, -14)$?

   A. 5
   B. 9
   C. 12
   D. 13
   E. 17

6. Triangle $\triangle LMN$ is an equilateral triangle. If angle $\angle L$ has a measure of 60°, and if side *MN* has a length of 12 millimeters, then which of the following statements are true ?

   I. $\triangle LMN$ is an acute triangle
   II. $\angle N$ is greater than 90°
   III. Side *LM* has a length of less than 12 millimeters

   F. I only
   G. II only
   H. III only
   J. I and III only
   K. I, II, and III

7. In the figure below, $\triangle MNO$ and $\triangle PQR$ are similar triangles with the given side lengths in miles. What is the perimeter, in miles, of $\triangle PQR$?

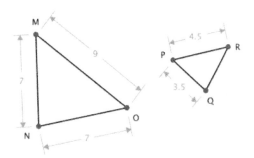

A. 3.5
B. 7.5
C. 11.5
D. 16
E. 23

Good to Know #3: Absolute Value

Absolute Value is a concept that most students have seen and worked with before, but it is time for a refresher. Absolute value is represented by two vertical lines with a numerical value or variable in between, like these:

$$|-2| \quad |3| \quad |y|$$

Here is the simplest explanation of this concept: whatever comes between the bars is made positive, and the bars are removed. Here's a technical, but also simple, meaning of absolute value: it simply represents the distance from 0. Thus, in the above two examples:

The value of $|-2|$ is 2, simply because -2 is 2 away from 0.

The value of $|3|$ is 3, simply because 3 is a total of 3 away from 0.

No matter what y equals, the absolute value of y will be a positive y. So, if $y = -10$ or 10, the value of the absolute value of y in that case is 10, simply because -10 is 10 units away from 0, and 10 is 10 units away from 0.

Unfortunately, it is extremely unlikely that the ACT will ask you to find the absolute value of -3 as one of its 60 questions. Here are a few examples that feature the concept that are more true to the ACT itself.

8. What is $|m - 11|$ when $m = 7$?

    F. -18
    G. -4
    H.   4
    J.   7
    K.   18

9. For all nonzero values of j and k, the value of which of the following expressions is *always* negative ?

A. $\dfrac{|j|}{|k|}$

B. $\dfrac{-j}{-|k|}$

C. $\dfrac{-|j|}{|k|}$

D. $-\dfrac{|j|}{k}$

E. $-\dfrac{j}{k}$

10. Which of the following expressions, if any, is equivalent to $|-x|$?

F. $\dfrac{|x|}{|x|^2}$

G. $-\dfrac{|x|^2}{|x|}$

H. $-x$

J. $\dfrac{|-x|}{|-x|^2}$

K. $\sqrt{(-x)^2}$

Good to Know #4: Inequalities

Inequality Basics

You can expect, on average, 1 question on the ACT Math that tests or requires your understanding of inequalities. An inequality is like an algebraic equation in that it will have one or more variables, but instead of an equal sign, they are related to each other by one of four signs: greater than, less than, greater than or equal to, or less than or equal to. Look at this simple inequality:

$$x > 5$$

All this means is that every possible value of x must be greater than 5: it can be 100, 17, 6, or even 5.1, but it can't be 5 or less. Similarly:

$$x \geq 14$$

All this means, like the last one, is that x can be any number greater than 14, but it could also *be* 14; the line beneath the "greater than" symbol means "or equal to."

If you flip the signs, the explanations are the same. Look at this simple inequality:

$$x < 9$$

All this means is that every possible value of x must be less than 9. Its value could be 8, 0, or -418, and everything up to, but not including, 9. Lastly, here is one featuring a less than or equal to sign:

$$x \leq 20$$

Again, simple idea: the value of x can be anything less than 20, but can also include 20 as well.

Simplifying and Switching Signs

The only remaining thing about inequalities you might need to know is how to solve an equation or simplify an inequality, and what makes the sign "switch" from facing one side to facing another. Imagine you were asked to simplify the following inequality, solving it in terms of x:

$$-x + 3 - 2x < 6$$

You can treat this the exact same way you would treat an equation with an equal sign. First let's combine like terms to get $-3x + 3 < 6$. Next, we can subtract 3 from both sides and end up with $-3x < 3$. To solve for x, what comes next ought to seem pretty clear: we have to divide both sides by negative 3. However, with inequalities, there's a rule here we have to remember: if you divide or multiply both sides of an inequality by a negative number, and only a negative number, then the sign must "switch." This *doesn't* happen when adding/subtracting negative numbers to/from both sides, but *only* with multiplication or division of negative numbers. Thus, if we divide both sides by -3, we end up with the following: $x > -1$. Note that if this were $\leq$ or $\geq$, you wouldn't do anything to the "or equal to" part; it remains; just switch it from facing one way to another!

11. Which of the following inequalities orders the numbers $\frac{3}{8}$, 0.35 , and 0.04 from least to greatest?

   A. $0.35 < \frac{3}{8} < 0.04$

   B. $0.04 < \frac{3}{8} < 0.35$

   C. $\frac{3}{8} < 0.04 < 0.35$

   D. $0.04 < 0.35 < \frac{3}{8}$

   E. $0.35 < 0.04 < \frac{3}{8}$

12. Which of the following inequalities is equivalent to $-2x - 4y \le 6y + 2$?

F. $x \le -5y - 1$
G. $x \ge -5y - 1$
H. $x \le 5y + 1$
J. $x \ge 5y + 1$
K. $x > -5y - 1$

13. Charlotte owns a bakery on a crowded avenue in the big city. The number of cookies, c, that she sells on any given weekday relative to her largest sales day (Saturday) satisfies the inequality $|c - 30| \le 45$. If a negative value of c denotes a decrease in sales from the previous Saturday, which of the following numbers of cookies sold on a Wednesday is NOT within the range of this inequality?

A. -40
B. -15
C. 0
D. 30
E. 70

Good to Know #5: Parabolas

Parabolas are shapes you probably learned about for the first time in Algebra I, but for many of you, that was a long time ago. On average, one ACT Math question per test requires you to be able to work with these shapes in one way or another, and it is the purpose of this small lesson to refresh you on what's most important. Before I sat down and conducted my own research over previous ACT Math tests, I used to think that parabola questions were far more common on the ACT Math test than they really are. Thus, they have landed in the *Good to Know* category instead of the *Have to Know* category.

A parabola is a shape that results from graphing a quadratic equation; a quadratic equation is a trinomial in which a variable, usually x, is raised to the second power, like this:

$$y = 4x^2 + 4x - 8$$

This might be bringing back bad memories of the Quadratic Formula, but don't worry, it's not necessary to memorize the Quadratic Formula to get a parabola question right on the ACT!

Here is what the quadratic we just came up with looks like when graphed:

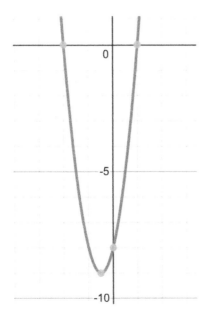

This shape is usually represented by two arrows on the lines that stretch upwards since they go on forever. There are a couple of things about this that you should know.

First are the *solutions*. Many students have no idea what that means, and are often faced with questions that ask for the solution set of a quadratic, or ask for the number of solutions for a quadratic, or something like that. Well, for any quadratic, the solutions are where the parabola crosses the x-axis. In this graph pictured, here, the parabola crosses the x-axis at -2 and 1, which are the two solutions.

It is possible, however, for a parabola to have only one solution. That would be when the "tip" of the parabola (minimum for an upwards moving parabola, maximum for a downwards moving parabola) is actually on the x-axis. Lastly, it is also possible for a parabola to have no solutions. In that case, the parabola does not cross the x-axis at all.

So, let's assume you've been given a quadratic or the formula for a parabola, like this one: $y = x^2 - 6x + 9$, and you are asked to find the solutions. One way that was probably drilled into your brain in Algebra was to use the Quadratic Formula. If you have the Quadratic Formula memorized, then go for it, but the Quadratic Formula is better used on quadratics that can't be factored easily, unlike most (or probably all) that you'll see on the ACT.

DO NOT binge study the Quadratic Formula…there are easier ways to find the solution or solutions (if there are any) for a parabola like this one, which will be best explained through our first example. First, there is graphing. On your graphing calculator, hit buttons in this order (using the trinomial from above, $y = x^2 - 6x + 9$, as an example):

1: Y= **2:** X,T,Θ,n **3:** ^ **4:** 2 **5:** - **6:** 6 **7:** X,T,Θ,n **8:** + **9:** 9 **10:** GRAPH

Anywhere the parabola crosses the x-axis, you have your solutions (in this case, the parabola never truly "crosses" the x-axis; rather, it "touches" the x-axis at $x = 3$, which is our one solution then).

The second way, which is usually my default way to solve these, is to factor the trinomial into two binomials, then set each of these equal to zero. To factor a trinomial like this one (let's remember the trinomial we're dealing with: $y = x^2 - 6x + 9$), you first identify two numbers that *multiply* to give you your third term (in this case, 9) that can also be added to equal the coefficient in front of the x in your second/middle term (in this case, -6). One thought is that $3 \times 3 = 9$, but $3 + 3 = 6$, not -6, so try again. However, notice that $(-3) \times (-3) = 9$, and $(-3) + (-3) = -6$. Thus, -3 and -3 become the second terms in our two binomials, both added to x. Factored, our trinomial now looks like:

$$y = x^2 - 6x + 9 = (x - 3)(x - 3)$$

Now that we have our two binomials $(x - 3)$ and $(x - 3)$, we should set each of them equal to 0 and solve each individually.

$(x - 3) = 0$ $\qquad\qquad\qquad\qquad\qquad\qquad$ $(x - 3) = 0$

$x = 3$ $\qquad\qquad\qquad\qquad\qquad\qquad\qquad\quad$ $x = 3$

It may seem strange that our "two" solutions are the same, but there is nothing strange about it at all; all this means is that there is only 1 solution. The parabola has its vertex at $x = 3$, meaning it only has one solution. If you were to graph this on a graphing calculator, you would see a parabola with its "tip" at 3.

I think we've said enough about the parabola; let's get into a few examples based on recent ACT tests:

14. What is the mean of the 2 solutions of the equation $x^2 - 10x - 24$?

    F. -12
    G. -5
    H.   0
    J.   5
    K.   7

15. What is the solution set of the equation $x(x - 1) = 2x^2 + 9x + 25$?

    A. $\{-5\}$
    B. $\{-5, 2.5\}$
    C. $\{-2.5, 2.5\}$
    D. $\{5\}$
    E.   The set of all real numbers

16. The 3 parabolas graphed in the standard (x, y) coordinate plane below are from a family of parabolas. A general equation that defines this family of parabolas contains the variable z in addition to x and y. For the parabola with the smallest minimum, $z = 2$; for the parabola with a minimum between the other two, $z = 4$; and for the parabola with the largest minimum, $z = 6$. Which of the following could be a general equation that defines this family of parabolas?

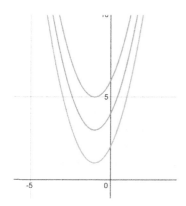

F. $y = zx^2 + 2x - 1$

G. $y = x^2 + zx + 5$

H. $y = x^2 + 2x + z$

J. $y = x^2 + 2x - z$

K. $7 = -x^2 - zx + 5$

Good to Know #6: Trig Graphs and Wave Familiarity

Usually, though not always, ACT Math questions that mention or show figures featuring waves have specifically to do with the graphs of sine and cosine, which are waves (unlike tangent, which is not a wave!). In this little lesson overall, though, we will discuss the vocabulary around waves, like wavelength and amplitude. I think the best way to teach these things is by analyzing the graph of sine, then cosine, but again, the purpose of this book is not to examine each and every possible math concept that could conceivably be asked about or required on any given ACT Math test; that kind of book would be impossibly long.

What you see here is a graph of sine and cosine. If you've never seen this, it can be intimidating. Before we talk about these trig functions in particular, we should go over basic wave vocabulary. That's a good first

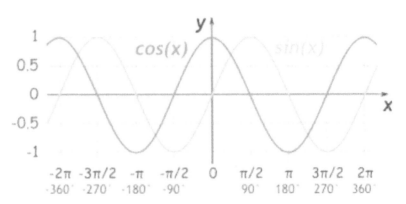

step because it's not uncommon for you to get an ACT Math question where you simply have to find the amplitude, period, crest, trough, or wavelength of a wave.

- **Crest:** the height of the tip of a wave; how far "up" it goes (for both sin(x) and cos(x), this is 1).

- **Trough:** the depth of the tip of a wave; how far "down" it goes (for both sin(x) and cos(x), this is -1).

- **Period/wavelength:** the length or width of a wave from crest to crest or trough to trough. For sin(x) and cos(x), the period/wavelength is 2π.

- **Amplitude:** the height of a wave, from the *x*-axis to the crest (or, the depth of a wave, from the *x*-axis to the trough). For both sin(*x*) and cos(*x*), this is 1.

For sine and cosine, if need be, you are able to graph these on your graphing calculator. Before you do so, hit "Mode" and make sure your calculator is set to radians, not degrees (as a side note, this would be the only conceivable situation in which your calculator would be set to radians; MAKE SURE before the test begins that your calculator is set to DEGREES, otherwise, you will be thoroughly lost on many problems).

Here is how to graph sine (once your calculator is set to radians), for example, step by step. In your calculator, hit these buttons in order:

1: Y=   **2:** SIN   **3:** X,T,Θ,n   **4:**)   **5:** GRAPH

You'll see a sine wave pop up. This would only be necessary if a question asks you what happens to the graph of a sine wave when the equation is altered with a new number in parentheses after sine (such as sin(3*x*), with a number before sine (multiplied by sine, in other words, like 4sin(*x*)), or if a number is added to the end of the equation (such as sin(*x*)+2). If you've got the time, you can play with these in your calculator. In the mean time, here are a couple of examples based on how these types of wave questions have been asked in previous ACT's.

17. For four days, Olivia charts the times for high and low tide for Flint Bay. On Day 1, high tide occurred at 1:15 PM and low tide occurred at 11:45 PM; on Day 2, high tide occurred at 12:30 PM and low tide occurred at 11:00 PM; on Day 3, high tide occurred at 11:45 AM and low tide occurred at 10:15 PM; and on Day 4; high tide occurred at 11:00 AM and low tide occurred at 9:30 PM. What is the average period of the wave created by Olivia's charts?

    A.   21 hours and 15 minutes
    B.   21 hours and 45 minutes
    C.   22 hours and 45 minutes
    D.   23 hours and 15 minutes
    E.   24 hours and 45 minutes

18. Consider the function $f(x) = c \sin x$, where c is a real number. As c increases, what happens to the wavelength and the amplitude of the resulting graph?

    F. The period increases; the amplitude decreases.
    G. The period stays the same; the amplitude increases.
    H. The period decreases; the amplitude stays the same.
    J. The period and the amplitude both stay the same.
    K. The period and the amplitude both increase.

Good to Know #7: Overlapping Line Segments and Categories

I don't really know what to call this type of question besides *Overlapping Line Segments or Categories*. This represents a question that you would probably never actually have in math class, but tests your reasoning skills. The ACT likes this kind of question and, if I were to place a bet, I'd say you'd see one on your next ACT Math test.

In these kinds of questions, sometimes a line segment is either described or given, and it features usually 4 points, probably labeled *A*, *B*, *C*, and *D* (such as in #19 below). The distance between some of these points are given, and you'll need to analyze the line in the right way to determine a distance between two other points that is not yet given. While there are reasoning ways to solve these kinds of problems, for stuck students, there is always the *Drawn to Scale* mini-strategy (if you skipped that, go back and check it out in Step 2!). Because some line lengths will be given, you can used the edge of your answer sheet as a ruler, then compare to the line the length of which you are trying to find.

Another way this kind of question is asked is that some people are described as doing one thing (such as taking a Spanish class), another group of people is described as doing another (such as taking a French class), and you have determine how many do either or both. Instead of analyzing here exactly how to solve this kind of problem, let's let the examples below do the talking, one of each type described above. Try each one yourself first, reasoning your way through it, before you check answers and read the answer explanations.

19. Points *B* and *C* lie on *AD*. The length of *AD* is 45 units; *AC* is 27 units long; and *BD* is 26 units long. How many units long, if it can be determined, is *BC* ?

- **A.** 8
- **B.** 11
- **C.** 18
- **D.** 19
- **E.** Cannot be determined from the given information

20. Mr. East takes a poll in his class of 25 students. He finds that 15 of them play a Spring sport and that 17 of them play a Fall sport. Given this information, what is the minimum number of students in the class who play both a Spring and a Fall sport?

    F. 0

    G. 2

    H. 7

    J. 15

    K. 17

Good to Know #8: Matrices

A matrix in math is a set of numbers arranged in rows and columns, like this:

$$\begin{bmatrix} 3 & 2 & -1 \\ -4 & 2 & 1 \\ 5 & -3 & 7 \end{bmatrix}$$

For our purposes, there are two main things it's *Good to Know* about matrices: how to add/subtract them, and how to multiply them.

Let's start with a simple **addition**. We will use two matrices that have the same dimensions, which is the number of rows (rows run left to right) × the number of columns (columns run up and down), like this:

$$\begin{bmatrix} 0 & 4 \\ -3 & 7 \end{bmatrix} + \begin{bmatrix} -2 & -1 \\ 4 & -2 \end{bmatrix} = \begin{bmatrix} -2 & 3 \\ 1 & 5 \end{bmatrix}$$

The only way, in fact, to add or subtract matrices is if they have the same dimensions, otherwise, it is undefined. Above, you can see I simply added one location at a time. The top-left corner of each matrix is added together, $(0 + -2)$, which equals the top-left corner of the resulting matrix (-2).

As for **multiplication**, there is a strange rule that must be remembered: two matrices can only be multiplied if the number of columns in the first matrix equals the number of rows in the second matrix. If not, the answer is undefined. Here is an example of this:

$$[-3 \quad 4 \quad 0] \times \begin{bmatrix} 2 \\ 8 \\ -7 \end{bmatrix} =$$

The first of these matrices is a 1×3 (1 row and 3 columns), and the second is a 3×1 (3 rows and 1 column). Because the number of columns in the first (3) matches the number of rows in the second (also

3), they *can* be multiplied. The size of the resulting matrix will be the exact opposite; because there is one *row* in the first and one *column* in the second, respectively, the result will be a matrix that is 1×1 after finding the dot product.

$$[(-3 \times 2) + (4 \times 8) + (0 \times -7)] = [-6 + 32 + 0] = [26]$$

This would be the dot product of row 1 of the first, times column 1 of the second. In the examples below, you'll see a matrix multiplication problem that is a bit different. But remember: if the columns in the 1st match the rows in the 2nd, they can be multiplied; the result will be a matrix of size (rows in 1st) × (columns in 2nd). I remember this by the letters **crrc.** Let's make up a weird sentence to remember this by...how about, "**C**alm **R**ivers **R**eveal **C**rocs." CRRC: columns = rows, rows × columns. Hey if it works, right?

Now, let's look at some examples based on recent ACT tests:

21. Which of the following matrices is equivalent to
$$\begin{bmatrix} -6 & 9 \\ -8 & 4 \end{bmatrix} - \begin{bmatrix} 10 & -4 \\ -1 & 0 \end{bmatrix}?$$

A. $\begin{bmatrix} 4 & 5 \\ -9 & 4 \end{bmatrix}$

B. $\begin{bmatrix} -16 & 13 \\ -7 & 4 \end{bmatrix}$

C. $\begin{bmatrix} 60 & -36 \\ 8 & 0 \end{bmatrix}$

D. $\begin{bmatrix} -16 & 5 \\ -9 & 0 \end{bmatrix}$

E. $\begin{bmatrix} 4 & 13 \\ 7 & 4 \end{bmatrix}$

22. Which of the following matrices is equal to $3 \begin{bmatrix} 0 & -2 \\ 6 & 5 \end{bmatrix}$?

F. $\begin{bmatrix} 0 & -\frac{2}{3} \\ \frac{1}{2} & \frac{3}{5} \end{bmatrix}$

G. $\begin{bmatrix} 3 & 1 \\ 9 & 8 \end{bmatrix}$

H. $\begin{bmatrix} 0 & -\frac{3}{2} \\ 2 & \frac{5}{3} \end{bmatrix}$

J. $\begin{bmatrix} 0 & -6 \\ 18 & 15 \end{bmatrix}$

K. $\begin{bmatrix} 18 & 9 \end{bmatrix}$

23. What is the matrix product $\begin{bmatrix} -4 \\ x \\ 2x \end{bmatrix} \begin{bmatrix} x & 3 & 0 \end{bmatrix}$?

A. $\begin{bmatrix} -x \end{bmatrix}$

B. $\begin{bmatrix} -x^2 + 9x - 12 \end{bmatrix}$

C. $\begin{bmatrix} -x^2 \\ 9x \\ -12 \end{bmatrix}$

D. $\begin{bmatrix} -4x & -12 & 0 \\ x^2 & 3x & 0 \\ 2x^2 & 6x & 0 \end{bmatrix}$

E. The product is undefined

Good to Know #9: Tricky Conversions

Another *Good to Know* ACT Math skill is the ability to convert from one unit of measure (whether it be time or distance), and perhaps even back again in the other direction (such as feet to inches, hours to minutes, etc.). One way the ACT likes to trip up students is to give them a math question in inches, then require the answer in feet, or something similar. Of course, there are 12 inches in 1 foot. But how long is 3.75 feet? Some students are too quick and say, "3 feet and 7.5 inches," but that's not the case (and, of course, one of the answer choices is going to match up well with that error). 3.75 feet, rather, is 3 feet and 3 quarters of 1 foot, or 3 feet 9 inches.

Give the following examples your best shot! Remember to take your time and don't trip up making simple mistakes.

24. A board (shown below) 7 feet 4 inches long is cut into 2 equal parts. What is the length, to the nearest inch, of each part?

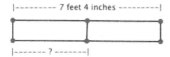

| |------ 7 feet 4 inches ------| |

| |----- ? -----| |

   F.   3 feet 5 inches
   G.   3 feet 7 inches
   H.   3 feet 8 inches
   J.   4 feet 0 inches
   K.   4 feet 2 inches

25. Samuel is the facilities director at a high school. After measuring the floor of the cafeteria, he realizes that he will need 14,400 square feet of new tile. However, the type of tile that he needs to purchase is only sold by the square yard. How many square yards of tile will Samuel need to cover the floor of the cafeteria?

   A.   240
   B.   480
   C.   1,600
   D.   3,600
   E.   4,800

26. Clarence is cruising down the highway on his motorcycle at 40 miles per hour. At that rate, how many miles will Clarence drive in 16 minutes?

F. $10\dfrac{2}{3}$

G. $10\dfrac{3}{4}$

H. 11

J. $12\dfrac{1}{2}$

K. 16

Good to Know #10: Logarithms and Exponents

Logarithms

Logarithms is a scary word, and the form of a logarithm usually strikes fear and confusion into the typical ACT test taker. However, if you can grasp a basic understanding of a logarithm, you will be in a great place, and getting a basic grasp is much simpler than you think. I wouldn't say that if it wasn't true. It's as simple as this: if you understand exponents, you can understand the basics of logarithms.

Take, for example, this exponent: 2^5. You know what that means: $2 \times 2 \times 2 \times 2 \times 2$, which is 32. Pretty simple, thus, we can write it like this: $2^5 = 32$.

However, what if we didn't know what the exponent was? In other words, what if we had an equation that looked like this: $2^x = 32$? Well, it is logarithms that allow you to solve this equation for x, to find a missing exponent. This is what it looks like:

$$\log_2 32 = x$$

This is simply asking: with a base of 2, what is the value of the exponent x when 2 raised to the x power equals 32?

There is a way to type logs into your calculator to figure out exponents, such as in the example above. Sometimes, however, figuring out how to properly do this on your calculator is more difficult than just writing it on paper and then using the basics of your calculator to solve. If I thought you needed to know how to type this into a calculator for the purposes of ACT Math, I would tell you, as I have before. Chances are, if you play around with your calculator and the LOG button, you will end up confused. That is because the LOG function on your calculator is automatically set to a base of 10 (as in, 10 raised to a power). You will have to go into your MATH options and find "Logbase" to change that. This is confusing and time-consuming, and unless you've already got this calculator skill mastered, keep reading.

Instead, do what I alluded to in the above paragraph. Use your calculator's basics and *Backsolving* until you get the right answer. For example, let's say you were asked to find the value of x in the following:

$$\log_3 114 = x$$

When written without the *log*, the equation looks like this: $3^x = 114$. Thus, 3 raised to the power of what exponent will give us 114? Well, you are going to be given 5 answer choices, right? Why not go through them and see which one fits? Let's say **C** was 3.75. Well, when I type in my calculator 3 ^ 3.75 and hit =, I get a value of 61.55; not big enough, so I need to go higher. Answer choice D is 4.31. I type in 3 ^ 4.31, and sure enough, that's the correct answer.

Recently, I saw some students in my classes working on logs for their Algebra II class. They were solving lots of complicated equations in which log functions were being multiplied by each other, divided by each other, etc. I have never seen that kind of question on the ACT Math test. It doesn't mean it can't happen, but it means that going through all of that here in preparation for ACT Math is unnecessary. If you've got the basics outlined above, you're good to go!

Exponents

While we're here, let's review some basics of exponents. We reviewed some of this a bit in previous examples in other lessons, but here is a refresher. It might have been a while since you used these, but they can certainly be helpful.

First, negative exponents. A negative exponent simply means that the term needs to be moved from the numerator into the denominator, or vice versa. For example: $3^{-3} = \dfrac{1}{3^3} = \dfrac{1}{9}$.

Second, any number except for 0 raised to the power of 0 always =1. For your sanity and mine, let's not spend 15 minutes reviewing why that is the case, but here are some examples: $(-44)^0 = 1$, $7^0 = 1$, and for all values of x that do not equal 9, $\left(\dfrac{x+2}{x-9}\right)^0 = 1$.

With that said, let's get into a couple of examples that test your understanding:

27. Which of the following is a value of x that satisfies $\log_x 343 = 3$?

   A. 3
   B. 5
   C. 7
   D. 9
   E. 11

28. When $\log_4 x = -3$, what is x ?

   F. -9

   G. -3

   H. $-\dfrac{1}{8}$

   J. $\dfrac{1}{64}$

   K. $\dfrac{1}{4}$

29. What is the value of $\dfrac{\frac{1}{3^{-3}}}{3}$?

   A. -9
   B. -3
   C. 9
   D. 27
   E. 81

30. Simplify $\dfrac{a^{-3}b^2c^{-4}}{a^2b^{-2}c^{-1}}$.

   F. $\dfrac{b^4}{a^5c^3}$

   G. $\dfrac{b^4}{a^6c^5}$

   H. $\dfrac{1}{a^6c^5}$

   J. $\dfrac{1}{a^5c^3}$

   K. $a\,c^3$

Good to Know #11: Formula of a Circle

Again, there are many, many additional categories or types of math questions that could be asked on ACT day, but to cover every possibility thoroughly would require a redo of every math lesson you could possibly have had from 6th to 12th grade, and then some. You can't possibly prepare anew for every one of these possibilities, but the more you practice, the more likely you are to increase your knowledge, understanding, and experience, and thus up your score. Indeed: if you can learn and master the 24 ACT Math *Have to Know* and *Good to Know* math categories and lessons as presented in this book, there is little doubt that you will succeed on test day.

The last type of math knowledge that I can put into the *Good to Know* category is that of the formula or equation of a circle. Again, being in this category simply means that there's a good chance you will have at least one question on ACT day about it, or one question that requires your knowledge of it as a step towards a right answer…it's not guaranteed. What *is* guaranteed is the material we covered on circles back in *Have to Know* Lesson 13.

Let's keep this as simple as possible. The formula for a circle is as follows:

$$(x - h)^2 + (y - k)^2 = r^2$$

The coordinate (h, k) is the center of the circle, and r is the radius.

So, if we had a circle with its center at $(1, 4)$ and a radius of 3, its formula would look like this:

$$(x - 1)^2 + (y - 4)^2 = 9$$

With that out of the way, let's go through a few examples relative to this topic that are the kinds of questions typical of the ACT.

31. What is the formula of a circle that is centered on $(-1, 3)$ and has a radius of 5 ?

  A. $(x + 1)^2 + (y - 3)^2 = 5$
  B. $(x - 1)^2 + (y + 3)^2 = 5$
  C. $(x + 1)^2 + (y - 3)^2 = 25$
  D. $(x - 1)^2 + (y + 3)^2 = 25$
  E. $(x - 1)^2 + (y - 3)^2 = 25$

32. Consider the following three circles:

  I. A circle centered at $(-2, -2)$ passing through $(6, -2)$
  II. A circle with a circumference of 16π
  III. A circle with the equation $(x - 9)^2 + (y + 3)^2 = 64$

  Which of the circles has an area of 64π ?

  F. II only
  G. I and II only
  H. I and III only
  J. II and III only
  K. I, II, and III

33. In the standard (x, y) coordinate plane, Circle P is represented by the formula $(x - 2)^2 + (y - 5)^2 = 49$ and passes through which of the following points ?

  A. $(2, -2)$
  B. $(2, 5)$
  C. $(-2, 2)$
  D. $(5, -3)$
  E. $(9, 12)$

Step 5 Correct Answers

1: C	12: G	23: D
2: K	13: A	24: H
3: E	14: J	25: C
4: J	15: A	26: F
5: D	16: H	27: C
6: F	17: D	28: J
7: C	18: G	29: C
8: H	19: A	30: F
9: C	20: H	31: C
10: K	21: B	32: K
11: D	22: J	33: A

ACT Math *Good to Know* practice answer explanations begin on page 310.

STEP 6

Full-Length Practice Tests

Practice Test Introduction

The two practice tests that follow below are designed to mimic real ACT Math tests as closely as possible. They include, like a real ACT Math test, a multiplicity of *Have to Know* questions, a large handful of *Good to Know* questions, and a scattering of *Possibly Might Have to Know* material. Though this book does not feature formal lessons on this last category, if you have completed the book to this point, you have encountered many in the example questions.

When I say the following tests mimic real ACT Math tests, I mean that is also true in the details. Each question has 5 answer choices; each answer choice is used exactly 6 times; the first third is the easiest third, the middle third is of middle difficulty, and the final third is the most difficult third; some problems feature given diagrams, some describe them and require the test taker to draw them; etc.

This is another opportunity to formally test your math knowledge and ACT Math capabilities. Do this test in a quiet space. Set a 60 minute timer. Utilize the 4 ACT Math mini-strategies, but most importantly, implement the *Two Pass* strategy from Step 1 by circling and skipping questions that you foresee will pose great difficulties and cost you a lot of time off the bat; bank that time for the end, ensuring you given every question a shot.

Following each test, you will find the list of correct answers, and explanations for each question can be found in the back of the book. Practice Test 1 explanations begin on page 318, and Practice Test 2 explanations begin on page 334.

Best of luck! But if you've made it this far through this book, you probably don't need luck!

PRACTICE TEST 1
60 Minutes, 60 Questions

MATHEMATICS TEST

60 Minutes — 60 Questions

DIRECTIONS: Solve each problem, choose the correct answer, and then fill in the corresponding oval on your answer document.

Do not linger over problems that take too much time. Solve as many as you can; then return to the others in the time you have left for this test.

You are permitted to use a calculator on this test. You may use your calculator for any problems you choose, but some of the problems may best be done without using a calculator.

Note: Unless otherwise stated, all of the following should be assumed.

1. Illustrative figures are NOT necessarily drawn to scale.
2. Geometric figures lie in a plane.
3. The word *line* indicates a straight line.
4. The word *average* indicates arithmetic mean.

---

1. Chip sold 28 candy bars for $1.30 each. With the money from these sales, he bought 3 fishing poles and had $13.90 left over. What was the average amount Chip paid for each fishing pole?

   A. $3.90
   B. $5.63
   C. $7.50
   D. $11.23
   E. $22.50

2. Roberto left his home at 6:00 a.m. on Saturday and traveled 880 miles. When he arrived at his destination, it was 10:00 p.m. on the same day. Given that his home and his destination are in the same time zone, which of the following is closest to his average speed, in miles per hour, for this trip?

   F. 59
   G. 55
   H. 52
   J. 19
   K. 9

3. For her dog walking business, Sylvia charges a $12.00 fee plus $1.25 for each block that she walks a dog. If Sylvia is paid $29.50 for the dog she walked today, then how many blocks did she walk the dog?

   A. 9.6
   B. 14.0
   C. 16.0
   D. 17.5
   E. 23.6

4. A point at $(4, -6)$ in the standard (x, y) coordinate plane is translated down 5 coordinate units and right 9 coordinate units. What are the coordinates of the point after the translation?

   F. $(-1, -15)$
   G. $(-1, -9)$
   H. $(-5, 9)$
   J. $(13, -5)$
   K. $(13, -11)$

DO YOUR FIGURING HERE.

5. Which of the following matrices is equal to $\begin{bmatrix} 4 & 9 \\ -3 & 7 \end{bmatrix} + \begin{bmatrix} -8 & 3 \\ 4 & 0 \end{bmatrix}$?

A. $\begin{bmatrix} -4 & 12 \\ 1 & 7 \end{bmatrix}$

B. $\begin{bmatrix} 12 & 6 \\ -7 & 7 \end{bmatrix}$

C. $\begin{bmatrix} -4 & 6 \\ 7 & 0 \end{bmatrix}$

D. $\begin{bmatrix} -2 & 3 \\ -1 & 0 \end{bmatrix}$

E. $\begin{bmatrix} -8 & 9 \\ 4 & 7 \end{bmatrix}$

6. The square root of a certain number is approximately 7.48921. The certain number is between what two integers?

F. 2 and 3
G. 3 and 4
H. 7 and 8
J. 14 and 15
K. 49 and 64

7. When points $A(2, -4)$ and B are graphed in the standard (x, y) coordinate plane, the midpoint of $\overline{AB}$ will be $(4, 1)$. What will be the coordinates of point B?

A. $(6, 6)$
B. $(3, 6)$
C. $(6, -3)$
D. $(-2, -5)$
E. $(-2, -7)$

8. There is to be a race between 20 total cars: 12 white, 4 green, 3 red, and 1 orange. If all cars are otherwise equal, what is the probability that the winner of the race is NOT a green car?

F. $\dfrac{1}{10}$

G. $\dfrac{1}{5}$

H. $\dfrac{1}{2}$

J. $\dfrac{4}{5}$

K. $\dfrac{9}{10}$

DO YOUR FIGURING HERE.

9. David's bookshelves have on them 207 books, which is 30 more than 3 times the number of books he had on them last year. How many books did David have on the bookshelves last year?

    A. 21
    B. 39
    C. 54
    D. 59
    E. 69

10. A function, f, is defined by $f(x, y) = -(x^3) + 3y$. What is the value of the function $f(2, -1)$?

    F. -11
    G. -5
    H. 5
    J. 7
    K. 11

11. Points B and C lie on $\overline{AD}$ as shown below. The length of $\overline{AD}$ is 34 units; $\overline{AC}$ is 21 units long; and $\overline{BD}$ is 24 units long. How many units long is $\overline{BC}$?

    A. 5
    B. 11
    C. 17
    D. 19
    E. 20

12. What are the values for y that satisfy the equation $(y + m)(y - n) = 0$?

    F. m and n
    G. m and $-n$
    H. $-m$ and $-n$
    J. $-m$ and n
    K. mn

13. What is the solution set for x if $x^2 = 7x(x - 0) - 54$?

    A. $\{-4\}$
    B. $\{5\}$
    C. $\{9\}$
    D. $\{-2, 2\}$
    E. $\{-3, 3\}$

Use the following information to answer questions 14-16.

In the figure below, E is the center of the circle, and FG is a diameter. Point H lies on the circle, I lies outside the circle on $\overleftrightarrow{FG}$, $\overleftrightarrow{IK}$ is tangent to the circle at J, and $\overline{KF}$ is perpendicular to $\overline{FG}$.

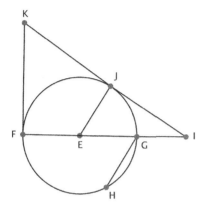

14. Which of the following angles or minor arcs has the greatest degree measure?

   F. $\angle FKJ$

   G. $\angle FGH$

   H. $\overset{\frown}{FJ}$

   J. $\overset{\frown}{JG}$

   K. $\overset{\frown}{GH}$

15. If segment $\overline{EJ}$ is perpendicular to $\overline{KI}$, and if $\overline{EJ}$ has a slope of $\frac{3}{2}$, what is the slope of $\overline{KI}$?

   A. $-\frac{3}{2}$

   B. $-\frac{2}{3}$

   C. $\frac{2}{3}$

   D. $\frac{3}{2}$

   E. 3

16. If segment $\overline{KF}$ is 20 units long, and the diameter of the circle centered at E is 22 units, then what is the area of the circle that lies within $\triangle KFI$?

    F. 11π
    G. 22π
    H. 60.5π
    J. 91π
    K. 121π

---

17. On a map, $\dfrac{1}{5}$ centimeters represents 14 kilometers. Two mountains that are $3\dfrac{2}{5}$ centimeters apart on this map are how many actual kilometers apart?

    A. 47.6
    B. 119
    C. 224
    D. 238
    E. 476

18. Candace rides her bike at a rate of 11 miles per hour. At that rate, how many miles will she ride in 11 minutes, rounded to the nearest mile?

    F. 2
    G. 3
    H. 4
    J. 22
    K. 121

19. John's teacher hands him a calculator with a pre-programmed linear function, but John does not know what the function is. When 3 is entered, the calculator displays the value 7. When 12 is entered, the calculator displays the value 28. Which of the following expressions explains what the calculator will display when any number, z, is entered?

    A. $\dfrac{3}{7}z$

    B. $7z$

    C. $\dfrac{7}{3}z$

    D. $z + 4$

    E. $2z + 4$

20. In the figure below, V is on $\overleftrightarrow{WX}$ and Y is on $\overleftrightarrow{WZ}$. What is the measure of $\angle VWY$?

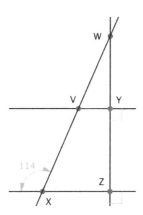

   F.   12°
   G. 24°
   H. 66°
   J.   114°
   K. 156°

21. A certain stock was valued at $500 per share at 8:00 a.m. The value of the stock dropped by 5% each hour for three straight hours before rising back to a value of $500 by the end of the fourth hour. What percent did the stock rise in the fourth hour, rounded to the nearest percent?

   A. 5
   B. 10
   C. 15
   D. 16
   E. 17

22. On a certain race track, riders are given scores based on their average times across 6 races. These scores are assigned according to the chart below.

Average (seconds)	Score
55.10 or more	Poor
51.10-55.09	Fair
46.10-51.09	Average
43.00-46.09	Good
42.99 or less	Superior

If Ethan records times of 42.50, 45.50, 45.00, 51.25, and 47.75 seconds in his first 5 races, then which of the following times in his sixth and last race would cause Ethan to receive a score of Good for the season?

   F. 44.00
   G. 45.00
   H. 46.00
   J.   48.00
   K. 50.00

DO YOUR FIGURING HERE.

23. Given $x = \dfrac{y}{y-1}$ and $y < -2$, which of the following is a possible value of x ?

    A. -1.71
    B. -0.71
    C. 0.00
    D. 0.71
    E. 1.71

24. The set of all possible integers divisible by both 21 and 49 is infinite. What is the least possible integer in this infinite set?

    F. 7
    G. 49
    H. 70
    J. 147
    K. 294

25. Richard's caddy assures him that when he strikes the ball with his 9-iron, the ball will land within a certain area. If this area consists of 198 square feet of green, 94 square feet of fringe, 134 square feet of sand trap, and 124 square feet of rough, then which of the following is the best estimate of the probability that the ball will land in a sand trap when Richard strikes the ball?

    A. 13.4%
    B. 24.4%
    C. 28.7%
    D. 32.2%
    E. 33.3%

26. A parallelogram has a perimeter of 102 inches, and 1 of its sides measures 22 inches. If it can be determined, what are the lengths, in inches, of the other 3 sides?

    F. 22, 21, 21
    G. 22, 22, 22
    H. 22, 29, 29
    J. 22, 30, 30
    K. Cannot be determined from the given information

27. On a certain softball field, home plate is equivalent to the origin $(0, 0)$ in the standard (x, y) coordinate plane, the first base line is equivalent to the positive x-axis, and the third base line is equivalent to the positive y-axis. Hitting a ball into Quadrant I is fair, and any other hit is foul. If Carla hits a fair ball from home plate that, when graphed, travels 40 feet and 96 feet down the first and third base lines, respectively, then how far did the ball travel?

    A. 104 feet
    B. 114 feet
    C. 118 feet
    D. 133 feet
    E. 136 feet

DO YOUR FIGURING HERE.

28. In the isosceles triangle △*ABC* shown below, the measure of ∠*B* is 72°. If it can be determined, what is the measure of ∠*C* ?

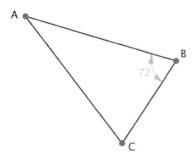

F. 36°
G. 46°
H. 72°
J. 108°
K. Cannot be determined from the given information

29. A manufacturer builds 3 different models of bicycles (X, Y, and Z). They order all of the frames, wheels, and accessories packages from a certain supplier for a fixed price. The table below gives the prices of these bicycle components for each of the three bicycle models.

Model	Frame Price	Wheel Price (for 1 wheel)	Accessories Package Price
X	$55	$20	$24
Y	$58	$24	$24
Z	$70	$33	$24

The manufacturer gets an order for 2 X's, 7 Y's, and 5 Z's. If each bicycle needs 2 wheels, what will be the cost to the manufacturer to purchase the components necessary to build these bicycles?

A. $1,575
B. $1,893
C. $1,948
D. $2,008
E. $2,118

30. A board 7 feet 3 inches long is cut into 3 equal parts. What is the length, to the nearest inch, of each part?

F. 2 feet 4 inches
G. 2 feet 5 inches
H. 2 feet 9 inches
J. 3 feet 1 inch
K. 5 feet 5 inches

31. In the standard (x, y) coordinate plane, H' is the image resulting from the reflection of the point $H(-4, 2)$ across the x-axis. What are the coordinates of H' ?

- **A.** $(4, 2)$
- **B.** $(4, -2)$
- **C.** $(-2, 4)$
- **D.** $(-4, -2)$
- **E.** $(-2, -4)$

32. Which of the following expressions is equivalent to $-\dfrac{1}{x^z} \times \dfrac{1}{21^z}$?

- **F.** $(-x \times 21)^{-2z}$
- **G.** $-(x \times 21)^{2z}$
- **H.** $(-x \times 21)^{z}$
- **J.** $-(x \times 21)^{z}$
- **K.** $(-x \times 21)^{-z}$

33. To increase the mean of 5 numbers by 7, how much would the sum of the 5 numbers have to increase?

- **A.** $\dfrac{5}{7}$
- **B.** $\dfrac{7}{5}$
- **C.** 1
- **D.** 12
- **E.** 35

34. Genevieve was training for a marathon. On her first practice run, she ran 11 blocks before stopping for the day. On the next day, she ran a second practice run that was $\dfrac{3}{5}$ farther than the distance of her practice run the previous day, then repeated the same $\dfrac{3}{5}$ increase in distance on her practice runs for the next two consecutive days. How many blocks did Genevieve run on her 4th day of training?

- **F.** 28.1600 blocks
- **G.** 30.8000 blocks
- **H.** 45.0560 blocks
- **J.** 70.4000 blocks
- **K.** 72.0896 blocks

Use the following information to answer questions 35-37.

DO YOUR FIGURING HERE.

A professional baseball league is training a new umpire to replace one who is entering into retirement. When watching film, the retiring umpire is 100% accurate in properly calling pitches 'balls' or 'strikes' and 100% accurate in properly calling a player 'safe' or 'out' in close calls at first base. The umpire in training, on the other hand, is much less accurate. Both umpires were shown video of 1,000 pitches and 1,000 close calls at first base then asked to analyze them. Their conclusions are provided in the table below.

	Strikes	Balls	Safe	Out
Retiring Umpire	319	681	421	579
New Umpire	393	607	502	498

35. The new umpire is paid $35 per hour for watching and analyzing the video clips. If each clip lasts, on average, 8 seconds, then about how much money will the new umpire be paid for watching and analyzing the video clips?

A. $57.14
B. $77.78
C. $155.56
D. $187.50
E. $311.11

36. What percent of the new umpire's strike calls were inaccurate?

F. 39.3%
G. 31.9%
H. 19.1%
J. 18.8%
K. 0.0%

37. Two of the videos watched and analyzed by both the new umpire and the retiring umpire will be chosen at random. To the nearest 0.001, what is the probability that both of the chosen clips were incorrectly labeled by the new umpire?

A. 0.310
B. 0.155
C. 0.134
D. 0.012
E. 0.006

38. David is a scientist in a laboratory on a college campus and reads a sign that says that if the pressure within a certain container exceeds 255 Pascal, that he should notify the Chemistry department. David knows that the ideal gas pressure formula is given as $P = \dfrac{nRT}{V}$, in which V is the volume, n is the number of moles, R is a constant equal to 0.082, and T is the temperature. If the number of moles in this container is 550, the temperature is 220 K, and the volume is 42 liters, what is the gas pressure of the container, rounded to the nearest Pascal?

F.   24 Pascal
G.   110 Pascal
H.   114 Pascal
J.   236 Pascal
K.   2,362 Pascal

39. In the standard (x, y) coordinate plane, where does the graph of the equation $y = \dfrac{-(x+3)(x^2 - x - 6)}{(x+2)}$ cross the x-axis ?

A. $x = -3,\ x = 3$
B. $x = -2,\ x = 2$
C. $x = -1,\ x = 1$
D. $x = 2,\ x = 3$
E. $x = 0,\ x = 4$

40. When graphed, what is the amplitude of the function $f(x) = \dfrac{2}{3}\sin(2x - \pi)$?

F. $\dfrac{1}{3}$

G. $\dfrac{2}{3}$

H. $\dfrac{3}{2}$

J.   2

K. $2 - \pi$

41. In the standard (x, y) coordinate plane, point N lies at the origin, point M lies at point $(3, 4)$, and point O lies at point $(8, 0)$. What is the length, in coordinate units, of the altitude of the triangle formed by the 3 points?

A.   3
B.   4
C.   5
D.   7
E.   8

42. A car rental company has 120 cars in its lot to rent to customers. Based on over ten years of car rental data, the company created the table below showing the daily rental rates and their probabilities of occurring on any day of the year. Based on the probability distribution in the table, to the nearest whole number, what is the expected number of cars that will be rented on any given day?

Rental rate	Probability
0.25	0.10
0.50	0.20
0.75	0.40
0.90	0.20
1.00	0.10

F. 85
G. 88
H. 90
J. 94
K. 95

43. What is the degree measure of the smaller of the 2 angles formed by the 2 lines in the figure below?

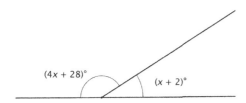

$(4x + 28)°$ $(x + 2)°$

A. 30°
B. 32°
C. 55°
D. 148°
E. 150°

44. Let a equal $3b + 7 - 4c$. What happens to the value of a if the value of b decreases by 2 and the value of c increases by 1 ?

F. It increases by 11.
G. It increases by 8.
H. It is unchanged.
J. It decreases by 1.
K. It decreases by 10.

45. A retreat center has 11 rooms set aside for small groups. Each room can fit up to 12 people each. If 90 employees of a company that is using the retreat center are sent to the rooms, and each room has a minimum of 2 employees, what is the greatest possible number of rooms that can be filled with 12 people?

    A.   0
    B.   3
    C.   4
    D.   6
    E.   7

46. Charlotte works for an industrial kitchen and is in charge of properly mixing ingredients for a new recipe. The recipe calls for 400 ounces of water for every 5 cups of flour. Given this ratio, how many gallons should Charlotte add for 25 liters of flour?

(Note: 1 gallon = 128 fluid ounces;
1 liter = 4.22675 cups)

    F. $\dfrac{(400)(25)(4.22675)}{(5)(128)}$

    G. $\dfrac{(5)(25)(4.22675)}{(400)(128)}$

    H. $\dfrac{(400)(25)(5)}{(4.22675)(128)}$

    J. $\dfrac{(400)(5)(4.22675)}{(25)(128)}$

    K. $\dfrac{(5)(128)}{(400)(25)(4.22675)}$

47. Which of the following expressions, if any, are *not* always equal to x ?

    I. $\dfrac{x^2}{x^{-1}}$

    II. $|-x|$

    III. $-\sqrt{(-x)^2}$

    A.   I only
    B.   I and II only
    C.   I and III only
    D.   II and III only
    E.   I, II, and III

48. How many integer values of a are there that cause the fraction $\dfrac{3}{a}$ to lie between 0.480 and 0.205 ?

- **F.** 3
- **G.** 7
- **H.** 8
- **J.** 9
- **K.** 10

49. Jacob is competing in a bass fishing tournament, which averages the weight of a competitor's 5 largest fish. The average weight of his first 4 fish is exactly a ounces. How many ounces higher than a must Jacob's 5th fish weigh in order to raise the average weight of the 5 fish to $a + 3$ ounces?

- **A.** 3
- **B.** 4
- **C.** 12
- **D.** 15
- **E.** 16

50. The intersection of lines c and d forms the angles $\angle W$, $\angle X$, $\angle Y$, and $\angle Z$. The measure of $\angle Z$ is 1100% larger than the measure of $\angle W$. If it can be determined, what is the measure of $\angle W$?

- **F.** $5°$
- **G.** $15°$
- **H.** $165°$
- **J.** $175°$
- **K.** Cannot be determined from the given information

51. A sequence is defined for all positive integers by $s_n = \dfrac{1}{2}s_{(n+1)} + |n| + 4$ and $s_4 = 77$. What is s_1 ?

- **A.** 25.250
- **B.** 23.875
- **C.** 21.125
- **D.** 19.750
- **E.** 19.375

52. If x is an integer less than -2, which of the following orders the expressions $-x^3$, $-\dfrac{1}{x^2}$, and $|x|$?

- **F.** $-\dfrac{1}{x^2} < |x| < -x^3$

- **G.** $-\dfrac{1}{x^2} < -x^3 < |x|$

- **H.** $-x^3 < -\dfrac{1}{x^2} < |x|$

- **J.** $-x^3 < |x| < -\dfrac{1}{x^2}$

- **K.** $|x| < -\dfrac{1}{x^2} < -x^3$

53. What is the 333rd digit after the decimal point in the repeating decimal $0.\overline{740231}$?

    A. 0
    B. 1
    C. 2
    D. 4
    E. 7

54. A local charity is trying to determine how many t-shirts to print and sell at an upcoming event. The charity has determined, based on past events, that 15% of those on their email list will attend. If the charity also estimates that, using the same historical data, $\frac{1}{6}$ of all attendees will purchase a t-shirt, then about how many t-shirts should be printed if an invite to the event was sent to 122,000 unique emails on the charity's email list ?

    F.   Between 2,500 and 2,600
    G.   Between 3,000 and 3,100
    H.   Between 10,900 and 11,000
    J.   Between 18,250 and 18,350
    K.   Between 20,300 and 20,400

55. If $i = \sqrt{-1}$, then $\dfrac{(-3i + 1)(2i + 2)}{4} = ?$

    A. 2

    B. 3

    C. $2 + \dfrac{1}{i}$

    D. $-2 + i$

    E. $2 - i$

56. Triangles $\triangle ABC$ and $\triangle XYZ$ are similar, right triangles. $\triangle ABC$ has a hypotenuse 10 inches long, and $\triangle XYZ$ has a hypotenuse 5 inches long. $\triangle ABC$ has one angle that is 53.13°, the opposite side of which measures 8 inches. What is the perimeter of $\triangle XYZ$, in inches ?

    F.   8.5
    G.   9
    H.   10.5
    J.   11.5
    K.   12

57. If the length of the base of a triangle is increased by 10% and the height is decreased by 35%, the area of the resulting triangle is smaller than the area of the original triangle by what percent?

    A. 71.5%
    B. 45.0%
    C. 28.5%
    D. 22.5%
    E. 20.0%

58. A twelve-sided dice, with sides numbered 1-12, and a six-sided dice, with sides numbered 1-6, are rolled across a table. What is the probability that the sum of the numbers on the two die is 15?

    F. $\dfrac{1}{72}$

    G. $\dfrac{1}{36}$

    H. $\dfrac{1}{24}$

    J. $\dfrac{1}{18}$

    K. $\dfrac{5}{72}$

59. Michael calculates that he will need 5,625 square feet of wood floors in the new home he is building. However, the wood that he is looking to purchase is priced by the square *yard*. How many square yards of wood floor does he need?

    A. 625
    B. 735
    C. 920
    D. 1,750
    E. 1,875

60. For all $x > 0$, which of the following expressions is NOT equivalent to $\sqrt[3]{\sqrt[3]{\sqrt[3]{\sqrt[3]{x^3}}}}$?

    F. $\sqrt[3]{\sqrt[3]{x}}$

    G. $\sqrt[18]{x^2}$

    H. $\sqrt[9]{x}$

    J. $x^{\frac{1}{9}}$

    K. $x^{\frac{1}{6}}$

PRACTICE TEST 2
60 Minutes, 60 Questions

MATHEMATICS TEST

60 Minutes — 60 Questions

DIRECTIONS: Solve each problem, choose the correct answer, and then fill in the corresponding oval on your answer document.

Do not linger over problems that take too much time. Solve as many as you can; then return to the others in the time you have left for this test.

You are permitted to use a calculator on this test. You may use your calculator for any problems you choose,

but some of the problems may best be done without using a calculator.

Note: Unless otherwise stated, all of the following should be assumed.

1. Illustrative figures are NOT necessarily drawn to scale.
2. Geometric figures lie in a plane.
3. The word *line* indicates a straight line.
4. The word *average* indicates arithmetic mean.

---

1. The cost for a certain town's greatest internet service is a onetime fee of $225, plus a weekly fee of $20. Elisa wrote a $705 check to pay for the internet service for a number of weeks, including the onetime fee. How many weeks of membership did she pay for?

   A. 6
   B. 9
   C. 24
   D. 31
   E. 35

2. A certain company prints signs for political parties. For orders of 1 to 250 signs, the company charges $2.50 per sign, but for orders of 251 or more signs, the company charges $2.15 per sign. A political party that ordered 425 signs was accidentally charged $2.50 per sign. What is the total refund that the sign company owes the political party?

   F. $42.50
   G. $148.75
   H. $191.25
   J. $212.50
   K. $425.00

3. A bus is driving from Charlotte, NC to Austin, TX. Abraham and Rachel board the bus at 5:45 a.m., and the bus departs at exactly 6:00 a.m. At 7:30 a.m., Abraham checks a map and sees that the bus has traveled exactly 90 miles. At this rate, how far will the bus travel in 4 hours?

   A. 150 miles
   B. 180 miles
   C. 220 miles
   D. 240 miles
   E. 360 miles

DO YOUR FIGURING HERE.

4. A local restaurant offers 17 different meal options, and 1 of them is Christopher's favorite meal. On his next visit, he decides to let his waitress choose a meal on his behalf at random, as long as it is not spicy. If the restaurant offers 5 spicy meals, what are the odds that the waitress chooses Christopher's favorite meal?

F. $\dfrac{1}{12}$

G. $\dfrac{5}{17}$

H. $\dfrac{5}{16}$

J. $\dfrac{6}{17}$

K. $\dfrac{5}{12}$

5. Mr. Schmidt has 21, 27, 22, 25, and 21 pupils in his first five classes of the school day. Solving which of the following equations for p gives the number of students he needs in his 6th class of the day to average exactly 24 students per class?

A. $\dfrac{(21 + 27 + 22 + 25 + 21)}{5} + p = 24$

B. $\dfrac{(21 + 27 + 22 + 25 + 21)}{6} + p = 24$

C. $\dfrac{(21 + 27 + 22 + 25 + 21 + p)}{6} = \dfrac{24}{6}$

D. $\dfrac{(21 + 27 + 22 + 25 + 21 + p)}{5} = 24$

E. $\dfrac{(21 + 27 + 22 + 25 + 21 + p)}{6} = 24$

6. What is $x^2 - |7 - x| - (-x)$ when $x = 11$?

F. 106
G. 114
H. 125
J. 128
K. 136

7. Consider the equation $m - n = \dfrac{9}{4}n + 3$. For what value of n is the value of m equal to 16 ?

A. 4.00
B. 6.75
C. 10.40
D. 10.50
E. 42.25

8. After a survey, Gary made the pie chart below to show the different tastes in candy among the student body from among four options: chocolate, gummies, hard candies, or gum. After making the chart, he measures the angles of the different pieces of the pie. If more students voted for chocolate than any other option, then what percent of the student body prefers chocolate, rounded to the nearest percent?

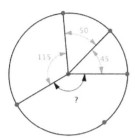

   F.   25%
   G.   32%
   H.   38%
   J.   42%
   K.   Cannot be determined from the given information

9. A homeowner precisely measures, in feet, the lengths and widths of an L-shaped hallway in his home. Assuming all walls meet at 90° angles, what is the square footage of the homeowner's hallway?

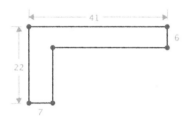

   A.   76
   B.   358
   C.   372
   D.   400
   E.   902

10. Given that $f(x) = 4x - 2$ and $g(x) = \dfrac{x^3}{2}$, what is the value of $f(g(2))$?

   F.   6
   G.   14
   H.   16
   J.   30
   K.   108

11. In the standard (x, y) coordinate plane, the point $(0, -3)$ is the midpoint of AB. Point A has coordinates $(-3, 6)$. What are the coordinates of point B?

A. $(-1.5, 1.5)$
B. $(-3, -6)$
C. $(3, -12)$
D. $(-6, 15)$
E. $(1.5, -1.5)$

12. Aaron can type 112 words per minute. What is the number of hours it takes him to type 8,400 words?

F. $1\frac{1}{15}$

G. $1\frac{1}{8}$

H. $1\frac{1}{4}$

J. $7\frac{1}{4}$

K. $7\frac{1}{2}$

13. Carlos scored 37 points in the state championship basketball game. If all of his points came from 2 and 3 point shots, and if he made a total of 15 shots, then how many 2 point shots did he make?

A. 7
B. 8
C. 9
D. 10
E. 11

14. Diana puts 30 poker chips into a hat, 13 of which are blue, 11 of which are green, and 6 of which are black. How many additional black poker chips must be put into the hat so that the probability of drawing a black poker chip is $\frac{5}{11}$?

F. 1
G. 4
H. 5
J. 13
K. 14

15. What is 4% of 6.71×10^{-3}?

A. 0.00002684
B. 0.0002684
C. 0.0016775
D. 0.002684
E. 0.016775

DO YOUR FIGURING HERE.

16. The volume of a cone is $\pi r^2 \dfrac{h}{3}$, where r is the radius of the sphere and h is the height of the cone. What is the volume, in cubic feet, of a cone with a height of 1 and a *diameter* of 12 feet?

   F. 12π
   G. 16π
   H. 38π
   J. 48π
   K. 151π

17. What is the product of the two solutions of the equation $x^2 - 10x + 21 = 0$?

   A. -21
   B. -10
   C. -4
   D. 10
   E. 21

18. The radius of a certain circle is $3x - 2$. The diameter of the same circle is $5x + 1$. What is the area of this circle?

   F. 5π
   G. 13π
   H. 25π
   J. 169π
   K. 676π

19. Imidacloprid, a neonicotinoid chemical that acts on the central nervous system of insects, is the active ingredient in many pets' flea medication. A dosage of 3.20 ml is recommended for dogs weighing 70 pounds or more, and to avoid over-dosing, the dosage decreases by 0.04 ml per pound from 3.20 ml. To the nearest 0.01 ml, what is the recommended dosage for a dog weighing 42 pounds?

   A.   1.52 ml
   B.   1.68 ml
   C.   1.72 ml
   D.   2.08 ml
   E.   2.80 ml

20. In the figure below, all segments that meet do so at right angles. What is the area, in square units, of the shaded region?

   F.   3

   G.   4

   H.   6

   J.   9

   K.   14

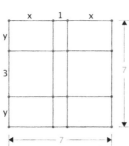

21. Which of the following is a value of x that satisfies $\log_x 125 = 3$?

A. 5
B. 15
C. 25
D. 41
E. 375

22. If a and b are positive integers, such that the greatest common factor of a^3b^2 and $a\,b^3$ is 24, then which of the following could b equal?

F. 36
G. 24
H. 8
J. 6
K. 2

23. A line contains the points F, G, H, and J. Point G lies between points F and H. Point J lies between points H and G. If segment JH is 8 units long, and if segment FG is 10 units long, then which of the following inequalities *must* be true about the lengths of these segments?

A. $\overline{GJ} < 8$

B. $8 > \overline{FG}$

C. $\overline{GH} < 10$

D. $\overline{GJ} < 10$

E. $8 < \overline{GH}$

24. One bird makes a call every 3 seconds. A second bird makes a call every 7 seconds. At a certain moment, both birds call at the same time. How many seconds elapse until the 2 birds next call at the same time?

F. 10
G. 21
H. 28
J. 41
K. 42

25. A rectangular painting is being mounted to a wall in a city museum. The painting measures 105 inches from the top left corner of the frame to the bottom right corner of the frame. If the painting is 84 inches wide, then how tall is the painting in inches?

A. 21
B. 63
C. 84
D. 85
E. 86

DO YOUR FIGURING HERE.

26. If 3 times a number n is added to -12, the result is positive. Which of the following gives the possible value(s) for n ?

   F. All $n > 4$

   G. All $n < -4$

   H. All $n > \dfrac{1}{4}$

   J. 4 only

   K. $-\dfrac{1}{4}$ only

27. For all $x > 8$, $\dfrac{(x^2 - 10x + 16)(x + 3)}{(x^2 - 5x - 24)(x - 2)} = ?$

   A. 0

   B. $\dfrac{4}{5}$

   C. 1

   D. $\dfrac{x - 8}{x + 8}$

   E. $\dfrac{x + 8}{x - 8}$

28. On Tuesdays at Camilla's favorite bakery, the amount of money in the cash register at any given time, m, satisfies the inequality $|m + \$25| \le \$175$. If a negative number denotes a decrease in sales from the previous day, then which of the following dollar amounts is NOT in this range?

   F. $-\$205$
   G. $-\$160$
   H. $-\$25$
   J. $\$0$
   K. $\$150$

29. Zeke wants to cook a meal consisting of one meat dish, one vegetable dish, and one dessert. While reading through cookbooks, Zeke feels comfortable cooking 80 different meat dishes, 55 different vegetable dishes, and 22 different desserts. How many meals, each consisting of one meat dish, one vegetable dish, and one dessert, is Zeke comfortable cooking?

   A. 22
   B. 58
   C. 80
   D. 157
   E. 96,800

DO YOUR FIGURING HERE.

30. In the standard (x, y) coordinate plane, which of the following lines best approximates the data points $(3, 5)$, $(1, 4)$, $(-4, 3)$, $(-5, 2.5)$, $(5, 6)$, and $(2, 4.5)$?

F. $y = -\left(\dfrac{1}{3}\right)x + 4$

G. $y = 3x + 4$

H. $y = \left(\dfrac{1}{3}\right)x + 4$

J. $y = 4x - 1$

K. $y = -\left(\dfrac{2}{3}\right)x - 1$

31. For all x and $y \neq 0$, what is the value of $\left(\dfrac{\frac{x^3}{-(y^{-2})}}{(-(xy)^4)}\right)^0$?

A. $x^7 y^5$

B. $-(x^7 y^5)$

C. $(xy)^2$

D. 1

E. 0

32. If $0° < \theta < 90°$ and $\cos\theta = \dfrac{12}{13}$, then $\sin\theta = $?

F. $-\dfrac{5}{12}$

G. $\dfrac{5}{13}$

H. $\dfrac{5}{12}$

J. $\dfrac{13}{12}$

K. $\dfrac{13}{5}$

33. Lila drew a picture for her mother for Valentine's Day that is 8 inches long and 10 inches wide. The picture is too large to fit in the frame, so Lila is going to cut the picture down slightly to have an area that is 70% of the area of the original drawing. The length of Lila's new picture will be 87.5% the length of the original picture. How many inches wide will the new picture be?

A. 8

B. 7.5

C. 7

D. 6.5

E. 6

Use the following information to answer questions 34-36.

Mr. Oberlee decides that he will give bonus points to any student who brings in a pie to share with the rest of math class on March 14th. Of his 25 students, only 11 of them brought in a pie to share with the class. Below are three circles that represent the three pies that were voted by the class as the most delicious.

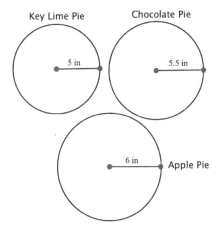

Key Lime Pie

Chocolate Pie

5 in

5.5 in

6 in   Apple Pie

34. Mr. Oberlee traces the Chocolate Pie with its center at the origin on a poster that features the standard (x, y) coordinate plane drawn with one inch per square unit. Which of the following formulas best represents the pie's tracing?

  F. $(x - 5.5)^2 + (y - 5.5)^2 = 11$
  G. $(x + 5.5)^2 + (y + 5.5)^2 = 11$
  H. $(x - 5.5)^2 + (y - 5.5)^2 = 30.25$
  J. $x^2 + y^2 = 5.5$
  K. $x^2 + y^2 = 30.25$

35. The area of the Chocolate Pie is equivalent to which of the following percentages, rounded to the nearest hundredth of a percent?

  A. 84.03% of the Apple Pie
  B. 121.00% of the Apple Pie
  C. 69.44% of the Key Lime Pie
  D. 119.01% of the Apple Pie
  E. 82.64% of the Key Lime Pie

36. Which of the following inequalities or expressions properly orders the areas of these 3 pieces of pie:

Piece 1: Key Lime Pie cut with an interior angle of 25°
Piece 2: Chocolate Pie cut with an interior angle of 20°
Piece 3: Apple Pie cut with an interior angle of 25°

   F.   Piece 1 = Piece 2 = Piece 3
   G.   Piece 1 = Piece 3 < Piece 2
   H.   Piece 3 < Piece 1 < Piece 2
   J.   Piece 1 < Piece 2 < Piece 3
   K.   Piece 2 < Piece 1 < Piece 3

37. In the figure below, $\overline{AB} \parallel \overline{CD}$, and $\overline{CB}$ bisects $\angle ABD$. If the measure of $\angle ABD$ is 118°, what is the measure of $\angle BCD$?

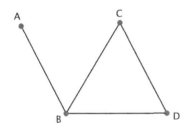

   A.   49°
   B.   52°
   C.   59°
   D.   62°
   E.   Cannot be determined from the given information

38. Much of the grass in Paulo's front yard has died, and he decides to replace it. The total area of grass that needs replacing is 1,350 square feet. If the local hardware store sells grass squares that are 25 inches by 25 inches, then what is the minimum number of grass squares that Paolo must purchase to replace the dead grass in his front yard?

   F.   54
   G.   311
   H.   312
   J.   195
   K.   1,944

39. A group of concerned citizens tests the levels of Halo-acetic acids in a community's drinking water. Across ten testing sites, the group discovered 0.06, 0.05, 0.11, 0.10, 0.05, 0.05, 0.09, 0.06, 0.11, and 0.05 ppb (parts per billion), respectively. Given this data set, which of the following two values are equal?

   A.   The mean and the mode
   B.   The mode and the range
   C.   The median and the mode
   D.   The median and the range
   E.   The mean and the range

Use the following information to answer questions 40-42.

Chandra is reading a book about famous Italian landmarks and learns the following facts about the Leaning Tower of Pisa in Pisa, Italy. First, she learns that the tower is 183.25 feet tall on the lowest side and 185.92 feet tall on the highest side. Second, she learns that the tower stands at an angle of 86.03° to the ground on the low side and 93.97° on the high side. Third, she learns that the tower weighs 16,000 tons.

*Note: 1 ton = 2,000 pounds

40. Solving which of the following equations would result in the height of the tower if it were to stand perpendicular to the ground?

F. $\dfrac{185.92}{\cos(86.03)}$

G. $\dfrac{183.25}{\cos(86.03)}$

H. $\dfrac{185.92}{\tan(86.03)}$

J. $\dfrac{183.25}{\sin(86.03)}$

K. $\dfrac{185.92}{\sin(86.03)}$

41. If the book averages 350 words per page, and if Chandra reads at a rate of x words per minute, then how many minutes will it take her to read 15 pages?

A. $\dfrac{350x}{15}$

B. $\dfrac{x}{350(15)}$

C. $\dfrac{15x}{350}$

D. $\dfrac{350}{15x}$

E. $\dfrac{350(15)}{x}$

42. Suppose another city wishes to build a new tower of the exact same weight of the original Tower of Pisa. This new tower will have an average diameter of 50 feet from top to bottom and will be exactly 185 feet tall. What would be this new tower's resulting pounds per cubic foot, rounded to the nearest pound?

F. 55
G. 64
H. 88
J. 276
K. 277

43. What are the values of x and y if $3x + 2y = 14$ and $4x - y = -29$?

   A. $x = 2$ and $y = 4$
   B. $x = -4$ and $y = 13$
   C. $x = 4$ and $y = -13$
   D. $x = -2$ and $y = -4$
   E. $x = -2$ and $y = -21$

44. Given $15x = 5y^5 - 25$, which of the following is an expression for y in terms of x ?

   F. $y = 3x + 5$

   G. $y = 3(x^{\frac{1}{5}}) - 5$

   H. $y = (3x - 5)^{\frac{1}{5}}$

   J. $y = (3x + 5)^{\frac{1}{5}}$

   K. $y = (3x + 5)^5$

45. If an equilateral triangle has a height of 20 inches, what is its area rounded to the nearest square inch?

   A. 101
   B. 200
   C. 231
   D. 400
   E. 462

46. What is the result if the mean of the first 6 prime numbers is multiplied by the mean of the factors of 10?

   F. $9\frac{9}{10}$

   G. $18\frac{9}{10}$

   H. $21\frac{3}{4}$

   J. $27\frac{3}{10}$

   K. $35\frac{1}{10}$

47. Four matrices are given below.

$$A = [4 \quad 5] \qquad B = \begin{bmatrix} -2 \\ 8 \end{bmatrix} \qquad C = \begin{bmatrix} 6 & 0 \\ 0 & 0 \end{bmatrix} \qquad D = \begin{bmatrix} -4 & 4 \\ -2 & 2 \\ -3 & 3 \end{bmatrix}$$

Which of the following matrix products is undefined?

   A. AB
   B. BA
   C. DB
   D. BD
   E. DC

48. For all nonzero values of a, $\dfrac{8a^{16} - 6a^4}{2a^2} = ?$

    F. $(4a^4 - 3)$

    G. $\dfrac{a^2(4a^{12} - 3)}{a}$

    H. $\dfrac{a^2(4a^{12} - 3)}{a^2}$

    J. $a^2(4a^4 - 3)$

    K. $a^2(4a^{12} - 3)$

49. Molly wants to bake chocolate chip cookies for her friends. The recipe calls for $1\frac{3}{4}$ cups of chocolate chips for every $2\frac{1}{8}$ cups of butter. If Molly uses this ratio as called for in the recipe, but decides to use all of the $2\frac{1}{3}$ cups of chocolate chips she has at hand, then how many cups of butter will Molly need?

    A. $2\frac{5}{6}$

    B. 3

    C. $3\frac{1}{10}$

    D. $3\frac{2}{3}$

    E. $4\frac{1}{5}$

50. Donald is a new coach who wants to get to know his football team better. When he asks them to raise their hands if any of them play a winter sport, 29 raise their hands. When he asks them to raise their hands if any of them play a spring sport, 31 of them raise their hands. If there are 55 members of the football team, then what is the minimum number of football players who play both a winter and a spring sport?

    F. 0
    G. 5
    H. 15
    J. 29
    K. 31

51. An inspector found that 193 laptops made by Chip Computers had 0 defects, 111 laptops had 1 defect, 152 laptops had 2 defects, 105 laptops had 3 defects, and 53 laptops had 4 defects. If the inspected laptops represent an accurate sample size, then which of the following fractions best approximates the likelihood that a Chip Computer has 2 or fewer defects?

    A. $\dfrac{1}{4}$

    B. $\dfrac{1}{2}$

    C. $\dfrac{2}{3}$

    D. $\dfrac{37}{50}$

    E. $\dfrac{23}{25}$

52. In the figure below, all line segments are either horizontal or vertical, and the dimensions given are in meters. What is the perimeter, in meters, of the figure?

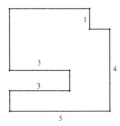

    F. 19
    G. 20
    H. 22
    J. 26
    K. 27

53. Yuriy's New Year resolution is to take more steps. On his first day, he took 1,000 steps. On each successive day, he added 50 more steps than the total steps he took the day before. If Yuriy met his exact step goals for each day, then how many steps total did he take in his first 10 days?

    A. 10,500
    B. 12,000
    C. 12,250
    D. 13,600
    E. 13,800

54. What is the area, in square units, of the parallelogram created by the following lines: $y = 2\frac{1}{2}x + 2$, $y = 2\frac{1}{2}x - 8$, $y = 2$, and $y = 7$?

    F. 20
    G. 22
    H. 23
    J. 26
    K. 28

DO YOUR FIGURING HERE.

55. For all $y \neq 0$, which of the following expressions is

equivalent to $\dfrac{(-\sqrt{y} - 3)(y + 5\sqrt{y} + 4)}{(\sqrt{y} + 1)(y - 4\sqrt{y} - 21)}) = ?$

A. $\sqrt{y}$

B. $-\sqrt{y}$

C. $\dfrac{\sqrt{y}}{\sqrt{y} + 7}$

D. $\dfrac{\sqrt{y} + 4}{\sqrt{y} - 7}$

E. $\dfrac{-\sqrt{y} - 4}{\sqrt{y} - 7}$

56. When $y = \cos(x)$ is graphed on the standard (x, y) coordinate plane, the result is a wave with an amplitude of 1 and a period of 2π. How does this wave compare to that of $y = 3\cos(\dfrac{x}{2})$?

F. It has three times the amplitude and twice the period.
G. It has three times the amplitude and half the period.
H. It has twice the amplitude and thee times the period.
J. It has one-third the amplitude and half the period.
K. It has half the amplitude and three times the period.

57. In a standard deck of cards there are a total of 52 cards: 4 aces, 12 face cards, and 4 cards of every number 2 through 10 (4 cards with a 2, 4 cards with a 3, and so on up to 4 cards with a 10). Harriet wins a chance to draw a card at random. If she draws an ace, she will be awarded $150, if she draws a face card, she will be awarded $100, and if she draws any other card, she will be awarded $10. What is the expected outcome of Harriet's award, rounded to the nearest whole dollar?

A. $10
B. $42
C. $49
D. $85
E. $125

58. A certain rectangle's width and length are whole numbers in millimeters. In addition, the rectangle's width is greater than the rectangle's length. Lastly, the rectangle has an area of 240 square millimeters. Which of the following perimeters is *not* possible for this rectangle?

F. 482
G. 113
H. 68
J. 64
K. 62

59. Three lines with different slopes are graphed in the standard (x, y) coordinate plane. Which of the following is *not* possible?

A. Two of the lines never cross the x-axis.
B. The three lines have the same y-intercept.
C. The three lines intersect at the origin.
D. One of the lines never crosses the y-axis.
E. One of the lines is $x = 0$.

60. A new hotel is considering different dimensions for a grand ball room. Originally, the ball room was to have a length of 300 feet, a width of 150 feet, and a ceiling height of 20 feet. However, upon seeing the plans, the owner of the hotel determines that the length and width of the room should both be increased by 25%. What will be the resulting increase, to the nearest 1%, in the volume of the grand ball room?

F. 25%
G. 26%
H. 42%
J. 50%
K. 56%

Practice Test 1 Correct Answers

1: C	21: E	41: B
2: G	22: F	42: F
3: B	23: D	43: B
4: K	24: J	44: K
5: A	25: B	45: D
6: K	26: H	46: F
7: A	27: A	47: C
8: J	28: H	48: H
9: D	29: C	49: D
10: F	30: G	50: G
11: B	31: D	51: E
12: J	32: K	52: F
13: E	33: E	53: A
14: H	34: H	54: G
15: B	35: C	55: E
16: H	36: J	56: K
17: D	37: E	57: C
18: F	38: J	58: J
19: C	39: A	59: A
20: G	40: G	60: K

Practice Test 2 Correct Answers

1: C	21: A	41: E
2: G	22: K	42: H
3: D	23: E	43: B
4: F	24: G	44: J
5: E	25: B	45: C
6: J	26: F	46: H
7: A	27: C	47: D
8: J	28: F	48: K
9: B	29: E	49: A
10: G	30: H	50: G
11: C	31: D	51: D
12: H	32: G	52: J
13: B	33: A	53: C
14: K	34: K	54: F
15: B	35: A	55: E
16: F	36: K	56: F
17: E	37: C	57: B
18: J	38: H	58: G
19: D	39: D	59: A
20: H	40: J	60: K

Practice Test 1 answer explanations begin on page 318; Practice Test 2 answer explanations begin on page 334.

The ACT Science
System

Six Steps to ACT Science Perfection

Introduction to ACT Science

The ACT Science test consists of 6 passages, each of which is followed by 6 or 7 questions; you are given 35 minutes to answer these 40 questions to the best of your ability, which equates to 5 minutes and 50 seconds per passage (that may sound like a lot, but anyone who has taken the test knows the truth that the time will fly by!). The passages themselves are drawn from a diverse array of science topics, including physics, chemistry, geology, biology, astronomy, etc., but in no particular order.

There are three types or categories of ACT Science passages that will be discussed in this book, and they are as follows:

1) Data Representation - two of the six passages will be in the category of Data Representation; each of these passages is followed by 6 questions. Essentially, these passages present lots of data in the form of graphs, charts, tables, diagrams, etc., and it will mostly be your responsibility to read, find, and interpret that data. What's also important about this type of passage is what it is missing, which is multiple experiments or studies to compare and contrast. In that sense, these two passages are *simpler* in structure.

2) Research Summary - three of the six passages will be in the category of Research Summary; each of these passages is followed by 7 questions (thus, 21 total questions or over half of all ACT Science questions follow these passages). Essentially, these passages also present lots of data in the form of graphs, charts, tables, diagrams, etc., but they also include descriptions and results from multiple experiments or studies.

In general, I will not make a big fuss in this book in distinguishing the two types of passages presented above, though there will be some discussion in the matter. More on this in Step 1.

3) Conflicting Viewpoints - one of the six passages will be in the category of Conflicting Viewpoints; this passage is followed by 7 questions. This passage is unique in that it rarely features any data presented in

graphs and tables; rather, it focuses on a disagreement between two or more scientists about a particular topic. Typically, this passage features only written words in the form of paragraphs. While many students are caught off guard by this passage and do not know how to hit this curveball, you, on the other hand, will be prepared; Step 4 is dedicated to this kind of passage.

What This Test Isn't

There are many students who excel in science class in high school and perform poorly on the ACT Science test. If this is you, you are not alone. In high school, there are lots of ways to boost your grade, including doing homework, studying for tests and quizzes, participating in class, cleaning your lab station well, presenting results effectively as a group, doing that random extra credit assignment that your teacher offered at the end of the quarter, and the list goes on and on. Unfortunately, the ACT Science test is really none of those things; it is not really like any test you have ever taken before. Think about it: when was the last time your teacher gave you a *timed* test requiring you to analyze material you had never seen?

Even the name of this test is a bit deceiving in that you will not really be *doing* any science (which is really what science *is*, since science is a method to acquiring knowledge). For example, I remember in my sophomore year of high school that I was the class pro at balancing chemical equations. Students from around the class would bring me equations they were stumped on and I would be able to piece together the atoms in a matter of seconds (using mols, on the other hand, was quite a chemistry struggle for me!). This is a *skill* in science; but the ACT Science Test is not about testing these kinds of scientific skills. It's not really about how much science you know, either, as *very few* of the questions require any kind of previous science knowledge at all (and even these questions rely on basic scientific ideas, like the difference between a meter and a millimeter).

Instead, this test is more true to its old name: *Science Reasoning*. This means that the subject matter is scientific, and you have to reason your way through it given the information before you. 'Reasoning' might sound like a scary word, but it isn't. It simply means that you have to think your way to correct answers sometimes, which can often mean eliminating answers you know to be wrong one at a time until you're left with just one. And even then, most of this reasoning involves reading data off of a chart or table and then taking one additional step (like comparing it to another piece of data or reaching a conclusion about all of the data, etc.).

Strategy

Strategy for taking the ACT Science test in the most effective and efficient way comes down to reading through the passage as fast as you can remembering a couple of things to do and avoid. This kind of "fast reading" is called *active reading*. For the purposes of ACT Science, this means that you have your pencil in hand and are *willing* or *choosing* to read over everything quickly and well. If you are familiar with what I say about active reading in The ACT Reading System, then you might be surprised that I am not making as big of a deal here as I did there. In fact, the ability to active read is Step 1 in The ACT Reading System. With ACT Science, however, there's typically *not* a lot to read. This means that what you do with the information before you is more critical, and is summed up by the following list of things to do and to avoid:

Do:

- Read quickly - as has been said, you don't want to be sitting there tired with your head leaning on your arm as if you're about to fall asleep. This is going to cause you to read very slowly and without any kind of comprehension. Those who choose (using their will power!) to read quickly and alertly are at a significant advantage over the student half asleep yawning and sighing his way through the test.

- Underline/circle key words and ideas - when you come to a seemingly key word being defined in the passage, circle it or underline it or both. This draws the attention of your mind to that information.

- Annotate or doodle to extract trends/relationships - make use of the margins. Next to written paragraphs, if you are told that as a certain chemical is burned at higher and higher temperatures, the color changes from purple to red to pink to white, jot in the margins something like this: **temp ↑ purp. to white**. This takes an idea and concretizes it into something manageable.

- Notice data trends along *x* and *y* axes - though you don't have time to analyze each piece of data or information in every table and graph, you can notice trends. In a graph, you may notice that a trend goes up, then decreases (for example). In a table, notice that as one data set decreases, another also decreases. In other words, a brief overview of the data is called for, though not a thorough review.

Avoid:

- "Sticker shock" - this is a phrase that refers to the shock of seeing the higher-than-expected price of something you want to buy. Although you don't want to buy anything during the ACT Science test, you can still be left with a terrible shock each time you turn the page. When you do so, what you'll likely see with most of the passages is diagrams, charts, data, and scientific words and terms that you've never heard, don't recognize, and that just plain look scary. However: *no student taking the ACT Science test has ever seen this stuff either*. You are on the same level as everyone in the room. Again, *the ACT is expecting you to have little to no previous science knowledge; the fact that you don't know what is before you is absolutely irrelevant!* It doesn't matter if it's physics or chemistry or about animals or outer space: you will not be familiar with any of what you see before you, and that's the point.

But, here's the silver lining: *it all makes sense*. What you see in front you in that ACT Science passage is something that is ordered, organized, and the result of a science experiment or experiments. It is well thought out. It is, by its nature, *sensical*, not nonsensical. Your reaction to what you see initially is confusion, but what you're looking at *isn't* confusion. That's why you have to read it!

- Pronouncing scientific terms - during the ACT Science test, you are going to come across lots of scientific terms that, again, you've probably never heard and could barely pronounce. For example: *Azeotropic distillation*, or *Klebsiella pneumoniae*, or *Coma Berenices*. You don't need to correctly pronounce these words; just call them "Az" and "Kleb" and "Coma B" in your mind.

- Memorizing data - during your first read through the passage, you don't have to memorize data presented to you in tables, graphs, charts, etc. Instead, simply glance over these means of presenting data to come to a basic understanding of the data itself. Look for what is along the x-axis, what is along the y-axis, and what trends may be obvious in the data.

- Getting hung up on very difficult questions - let's face it: some of the ACT Science questions are going to be purposefully at a higher level of difficulty. You can expect roughly 2-3 of these types of questions on your next ACT Science test; they require an understanding of the passage, an understanding of data, and some deep reasoning skills (more on these in Step 5). Give them your best shot, of course, but remember that if you spend 2 minutes on 2 of these questions, that's 4 minutes gone, almost guaranteeing that you will not give yourself sufficient time on easier questions at the end of the test in the final passage. Have the wisdom to circle these questions after making a guess so you can return to them if you have spare time at the end of the test.

Another "Strategy"

The ACT exam will begin at 8:00 AM (unless you're in some kind of situation that is an exception). This means that sometime around 11:00 AM the ACT Science exam will begin. This means that you've already taken a 45 minute long ACT English test (with 75 questions), a 60 minute long ACT Math test (with 60 questions), and a 35 minute long ACT Reading test (with 40 questions). Needless to say, you are worn out. You need a nap or an energy drink or a day at the beach or a nice long hug or all of the above.

However, what this means is that *most students make the major mistake of not choosing to stick it out through the ACT Science test*! The vast majority of ACT students in the room aren't aware that they are tired and fading. This leads not only to careless mistakes which sometimes can't be avoided, but one major mistake that can be avoided: *guessing just because they're tired*. You know the feeling. You're on number 22 of the ACT Science test and it's asking about some molecule you've never heard of and what it does when exposed to some chemical and you just don't *feel like* figuring it out so you glance over the answers and put C.

You've been there, right? It's the effect of being overtired and just plain over it.

However, think of it like this: even if you do that only 8 times, chances are that you will get 6 of those 8 questions incorrect. That doesn't sound like a big deal. However, getting those six questions wrong... *could drop your ACT Science score as many as SEVEN POINTS!*

Did you hear that? As many as SEVEN POINTS, and a minimum of FOUR POINTS! A drop of 4 points on the ACT Science test will mean a 1 point decrease in your overall ACT score, but a drop of 7 points will mean a 2 point decrease in your overall ACT score.

Now, reverse your thinking: if you can stick with it and try on these questions and get most of them correct, you are raising your ACT score by a point or two. So, how to avoid this over-exhausted-guessing-spree?

a) - the basics. Get a good sleep the night before, wake up early enough to eat a good, balanced breakfast before the ACT (NOT a bowl of sugary cereal and an energy drink, but eggs, bacon, and fruit), and a good snack on the break. Between ACT Math and Reading, you will get a break of 10 minutes. That's not very long, but it's long enough to get a bit of a recharge. Don't eat a bag of salty chips; eat a protein bar or an apple or something like that.

b) - take a good, deep, long breath between each of the ACT Science passages while committing yourself to do your best on this one passage before you. This five-second investment will take you far and help eliminate the temptation to guess all the time out of exhaustion.

Timing

Keeping time on the ACT Science test is relatively straightforward. As has been said, each test requires you to use an average of 5 minutes and 50 seconds per passage. That's difficult to do, since keeping track of whether or not 5 minutes and 50 seconds or 6 minutes has gone by. It is easier to remember that you have 6 minutes for each passage except for one; in other words, one of the Data Representation passages (the ones with only data that have only 6 questions after them) should only take you 5 minutes.

Unfortunately, one mistake that many students make is that they start guessing when they hear "Five minutes remaining!" However, this call isn't a signal to the end of the test, but rather simply a five minute warning; this is not the time to start guessing, seeing as it will take you about 5 minutes to complete an entire passage!

STEP 1

Reading, Analyzing, and

Interpreting Data

As has been said, the ACT Science test does not require that you have much previous scientific knowledge. Instead, it is testing your reasoning skills. However, even those reasoning skills are built upon a more basic scientific or mathematic skill: reading, analyzing, and comparing information off of charts, tables, and graphs. This skill is *the most necessary skill* on the ACT Science test.

It's All About the Data

There is often a lot going on in any given ACT Science passage. Sometimes, you have a diagram of some process or scientific object, like a cell or animal. Sometimes there might be a very complicated-looking equation shoved in there somewhere (but don't worry: any math required on the ACT is so basic that you are not allowed to use a calculator; usually these equations, if present, are designed to scare the student). Sometimes you have paragraphs of information that feature multiple definitions of very scientific words you may have never heard before.

The *good news* is that the number one thing that will move the needle on your ACT Science score the most involves none of these things. Instead, it involves your ability to look at the graphs, charts, and tables and read them properly, pulling out the correct information and perhaps inferring to a correct answer or comparing the data to another piece of data. In fact, about 60% of all ACT Science questions require this skill in one way or another...so it's important!

Passage Types and Data

In the introduction to ACT Science, I differentiated between three "types" of ACT Science Passages: Data Representation, Research Summaries, and Conflicting Viewpoints. Most of the time, the Conflicting Viewpoints passage (again, more discussion on this in Step 4) features no data, charts, tables, or graphs, making it mostly irrelevant for our current discussion under Step 1. It is the former two that need a bit more discussion.

Data Representation passages do just that: they represent a bunch of data from one kind of experiment or topic. Often, data in this passage is presented in different ways. For example, you might have a pie chart called "Figure 1," a table of data called "Table 1," and a graph of other data called "Figure 2." These types of passages are *typically* the "easiest," and because they only have 6 questions that follow them as opposed to 7, they should usually take a bit less time too.

Research Summaries passages, like Data Representation Passages, feature lots of data presented in charts, graphs, and tables. However, these passages feature multiple trials, experiments, or studies that have overlapping variables. For example, you may have a Trial 1 that tests the rate of growth of various plants watered with a sports drink, a Trial 2 that tests the rate of growth of these same plants watered with an energy drink, and a Trial 3 that tests the rate of growth of these same plants watered with coffee (and all three trials will be compared to a control group grown with water). What's happening here is that the **independent variable** (meaning, what the scientists control, in this case, what is being used to water the plants) is changing from trial to trial. This is resulting in new data, or values for the **dependent variable** (in this case, the rate of growth of the various plants). Some of the questions will require you to compare these one to the other.

The Practice That Follows

Now, it is time to put into practice this number 1 skill. You will be presented with 6 ACT Science passages (called Passage I, II, III, IV, V, and VI) in a row, just like on the real ACT. Each and every question associated with these passages in Step 1 have to do exclusively with this skill. In other words, other elements of the passage (most especially what is defined, given, or described in the written portion) are unnecessary for getting these questions correct. Importantly, I will be using *these same passages* to ask new, different types of questions in Step 2, Step 3, and Step 5 as well.

So, without further ado, let's practice this skill. Remember: each question is exclusively about the data!

Passage I

Most of the water consumption within the United States is used by the agricultural industry for food production. This heavily contributes to the overuse of groundwater aquifers. Therefore, finding alternative resources of water for agricultural production is necessary to lessen the looming threat of food and water scarcity. One issue is that alternative ·water sources in certain regions often contain a higher concentration of salt compared to groundwater aquifers, and many food crops are not selected for traits like tolerance to salt. In recent years, new varieties, also called *variants*, of crops have been selected mostly for commercial benefit, with little regard for producing varieties that can withstand changes in salt concentrations. As a result, a group of researchers sought to determine plant variants that are resilient to waters with higher salt concentrations.

Researchers first tested the salt tolerance in variants of two regularly consumed crops, tomato and pepper, by testing the consumable yields of each plant when grown in the same soil. The control for the experiment was freshwater from a ground water aquifer, while the experimental condition was done with water containing a higher salt content. The results are recorded in Table 1 (tomato) and Table 2 (pepper) below.

Fruit yield (grams)		
Tomato variant	Control	Experimental
Bloody Butcher	2785	1719
Juane Flamme	2317	1355
Quarter Century	1415	928

Table 1

Fruit yield (grams)		
Pepper variant	Control	Experimental
California Wonder	2591	1993
Thai Hot	295	291
Ancho	1514	1489

Table 2

The researchers next tested the concentration of sodium within the plant tissue of the different variants for both the control and saltwater (experimental) groups. Their findings are recorded in Figure 1 (tomato) and Figure 2 (pepper) below in millimoles per kilogram.

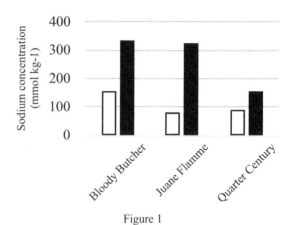

Figure 1

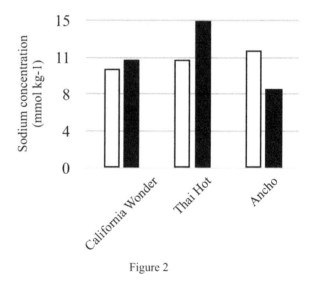

Figure 2

1. Based on Figures 1 and 2, which variety of fruit saw the greatest difference in sodium concentration between the control and experimental groups?

   A. Bloody Butcher
   B. Juane Flamme
   C. Thai Hot
   D. Ancho

2. According to Tables 1 and 2, which plant variety yielded the most fruit with experimental watering relative to the control?

    F. Bloody Butcher
    G. Juane Flamme
    H. California Wonder
    J. Thai Hot

3. If a higher sodium concentration results in a saltier taste, then which variety of fruit's experimental yield will taste less salty than the control?

    A. Bloody Butcher
    B. Juane Flamme
    C. California Wonder
    D. Ancho

4. Based on Figures 1 and 2, which variety of fruit contains the highest sodium concentration in mmol/kg-1?

    F. Bloody Butcher
    G. Juane Flamme
    H. Thai Hot
    J. Ancho

Passage II

A group of high school students investigated the momentum of carts rolling down an inclined plane across a designated finish line. The students used three carts, labeled Cart A, Cart B, and Cart C. Cart A had a mass of 12.5 kg, Cart B had a mass of 21.8 kg, and Cart C had a mass of 34.7 kg. They conducted five trials, progressively increasing the release height of the carts. The purpose of the experiment was to explore how changes in release height affect the velocity and momentum of the carts.

Velocity is a fundamental concept in physics that represents the speed of an object in a specific direction. In this experiment, velocity was measured as each cart crossed the finish line, but can also be determined using the equation $v = \sqrt{2gh}$, where v is the velocity, g is the acceleration due to gravity (approximately 9.8 m/s²), and h is the release height of the cart.

Momentum is a property of a moving object that depends on its mass and velocity. It describes the quantity of motion possessed by an object and is calculated by multiplying the mass of the object by its velocity. The equation for momentum is given as $p = mv$, where p represents the momentum, m is the mass of the object, and v denotes the velocity.

After collecting data, the students calculated the momentum for each cart and trial. Figure 1 shows the recorded velocity for each cart as it crossed the finish line, and Figure 2 shows the calculated momentum for each cart as it crossed the finish line.

Key:

■ Cart A
▲ Cart B
● Cart C

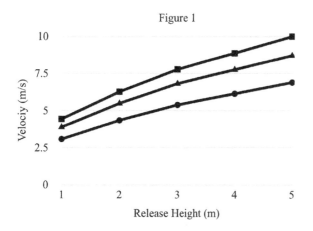

Figure 1

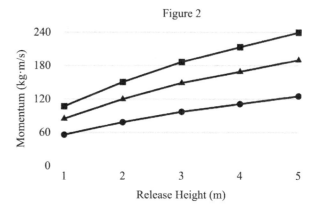

Figure 2

5. If Cart B were to be released from a height of 4.5 meters, it would be expected to cross the finish line with an expected momentum of:

   A. 8.5 kg·m/s
   B. 160 kg·m/s
   C. 180 kg·m/s
   D. 200 kg·m/s

6. According to Figure 1, the smallest difference in velocity recorded between the three carts resulted from a release height of:

   F. 1 meter
   G. 2 meters
   H. 3 meters
   J. 5 meters

7. One of the students decides to conduct a sixth trial in which Cart C is released from a height of 8 meters. Is it likely that it will record a velocity greater than 7.5 m/s as it crosses the finish line?

   A. Yes: an increase of 1 or more m/s is expected, enough to reach the milestone.
   B. Yes: the cart has already reached this milestone, and a drop in velocity is unexpected.
   C. No: based on its current trajectory, it is unlikely that the cart will reach the milestone.
   D. No: the mass of the cart would have to be significantly increased to mathematically have a chance to reach the milestone.

8. Which of the following carts had the highest velocity as it crossed the finish line?

   F. Cart A released at a height of 1 meter
   G. Cart A released at a height of 2 meters
   H. Cart B released at a height of 3 meters
   J. Cart C released at a height of 4 meters

Passage III

The *Mpemba Effect* refers to a curious phenomenon in which hot water freezes faster than cold water under certain circumstances. Several proposed explanations have been put forth to shed light on the Mpemba Effect. One possibility relates to the evaporation of the hot water during the cooling process. As hot water is exposed to lower temperatures, it undergoes rapid evaporation, resulting in a reduction in its volume. This reduction in volume leads to an increase in the concentration of dissolved solids in the remaining water. Consequently, the higher concentration of dissolved solids may lower the freezing point of the hot water, allowing it to freeze more rapidly.

A group of students designed an experiment to test the Mpemba Effect. They collected four beakers and labeled them A, B, C, and D. *Thermocouples*, or thermoelectric devices for measuring temperature, were placed in the bottom of each beaker. Beakers A and B were filled with distilled (purified) water, and beakers C and D were filled with tap water. The water in beakers A and C was heated to 50 degrees Celsius, and the water in beakers B and D was left at room temperature (around 30 degrees Celsius).

The students recorded the temperature of each beaker after placing it in a freezer with a temperature of -18° Celsius until it had reached 0° Celsius, the freezing point of water. The observations of the students are given below. Table 1 corresponds to beaker A, Table 2 to beaker B, Table 3 to beaker C, and Table 4 to beaker D.

Table 1 (Beaker A)

Time Elapsed (minutes)	Temperature (°C)
0	50
5	42
10	36
15	30
20	25
25	21
30	17
35	13
40	10
45	8
50	5
55	2
60	0

Table 2 (Beaker B)

Time Elapsed (minutes)	Temperature (°C)
0	30
5	26
10	23
15	20
20	18
25	17
30	14
35	12
40	10
45	8
50	6
55	5
60	4
65	3
70	0

Table 3 (Beaker C)

Time Elapsed (minutes)	Temperature (°C)
0	50
5	44
10	38
15	33
20	28
25	24
30	20
35	17
40	14
45	11
50	8
55	5
60	3
65	0

Table 4 (Beaker D)	
Time Elapsed (minutes)	Temperature (°C)
0	30
5	26
10	22
15	19
20	18
25	17
30	15
35	13
40	11
45	10
50	8
55	6
60	4
65	2
70	1
75	0

9. If all four beakers had been placed in the freezer at the exact same time, and the temperatures were checked after 70 minuted had elapsed, what percent of the beakers would read a temperature of 0° Celsius or colder?

    A. 0%
    B. 25%
    C. 75%
    D. 100%

10. If the beakers' temperatures had been checked in 1 minute intervals instead of 5 minute intervals, then the temperature of Beaker C after 37 minutes had elapsed would be expected to be about:

    F. 11° Celsius
    G. 16° Celsius
    H. 18° Celsius
    J. 21° Celsius

11. Which beaker saw the greatest drop in temperature between 10 minutes having elapsed and 45 minutes having elapsed?

    A. Beaker A
    B. Beaker B
    C. Beaker C
    D. Beaker D

12. Which beaker held water that took the most amount of time to drop from 20° Celsius to 0° Celsius?

    F. Beaker A
    G. Beaker B
    H. Beaker C
    J. Beaker D

Passage IV

Real-time polymerase chain reaction (PCR) *analysis* is a laboratory technique that can be used to help determine if a specific type of DNA is present in a sample. This technique works by increasing the total amount of DNA present in a sample, a step called *amplification*, and then detecting if the DNA matches the target DNA.

Detection of the target DNA is determined by the *cycle threshold* (CT) value. The CT value is the number of cycles of amplification that is needed for a specific DNA sequence to be detected in a sample. The lower the CT value, the more likely it is that the sample contains the DNA of interest. Most real-time PCR analyses undergo a total of 40 cycles of amplification.

While this technique is often used for medical purposes, it also has applications in food safety. Due to the safety concerns regarding food allergens, scientists will use real-time PCR to search for the DNA of common allergen causing ingredients in commercial products to ensure that the package label is accurate. One common and often dangerous food allergy is an allergy to peanuts. If a person is severely allergic to peanuts and unknowingly ingests even a small amount, it could be deadly. Therefore, scientists completed real-time PCR analysis to test commercial food products for DNA that matches the peanut.

Table 1 shows commercial food products, their current package labels for allergens, and the CT values discovered by a researcher for each following real-time PCR analysis to detect peanut DNA. An N.D. value means that there was no detection of the target DNA after 40 cycles of amplification.

Table 1		
Food	Food Packaging Allergen Declaration	Peanut CT Value
Cereal bar I	Peanut, hazelnut	17.97
Cereal bar II	Almond and tree nuts	32.40
Cereal bar III	Hazelnut, almond and peanut traces	33.74
Cereal bar IV	May contain tree nut traces	35.90
Chocolate with pistachio	Pistachio, almond, hazelnut, tree nut traces	36.80
Sausage with walnut	Walnuts	N.D.
Chocolate	Almond and hazelnut traces	37.99
Cookies with fiber	Not declared	32.25

Table 2 displays example CT values and the likelihood of the values causing an allergic reaction in an individual with peanut allergy (if testing for peanut DNA).

Table 2	
Example CT Value	Likelihood of Causing Peanut Allergic Reaction
≤ 29	High
30-35	High to moderate
36-40	Low to none

13. A scientist finds that a new type of energy bar contains a CT value of 39.7. Should the manufacturer label the bar as likely to cause a peanut-triggered allergic reaction?

   A. Yes: the higher the CT value, the more likely the bar will trigger an allergic reaction.
   B. Yes: a CT value that ends in a decimal is more likely to cause a reaction than those that are whole numbers.
   C. No: a CT value between 36 and 40 is extremely unlikely to cause such an allergic reaction.
   D. No: any CT value less than 50 has a 0% likelihood in triggering such an allergic reaction.

14. How many of the foods tested by the researcher possesses a high likelihood to trigger an allergic reaction if consumed by someone with a severe peanut allergy?

   F. 1
   G. 2
   H. 6
   J. 7

15. What percent of the foods tested by the researcher that have a high to moderate likelihood of causing a peanut allergic reaction state the presence of peanuts in their food packaging?

   A. 0%
   B. 33%
   C. 50%
   D. 67%

16. A food company creates a new cereal bar and declares on the food packaging that it may contain traces of tree nuts and walnuts. It would be expected that such a cereal bar, if tested by the researcher, would generate a CT value of:

   F. 0-15
   G. 15-25
   H. 25-30
   J. 30-40

Passage V

Enzymes are substances that act as a catalyst to speed up biochemical reactions. When a *substrate* binds to the active site of an enzyme, a reaction can occur in which the substrate is converted into one or more products. The digestive enzyme, Trypsin, catalyzes the process of breaking down proteins in the small intestine into amino acids, which can then be absorbed into the blood stream. Importantly, any physical or chemical changes to an enzyme's environment, such as changes in temperature, pH, and salt concentration, can alter its ability to function by denaturing or inactivating the enzyme.

Two experiments sought to compare the ability of Trypsin to generate products (amino acids) at two different pH levels. For each experiment, four vials were made to contain 1mM of Trypsin and differing concentrations of substrate. The values of light absorbance for each sample were recorded every 30 seconds for 2.5 minutes using a *spectrophotometer*, an apparatus for measuring the intensity of light. The measured absorbance values were collected at a wavelength that corresponds to the relative amount of product that was generated in the samples. In other words, a higher absorbance value at the indicated wavelength would mean more product was made by the Trypsin.

Experiment 1

Four vials were made to contain 1mM of Trypsin and differing levels of substrate concentration maintained at a pH of 8. The absorbance values after each 30 second time period for each substrate level is recorded in Table 1.

Absorbance value					
Substrate level (mM)	0.5 min	1 min	1.5 min	2 min	2.5 min
0.04	0.023	0.035	0.053	0.069	0.082
0.09	0.039	0.082	0.125	0.154	0.184
0.15	0.067	0.137	0.199	0.261	0.310
0.24	0.115	0.239	0.340	0.431	0.511

Table 1

Experiment 2

Four vials were made to contain 1mM of Trypsin and differing levels of substrate concentration maintained at a pH of 6. The absorbance values after each 30 second time period for each substrate level is recorded in Table 2.

Absorbance value					
Substrate level (mM)	0.5 min	1 min	1.5 min	2 min	2.5 min
0.04	0.006	0.011	0.017	0.023	0.027
0.09	0.014	0.028	0.042	0.055	0.068
0.15	0.027	0.053	0.078	0.102	0.149
0.24	0.060	0.090	0.145	0.190	0.233

Table 2

17. After 2 minutes of interaction, a vial with a pH of 8 containing 1mM of Trypsin and a substrate level of 0.09mM will result in an absorbance level of:

   A. 0.068
   B. 0.055
   C. 0.154
   D. 0.184

18. A vial containing 1mM of Trypsin and a substrate level of 0.15 with a pH value of 6 would result in an absorbance level of 0.040 after roughly:

   F. 30 seconds of interaction.
   G. 45 seconds of interaction.
   H. 60 seconds of interaction.
   J. 75 seconds of interaction.

19. Which of the following substrate levels resulted in the highest average absorbance value across the five time measurements?

   A. 0.04mM interacting with 1mM of Trypsin at a pH level of 6
   B. 0.24mM interacting with 1mM of Trypsin at a pH level of 6
   C. 0.15mM interacting with 1mM of Trypsin at a pH level of 8
   D. 0.24mM interacting with 1mM of Trypsin at a pH level of 8

20. If measurements were taken every 15 seconds, then it would be expected that an absorbance value of 0.062 would be measured:

   F. after a substrate level of 0.04 interacted with 1mM of Trypsin at a pH of 8 for 1.25 minutes.
   G. after a substrate level of 0.09 interacted with 1mM of Trypsin at a pH of 8 for 1.25 minutes.
   H. after a substrate level of 0.04 interacted with 1mM of Trypsin at a pH of 6 for 2.25 minutes.
   J. after a substrate level of 0.09 interacted with 1mM of Trypsin at a pH of 6 for 2.25 minutes.

Passage VI

With the traditional *optical microscope*, the user looks into the eyepieces to view a sample or specimen. The objective lens focuses light from the sample into the eyepieces. The eyepiece lens and the objective lens both provide magnification, but the latter more so. The condenser lens helps to concentrate light on the sample for easy viewing. Figure 1 displays the visual path of an optical microscope.

While the more advanced *fluorescent microscope* shares some similarities to the optical microscope, one key difference is that fluorescent microscopes utilize a process called *photoluminescence*. This is where molecules in a sample can be put into an excited state and absorb energy from a high intensity light, causing the molecules to emit light at a longer wavelength. The filter then works by separating any surrounding light, so only the fluorescence emitted by the molecules in a sample can be visualized. The detector can be used to display the fluorescent sample on a digital screen for easy viewing. Figure 2 displays the visual path of a fluorescent microscope.

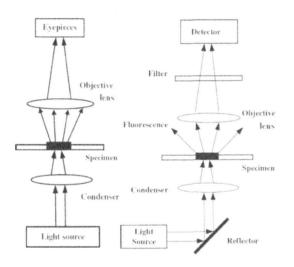

Figure 1   Figure 2

A teacher sought to test a group of students' ability to distinguish neutrophil white blood cells within a blood sample using both optical (Study 1) and fluorescent (Study 2) microscopes. To distinguish a neutrophil under the optical microscope, the students were to look for a round cell body with a multi-lobed nucleus that is around 12-14 μm in diameter. For the fluorescent microscope, the blood sample was treated with an antibody that causes only neutrophil cells to fluoresce green.

Table 1 displays the results of Study 1, consisting of each student's answer for the number of neutrophils found in a blood sample and the percentage of correct cells that were identified using the optical microscope. Table 2 displays the results of Study 2, consisting of each student's answer for the number of neutrophils found in a blood sample and the percentage of correct cells that were identified using the fluorescent microscope.

Optical Microscope	Neutrophil count	Percent correct
Student 1	5	33%
Student 2	8	53%
Student 3	10	67%
Student 4	4	27%

Table 1

Fluorescent Microscope	Neutrophil count	Percent correct
Student 1	13	76%
Student 2	16	94%
Student 3	17	100%
Student 4	13	76%

Table 2

21. Suppose the teacher will present an award to the student who is most proficient at finding neutrophils under both microscopes. Which student is most likely to receive the award based on the results of Study 1 and Study 2?

   A. Student 1
   B. Student 2
   C. Student 3
   D. Student 4

22. How many neutrophils were present in the blood samples in Study 1 and Study 2 combined?

   F. 17
   G. 28
   H. 30
   J. 32

23. If a fifth student counts neutrophils under the optical microscope and finds 47% of the total, then the amount of neutrophils found by her would be:

   A. 6
   B. 7
   C. 8
   D. 9

24. Which of the students, if any, displayed an ability to better identify neutrophils under an optical microscope compared to a fluorescent microscope?

    F.   Student 1
    G.   Student 3
    H.   Student 4
    J.   None of the students displayed this ability.

Step 1 Correct Answers

Passage I:	Passage II:	Passage III:	Passage IV:	Passage V:	Passage VI:
1: B	5: C	9: C	13: C	17: C	21: C
2: J	6: F	10: G	14: F	18: G	22: J
3: D	7: A	11: A	15: B	19: D	23: B
4: F	8: H	12: J	16: J	20: J	24: J

Stumped on any? You can find the explanations for each of these questions beginning on page 351.

STEP 2

Reading and Applying Written

Descriptions

A lot (and I really do mean *a lot*) of ACT tutors and instructors (or high school science teachers who don't know any better) often tell students that all they need to do is what we did in Step 1: read data and answer questions about it. I wish, so badly, that that were true; it would make this test a whole lot easier and your preparation a lot simpler. However, it simply isn't true (I know: I've researched the ACT more than anyone): you will need the written information if you want to do your best on the ACT Science test. And, because I want you to do your best, I have included a step dedicated to your ability to do just that.

As has been noted (and as you've seen from the previous passages), there can often be a good bit of reading to get through in order to properly understand an ACT Science passage. Though we haven't discussed it in any in depth, there is also usually 1 passage that is exclusively written words (the Conflicting Viewpoints passage; more on the in Step 4). Because of this, the second most important skill in the ACT Science test is your ability to read, understand, and apply what is described in the written descriptions. In fact, about 25% of ACT Science questions require that you *merely* reference the written descriptions (in other words, the percentage of questions that require an understanding of written material is far greater than 25%).

Diagrams

On occasion, an ACT Science passage will feature a diagram of some kind. These diagrams do not give data, of course. Rather, they show the layout of an experiment, how some kind of apparatus works, etc. I consider these diagrams to be a part of the written material that we are discussing here in Step 2 since there is no data within them to study as we did in Step 1. You will notice (if you haven't already) that one of the practice passages that follows contains a couple of diagrams.

Sticker Shock

In the introduction to this book I spoke briefly about "sticker shock." What I meant was this: often, when students take the ACT Science test, they are shocked/scared/etc. about what they initially see when they flip the page to a new science passage: graphs, diagrams, charts, figures, and scientific terminology that they have never come across in all their years studying science. However, *no one* taking the ACT has seen this stuff. Just because you aren't familiar with a word that comes up in the written portion of the passage doesn't mean you're stupid or the only one; I guarantee the student to your left and your right are thinking the exact same thing.

Active Reading

To get through the written information properly, follow these steps. First, take a deep breath, which gets much-needed oxygen flowing to the brain. Second, take a good posture and have your pencil in hand. Third, read quickly, but for general understanding; don't get caught up on every single word or detail that comes up. If a particular passage needs you to know or understand a word and its meaning, the test makers usually do two things: 1) italicize the word, and 2) define the word. These are clues that this is important and need to be underlined or circled. Other items in the written passage may or may not be important. For example, a scary looking equation is probably not important and certainly won't be solved (remember: no calculator on the ACT Science test, so no difficult math either).

The Purpose of this Step and the Practice that Follows

The purpose of this step is simple: to get you used to reading and understanding the written descriptions that are a part of each ACT Science passage. Each of the questions that follow ask exclusively about the written portion of each passage and DO NOT require a reference to the data that is presented in charts/ tables/graphs (as was the case in Step 1). Of course, there is overlap between these two portions of the passage; there are many questions that will require you to find data and also understand something from the passage. However, due to the importance of that skill, it has its own step: Step 3.

So, let's practice this skill or reading, interpreting, and applying information from the written portions of these passages. Remember: each question is *exclusively* about the *written* material (not the data)!

Passage I

Most of the water consumption within the United States is used by the agricultural industry for food production. This heavily contributes to the overuse of groundwater aquifers. Therefore, finding alternative resources of water for agricultural production is necessary to lessen the looming threat of food and water scarcity. One issue is that alternative water sources in certain regions often contain a higher concentration of salt compared to groundwater aquifers, and many food crops are not selected for traits like tolerance to salt. In recent years, new varieties, also called *variants*, of crops have been selected mostly for commercial benefit, with little regard for producing varieties that can withstand changes in salt concentrations. As a result, a group of researchers sought to determine plant variants that are resilient to waters with higher salt concentrations.

Researchers first tested the salt tolerance in variants of two regularly consumed crops, tomato and pepper, by testing the consumable yields of each plant when grown in the same soil. The control for the experiment was freshwater from a ground water aquifer, while the experimental condition was done with water containing a higher salt content. The results are recorded in Table 1 (tomato) and Table 2 (pepper) below.

Fruit yield (grams)		
Tomato variant	Control	Experimental
Bloody Butcher	2785	1719
Juane Flamme	2317	1355
Quarter Century	1415	928

Table 1

Fruit yield (grams)		
Pepper variant	Control	Experimental
California Wonder	2591	1993
Thai Hot	295	291
Ancho	1514	1489

Table 2

The researchers next tested the concentration of sodium within the plant tissue of the different variants for both the control and saltwater (experimental) groups. Their findings are recorded in Figure 1 (tomato) and Figure 2 (pepper) below in millimoles per kilogram.

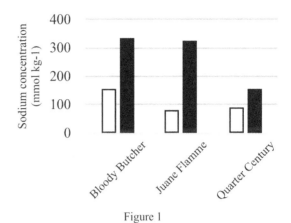

Figure 1

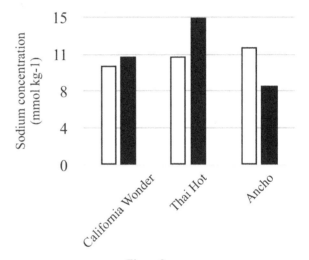

Figure 2

1. Why did the experimental group of tomatoes and peppers test for a higher concentration of salt than the control group?

   A. Because the groundwater aquifers from which they were watered typically contain a heavy concentration of salt.
   B. Because the alternative water sources from which they were watered typically contain a heavy concentration of salt.
   C. Because the soil in which they were grown featured a high concentration of sodium and sodium-containing minerals.
   D. Because tomatoes and peppers are more likely to absorb salt when watered from groundwater aquifers.

2. Which of the following is, agriculturally speaking, an example of a *variant*?

    F. A groundwater aquifer
    G. The California Wonder
    H. Salt
    J. The pepper

3. Which of the factors listed below were the same for both the control and experimental groups?

    I. The variants of crops tested
    II. The source of the water
    III. The soil in which the plants were grown

    A. I only
    B. I and III only
    C. II and III only
    D. I, II, and III

Passage II

A group of high school students investigated the momentum of carts rolling down an inclined plane across a designated finish line. The students used three carts, labeled Cart A, Cart B, and Cart C. Cart A had a mass of 12.5 kg, Cart B had a mass of 21.8 kg, and Cart C had a mass of 34.7 kg. They conducted five trials, progressively increasing the release height of the carts. The purpose of the experiment was to explore how changes in release height affect the velocity and momentum of the carts.

Velocity is a fundamental concept in physics that represents the speed of an object in a specific direction. In this experiment, velocity was measured as each cart crossed the finish line, but can also be determined using the equation $v = \sqrt{2gh}$, where v is the velocity, g is the acceleration due to gravity (approximately 9.8 m/s²), and h is the release height of the cart.

Momentum is a property of a moving object that depends on its mass and velocity. It describes the quantity of motion possessed by an object and is calculated by multiplying the mass of the object by its velocity. The equation for momentum is given as $p = mv$, where p represents the momentum, m is the mass of the object, and v denotes the velocity.

After collecting data, the students calculated the momentum for each cart and trial. Figure 1 shows the recorded velocity for each cart as it crossed the finish line, and Figure 2 shows the calculated momentum for each cart as it crossed the finish line.

Key:

- Cart A
- Cart B
- Cart C

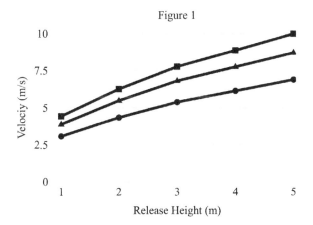

Figure 1

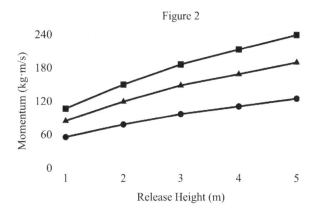

Figure 2

4. Which of the following correctly orders the events in the experiment?

    F. Students took data, then calculated the momentum, then calculated the velocity.
    G. Students released a cart, then measured the velocity, then calculated the momentum.
    H. Students made a hypothesis about each cart's velocity and momentum, then measured each as the cart crossed the finish line.
    J. Students calculated momentum, then made a hypothesis about the velocity, then calculated the velocity.

5. What action was taken in the experiment to ensure that both the velocity and momentum of each cart as it crossed the finish line would differ from the other two carts when released from the same height?

    A. The carts' wheels featured different tread patterns.
    B. The carts' wheels were different widths.
    C. The carts differed in volume.
    D. The carts differed in mass.

6. Which of the following is dependent upon the value of the acceleration due to gravity (approximately 9.8 m/s²)?

    I. Mass
    II. Velocity
    III. Momentum

    F. II only
    G. III only
    H. II and III only
    J. I, II, and III

Passage III

The *Mpemba Effect* refers to a curious phenomenon in which hot water freezes faster than cold water under certain circumstances. Several proposed explanations have been put forth to shed light on the Mpemba Effect. One possibility relates to the evaporation of the hot water during the cooling process. As hot water is exposed to lower temperatures, it undergoes rapid evaporation, resulting in a reduction in its volume. This reduction in volume leads to an increase in the concentration of dissolved solids in the remaining water. Consequently, the higher concentration of dissolved solids may lower the freezing point of the hot water, allowing it to freeze more rapidly.

A group of students designed an experiment to test the Mpemba Effect. They collected four beakers and labeled them A, B, C, and D. *Thermocouples*, or thermoelectric devices for measuring temperature, were placed in the bottom of each beaker. Beakers A and B were filled with distilled (purified) water, and beakers C and D were filled with tap water. The water in beakers A and C was heated to 50 degrees Celsius, and the water in beakers B and D was left at room temperature (around 30 degrees Celsius).

The students recorded the temperature of each beaker after placing it in a freezer with a temperature of -18° Celsius until it had reached 0° Celsius, the freezing point of water. The observations of the students are given below. Table 1 corresponds to beaker A, Table 2 to beaker B, Table 3 to beaker C, and Table 4 to beaker D.

Table 1 (Beaker A)	
Time Elapsed (minutes)	Temperature (°C)
0	50
5	42
10	36
15	30
20	25
25	21
30	17
35	13
40	10
45	8
50	5
55	2
60	0

Table 2 (Beaker B)	
Time Elapsed (minutes)	Temperature (°C)
0	30
5	26
10	23
15	20
20	18
25	17
30	14
35	12
40	10
45	8
50	6
55	5
60	4
65	3
70	0

Table 3 (Beaker C)	
Time Elapsed (minutes)	Temperature (°C)
0	50
5	44
10	38
15	33
20	28
25	24
30	20
35	17
40	14
45	11
50	8
55	5
60	3
65	0

Table 4 (Beaker D)	
Time Elapsed (minutes)	Temperature (°C)
0	30
5	26
10	22
15	19
20	18
25	17
30	15
35	13
40	11
45	10
50	8
55	6
60	4
65	2
70	1
75	0

7. One factor that may cause hot water to freeze faster than cold water is:

   A. a lower presence of dissolved solids before undergoing rapid evaporation.
   B. a higher presence of dissolved solids before undergoing rapid evaporation.
   C. a lower presence of dissolved solids after undergoing rapid evaporation.
   D. a higher presence of dissolved solids after undergoing rapid evaporation.

8. Given the definition of the Mpemba Effect in the passage, which of the following is an assumption made by the students conducting the experiment?

   F. That boiling water is "hot" water.
   G. That water measuring a temperature of 30° Celsius is "hot" water.
   H. That room temperature water is "cold" water.
   J. That water measuring a temperature of 50° Celsius is "cold" water.

9. Which of the following was not one of the water varieties tested in the study?

   A. A beaker of tap water heated to 50° Celsius then placed in a freezer set to -18° Celsius.
   B. A beaker of purified water kept at 30° Celsius then placed in a freezer set to -18° Celsius.
   C. A beaker of salt water heated to 50° Celsius then placed in a freezer set to -18° Celsius.
   D. A beaker of tap water kept at 30° Celsius then placed in a freezer set to -18° Celsius.

Passage IV

Real-time polymerase chain reaction (PCR) *analysis* is a laboratory technique that can be used to help determine if a specific type of DNA is present in a sample. This technique works by increasing the total amount of DNA present in a sample, a step called *amplification*, and then detecting if the DNA matches the target DNA.

Detection of the target DNA is determined by the *cycle threshold* (CT) value. The CT value is the number of cycles of amplification that is needed for a specific DNA sequence to be detected in a sample. The lower the CT value, the more likely it is that the sample contains the DNA of interest. Most real-time PCR analyses undergo a total of 40 cycles of amplification.

While this technique is often used for medical purposes, it also has applications in food safety. Due to the safety concerns regarding food allergens, scientists will use real-time PCR to search for the DNA of common allergen causing ingredients in commercial products to ensure that the package label is accurate. One common and often dangerous food allergy is an allergy to peanuts. If a person is severely allergic to peanuts and unknowingly ingests even a small amount, it could be deadly. Therefore, scientists completed real-time PCR analysis to test commercial food products for DNA that matches the peanut.

Table 1 shows commercial food products, their current package labels for allergens, and the CT values discovered for each following real-time PCR analysis to detect peanut DNA. An N.D. value means that there was no detection of the target DNA after 40 cycles of amplification.

Table 1		
Food	Food Packaging Allergen Declaration	Peanut CT Value
Cereal bar I	Peanut, hazelnut	17.97
Cereal bar II	Almond and tree nuts	32.40
Cereal bar III	Hazelnut, almond and peanut traces	33.74
Cereal bar IV	May contain tree nut traces	35.90
Chocolate with pistachio	Pistachio, almond, hazelnut, tree nut traces	36.80
Sausage with walnut	Walnuts	N.D.
Chocolate	Almond and hazelnut traces	37.99
Cookies with fiber	Not declared	32.25

Table 2 displays example CT values and the likelihood of the values causing an allergic reaction in an individual with peanut allergy (if testing for peanut DNA).

Table 2	
Example CT Value	Likelihood of Causing Peanut Allergic Reaction
≤ 29	High
30-35	High to moderate
36-40	Low to none

10. In PCR analysis and application, scientists assume:

  F. that 40 cycles of amplification is sufficient to determine the presence of a certain DNA in a sample.
  G. that ingesting even a small amount of peanut DNA can be deadly for a person with a severe peanut allergy.
  H. that the technique can be used to determine the presence of certain DNA in a sample.
  J. that all commercially available products contain at least a small trace of peanut DNA.

11. Imagine a laboratory can perform real-time polymerase chain reaction analysis via amplification of DNA once per day and only on weekdays. How many weeks maximum would the lab need to determine the cycle threshold value of a sample?

  A. 5
  B. 7
  C. 8
  D. 10

12. Food producers who desire that those with a severe peanut allergy to be able to consume their product would like a CT value that is:

  F. low: a low CT score means that few iterations of PCR analysis were necessary to detect potentially harmful DNA.
  G. low: a low CT score means that many iterations of PCR analysis were necessary to detect potentially harmful DNA.
  H. high: a high CT score means that few iterations of PCR analysis were necessary to detect potentially harmful DNA.
  J. high: a high CT score means that many iterations of PCR analysis were necessary to detect potentially harmful DNA.

Passage V

Enzymes are substances that act as a catalyst to speed up biochemical reactions. When a *substrate* binds to the active site of an enzyme, a reaction can occur in which the substrate is converted into one or more products. The digestive enzyme, Trypsin, catalyzes the process of breaking down proteins in the small intestine into amino acids, which can then be absorbed into the blood stream. Importantly, any physical or chemical changes to an enzyme's environment, such as changes in temperature, pH, and salt concentration, can alter its ability to function by denaturing or inactivating the enzyme.

Two experiments sought to compare the ability of Trypsin to generate products (amino acids) at two different pH levels. For each experiment, four vials were made to contain 1mM of Trypsin and differing concentrations of substrate. The values of light absorbance for each sample were recorded every 30 seconds for 2.5 minutes using a *spectrophotometer*, an apparatus for measuring the intensity of light. The measured absorbance values were collected at a wavelength that corresponds to the relative amount of product that was generated in the samples. In other words, a higher absorbance value at the indicated wavelength would mean more product was made by the Trypsin.

Experiment 1

Four vials were made to contain 1mM of Trypsin and differing levels of substrate concentration maintained at a pH of 8. The absorbance values after each 30 second time period for each substrate level is recorded in Table 1.

Absorbance value					
Substrate level (mM)	0.5 min	1 min	1.5 min	2 min	2.5 min
0.04	0.023	0.035	0.053	0.069	0.082
0.09	0.039	0.082	0.125	0.154	0.184
0.15	0.067	0.137	0.199	0.261	0.310
0.24	0.115	0.239	0.340	0.431	0.511

Table 1

Experiment 2

Four vials were made to contain 1mM of Trypsin and differing levels of substrate concentration maintained at a pH of 6. The absorbance values after each 30 second time period for each substrate level is recorded in Table 2.

Absorbance value					
Substrate level (mM)	0.5 min	1 min	1.5 min	2 min	2.5 min
0.04	0.006	0.011	0.017	0.023	0.027
0.09	0.014	0.028	0.042	0.055	0.068
0.15	0.027	0.053	0.078	0.102	0.149
0.24	0.060	0.090	0.145	0.190	0.233

Table 2

13. What did each vial in the experiment have in common?

   A. The Trypsin level
   B. The substrate level
   C. The pH
   D. The absorbance value

14. In the experiments, a higher absorbance value at the indicated wavelength means:

   F. less product was made by the Trypsin.
   G. less enzymes were present in the vial.
   H. more substrates were catalyzed by Trypsin enzymes.
   J. more substrates had failed to react with an enzyme.

15. If the scientists wanted to conduct further experiments testing how Trypsin responds to chemical or physical changes to its environment besides pH, then one additional change that could be made to the vials might include:

   A. a change in temperature.
   B. a change in substrate levels.
   C. a change in enzyme.
   D. a change in Trypsin levels.

Passage VI

With the traditional *optical microscope*, the user looks into the eyepieces to view a sample or specimen. The objective lens focuses light from the sample into the eyepieces. The eyepiece lens and the objective lens both provide magnification, but the latter more so. The condenser lens helps to concentrate light on the sample for easy viewing. Figure 1 displays the visual path of an optical microscope.

While the more advanced *fluorescent microscope* shares some similarities to the optical microscope, one key difference is that fluorescent microscopes utilize a process called *photoluminescence*. This is where molecules in a sample can be put into an excited state and absorb energy from a high intensity light, causing the molecules to emit light at a longer wavelength. The filter then works by separating any surrounding light, so only the fluorescence emitted by the molecules in a sample can be visualized. The detector can be used to display the fluorescent sample on a digital screen for easy viewing. Figure 2 displays the visual path of a fluorescent microscope.

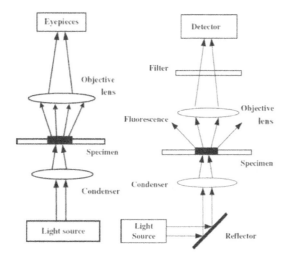

Figure 1   Figure 2

A teacher sought to test a group of students' ability to distinguish neutrophil white blood cells within a blood sample using both optical (Study 1) and fluorescent (Study 2) microscopes. To distinguish a neutrophil under the optical microscope, the students were to look for a round cell body with a multi-lobed nucleus that is around 12-14 μm in diameter. For the fluorescent microscope, the blood sample was treated with an antibody that causes only neutrophil cells to fluoresce green.

Table 1 displays the results of Study 1, consisting of each student's answer for the number of neutrophils found in a blood sample and the percentage of correct cells that were identified using the optical microscope. Table 2 displays the results of Study 2, consisting of each student's answer for the number of neutrophils found in a blood sample and the percentage of correct cells that were identified using the fluorescent microscope.

Optical Microscope	Neutrophil count	Percent correct
Student 1	5	33%
Student 2	8	53%
Student 3	10	67%
Student 4	4	27%

Table 1

Fluorescent Microscope	Neutrophil count	Percent correct
Student 1	13	76%
Student 2	16	94%
Student 3	17	100%
Student 4	13	76%

Table 2

16. According to their descriptions, which of the following is a difference between optical and fluorescent microscopes?

F. The optical microscope utilizes a process called photoluminescence.
G. The fluorescent microscope makes use of less lenses to focus on a specimen than does the optical microscope.
H. Under an optical microscope, molecules in a sample are put into an excited state.
J. The eyepiece of the fluorescent microscope provides additional magnification.

17. According to Figure 2, the part of the fluorescent microscope responsible for separating out unnecessary light is placed relative to the path of light:

A. immediately prior to the objective lens.
B. immediately prior to the detector.
C. immediately after the condenser.
D. immediately after the reflector.

18. One precondition for the obtaining of accurate results from the studies was that:

    F. the antibody in Study 1 would cause all blood cells but neutrophil cells to fluoresce green.

    G. five minutes per student per microscope is sufficient time to count neutrophil cells.

    H. the antibody in Study 2 would only cause neutrophil cells to fluoresce green.

    J. square neutrophil cells with a single-lobed nucleus were not to be considered in either study.

Step 2 Correct Answers

Passage I:	Passage II:	Passage III:	Passage IV:	Passage V:	Passage VI:
1: B	4: G	7: D	10: F	13: A	16: G
2: G	5: D	8: H	11: C	14: H	17: B
3: B	6: H	9: C	12: J	15: A	18: H

Stumped on any? You can find the explanations for each of these questions beginning on page 354.

STEP 3

Pairing a Passage's Written

Descriptions and Data

In Step 1, you practiced simply reading charts, tables, graphs, etc. in order to find data and apply it in a relevant way to determine an answer. In Step 2, you practiced reading through and thinking about the passage's written information in order to answer questions correctly. Here, we combine these two skills to take your preparation to the next level.

Putting It Together

One of the reasons for active reading on your initial read through of the passage, as has been said, is so that you can have the time to find proper information (either data from charts/tables/graphs or information in the written section, including a diagram on occasion). Here, it is time to realize that you may have to do both of those things. While, strictly speaking, only 12% to 15% of the questions require this two step process, the reason the ability to reference both is Step 3 instead of 4 or 5 is that it reinforces the two main skills associated with the ACT Science test from Steps 1 and 2.

The Following Practice

I think you are used to this by now. The following practice passages are the same as those featured in Step 1 and Step 2. Notice how they may require more of you than simply reading data or finding information in the passage, but rather both.

So, without further ado, let's practice putting these two skills together!

Passage I

Most of the water consumption within the United States is used by the agricultural industry for food production. This heavily contributes to the overuse of groundwater aquifers. Therefore, finding alternative resources of water for agricultural production is necessary to lessen the looming threat of food and water scarcity. One issue is that alternative water sources in certain regions often contain a higher concentration of salt compared to groundwater aquifers, and many food crops are not selected for traits like tolerance to salt. In recent years, new varieties, also called *variants*, of crops have been selected mostly for commercial benefit, with little regard for producing varieties that can withstand changes in salt concentrations. As a result, a group of researchers sought to determine plant variants that are resilient to waters with higher salt concentrations.

Researchers first tested the salt tolerance in variants of two regularly consumed crops, tomato and pepper, by testing the consumable yields of each plant when grown in the same soil. The control for the experiment was freshwater from a ground water aquifer, while the experimental condition was done with water containing a higher salt content. The results are recorded in Table 1 (tomato) and Table 2 (pepper) below.

Fruit yield (grams)		
Tomato variant	Control	Experimental
Bloody Butcher	2785	1719
Juane Flamme	2317	1355
Quarter Century	1415	928

Table 1

Fruit yield (grams)		
Pepper variant	Control	Experimental
California Wonder	2591	1993
Thai Hot	295	291
Ancho	1514	1489

Table 2

The researchers next tested the concentration of sodium within the plant tissue of the different variants for both the control and saltwater (experimental) groups. Their findings are recorded in Figure 1 (tomato) and Figure 2 (pepper) below in millimoles per kilogram.

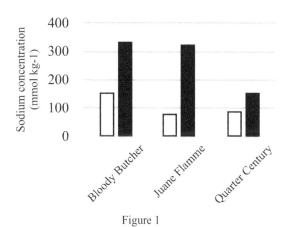

Figure 1

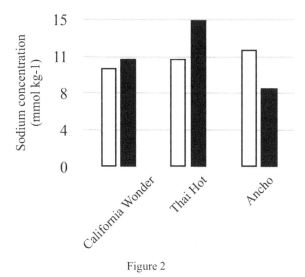

Figure 2

1. Based on sodium concentration alone, which variety of crop shows the most potential in helping to decrease agricultural dependence on groundwater aquifers?

A. Bloody Butcher
B. Juane Flamme
C. Thai Hot
D. Ancho

2. Which variety of fruit most likely has the most natural salty taste?

    F. Thai Hot
    G. Bloody Butcher
    H. California Wonder
    J. Juane Flamme

3. Which of the following varieties of fruit, based on Tables 1 and 2, demonstrates the greatest tolerance to salt in its water supply?

    A. Thai Hot
    B. Bloody Butcher
    C. California Wonder
    D. Juane Flamme

Passage II

A group of high school students investigated the momentum of carts rolling down an inclined plane across a designated finish line. The students used three carts, labeled Cart A, Cart B, and Cart C. Cart A had a mass of 12.5 kg, Cart B had a mass of 21.8 kg, and Cart C had a mass of 34.7 kg. They conducted five trials, progressively increasing the release height of the carts. The purpose of the experiment was to explore how changes in release height affect the velocity and momentum of the carts.

Velocity is a fundamental concept in physics that represents the speed of an object in a specific direction. In this experiment, velocity was measured as each cart crossed the finish line, but can also be determined using the equation $v = \sqrt{2gh}$, where v is the velocity, g is the acceleration due to gravity (approximately 9.8 m/s²), and h is the release height of the cart.

Momentum is a property of a moving object that depends on its mass and velocity. It describes the quantity of motion possessed by an object and is calculated by multiplying the mass of the object by its velocity. The equation for momentum is given as $p = mv$, where p represents the momentum, m is the mass of the object, and v denotes the velocity.

After collecting data, the students calculated the momentum for each cart and trial. Figure 1 shows the recorded velocity for each cart as it crossed the finish line, and Figure 2 shows the calculated momentum for each cart as it crossed the finish line.

Key:  Cart A
Cart B
Cart C

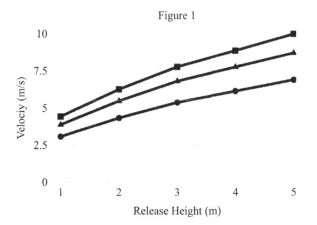

Figure 1

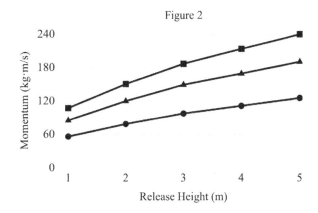

Figure 2

4. In this same experiment, a cart with a mass of 17 kg released from a height of 4 meters would be expected to have momentum as it crossed the finish line that measured approximately:

   F. 80 kg·m/s
   G. 140 kg·m/s
   H. 195 kg·m/s
   J. 245 kg·m/s

5. At a height of 2 meters, the value of p for a cart weighing 12.5 kg is approximately how much greater than the value of p for a cart weighing 34.7 kg?

   A. 30 kg·m/s
   B. 45 kg·m/s
   C. 55 kg·m/s
   D. 75 kg·m/s

6. Which of the following carts would have the least velocity as it crossed the finish line?

   F. A cart weighing 10 kg released from a height of 5 meters
   G. A cart weighing 10 kg released from a height of 2 meters
   H. A cart weighing 15 kg released from a height of 4 meters
   J. A cart weighing 35 kg released at a height of 3 meters

Passage III

The *Mpemba Effect* refers to a curious phenomenon in which hot water freezes faster than cold water under certain circumstances. Several proposed explanations have been put forth to shed light on the Mpemba Effect. One possibility relates to the evaporation of the hot water during the cooling process. As hot water is exposed to lower temperatures, it undergoes rapid evaporation, resulting in a reduction in its volume. This reduction in volume leads to an increase in the concentration of dissolved solids in the remaining water. Consequently, the higher concentration of dissolved solids may lower the freezing point of the hot water, allowing it to freeze more rapidly.

A group of students designed an experiment to test the Mpemba Effect. They collected four beakers and labeled them A, B, C, and D. *Thermocouples*, or thermoelectric devices for measuring temperature, were placed in the bottom of each beaker. Beakers A and B were filled with distilled (purified) water, and beakers C and D were filled with tap water. The water in beakers A and C was heated to 50 degrees Celsius, and the water in beakers B and D was left at room temperature (around 30 degrees Celsius).

The students recorded the temperature of each beaker after placing it in a freezer with a temperature of -18° Celsius until it had reached 0° Celsius, the freezing point of water. The observations of the students are given below. Table 1 corresponds to beaker A, Table 2 to beaker B, Table 3 to beaker C, and Table 4 to beaker D.

Table 1 (Beaker A)	
Time Elapsed (minutes)	Temperature (°C)
0	50
5	42
10	36
15	30
20	25
25	21
30	17
35	13
40	10
45	8
50	5
55	2
60	0

Table 2 (Beaker B)	
Time Elapsed (minutes)	Temperature (°C)
0	30
5	26
10	23
15	20
20	18
25	17
30	14
35	12
40	10
45	8
50	6
55	5
60	4
65	3
70	0

Table 3 (Beaker C)	
Time Elapsed (minutes)	Temperature (°C)
0	50
5	44
10	38
15	33
20	28
25	24
30	20
35	17
40	14
45	11
50	8
55	5
60	3
65	0

Table 4 (Beaker D)	
Time Elapsed (minutes)	Temperature (°C)
0	30
5	26
10	22
15	19
20	18
25	17
30	15
35	13
40	11
45	10
50	8
55	6
60	4
65	2
70	1
75	0

7. Based on the results of the experiment, which of the following would most likely be the last to reach a temperature of 0° Celsius?

   A. A gallon of tap water at room temperature placed in a freezer set at a temperature of -18° Celsius
   B. A gallon of purified water at room temperature placed in a freezer set at a temperature of -18° Celsius
   C. A gallon of tap water heated to 50° Celsius placed in a freezer set at a temperature of -18° Celsius
   D. A gallon of purified water heated to 50° Celsius placed in a freezer set at a temperature of -18° Celsius

8. Which of the beakers most likely underwent rapid evaporation?

   F. Beaker A
   G. Beaker B
   H. Beaker C
   J. Beaker D

9. Suppose a student repeated the experiment and put into Beaker E a mixture of tap and purified water. If the water was placed into the freezer at room temperature, it would be expected that the water would reach a temperature of 10° Celsius after:

   A. 40 minutes
   B. 42.5 minutes
   C. 45 minutes
   D. 47.5 minutes

Passage IV

Real-time polymerase chain reaction (PCR) *analysis* is a laboratory technique that can be used to help determine if a specific type of DNA is present in a sample. This technique works by increasing the total amount of DNA present in a sample, a step called *amplification*, and then detecting if the DNA matches the target DNA.

Detection of the target DNA is determined by the *cycle threshold* (CT) value. The CT value is the number of cycles of amplification that is needed for a specific DNA sequence to be detected in a sample. The lower the CT value, the more likely it is that the sample contains the DNA of interest. Most real-time PCR analyses undergo a total of 40 cycles of amplification.

While this technique is often used for medical purposes, it also has applications in food safety. Due to the safety concerns regarding food allergens, scientists will use real-time PCR to search for the DNA of common allergen causing ingredients in commercial products to ensure that the package label is accurate. One common and often dangerous food allergy is an allergy to peanuts. If a person is severely allergic to peanuts and unknowingly ingests even a small amount, it could be deadly. Therefore, scientists completed real-time PCR analysis to test commercial food products for DNA that matches the peanut.

Table 1 shows commercial food products, their current package labels for allergens, and the CT values discovered for each following real-time PCR analysis to detect peanut DNA. An N.D. value means that there was no detection of the target DNA after 40 cycles of amplification.

Table 1		
Food	Food Packaging Allergen Declaration	Peanut CT Value
Cereal bar I	Peanut, hazelnut	17.97
Cereal bar II	Almond and tree nuts	32.40
Cereal bar III	Hazelnut, almond and peanut traces	33.74
Cereal bar IV	May contain tree nut traces	35.90
Chocolate with pistachio	Pistachio, almond, hazelnut, tree nut traces	36.80
Sausage with walnut	Walnuts	N.D.
Chocolate	Almond and hazelnut traces	37.99
Cookies with fiber	Not declared	32.25

Table 2 displays example CT values and the likelihood of the values causing an allergic reaction in an individual with peanut allergy (if testing for peanut DNA).

Table 2	
Example CT Value	Likelihood of Causing Peanut Allergic Reaction
≤ 29	High
30-35	High to moderate
36-40	Low to none

10. Which of the following is *true* about the Cookies with fiber?

    F. Their likelihood of causing a peanut allergic reaction is low to none.
    G. They contain traces of DNA that can cause a peanut allergic reaction.
    H. There is a 0% chance that they will cause a peanut allergic reaction.
    J. Their cycle threshold value is not declared.

11. On average, how many cycles of amplification were needed to discover the presence of peanut DNA in the tested foods declared to contain peanuts and not just peanut traces?

    A. 4.1
    B. 12.03
    C. 17.97
    D. 35.90

12. According to the results of the analysis of the various foods, which is least likely to cause a peanut allergic reaction?

    F. Sausage with walnut
    G. Cereal bar I
    H. Chocolate
    J. Cookies with fiber

Passage V

Enzymes are substances that act as a catalyst to speed up biochemical reactions. When a *substrate* binds to the active site of an enzyme, a reaction can occur in which the substrate is converted into one or more products. The digestive enzyme, Trypsin, catalyzes the process of breaking down proteins in the small intestine into amino acids, which can then be absorbed into the blood stream. Importantly, any physical or chemical changes to an enzyme's environment, such as changes in temperature, pH, and salt concentration, can alter its ability to function by denaturing or inactivating the enzyme.

Two experiments sought to compare the ability of Trypsin to generate products (amino acids) at two different pH levels. For each experiment, four vials were made to contain 1mM of Trypsin and differing concentrations of substrate. The values of light absorbance for each sample were recorded every 30 seconds for 2.5 minutes using a *spectrophotometer*, an apparatus for measuring the intensity of light. The measured absorbance values were collected at a wavelength that corresponds to the relative amount of product that was generated in the samples. In other words, a higher absorbance value at the indicated wavelength would mean more product was made by the Trypsin.

Experiment 1

Four vials were made to contain 1mM of Trypsin and differing levels of substrate concentration maintained at a pH of 8. The absorbance values after each 30 second time period for each substrate level is recorded in Table 1.

Absorbance value					
Substrate level (mM)	0.5 min	1 min	1.5 min	2 min	2.5 min
0.04	0.023	0.035	0.053	0.069	0.082
0.09	0.039	0.082	0.125	0.154	0.184
0.15	0.067	0.137	0.199	0.261	0.310
0.24	0.115	0.239	0.340	0.431	0.511

Table 1

Experiment 2

Four vials were made to contain 1mM of Trypsin and differing levels of substrate concentration maintained at a pH of 6. The absorbance values after each 30 second time period for each substrate level is recorded in Table 2.

Absorbance value					
Substrate level (mM)	0.5 min	1 min	1.5 min	2 min	2.5 min
0.04	0.006	0.011	0.017	0.023	0.027
0.09	0.014	0.028	0.042	0.055	0.068
0.15	0.027	0.053	0.078	0.102	0.149
0.24	0.060	0.090	0.145	0.190	0.233

Table 2

13. Compared to the same vial at a pH of 6, a vial at a pH of 8 containing a substrate level of 0.15mM and 1mM of Trypsin:

   A. is experiencing more instances of the breaking down of amino acids into proteins.
   B. is experiencing more instances of the breaking down of proteins into amino acids.
   C. is experiencing less instances of the breaking down of amino acids into proteins.
   D. is experiencing less instances of the breaking down of proteins into amino acids.

14. Among the results of the experiments, the best conditions for maximizing the amount of product catalyzed by the enzyme Trypsin regardless of substrate level are:

   F. a pH of 6 for 0.5 minutes.
   G. a pH of 6 for 2.5 minutes.
   H. a pH of 8 for 0.5 minutes.
   J. a pH of 8 for 2.5 minutes.

15. If a spectrophotometer measured an absorbance value of 0.011 after 1 minute in a vial containing 0.24mM of substrate and 1mM of Trypsin, the pH of that same vial would be expected to be closest to:

   A. 4
   B. 6
   C. 7
   D. 9

Passage VI

With the traditional *optical microscope*, the user looks into the eyepieces to view a sample or specimen. The objective lens focuses light from the sample into the eyepieces. The eyepiece lens and the objective lens both provide magnification, but the latter more so. The condenser lens helps to concentrate light on the sample for easy viewing. Figure 1 displays the visual path of an optical microscope.

While the more advanced *fluorescent microscope* shares some similarities to the optical microscope, one key difference is that fluorescent microscopes utilize a process called *photoluminescence*. This is where molecules in a sample can be put into an excited state and absorb energy from a high intensity light, causing the molecules to emit light at a longer wavelength. The filter then works by separating any surrounding light, so only the fluorescence emitted by the molecules in a sample can be visualized. The detector can be used to display the fluorescent sample on a digital screen for easy viewing. Figure 2 displays the visual path of a fluorescent microscope.

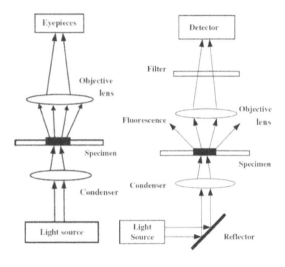

Figure 1   Figure 2

A teacher sought to test a group of students' ability to distinguish neutrophil white blood cells within a blood sample using both optical (Study 1) and fluorescent (Study 2) microscopes. To distinguish a neutrophil under the optical microscope, the students were to look for a round cell body with a multi-lobed nucleus that is around 12-14 μm in diameter. For the fluorescent microscope, the blood sample was treated with an antibody that causes only neutrophil cells to fluoresce green.

Table 1 displays the results of Study 1, consisting of each student's answer for the number of neutrophils found in a blood sample and the percentage of correct cells that were identified using the optical microscope. Table 2 displays the results of Study 2, consisting of each student's answer for the number of neutrophils found in a blood sample and the percentage of correct cells that were identified using the fluorescent microscope.

Optical Microscope	Neutrophil count	Percent correct
Student 1	5	33%
Student 2	8	53%
Student 3	10	67%
Student 4	4	27%

Table 1

Fluorescent Microscope	Neutrophil count	Percent correct
Student 1	13	76%
Student 2	16	94%
Student 3	17	100%
Student 4	13	76%

Table 2

16. In one of the studies, Student 4 did not count 4 oval cell bodies that had the proper nucleus sizes, even though they were true neutrophils. If she had done so, her percent correct would have been:

F. 33%
G. 53%
H. 93%
J. 100%

17. The utilization of photoluminescence had what effect on the results of the two studies?

A. It more than quartered some students' abilities to discover neutrophils.
B. It more than halved some students' abilities to discover neutrophils.
C. It more than doubled some students' abilities to discover neutrophils.
D. It more than quadrupled some students' abilities to discover neutrophils.

18. A student guessed before the studies that the more a microscope alters or affects light with additional steps and parts, the less accurate the results would be. Was this student correct in her guess?

    F. No: the fluorescent microscope, which affects light more than the optical microscope, yielded better results.

    G. No: the optical microscope, which affects light more than the fluorescent microscope, yielded better results.

    H. Yes: the fluorescent microscope, which affects light more than the optical microscope, yielded better results.

    J. Yes: the optical microscope, which affects light more than the fluorescent microscope, yielded better results.

Step 3 Correct Answers

Passage I:	Passage II:	Passage III:	Passage IV:	Passage V:	Passage VI:
1: D	4: H	7: A	10: G	13: B	16: G
2: G	5: D	8: F	11: C	14: J	17: C
3: A	6: J	9: B	12: F	15: A	18: F

Stumped on any? You can find the explanations for each of these questions beginning on page 357.

STEP 4

Conflicting Viewpoints

What Is Conflicting Viewpoints?

In the introduction to the book, I briefly mentioned that there are three types of passages in every ACT Science test. The first two have been discussed a bit more since then, but it is time to return to the third type, which is so different that it requires its own step in this book: Conflicting Viewpoints.

The Conflicting Viewpoints passage is something closer to an ACT Reading passage than it is the other ACT Science passages. I say that a bit tongue-in-cheek, but there's truth in it. The Conflicting Viewpoints passage almost never features any charts, diagrams, or data (though it could, and has in the past, so that's not a guarantee). Instead, it is much more likely to feature *only* words. There will be an opening paragraph (sometimes as short as a sentence, sometimes much longer) that introduces a broad topic on which there may be varying points of view in the scientific community (for example, if Pluto is a planet or not). Then, some number of scientists (as little as 2 and as many as 4) will present a contrary thesis with their reasons why they are correct in 1 or 2 paragraphs.

For example, Scientist 1 might believe that Pluto is a planet. He will then give all the reasons why he is correct on that. Scientist 2 might believe that Pluto is an exoplanet. She will then give all the reasons why she is correct on that. It may stop there, but as I said, there could be 3 or 4 scientists' ideas that are presented here. Scientist 3 then might believe that Pluto is a meteor, and Scientist 4 that it is a Dwarf Planet. I'm no expert on Pluto, so forgive me if I misrepresent what was once a planet in my childhood, but these kinds of differences is what you can expect to find in the Conflicting Viewpoints passage.

How to Read It

I have stressed the necessity of active (quick) reading to this point in the book, and it is now worth stressing once again. You don't need to read this passage *s l o w l y* in an attempt to memorize every reason, evidence, or statistic presented by any of the scientists. Instead, with your pencil in hand, quickly read through the passage. Underline each scientists' main idea or thesis statement; maybe even double-underline it or put a star next to it so it stands out. If something jumps out to you as important, underline it as well or circle what you think may be key words, especially if you think it's a key reason why this scientist believes what she does (aka, underline the main pieces of evidence). Avoid underlining everything: only what seems to be key.

Major ideas are more important than minor details. The major thesis of each scientist, the major similarities, and the major difference are much more important to focus on during your initial read. Remember: your first read through is designed to give you the time to go and find details if necessary.

The Questions

As there is rarely any data given as a part of these passages, the questions are not similar to those of Step 1 or 3 that require reference to charts/tables/graphs. Instead, it is much more likely that you will have a variety of questions (7 total) that test your understanding of each scientist's position. For example, one question will probably give you a piece of evidence or a discovery and ask which scientist's position it helps. Another question might give you a statement and ask which scientist most agrees with it. Another question will simply restate an idea from the passage and ask which scientist agrees. In other words, the questions focus mostly on the similarities and differences between the points of view.

The Following Passages

What follows here is two Conflicting Viewpoints passages. The questions are designed to mimic as accurately as possible the types of questions that you will see on ACT day. As has been said, more than likely the Conflicting Viewpoints passage that you encounter will present the points of view of two scientists. However, because it is possible that there may be more, each of the following passages presents three points of view on different topics to get you used to this kind of thinking. So, set a timer for 6 minutes (5 minutes 50 seconds if you're being precise!) for each passage, take a deep breath, and do your best on the following passages one at a time; doing so will give you a serious advantage!

Passage I

Fast radio bursts (FRBs) are intense bursts of radio waves originating from deep space. These bursts last for a very short duration, typically just a few milliseconds, but within that brief time, they release an enormous amount of energy. FRBs are detected as sudden and powerful spikes in radio signals across a range of frequencies. These signals are typically observed by radio telescopes and analyzed by astronomers. FRBs are challenging to study because they occur throughout the universe at unpredictable times and locations, making it difficult to anticipate sources. Three scientists discuss their theories regarding the origin of FRBs.

Scientist 1

FRBs are generated by highly magnetized, rapidly rotating neutron stars called magnetars. Neutron stars are extremely dense remnants of massive stars that have undergone a supernova explosion. Magnetars are a specific type of neutron star with an exceptionally strong magnetic field. An FRB occurs when the intense magnetic field of a magnetar becomes disrupted, leading to a burst of radio waves. The disruption occurs because the magnetic field lines of the magnetar become twisted and rearranged due to various instabilities, or starquakes, within the star. FRB 121102 for example, one of the only FRBs known to repeat, has been discovered to originate from a source surrounded by an intense magnetic field. This type of magnetic field is only otherwise found around a Milky Way magnetar.

Scientist 2

FRBs are caused by the merger of compact objects, such as when a neutron star merges with another neutron star, or a black hole and neutron star merge. Compact object mergers are cataclysmic events that can release enormous amounts of energy of all wavelengths. During such a merger, the intense gravitational forces and tidal interactions can cause the objects involved to collide violently, producing powerful electromagnetic emissions, including the radio waves characteristic of an FRB. This explains why the vast majority of FRBs (FRBs 121102 and 181906 excluded) do not repeat, but are rather one-time events containing the energy output of hundreds of millions of stars.

Scientist 3

FRBs have multiple origins, not merely one. This is due to the fact that there are a multitude of large-scale and hyper-energy-producing events across the universe. One of the multitude of sources of FRBs is certainly neutron stars, one of which has been detected as the probable source of FRB 121102 three billion light years away (well outside the Milky Way galaxy). On the other hand, it seems equally probable that other cataclysmic events (such as black hole and neutron star collisions, for example) produce waves of multiple wavelengths simultaneously. One such FRB known as FRB 171209 is also thought to be the source of a gamma ray burst known as GRB 110715A.

1. According to Scientist 2, FRB 181906:

   A. is the only example of an FRB that repeats.
   B. originates approximately 3 billion light years away.
   C. is caused by the violent collisions of cosmic objects.
   D. does not contain the energy output of multiple stars.

2. Which of the scientists rely on the existence of internal disruptions of neutron stars to explain the origins of all FRBs?

   F. Scientist 1 only
   G. Scientist 2 only
   H. Scientists 1 and 3 only
   J. Scientists 2 and 3 only

3. Suppose it were definitely discovered that the source of FRB 121102 was the collision of two black holes. This discovery would support the position of:

   A. Scientist 1 only.
   B. Scientist 2 only.
   C. Scientists 1 and 3 only.
   D. Scientists 2 and 3 only.

4. Which of the following discoveries would bolster the position of Scientist 1 relative to that of Scientist 2?

   F. That magnetars also release gamma rays
   G. That the merger of celestial objects can produce gamma rays but not radio waves
   H. An FRB that lasts more than a few milliseconds
   J. An FRB that repeats once every few years

5. Detailed surveys of star clusters in and near the Milky Way galaxy reveal that there is no direct evidence of any major merger of compact objects in its history. These results are *inconsistent* with the argument of which scientist?

   A. Scientist 1
   B. Scientist 2
   C. Scientist 3
   D. It is inconsistent with the positions of none of the 3 scientists.

6. All three scientists agree that which of the following plays a role in the generation of many FRBs?

   F. The extreme gravitational pull of black holes and superstars
   G. Instabilities, or starquakes, that take place within a neutron star
   H. The relatively small size of the Milky Way relative to the Andromeda galaxy
   J. The dense remnants of stars that have experienced supernova

7. If gravitational forces play a role in the intensity of starquakes, then which of the three scientists would agree that gravitational forces play a role in the origins of FRBs?

   A. Scientists 1, 2, and 3
   B. Scientists 1 and 3 only
   C. Scientists 2 and 3 only
   D. Scientist 1 only

Passage II

Humans, along with all other species, experience biological aging. Biological aging refers to the gradual deterioration of biological systems and functions over time. It is distinct from other types of aging, such as psychological aging and social aging. Biological aging is a natural process that occurs in living organisms, including humans. Biological aging is characterized by a progressive decline in various physiological processes, such as cellular metabolism, tissue repair, immune function, and organ functionality. Although it has been studied extensively, the reasons why the decline associated with aging occurs is still unknown. Three scientists debate competing theories that explain biological aging.

Scientist 1

Biological aging is a result of genetic programming and evolutionary mechanisms. Organisms have an inherent biological clock or aging "program" that influences the rate of aging. Aging is an adaptive trait coded into DNA that has evolved over time to optimize the allocation of resources and enhance the survival of the species. It is likely that various physiological factors, such as hormonal changes and the decline of repair mechanisms, are orchestrated by the aging program to regulate the aging process.

Scientist 2

Aging is primarily caused by the gradual accumulation of cellular damage over time. A multitude of factors contribute to the progressive decline in cellular and tissue function, such as oxidative stress, DNA mutations, and the accumulation of cellular waste products. As cells throughout the body are exposed to environmental stressors and waste from internal metabolic processes, damage occurs at the molecular level. Over time, this accumulated damage overwhelms the cellular repair mechanisms, leading to a decline in organ function and the onset of age-related diseases.

Scientist 3

The progressive shortening of telomeres, protective structures located at the ends of chromosomes, plays the most significant role in the aging process. Telomeres naturally shorten with each cell division due to the incomplete replication of DNA ends. As telomeres become critically short, cells can no longer divide and function properly, known as cellular senescence. This leads to a gradual decline in tissue regeneration and function. Telomere shortening acts as a "molecular clock" that contributes to the overall aging of organisms.

8. Which of the following scientists, if any, state(s) that DNA plays a role in the aging process?

   F. None of the 3 scientists
   G. Scientists 1 and 3 only
   H. Scientists 2 and 3 only
   J. All 3 of the scientists

9. Suppose it is discovered that those with thyroiditis, a condition that affects hormonal output, tend to age faster than those without the condition. This finding would most bolster the position(s) of:

   A. Scientist 1
   B. Scientist 2
   C. Scientist 3
   D. Scientists 2 and 3

10. If the shortening of telomeres over time were classified as "cellular damage," then which two scientists could both be correct in their assessment as to the cause of aging?

    F. Scientists 1 and 2
    G. Scientists 1 and 3
    H. Scientists 2 and 3
    J. Scientists 1, 2, and 3

11. According to the theory of Scientist 2, a medication that might slow the aging process would be one that:

    A. helps regulate and support proper hormonal production.
    B. slows the shortening of telomeres.
    C. helps cells to dispose of waste more permanently.
    D. increases the accumulation of cellular damage over time.

12. According to at least one scientist, cellular senescence:

    F. is necessary to slow aging and relies on environmental stressors and DNA mutations.
    G. is necessary to slow aging and relies on the proper functioning of telomeres.
    H. furthers the aging process and is rooted in the gradual shortening of telomeres.
    J. furthers the aging process and relies on the proper functioning of telomeres.

13. *Cellular stress response* (CRS) is a reaction to the changes or fluctuations of extracellular conditions that damage the structure and function of molecules. Exposure to harmful chemicals is known to trigger CRS. Which scientist(s) would recommend avoiding exposure to harmful chemicals to keep the aging process in check?

    A. Scientist 1
    B. Scientist 2
    C. Scientist 3
    D. Scientists 2 and 3

14. Suppose a fourth scientist claims that the aging process is the gradual effect of the normal functioning of the body at the cellular or chromosomal level as opposed to a genetically predetermined outcome. Which of the scientists would agree with this claim?

    F. Scientist 2 only
    G. Scientists 1 and 3
    H. Scientists 2 and 3
    J. Scientists 1, 2, and 3

Step 4 Correct Answers

Passage I:
1: C
2: F
3: D
4: G
5: D
6: J
7: A

Passage II:
8: J
9: A
10: H
11: C
12: H
13: B
14: H

Stumped on any? You can find the explanations for each of these questions beginning on page 360.

STEP 5

The More Complex Questions

While it is of course true that most of the questions on the ACT Science test mimic those taught and practiced thus far in this book, it is also true that each ACT Science test will feature a handful of "other" or you may think "more difficult" questions. These questions vary in their types and number on any given test. Some of these questions require you to convert that data before you into some new kind of chart or graph. Some of these questions require you to reach bigger conclusions from lots of data. Some of these questions require previous science knowledge. Some of these questions require complex or deep reasoning. Some of them require an unexpected step of some kind. Some of them require inference (reaching the most likely conclusion based on the data).

Although the percentage of any of these questions individually on any ACT Science test is low (as low as 0%; for any of the types in the above paragraph, you may have 0 total questions, or you may have 5), together they make up a substantial block of more difficult or rare questions that are worth preparing for. While some of that preparation may come from the practice tests featured at the end of this book, they are worth isolating into their own step for practice as well.

The Following Practice Passages

The following practice passages are the same as you have seen thus far in Steps 1, 2, and 3. You might think it a bit strange that I didn't just make this current information into Step 4 to keep them all in a row. However, remember that the purpose of this book is to prepare you for the ACT Science test in order of importance. If these questions were more important than a step on the Conflicting Viewpoints passage, then the order of steps would have reflected that.

Take a deep breath, and give the following variety of questions your best shot!

Passage I

Most of the water consumption within the United States is used by the agricultural industry for food production. This heavily contributes to the overuse of groundwater aquifers. Therefore, finding alternative resources of water for agricultural production is necessary to lessen the looming threat of food and water scarcity. One issue is that alternative water sources in certain regions often contain a higher concentration of salt compared to groundwater aquifers, and many food crops are not selected for traits like tolerance to salt. In recent years, new varieties, also called *variants*, of crops have been selected mostly for commercial benefit, with little regard for producing varieties that can withstand changes in salt concentrations. As a result, a group of researchers sought to determine plant variants that are resilient to waters with higher salt concentrations.

Researchers first tested the salt tolerance in variants of two regularly consumed crops, tomato and pepper, by testing the consumable yields of each plant when grown in the same soil. The control for the experiment was freshwater from a ground water aquifer, while the experimental condition was done with water containing a higher salt content. The results are recorded in Table 1 (tomato) and Table 2 (pepper) below.

Fruit yield (grams)		
Tomato variant	Control	Experimental
Bloody Butcher	2785	1719
Juane Flamme	2317	1355
Quarter Century	1415	928

Table 1

Fruit yield (grams)		
Pepper variant	Control	Experimental
California Wonder	2591	1993
Thai Hot	295	291
Ancho	1514	1489

Table 2

The researchers next tested the concentration of sodium within the plant tissue of the different variants for both the control and saltwater (experimental) groups. Their findings are recorded in Figure 1 (tomato) and Figure 2 (pepper) below in millimoles per kilogram.

Key
☐ control
■ experimental

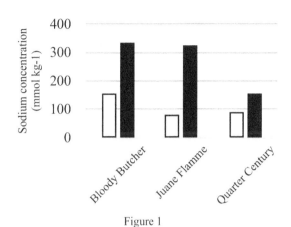

Figure 1

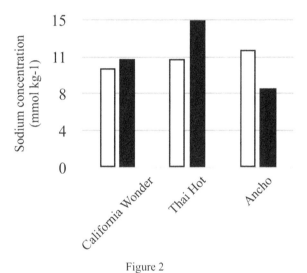

Figure 2

1. Better Boy is a variety of tomato that, when watered from a source low in salt, typically features a sodium concentration of 27.5 mmol/kg-1. What would be the expected sodium concentration of Better Boy if it were to be watered from an alternative source with a high concentration of salt?

   A. 0 mmol/kg-1
   B. 5 mmol/kg-1
   C. 75 mmol/kg-1
   D. 950 mmol/kg-1

2. Which of the following pie charts most accurately represents the total yield of the three tomato variants when watered from an underground aquifer?

F.

G.

H.

J.

3. A scientist breeds a tomato containing 50% of the DNA of both Bloody Butcher and Juane Flamme. If this new tomato were subjected to the same experiment, the amount of fruit it would yield if watered with a groundwater aquifer would most likely be closest to:

A. 1,525 grams
B. 2,525 grams
C. 2,785 grams
D. 5,000 grams

Passage II

A group of high school students investigated the momentum of carts rolling down an inclined plane across a designated finish line. The students used three carts, labeled Cart A, Cart B, and Cart C. Cart A had a mass of 12.5 kg, Cart B had a mass of 21.8 kg, and Cart C had a mass of 34.7 kg. They conducted five trials, progressively increasing the release height of the carts. The purpose of the experiment was to explore how changes in release height affect the velocity and momentum of the carts.

Velocity is a fundamental concept in physics that represents the speed of an object in a specific direction. In this experiment, velocity was measured as each cart crossed the finish line, but can also be determined using the equation $v = \sqrt{2gh}$, where v is the velocity, g is the acceleration due to gravity (approximately 9.8 m/s²), and h is the release height of the cart.

Momentum is a property of a moving object that depends on its mass and velocity. It describes the quantity of motion possessed by an object and is calculated by multiplying the mass of the object by its velocity. The equation for momentum is given as $p = mv$, where p represents the momentum, m is the mass of the object, and v denotes the velocity.

After collecting data, the students calculated the momentum for each cart and trial. Figure 1 shows the recorded velocity for each cart as it crossed the finish line, and Figure 2 shows the calculated momentum for each cart as it crossed the finish line.

Key: ■ Cart A
      ▲ Cart B
      ● Cart C

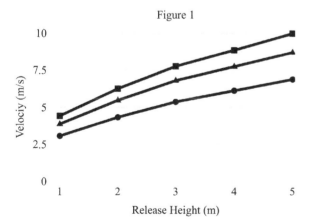

Figure 1

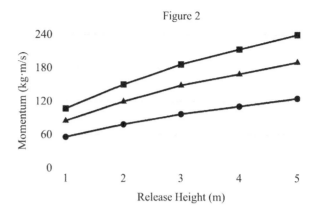

Figure 2

4. On the moon, the acceleration due to gravity is approximately 1.625 m/s², or 17% of that of earth. If students were to repeat the experiment on the moon with Cart B, what would be its approximate expected velocity when released from a height of 3 meters?

   F. 1.15 m/s
   G. 5.05 m/s
   H. 8.35 m/s
   J. 33.75 m/s

5. What was the velocity of Cart B as it crossed the finish line after being released from a height of 2 meters when expressed in *centimeters* per second?

   A. 5.48 cm/s
   B. 54.8 cm/s
   C. 548 cm/s
   D. 5,480 cm/s

6. Acceleration is defined as an object's change in velocity divided by the change in time over which this took place. If it took Cart A 1.5 seconds to reach the finish line from a release height of 5 meters, and assuming it was released from rest, then what was Cart A's acceleration when it crossed the finish line?

   F. −6.67 m/s²
   G. −3.33 m/s²
   H. 3.33 m/s²
   J. 6.67 m/s²

Passage III

The *Mpemba Effect* refers to a curious phenomenon in which hot water freezes faster than cold water under certain circumstances. Several proposed explanations have been put forth to shed light on the Mpemba Effect. One possibility relates to the evaporation of the hot water during the cooling process. As hot water is exposed to lower temperatures, it undergoes rapid evaporation, resulting in a reduction in its volume. This reduction in volume leads to an increase in the concentration of dissolved solids in the remaining water. Consequently, the higher concentration of dissolved solids may lower the freezing point of the hot water, allowing it to freeze more rapidly.

A group of students designed an experiment to test the Mpemba Effect. They collected four beakers and labeled them A, B, C, and D. *Thermocouples*, or thermoelectric devices for measuring temperature, were placed in the bottom of each beaker. Beakers A and B were filled with distilled (purified) water, and beakers C and D were filled with tap water. The water in beakers A and C was heated to 50 degrees Celsius, and the water in beakers B and D was left at room temperature (around 30 degrees Celsius).

The students recorded the temperature of each beaker after placing it in a freezer with a temperature of -18° Celsius until it had reached 0° Celsius, the freezing point of water. The observations of the students are given below. Table 1 corresponds to beaker A, Table 2 to beaker B, Table 3 to beaker C, and Table 4 to beaker D.

Table 1 (Beaker A)	
Time Elapsed (minutes)	Temperature (°C)
0	50
5	42
10	36
15	30
20	25
25	21
30	17
35	13
40	10
45	8
50	5
55	2
60	0

Table 2 (Beaker B)	
Time Elapsed (minutes)	Temperature (°C)
0	30
5	26
10	23
15	20
20	18
25	17
30	14
35	12
40	10
45	8
50	6
55	5
60	4
65	3
70	0

Table 3 (Beaker C)	
Time Elapsed (minutes)	Temperature (°C)
0	50
5	44
10	38
15	33
20	28
25	24
30	20
35	17
40	14
45	11
50	8
55	5
60	3
65	0

Table 4 (Beaker D)	
Time Elapsed (minutes)	Temperature (°C)
0	30
5	26
10	22
15	19
20	18
25	17
30	15
35	13
40	11
45	10
50	8
55	6
60	4
65	2
70	1
75	0

7. Suppose the students began with the hypothesis that the Mpemba Effect would *not* be seen in water that had been purified. Was the students' hypothesis falsified?

   A. Yes: the beaker of heated and purified water was the first to freeze.
   B. Yes: the beaker of room temperature purified water was the first to freeze.
   C. No: the beaker of heated and purified water was the first to freeze.
   D. No: the beaker of room temperature purified water was the first to freeze.

8. After the experiment is over, a student filled Beaker E with water and put it in the same freezer as Beakers A, B, C, and D. If it took the water 85 minutes to reach a temperature of 0° Celsius, which of the following could be true of the water prior to being put in the freezer?

   F. It was sourced from a freshwater spring and heated to a temperature of 50° Celsius.
   G. It was sourced from a freshwater spring and kept at room temperature.
   H. It was sourced from the ocean and heated to a temperature of 50° Celsius.
   J. It was sourced from the ocean and kept at room temperature.

9. Below is the formula for converting °Celsius into °Fahrenheit:

$$°F = (°C \cdot 1.8) + 32$$

   Which of the following temperatures in Fahrenheit was the temperature after 30 minutes had elapsed of the purified water that had been put into the freezer with an initial temperature of 50° Celsius?

   A. −30.1° F
   B. 1° F
   C. 62.6° F
   D. 100.1° F

Passage IV

Real-time polymerase chain reaction (PCR) *analysis* is a laboratory technique that can be used to help determine if a specific type of DNA is present in a sample. This technique works by increasing the total amount of DNA present in a sample, a step called *amplification*, and then detecting if the DNA matches the target DNA.

Detection of the target DNA is determined by the *cycle threshold* (CT) value. The CT value is the number of cycles of amplification that is needed for a specific DNA sequence to be detected in a sample. The lower the CT value, the more likely it is that the sample contains the DNA of interest. Most real-time PCR analyses undergo a total of 40 cycles of amplification.

While this technique is often used for medical purposes, it also has applications in food safety. Due to the safety concerns regarding food allergens, scientists will use real-time PCR to search for the DNA of common allergen causing ingredients in commercial products to ensure that the package label is accurate. One common and often dangerous food allergy is an allergy to peanuts. If a person is severely allergic to peanuts and unknowingly ingests even a small amount, it could be deadly. Therefore, scientists completed real-time PCR analysis to test commercial food products for DNA that matches the peanut.

Table 1 shows commercial food products, their current package labels for allergens, and the CT values discovered for each following real-time PCR analysis to detect peanut DNA. An N.D. value means that there was no detection of the target DNA after 40 cycles of amplification.

Table 1		
Food	Food Packaging Allergen Declaration	Peanut CT Value
Cereal bar I	Peanut, hazelnut	17.97
Cereal bar II	Almond and tree nuts	32.40
Cereal bar III	Hazelnut, almond and peanut traces	33.74
Cereal bar IV	May contain tree nut traces	35.90
Chocolate with pistachio	Pistachio, almond, hazelnut, tree nut traces	36.80
Sausage with walnut	Walnuts	N.D.
Chocolate	Almond and hazelnut traces	37.99
Cookies with fiber	Not declared	32.25

Table 2 displays example CT values and the likelihood of the values causing an allergic reaction in an individual with peanut allergy (if testing for peanut DNA).

Table 2	
Example CT Value	Likelihood of Causing Peanut Allergic Reaction
≤ 29	High
30-35	High to moderate
36-40	Low to none

10. Which of the following graphs best represents the relationship between the number of cycles of amplification needed for detection of a certain DNA sequence and the likelihood that that same DNA will cause an allergic reaction?

F.

G.

H.

J.

11. A lawmaker is proposing a fine of $100,000 per product on any company that manufactures a food with a High to Moderate likelihood of causing a peanut allergy that does not declare peanuts or peanut traces on their packaging. If the same company manufactured all of the products tested in Table 1, then how much money would the company owe in fines if the new law were to be passed?

    A. $100,000
    B. $200,000
    C. $300,000
    D. $400,000

12. It has been discovered that DNA has a half-life (the amount of time it takes for half of a substance to dissolve) of 521 years. Thus, in 1,042 years, it is likely that the CT value of a material with a current CT value of 40:

    F. would then have a CT value of 10.
    G. would then have a CT value of 20.
    H. would then have a CT value of 30.
    J. would then have a CT value greater than 40.

Passage V

Enzymes are substances that act as a catalyst to speed up biochemical reactions. When a *substrate* binds to the active site of an enzyme, a reaction can occur in which the substrate is converted into one or more products. The digestive enzyme, Trypsin, catalyzes the process of breaking down proteins in the small intestine into amino acids, which can then be absorbed into the blood stream. Importantly, any physical or chemical changes to an enzyme's environment, such as changes in temperature, pH, and salt concentration, can alter its ability to function by denaturing or inactivating the enzyme.

Two experiments sought to compare the ability of Trypsin to generate products (amino acids) at two different pH levels. For each experiment, four vials were made to contain 1mM of Trypsin and differing concentrations of substrate. The values of light absorbance for each sample were recorded every 30 seconds for 2.5 minutes using a *spectrophotometer*, an apparatus for measuring the intensity of light. The measured absorbance values were collected at a wavelength that corresponds to the relative amount of product that was generated in the samples. In other words, a higher absorbance value at the indicated wavelength would mean more product was made by the Trypsin.

Experiment 1

Four vials were made to contain 1mM of Trypsin and differing levels of substrate concentration maintained at a pH of 8. The absorbance values after each 30 second time period for each substrate level is recorded in Table 1.

Absorbance value					
Substrate level (mM)	0.5 min	1 min	1.5 min	2 min	2.5 min
0.04	0.023	0.035	0.053	0.069	0.082
0.09	0.039	0.082	0.125	0.154	0.184
0.15	0.067	0.137	0.199	0.261	0.310
0.24	0.115	0.239	0.340	0.431	0.511

Table 1

Experiment 2

Four vials were made to contain 1mM of Trypsin and differing levels of substrate concentration maintained at a pH of 6. The absorbance values after each 30 second time period for each substrate level is recorded in Table 2.

Absorbance value					
Substrate level (mM)	0.5 min	1 min	1.5 min	2 min	2.5 min
0.04	0.006	0.011	0.017	0.023	0.027
0.09	0.014	0.028	0.042	0.055	0.068
0.15	0.027	0.053	0.078	0.102	0.149
0.24	0.060	0.090	0.145	0.190	0.233

Table 2

13. Does the enzyme Trypsin function more effectively in a more basic or more acidic environment?

   A. Basic: the absorbance levels of the more basic vials are higher than the more acidic vials.
   B. Basic: the absorbance levels of the more basic vials are lower than the more acidic vials.
   C. Acidic: the absorbance levels of the more acidic vials are higher than the more basic vials.
   D. Acidic: the absorbance levels of the more acidic vials are lower than the more basic vials.

14. A scientist hypothesizes that persons whose liquid diet consists of mostly acidic drinks (orange juice, coffee, wine, etc.) will have a lesser concentration of amino acids in the blood stream than the person who mostly drinks water. Is the null hypothesis rejected by the findings of Experiments 1 and 2?

   F. No: the more basic vials had more substrate catalyzed into product than the acidic vials.
   G. No: the more acidic vials had more substrate catalyzed into product than the basic vials.
   H. Yes: the more basic vials had more substrate catalyzed into product than the acidic vials.
   J. Yes: the more acidic vials had more substrate catalyzed into product than the basic vials.

15. Which of the following is the dependent variable across both experiments?

   A. The substrate level
   B. The amount of Trypsin in each vial
   C. The absorbance value
   D. The pH levels of the vials

Passage VI

With the traditional *optical microscope*, the user looks into the eyepieces to view a sample or specimen. The objective lens focuses light from the sample into the eyepieces. The eyepiece lens and the objective lens both provide magnification, but the latter more so. The condenser lens helps to concentrate light on the sample for easy viewing. Figure 1 displays the visual path of an optical microscope.

While the more advanced *fluorescent microscope* shares some similarities to the optical microscope, one key difference is that fluorescent microscopes utilize a process called *photoluminescence*. This is where molecules in a sample can be put into an excited state and absorb energy from a high intensity light, causing the molecules to emit light at a longer wavelength. The filter then works by separating any surrounding light, so only the fluorescence emitted by the molecules in a sample can be visualized. The detector can be used to display the fluorescent sample on a digital screen for easy viewing. Figure 2 displays the visual path of a fluorescent microscope.

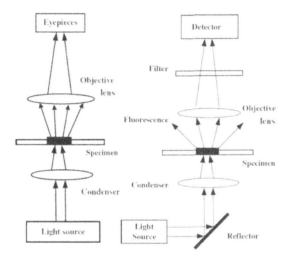

Figure 1   Figure 2

A teacher sought to test a group of students' ability to distinguish neutrophil white blood cells within a blood sample using both optical (Study 1) and fluorescent (Study 2) microscopes. To distinguish a neutrophil under the optical microscope, the students were to look for a round cell body with a multi-lobed nucleus that is around 12-14 μm in diameter. For the fluorescent microscope, the blood sample was treated with an antibody that causes only neutrophil cells to fluoresce green.

Table 1 displays the results of Study 1, consisting of each student's answer for the number of neutrophils found in a blood sample and the percentage of correct cells that were identified using the optical microscope. Table 2 displays the results of Study 2, consisting of each student's answer for the number of neutrophils found in a blood sample and the percentage of correct cells that were identified using the fluorescent microscope.

Optical Microscope	Neutrophil count	Percent correct
Student 1	5	33%
Student 2	8	53%
Student 3	10	67%
Student 4	4	27%

Table 1

Fluorescent Microscope	Neutrophil count	Percent correct
Student 1	13	76%
Student 2	16	94%
Student 3	17	100%
Student 4	13	76%

Table 2

16. Suppose Student 5 comes into class late and sits at his station to work without carefully reading the directions. If he identifies 45 neutrophil white blood cells when looking at the sample through the optical microscope, it is likely that he:

   F. mistakenly adjusted the reflector of the light source.
   G. ignored neutrophils that fluoresced green and counted dark-grey or black neutrophils instead.
   H. mistook each cell, no matter the shape or diameter of the nucleus, for a neutrophil cell.
   J. severely undercounted neutrophil cells due to a malfunction of the microscope itself.

17. For an additional study the following day, the teacher treats the blood sample with an antibody that turns multiple white blood cells blue. The student most likely to identify the most neutrophil cells correctly is the one who uses the fluorescent microscope and:

   A. searches for cells with a multi-lobed nucleus that have a diameter of around 12-14 μm.
   B. searches for cells with a multi-lobed nucleus that have a radius of around 12-14 μm.
   C. searches for cells that fluoresce closest to the blue-green side of the light spectrum.
   D. searches for cells that fluoresce closest to the blue-indigo side of the light spectrum.

18. If one μm is equal to one millionth of a meter, then about how large is the diameter of the nucleus of a neutrophil in meters?

    A.   0.0000013
    B.   0.000013
    C.   0.00013
    D.   0.0013

Step 5 Correct Answers

Passage I:	Passage II:	Passage III:	Passage IV:	Passage V:	Passage VI:
1: C	4: F	7: A	10: G	13: A	16: H
2: G	5: C	8: J	11: B	14: F	17: A
3: B	6: J	9: C	12: J	15: C	18: B

Stumped on any? You can find the explanations for each of these questions beginning on page 362.

STEP 6

Full-Length Practice Tests

I hope you have found this book to be valuable. It sums up and represents the best of ACT Science preparation, based off of thousands of hours of teaching, research into, and writing about the ACT itself. If you prepared from Step 1, then you have put first-things-first, second-things-second, and so on, ordering your preparation from most to least important based on the kinds of questions actually asked by the ACT. You haven't wasted your time memorizing the various categorizations of ACT Science question types or letting YouTube's algorithm throw endless videos at you over and over. Instead, you have spent your time wisely preparing through guided practice.

What follows now is two complete, full-length ACT Science practice tests. Let's quickly review strategies and what has been discussed before you set that timer and dive in.

1) Overall and Secondary Strategy

The ACT Science test will require that you use your time well and effectively. Taking "as much time as you need" on Passages I, II, III, and IV will all but guarantee that you will hear "Five minutes remaining!" when you're only halfway through Passage V, leaving you to guess entirely on Passage VI's questions. Instead, do your best to spend 5 minutes and 50 seconds (or, for the sake of simplicity, 6 minutes) on each passage. This means: 1) actively (quickly) reading the written portion of each passage as you circle/underline key terms and definitions and jot in the margins summaries of main ideas, and 2) glancing over data in charts/tables/graphs to get the main idea. This approach will guarantee you maximize the time you spend on the questions themselves, which is necessary: it takes *time* to get ACT Science questions correct because most (if not all) of them require you to look back into the passage for answers.

Secondarily, remember that this is the ACT's 4th quarter. That's cheesy, I know, but the idea works: you are tired, and if you give up, you very well may lose. Guessing can sometimes be acceptable on the ACT Science test (if a question is just too difficult and will require minutes you don't have, or if you are of course running out of time), but *never* just because you're tired and over it and want to go home and get back in bed for the rest of the day. Think about it like this: just about every time you guess, your ACT Science score is going down a point. Instead, take a deep breath prior to each individual passage and begin again.

2) It's All (Well, Mostly) About the Data

Except for the Conflicting Viewpoints passage (as discussed in Step 4), the ACT Science test's questions require you to read charts/tables/graphs properly more than anything else. Practice is the best way to get better at this skill. Again, on your first read through the passage, don't try to memorize this data: just glance over the x and y axes (in other words, see what's being measured) and look for any patterns in the data.

3) Questions that Require Previous Science Knowledge

It's not the time to go back and reread all of your previous science textbooks. You may go home and memorize the layer's of the earth's crust or the number of endangered lizard species in the United States, but questions that require you to have previous scientific knowledge are very rare. For most students, the few (or less) questions that require a foundation of science knowledge are not *too* difficult since, most often, it tests the basics. However, if you come to such a question, and have no idea, it's good to guess and save the time. If something clicks in you later, you can always come back.

That's it! For each of the following two practice tests, it is best to mimic the actual ACT as closely as possible. Set a 35 minute timer on your phone, put it on loud, then throw it in the hallway. Don't get up to get it, though you'll be tempted. Practice active reading and maximizing the time you spend on the actual questions (which is where ACT Science scores go up or down). Remember: practice really doesn't make perfect; instead, perfect practice *perfects*, meaning makes you better. So, practice as perfectly as you can!

Following each test, you'll find not only the correct answers on page 268, but also explanations for each question beginning on page 365 (Practice Test 1) and page 370 (Practice Test 2).

PRACTICE TEST 1
35 Minutes, 40 Questions

SCIENCE TEST
35 Minutes — 40 Questions

DIRECTIONS: There are several passages in this test. Each passage is followed by several questions. After reading a passage, choose the best answer to each question and fill in the corresponding oval on your answer document. You may refer to the passages as often as necessary.

You are NOT permitted to use a calculator on this test.

Passage I

Escherichia coli (*E. coli*) is a coliform bacterium that is commonly found in the lower intestine of warm-blooded organisms. Though most strains are harmless, some serotypes can cause food poisoning in their hosts. In humans, the bacterium is often transmitted through food items, such as undercooked hamburgers and unpasteurized milk. Scientists recently tested methods for minimizing the likelihood of ground beef becoming contaminated with *E. coli*.

Experiment 1

Scientists first studied the effects of radiation on ground beef. After taking an initial count of colony forming units (cfu/gm) of *E. coli*, ground beef was exposed to radiation for 15 minutes. Every 5 minutes, the ground beef was sampled to determine the death rate of *E. coli*, if any. Table 1 shows the results.

Table 1	
Time of exposure (minutes)	*E. coli* count
0	20,000 cfu/gm
5	15,000 cfu/gm
10	10,000 cfu/gm
15	5,000 cfu/gm

Experiment 2

Scientists also tested the effects of acid on *E. coli*. In this experiment, an initial count was done on a contaminated ground beef specimen, then 3 additional samples from the same specimen of beef were placed in a 10% vinegar-acidic solution for 5, 10, and 15 minutes, respectively. The results of the measured death rate of the *E. coli* are shown in Table 2.

Table 2	
Time of exposure (minutes)	*E. coli* count
0	25,000 cfu/gm
5	15,000 cfu/gm
10	10,000 cfu/gm
15	15,000 cfu/gm

Experiment 3

In the third experiment, four samples with 20,000 cfu/gm count *E. coli* were soaked in a vinegar-acidic solution for 5 minutes, then stored for 24 hours at varying temperatures before undergoing a final *E. coli* count. The results are shown below in Table 3.

Table 3	
Temperature of exposure (24 hours)	*E. coli* count
4°F	15,000 cfu/gm
20°F	30,000 cfu/gm
40°F	60,000 cfu/gm
50°F	70,000 cfu/gm

1. If another trial had been performed in Experiment 2 in which additional ground beef had been exposed to the vinegar-acidic solution for 20 minutes, the *E. coli* count most likely would have been:

   A. less than 5,000 cfu/gm.
   B. between 5,000 cfu/gm and 10,000 cfu/gm.
   C. between 10,000 cfu/gm and 15,000 cfu/gm.
   D. greater than 15,000 cfu/gm.

2. Suppose Experiment 3 had been repeated, but the 4 ground beef samples had been soaked in the vinegar-acidic solution for 10 minutes before a 24 hour storage. Would the *E. coli* count after 24 hours of storage at 50°F likely be greater or less than 70,000 cfu/gm?

   F. Greater, because the *E. coli* count after soaking would be lessened at the beginning of storage.
   G. Greater, because the *E. coli* count after soaking would be increased at the beginning of storage.
   H. Less, because the *E. coli* count after soaking would be lessened at the beginning of storage.
   J. Less, because the *E. coli* count after soaking would be increased at the beginning of storage.

3. An international beef distributor has decided to label any ground beef with a cfu/gm count of over 60,000 as *critical* and unfit for consumption. How many of the results of the 3 experiments are *critical*?

   A. 0
   B. 1
   C. 2
   D. 4

4. Which of the experiments exposed ground beef to radiation, if any?

   F. Experiment 1 only
   G. Experiment 2 only
   H. Experiments 1 and 2 only
   J. Experiments 1, 2, and 3

5. Is the relationship between the time of exposure to radiation and the *E. coli* count in ground beef a direct relationship or an inverse relationship?

   A. Direct; as the time of exposure to radiation increased, the *E. coli* count in the ground beef increased.
   B. Direct; as the time of exposure to radiation increased, the *E. coli* count in the ground beef decreased.
   C. Inverse; as the time of exposure to radiation increased, the *E. coli* count in the ground beef increased.
   D. Inverse; as the time of exposure to radiation increased, the *E. coli* count in the ground beef decreased.

6. Which of the following sequence of events is most likely to result in the lowest cfu/gm count of *E. coli* in a sample of ground beef?

   F. Expose it to radiation for 10 minutes, soak it in a vinegar-acidic solution for 10 minutes, then store it at 4°F for 24 hours.
   G. Expose it to radiation for 10 minutes, soak it in a vinegar-acidic solution for 15 minutes, then store it at 4°F for 24 hours.
   H. Expose it to radiation for 15 minutes, soak it in a vinegar-acidic solution for 15 minutes, then store it at 4°F for 24 hours.
   J. Expose it to radiation for 15 minutes, soak it in a vinegar-acidic solution for 10 minutes, then store it at 4°F for 24 hours.

7. Assume that an exposure to a vinegar-acidic solution for *greater than* 5 minutes creates an undesirable taste in ground beef. What percent of the results in Tables 1, 2, and 3 are undesirable?

   A. 16.67%
   B. 25%
   C. 33.33%
   D. 58.33%

Passage II

Glycene max is a soybean and species of legume native to East Asia. *G. max* usually undergoes *self-pollination* (in which both the egg and pollen are from the same *G. max* plant), but it is believed *cross-pollination* (in which the egg and pollen are from different *G. max* plants) could increase soybean yield. A study was conducted to examine the results of several pollination methods on bean yield and bean mass in a *G. max* population.

Before pollination could occur, 720 *G. max* flowering plants were separated into 3 equal groups of 240 each (Groups 1-3). The groups of *G. max* plants were then isolated from each other and placed into pollination cages to protect them from insects. Each group was then exposed to a different pollination method (see Table 1). The percent of plants that produced beans and the average mass per bean for each of the three groups were determined 4 weeks after the pollination occurred (see Figures 1 and 2, respectively).

Table 1	
Group	Pollination method
1	cross-pollination using wild bees
2	cross-pollination using honey bees
3	self-pollination*
*No pollinators were allowed to interact with the plants	

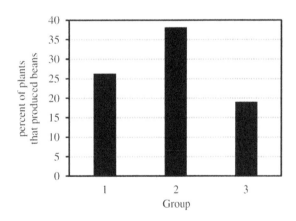

Figure 1

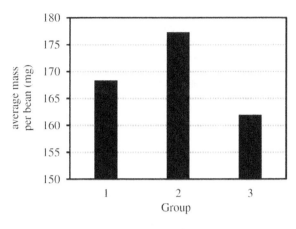

Figure 2

8. According to Figure 1, as bees are introduced into a population of *G. max* plants, the percent of plants that produces beans:

   F. increases.
   G. decreases.
   H. decreases, then increases.
   J. increases, then decreases.

9. When pollinators are not allowed to interact with *G. max* plants, which of the following occurs?

   I. Self-pollination
   II. The percent of plants producing beans is maximized
   III. The egg and pollen come from the same *G. max* plant

   A. I only
   B. I and II only
   C. I and III only
   D. II and III only

10. According to Figure 1, the number of bean-producing plants that resulted from cross-pollination using honey bees is approximately how many?

    F. 19
    G. 26
    H. 38
    J. 91

11. Based on the information in the passage, it can be reasonably expected that both the percent of plants producing beans and the average mass per bean could be lessened in the wild due to which of the following factors?

   A. The presence of honey bees.
   B. The presence of wild bees.
   C. A decrease in bees due to inclement weather.
   D. An increase in pollinators due to inclement weather.

12. Which of the following can be reasonably inferred from the passage?

   F. The bigger the plant, the bigger the bean.
   G. The smaller the plant, the bigger the bean.
   H. A healthy population of bees is good for *G. max* farmers.
   J. Self-pollinating plants are always poor investments for farmers.

13. A *G. max* soybean is chosen at random from the experiment and is found to weigh 179 mg. It is most likely that this soybean:

   A. is from Group 1 because self-pollinating *G. max* plants produce the largest soybeans.
   B. is from Group 2 because *G. max* plants pollinated using honey bees produce the largest soybeans.
   C. is from Group 2 because self-pollinating *G. max* plants produce the largest soybeans.
   D. is from Group 3 because *G. max* plants pollinated using honey bees produce the largest soybeans.

Passage III

There is debate about the genetic origins of human life on earth. It is widely agreed that the earliest fossil evidence of modern humans (*Homo sapiens*) first appeared in Africa 130,000 years ago and also that there is evidence of modern humans from the Near East dating to 90,000 years ago. However, there is disagreement about the process that led to the evolution of modern humans. During the process of evolution, mutations of DNA appear in offspring. While many mutations are harmful and detrimental to the individual, a few may be helpful in the survival of an individual. DNA coding for useful traits is passed onto offspring and over long periods of time enough of these genetic changes accumulates for the group of organisms to have evolved into a different species. Two scientists provided explanations as to how these DNA changes came about in the development of *Homo sapiens*.

Scientist 1

The evolution of *Homo sapiens* was a result of parallel evolution involving *Homo erectus* (a species preceding that of *Homo sapiens*) and an intermediary species of some sort, such as Neanderthals and/or Denisovans. This process occurred in Africa, Europe, and Asia with some genetic intermixing among some members of these various populations occurring before *Homo sapiens* killed off these populations. There is clear anatomical evidence for this theory seen when comparing certain minor anatomical features, such as skull shape and structure, of *Homo erectus* populations with modern humans from these areas. The anatomical differences are so minor as to be negligible, thus proving the Multi-Regional Hypothesis that modern humans evolved separately in populations of Africa, Europe, and Asia.

Scientist 2

The evolution of *Homo sapiens* occurred within one fairly small and isolated population of people, most likely in Africa. It is this population of people that would eventually spread across Asia, Africa, and Europe. As this spread took place, they displaced and replaced other humanoid populations, such as Neanderthals and Denisovans. When one looks at DNA evidence of living humans, especially that of mitochondrial DNA and the mutation rate of DNA, one can calculate with astonishing accuracy when modern humans diverged from a common ancestor. Most such calculations conclude that this divergence occurred approximately 200,000 years ago, which is far too recent to support the Multi-Regional Hypothesis. In addition, molecular biology also suggests that the Out of Africa Hypothesis, that the first modern humans evolved exclusively in Africa, is the truth of our origin as a species.

14. According to Scientist 2, the presence of *Homo sapiens* in the Near East 90,000 years ago is the result of:

    F. the migration of Neanderthals and Denisovans from a central point.

    G. the migration of *Homo sapiens* from a central point.

    H. the intermixing of Neanderthal and *Homo sapiens* populations in the Near East.

    J. genetic mutations of a *Homo erectus* population that already lived in the Near East.

15. Suppose an archaeologist discovered the remains of a *Homo erectus* individual from the Near East with a femur bone essentially identical to the femur bones of modern humans in the same area. This discovery provides support for the hypothesis of which scientist?

    A. Scientist 1 only

    B. Scientist 2 only

    C. Scientists 1 and 2

    D. This discovery supports the hypothesis of neither scientist

16. Suppose it were discovered that the earliest *Homo sapiens* bone fragments discovered in Africa featured as many anatomic similarities to modern Europeans as the earliest European *Homo sapiens* fragments. Would this discovery support Scientist 1's hypothesis?

    F. Yes; Scientist 1 accounts for such anatomic similarities, unlike Scientist 2.

    G. Yes; Scientist 1 believes that all *Homo sapiens* originated in Africa before spreading across the globe.

    H. No; Scientist 1 relies upon anatomic similarities being tied to individual locations and populations.

    J. No; Scientist 1 does not rely upon anatomical similarities to reach his hypothesis.

17. Suppose that the remains of a *Homo sapiens* individual were discovered in Europe dating to 215,000 years ago. This discovery would *weaken* which of the scientists' explanations?

    A. Scientist 1 only

    B. Scientist 2 only

    C. Scientists 1 and 2

    D. The discovery weakens the explanation of neither scientist

18. With which of the following statements would Scientists 1 and 2 both agree?

    F. At one point, *Homo sapiens* lived in the same area as other pre-modern humanoid species.

    G. All pre-modern humanoid species were killed off intentionally by early *Homo sapiens*.

    H. *Homo sapiens* resulted from the intermixing of pre-modern humanoid populations.

    J. *Homo sapiens* fossils are almost always indistinguishable from the fossils of pre-modern humanoid species.

19. Suppose the bones of a previously unknown humanoid species were discovered to have been living in the same time and place as some of the earliest *Homo sapiens*. With which of the following statements would both Scientists agree?

    A. There must be an earlier community of *Homo sapiens* undiscovered in Africa.
    B. *Homo sapiens* evolved from this species.
    C. *Homo sapiens* was most likely responsible for the killing off of this species.
    D. *Homo sapiens* migrated to this location from elsewhere.

20. Which of the following is a key difference between Scientist 1 and 2?

    F. Scientist 1 emphasizes anatomical data, while Scientist 2 emphasizes DNA analysis.
    G. Scientist 1 emphasizes DNA analysis, while Scientist 2 emphasizes anatomical data.
    H. Scientist 1 believes that *Homo sapiens* evolved from humanoid populations, while Scientist 2 does not.
    J. Scientist 2 believes that *Homo sapiens* evolved from humanoid populations, while Scientist 1 does not.

Passage IV

P. aurelia and *P. caudatum* are two species of *paramecium*, unicellular organisms that primarily occupy stagnant pools of fresh water. Paramecium are covered in *cilia*, hairlike extensions that act as flippers to push the organism through the water. When paramecium encounter negative or predatory stimuli, they use their cilia to rotate 180 degrees and flee. *P. aurelia* and *P. caudatum* have very similar food requirements and compete for survival when kept under similar conditions.

Experiment 1

In Experiment 1, a scientist measured the populations, *P*, of *P. aurelia* and *P. caudatum* when isolated in an unfiltered jar of fresh water kept at room temperature. At Day 0, 20 of each species were introduced to the environment. Population levels were measured every 5 days (P_5, P_{10}, P_{15}, etc.). The results are shown in Figure 1.

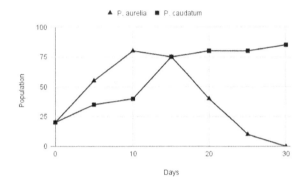

Figure 1

Experiment 2

In Experiment 2, a scientist measured the populations, *P*, of *P. aurelia* and *P. caudatum* when isolated in a room-temperature, unfiltered jar of fresh water that had been first given a bottom layer of 4 ounces of green algae. Population levels were measured every 5 days (P_5, P_{10}, P_{15}, etc.). The results are shown in Figure 2.

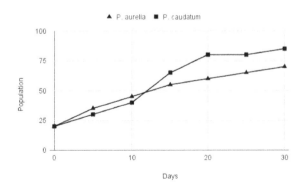

Figure 2

Experiment 3

In Experiment 3, the conditions of Experiment 2 were repeated with the addition of *Didinium nasutum*, a carnivorous unicellular ciliate that preys on paramecium. Aided by its toxicysts, *D. nasutum* paralyzes paramecium before consuming them through its expandable cytosome. Population levels for the three unicellular organisms were measured every 5 days (P_5, P_{10}, P_{15}, etc.). The results are shown in Figure 3.

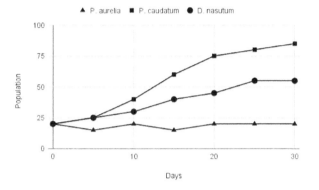

Figure 3

21. In the results of which experiment, if any, is there direct evidence that *P. aurelia* and *P. caudatum* are willing to consume other paramecium?

    A. Experiment 1
    B. Experiment 2
    C. Experiment 3
    D. None of the experiments has direct evidence that *P. aurelia* and *P caudatum* are willing to consume other paramecium.

22. Which of the following statements regarding *P* best describes a difference between Experiment 2 and Experiment 3?

    F. The presence of *D. nasutum* affects the P_0 through P_{30} of *P. caudatum* more than the P_0 through P_{30} of *P. aurelia*.
    G. The presence of *D. nasutum* affects the P_0 through P_{30} of *P. aurelia* more than the P_0 through P_{30} of *P. caudatum*.
    H. The presence of green algae affects the P_0 through P_{30} of *P. caudatum* more than the P_0 through P_{30} of *D. nasatum*.
    J. The presence of green algae affects the P_0 through P_{30} of *P. aurelia* more than the P_0 through P_{30} of *D. nasatum*.

23. If Experiment 3 were repeated with the addition of *Tetrahymena pyriformis*, which preys on *D. nasutum*, with a $P_0 = 20$, then it could be reasonably expected that the P_{25} of *P. aurelia* would be:

A. Greater than the P_{25} of *P. aurelia* in Experiment 3.
B. Less than the P_{25} of *P. aurelia* in Experiment 3.
C. Greater than the P_{25} of *P. caudatum* in Experiment 3.
D. Greater than the P_{25} of *D. nasutum* in Experiment 3.

24. Compared to Experiment 1, was the P_{20} of *P. aurelia* and *P. caudatum* greater than, less than, or equal to the P_{20} of both species in Experiment 2?

	P. aurelia	P. caudatum
F.	Greater than	Less than
G.	Less than	Equal to
H.	Greater than	Equal to
J.	Equal to	Greater than

25. Between all three experiments, the value of which of the following represents the lowest total number of paramecium after at least 20 days of population growth or decrease?

A. P_{20} of Experiment 1
B. P_{30} of Experiment 1
C. P_{20} of Experiment 2
D. P_{30} of Experiment 3

26. If it can be inferred, which of the following values is most likely the greatest?

F. The number of *P. aurelia* paralyzed by toxicysts in Experiment 3
G. The number of *P. caudatum* paralyzed by toxicysts in Experiment 3
H. The P_{30} of *P. aurelia* in Experiment 3
J. The P_{25} of *P. aurelia* in Experiment 3

27. Suppose green algae is rendered nutrient free after 50 days of isolation in room-temperature water. If Experiment 2 were carried out through 80 days, then which of the following could *not* be reasonably inferred?

A. At P_{80}, the population of *P. aurelia* would be approaching 0.
B. At P_{65}, the population of *P. aurelia* would begin to decline sharply.
C. At P_{60}, the population of *P. caudatum* would begin to level off.
D. At P_{70}, the population of *P. caudatum* would begin to decline sharply.

Passage V

A *solute* is any substance that is dissolved into another substance, which is called the *solvent*. A scientist tested the *solubility* (a measure of how much solute will dissolve into the solvent) of seven different substances. The solubility of a substance is defined as the concentration of dissolved solute that is in equilibrium with the solvent. Table 1 records the concentration in grams of dissolved substances in 100 grams (g) of water at various temperatures. The concentrations are expressed in grams of solute per 100 grams of water (H_2O).

When the mass of solvent (m_{sv}) is divided by the mass of solute (m_{su}), the result is the amount of solvent necessary to dissolve one unit mass of solute at 20°C. This measurement, m_{sv}/m_{su}, is used for descriptive purposes. Table 2 lists these terms and their accompanying measurements. Table 3 lists the m_{sv}/m_{su} values for the seven substances listed in Table 1.

Temp (°C)	$Na_2C_2O_4$	$NaNO_3$	HCl	$CaSO_4 \cdot 2H_2O$	$FeSO_4$	NaCl	NH_3
0	2.69	72	83	0.223	16	37	90
20	3.41	86	72	0.255	29	37	55
40	4.18	105	63	0.265	40	38	36
60	4.93	125	55	0.244	60	38	23
80	5.71	145	48	0.234	87	39	14
100	6.5	165	43	0.205	80	40	8

Table 1

Descriptive Term	m_{sv}/m_{su} Range
Very soluble	< 1
Freely soluble	1 to 10
Soluble	10 to 30
Sparingly soluble	30 to 100
Slightly soluble	100 to 1,000
Very slightly soluble	1,000 to 10,000
Practically insoluble	> 10,000

Table 2

Substance	m_{sv}/m_{su}
$Na_2C_2O_4$	29.3
$NaNO_3$	1.16
HCl	1.39
$CaSO_4 \cdot 2H_2O$	392.16
$FeSO_4$	3.45
NaCl	2.70
NH_3	1.82

Table 3

28. Before testing the solubility, the scientist hypothesized that exactly one of the seven substances would be considered *very soluble*. Was this hypothesis consistent with the results of the experiment?

   F. No; more than one of the seven substances is to be considered very soluble.
   G. No; none of the seven substances is to be considered very soluble.
   H. No; there is not enough data available to reach a conclusion about the appropriate descriptive term for any of the seven substances.
   J. Yes; exactly one of the seven substances is to be considered very soluble.

29. How many grams of Hydrogen Chloride (HCl) will dissolve into 100 grams of water at 60°C?

   A. 43
   B. 48
   C. 55
   D. 63

30. Based on Tables 2 and 3, what fraction of the seven substances deserves to be described as *freely soluble*?

   F. $\dfrac{6}{7}$

   G. $\dfrac{5}{7}$

   H. $\dfrac{2}{7}$

   J. $\dfrac{1}{7}$

31. If *solubility equipollence* is reached when 100 grams of a solute dissolve into 100 grams of a solvent, then it could be reasonably inferred that Sodium Nitrate ($NaNO_3$) reaches *solubility equipollence* in water at approximately what temperature?

   A. 15°C
   B. 35°C
   C. 60°C
   D. 140°C

32. Before testing the solubility, the scientist hypothesized that any substance containing sodium (Na) was *freely soluble*. What this hypothesis consistent with the results of the experiment?

   F. Yes; both substances tested that contain sodium yielded a m_{sv}/m_{su} between 1 and 10.
   G. Yes; both substances tested that contain sodium yielded a m_{sv}/m_{su} between 1 and 10.
   H. No; none of the three substances tested that contain sodium yielded a m_{sv}/m_{su} between 1 and 10.
   J. No; only two of the three substances tested that contain sodium yielded a m_{sv}/m_{su} between 1 and 10.

33. The scientist creates the following line chart from some of the data gathered in Table 1:

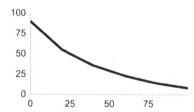

   If the *x*-axis measures °C and the *y*-axis measures dissolved g of the solute/100 g H_2O, the line chart represents the data of which solute?

   A. Ammonia (NH_3)
   B. Iron (II) sulfate ($FeSO_4$)
   C. Sodium nitrate ($NaNO_3$)
   D. Sodium oxalate ($Na_2C_2SO_4$)

Due to their rapid reproduction rates, two species of fly were used by students at a local university to study genetics. For each study, both the *genotype*, the genetic makeup of an organism, and the *phenotype*, the observable characteristics of a genotype, were observed and recorded across three generations.

Study 1

Drosophila melanogaster, the common fruit fly, was first studied. *D. melanogaster* most commonly inherits and passes on a red eye color. However, there are many other eye color possibilities due to loss of one or more of the pigments normally synthesized and combined to produce red. Students were interested in understanding what effect a breeding of *D. melanogaster* with *homozygous* (identical) *alleles* (genetic variations) of a red and brown phenotype would have on descendants after two subsequent generations.

All specimens in the parental (P) generation possess homozygous alleles, a breeding of which results in a population (F_1) consisting entirely of *heterozygous* (a mix of dominant and recessive) alleles. A third generation (F_2) was then observed and compared to the students' expected outcomes. Students expected that 3/4 of F_2 would be of phenotype red and that 1/4 of F_2 would be of phenotype brown. Their findings are recorded in Table 1.

Table 1*					
	Phenotype	Genotype		Phenotype	Genotype
P	Red eye	BB	x	Brown eye	bb
F_1	Red eye	Bb	x	Red eye	Bb
			Observed numbers		Expected numbers
F_2	Red eye	B__	63		61.5
	Brown Eye	bb	19		20.5
	Total		82		82
*B is dominant; b is recessive; a blank means *undetermined*					

Study 2

Musca domestica, the common housefly, were also studied in a *dihybrid experiment*, one in which specimens containing two pairs of homozygous alleles are crossed. Dihybrid experiments can yield surprising results after two subsequent generations.

All specimens in the parental (P) generation possess two pairs of homozygous alleles, a breeding of which results in a population (F_1) consisting entirely of heterozygous alleles. This population consists entirely of genotypes with two gene pairs, both with a dominant and recessive allele, resulting in a dominant phenotype. A third generation (F_2) was then observed and compared to the students' expected outcomes. Students expected that 9/16 of F_2 would be of phenotype red, 3/16 would be of phenotype brown, 3/16 would be of phenotype sepia (dark brown), and 1/16 would be of a fourth phenotype resulting from a doubly homozygous recessive genotype. Their findings are recorded in Table 2.

Table 2*					
	Phenotype	Genotype		Phenotype	Genotype
P	Sepia eye	ddBB	x	Brown eye	DDbb
F_1	Red eye	DdBb	x	Red eye	DdBb
			Observed numbers		Expected numbers
F_2	Red eye	D__B__	67		64.7
	Sepia eye	ddB__	18		21.6
	Brown eye	D__bb	30		21.6
	_____ eye	ddbb	____		7.2
	Total		115		115
*B or D is dominant; b or d is recessive; a blank means *undetermined*					

34. How many generations, on average, were studied and utilized across the two studies?

F. 2
G. 3
H. 82
J. 197

35. Based on the tables, which of the following phenotype/genotype observations most deviated from the students' expected outcomes?

A. Brown eye/bb
B. Red eye/B__
C. Sepia eye/ddB__
D. Brown eye/D__bb

36. Based on the data, what is the most likely explanation for zero observed doubly homozygous recessive genotypes in Study 2?

    F. Based on the conclusions of Study 1, it is reasonable to infer that a doubly homozygous genotype ddbb is not a genetic possibility.

    G. Based on the students' expectations, it is unlikely that a sample size of 115 *Musca domestica* specimens would result in 1 or more doubly homozygous genotypes.

    H. The doubly homozygous genotype ddbb in the *Musca domestica* manifests as a brown eye phenotype.

    J. The doubly homozygous genotype ddbb in the *Musca domestica* has a direct relationship with the numbers of larvae that die prior to hatching.

37. The primary reason that each study required three generations of flies was to:

    A. ensure an intermixing of alleles sufficient enough to diversify the eye color phenotype.

    B. allow the fly populations to multiply to a large enough sample size to avoid a margin of error greater than $+-4\%$.

    C. create a population of flies at F_2 comprised entirely of homozygous alleles.

    D. create a population of flies at F_2 with at least 10% sepia eye phenotype.

38. Suppose a farmer purchased two white sheep, the offspring of which had offspring with other white sheep. If a lamb in this third generation were born with black wool, and if the genotype in sheep determining wool color consisted of two alleles, this would mean that:

    F. this lamb inherited a recessive black wool gene from its father and mother, resulting in a recessive heterozygous genotype.

    G. this lamb inherited a dominant black wool gene from its father and mother, resulting in a recessive heterozygous genotype.

    H. this lamb inherited a dominant black wool gene from its father and mother, resulting in a recessive homozygous genotype.

    J. this lamb inherited a recessive black wool gene from its father and mother, resulting in a recessive homozygous genotype.

39. Suppose a student argues that more research must be done on the second allele of F_2 fruit flies with a red phenotype eye color to ensure accuracy when comparing observed to expected numbers. Is this student correct?

    A. Yes; the field of genetics is almost unpredictable without accurate allele counts.

    B. Yes; determining if the second allele is dominant (B) or recessive (b) is necessary in distinguishing dominant or recessive phenotypes.

    C. No; one dominant allele (B) is enough to ensure accurate numbers in *D. melanogaster*.

    D. No; if the second allele is found to be recessive (b), it would be assumed that the phenotype is also recessive.

40. Which of the following pairs of pie charts accurately displays the observed numbers compared to the expected numbers for Study 2?

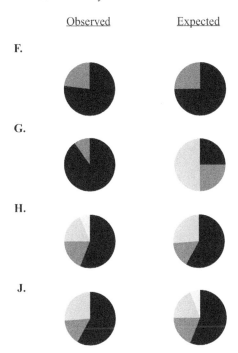

PRACTICE TEST 2
35 Minutes, 40 Questions

SCIENCE TEST
35 Minutes — 40 Questions

DIRECTIONS: There are several passages in this test. Each passage is followed by several questions. After reading a passage, choose the best answer to each question and fill in the corresponding oval on your answer document. You may refer to the passages as often as necessary.

You are NOT permitted to use a calculator on this test.

Passage I

Although the probability of life currently existing on Mars is low (as low as 0), many scientists are convinced that the Red Planet once sustained life. While current conditions on Mars include freezing temperatures and high radiation levels, there is evidence to suggest that ancient Mars had a climate that could support life.

One main factor in determining the potential for life on a planet includes the existence of water. Due to the global presence of sulfate and chloride salts on Mars today, it is thought that the planet once had *hypersaline*, or extremely salty, bodies of water. Interestingly, there are bodies of water currently existing on Earth that are comparable to those that are thought to have been present on ancient Mars. This type of environment is not suitable for the majority of living microorganisms, as extremely high salinity levels are often toxic to cells. Nevertheless scientists have been able to discover microorganisms on earth that are able to withstand these types of harsh conditions.

In the study below, scientists sought to determine the biological diversity present in a hypersaline lake that is thought to be analogous to those found on ancient Mars. Table 1 highlights the geochemical properties in the hypersaline lake.

Table 1	
Properties	
pH	~ 8.0 to 8.3
Salinity (%)	37.1
Organic carbon (%)	~ 1 to 3

Figure 1 illustrates the estimated organism diversity in the hypersaline lake.

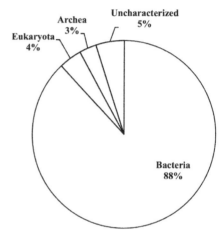

Figure 1

Figure 2 illustrates the estimated bacteria phyla diversity in the hypersaline lake.

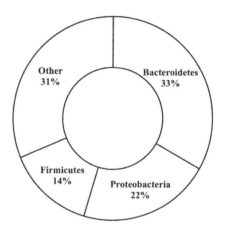

Figure 2

1. Based on the data in Figure 1 and Figure 2, about what percent of the estimated organism diversity in the hypersaline lake is made up of bacteroidetes?

   A. 12%
   B. 29%
   C. 33%
   D. 88%

2. According to the passage, if the salt levels of the lake were to be reduced over time, the overall percent of organism diversity in the lake occupied by bacteria would:

   F. decrease, because other types of life would be more likely to survive in the lake.
   G. decrease, because other types of life would be less likely to survive in the lake.
   H. increase, because other types of life would be more likely to survive in the lake.
   J. increase, because other types of life would be less likely to survive in the lake.

3. Consider the estimated organism and bacteria diversity in the hypersaline lake. Which of the following properly orders species based on percentage from lowest to highest occupation levels?

   A. Archea, Eukaryota, Proteobacteria, Firmicutes
   B. Eukaryota, Firmicutes, Proteobacteria, Bacteroidetes
   C. Firmicutes, Proteobacteria, Bacteroidetes, Archea
   D. Bacteroidetes, Proteobacteria, Eukaryota, Archea

4. The passage makes clear that one reason why current life on Mars is extremely improbable is due to:

   F. low radiation and high temperatures.
   G. high radiation and low temperatures.
   H. low levels of salinity in its lakes.
   J. high levels of salinity in its lakes.

5. A scientist reexamined the diversity of the life in the hypersaline lake and discovered the presence of the fungus *Wallemia ichthyophaga*. At most, *Wallemia i.* makes up what percent of the total diversity?

   A. 1%
   B. 2%
   C. 4%
   D. 5%

6. According to the passage, if it were discovered that life had once existed on Mars, it would most likely be:

   F. a bacteroidete that had grown and lived in a lake with little to no salt.
   G. a bacteroidete that had grown and lived in a hypersaline lake.
   H. a proteobacteria that had grown and lived in a lake with little to no salt.
   J. a proteobacteria that had grown and lived in a hypersaline lake.

Passage II

Athene cunicularia is a species of burrowing owl found throughout the open landscapes of both South and North America. Researchers hypothesized that *A. cunicularia* would favor prey of certain colors over others. This hypothesis was tested with three experiments using *Eublepharis macularius*, a species of gecko, which were purposefully bred with yellow, white, grey, purple, and brown skin. For each experiment, two geckos of each color were held in a large, open owl habitat that mimicked a forest, and the color of each gecko eaten by the owl was documented over a period of 24 hours. Every time the owl ate a gecko, another of the same color was added back into the habitat.

Experiment 1

In Experiment 1, ten wild-caught *A. cunicularia* were monitored one at a time in the habitat, having been placed there the same day as their capture. Figure 1 shows the average number of geckos of each color eaten over the 24 hour period.

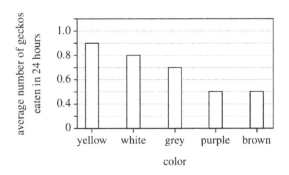

Figure 1

Experiment 2

In Experiment 2, ten wild-caught *A. cunicularia* were kept in the owl habitat for one month. Then, Experiment 1 was repeated. Figure 2 shows the average number of geckos of each color eaten over the 24 hour period.

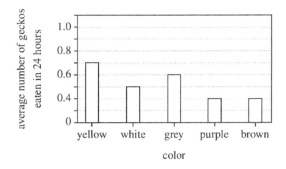

Figure 2

Experiment 3

In Experiment 3, ten *A. cunicularia* were hatched, raised, and bred in the laboratory. When they reached adulthood, Experiment 1 was repeated. Figure 3 shows the average number of geckos of each color eaten over the 24 hour period.

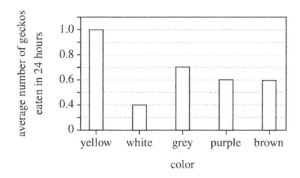

Figure 3

7. If the researchers had repeated the experiment with ten wild-caught owls that were kept in the habitat for two weeks, then the average number of yellow geckos eaten would have most likely been closest to:

   A. 0.5
   B. 0.6
   C. 0.7
   D. 0.8

8. As the time that the owls were held in captivity increased, the total number of geckos consumed:

   F. increased only.
   G. decreased only.
   H. increased then decreased.
   J. decreased then increased.

9. Given that wild geckos are not perfectly bred with pure colors, which of the following colors is least likely to be found thriving in the natural habitat of the *A. cunicularia*?

   A. Grayish-purple
   B. Brownish-purple
   C. Yellowish-white
   D. Grayish-white

10. If Experiment 3 were repeated, but *Eublepharis macularius* were not replaced as they were consumed, then the last gecko in the habitat would most likely be of what color?

    F. Yellow
    G. White
    H. Grey
    J. Purple

11. Based on the information in the passage, which of the following is likely to be true about *A. cunicularia*?

    A. The longer *A. cunicularia* is kept in captivity, the less it will tend to eat.
    B. There is no difference in the amount that wild and captive *A. cunicularia* tend to eat.
    C. Captive *A. cunicularia* tend to eat more than wild *A. cunicularia*.
    D. Wild *A. cunicularia* tend to eat more than captive *A. cunicularia*.

12. Which of the following is an assumption made by the researchers across all three experiments?

    F. That *A. cunicularia* prey upon a variety of animal types, including mammals, reptiles, and amphibians
    G. That *Eublepharis macularius* can only be bred into five color varieties
    H. That *A. cunicularia* are less likely to hunt for food in environments with little to no competition for the same prey
    J. That 24 hours is enough time to gather sufficient data on the eating preferences of *A. cunicularia*

13. If the owls used in Experiment 3 were released into the wild, and assuming *Eublepharis macularius* of each color were present in their new habitat, then which of the following changes to their preferences would be most likely?

    A. They would greatly increase their preference for white *Eublepharis macularius*.
    B. They would greatly decrease their preference for white *Eublepharis macularius*.
    C. They would greatly increase their preference for yellow *Eublepharis macularius*.
    D. They would greatly increase their preference for purple and brown *Eublepharis macularius*.

Passage III

Endocrine-disrupting chemicals (EDC's) have the potential to be detrimental to the reproductive health of aquatic organisms, as they have the ability to interfere with sex hormone production and secretion. Previous research has discovered that the minimum EDC concentration required to alter sex hormone levels (i.e. testosterone and estradiol) in aquatic animals is 1,000 ng/L. In addition to the concentration levels, the *half-life*, or the time required for the concentration of a chemical to be reduced by half, is also of concern. The longer the half-life of a chemical, the longer it takes for a chemical to be cleared from a sample.

In this study, scientists aimed to determine if significant amounts of EDC's could be found in the water and marine sediment of several bodies of water, all of which are found in the same greater habitat (within a 50 mile radius).

Table 1 shows the physical and chemical parameters of the sampled bodies of water in this study.

Table 1			
Sampling site #	Depth (m)*	Temperature (°C)	pH
1	-1.30	15.5	7.97
2	-0.50	15.9	7.99
3	-1.30	15.5	7.97
4	-0.30	15.6	8.08
5	-1.32	15.2	7.94
6	-2.10	15.4	7.92

*note: the deeper the stream, the lower the concentration of EDC's in water

Table 2 displays common EDC's and their corresponding concentration ranges found in the bodies of water (both water and marine sediment) over a 7-month period.

Table 2		
EDC	Concentration range in water (ng/L)	Concentration range in sediment (ng/L)
BPA	298-3,620	1,140-50,000
BADGE	2,140-28,000	4,290-61,000
BPAF	132-1,070	730-155,000
BPB	47-3,660	820-9,420

Table 3 displays the EDC's and their corresponding half-lives in both water and marine sediments.

Table 3		
EDC	Half-life in water (days)	Half-life in sediment (days)
BPA	37.5	337.5
BADGE	60.0	540.0
BPAF	180.0	1,600.0
BPB	38.0	340.0

14. According to Table 1, which body of water is most similar to sampling site #1?

F. Sampling site #6
G. Sampling site #5
H. Sampling site #3
J. Sampling site #2

15. According to Table 1, there is a direct relationship between:

A. water depth and temperature.
B. temperature and pH levels.
C. sampling site and temperature.
D. water depth and pH levels.

16. Tables 2 and 3 indicate that:

F. it is more difficult to remove EDC's from marine sediment than from water.
G. it is more difficult to remove EDC's from water than from marine sediment.
H. there is no overlap between the concentration ranges of various EDC's in water.
J. there is no overlap between the concentration ranges of various EDC's in marine sediment.

17. Suppose scientists also tested the streams for the EDC *polychlorinated biphenyls* and discovered a concentration range in water of 550-4,459 ng/L. A possible concentration range in sediment could be:

A. 61-383 ng/L
B. 202-28,704 ng/L
C. 3,355-49,049 ng/L
D. 4,459-172,390 ng/L

18. About how long would it take to reduce 75% of the amount of ng/L of BADGE from Sampling site #5?

    F.   60 days
    G. 120 days
    H. 540 days
    J.   1,080 days

19. Consider a hypothetical stream in the same greater habitat as the study. If this stream had a depth of -0.15 m, then what would be its likely concentration range of BPA in water?

    A. 200 ng/L
    B. 4,200 ng/L
    C. 32,000 ng/L
    D. 55,000 ng/L

Passage IV

The mission of the Voyager probes (Voyager 1 and 2) when they launched in 1977 was to explore Jupiter and its surrounding moons. Scientists could not begin to anticipate the discoveries they would make as they traveled through the solar system. As Voyager 2 approached Jupiter in the summer of 1979, images of Io (one of Jupiter's moons) revealed what appeared to be an erupting volcano on a celestial body otherwise devoid of an atmosphere or any form of liquid. As it revealed the only known active volcano beyond earth, the discovery was quite remarkable. Additional photographs revealed Io to be an incredibly geologically active world with extensive sulfur deposits on its surface. Two scientists document their disagreements about the fundamental reasons for and chemical compositions of the volcanoes of Io.

Scientist 1

Io is Jupiter's innermost Galilean moon, meaning it was large enough to be one of the four moons visible to Galileo through his early telescope. It is, however, a relatively small celestial body with a diameter approximately one-quarter that of Earth. Despite its small size, it has become quite a geologic phenomenon. As a consequence of its proximity to Jupiter, it is caught in a gravitational tug-of-war between Jupiter and the other Galilean moons. This gravitational action is the core reason for Io's extreme volcanic activity, which is characterized by extensive flows of molten sulfur (which flows at a much lower temperature than molten lava) and other sulfur-rich compounds on the surface. This makes Io's volcanic activity quite different from the volcanic activity observed on Earth in that there is no molten rock flowing on Io, unlike our own planet.

Scientist 2

The volcanoes of Io are more similar to those found on Earth than may be thought possible by other scientists. Based upon the Voyager photographs, the existence of mountains 10km (or 6.2 miles) in height cannot be explained solely by the presence of sulfur, which liquifies at a relatively low temperature. Instead, mountains of that height require, geologically speaking, the presence of silica rocks, which means that these volcanoes must be similar in composition to those found on Earth. Though Io is far from the sun relative to Earth, the friction created beneath the surface of the moon caused by the extreme competitive gravitational pulls of Jupiter and the other Galilean moons is enough to melt rock into lava that would at least partially resemble that found on Earth. Though sulfur is undeniably present on the planet, both in volcanic flows and plumes, it is intermixed with molten silica rock.

20. Which of the scientists, if either, claimed that Io is subject to gravitational pulls in multiple directions?

F. Scientist 1 only
G. Scientist 2 only
H. Both Scientist 1 and Scientist 2
J. Neither Scientist 1 nor Scientist 2

21. Suppose it were discovered that high levels of friction have the ability to melt rock into a molten state. This finding would be most consistent with the explanation given by:

A. Scientist 1 only
B. Scientist 2 only
C. Both Scientist 1 and Scientist 2
D. Neither Scientist 1 nor Scientist 2

22. Based on Scientist 1's explanation, one factor that does *not* contribute to Io's extreme volcanic activity is:

F. its size relative to Earth.
G. the heavy presence of sulfur.
H. the gravitational pull of Jupiter.
J. the gravitational pull of other Galilean moons.

23. Given that sulfur is a lighter substance than silica rock, which of the following inequalities properly orders the expected height of the volcanic plumes from similarly sized volcanoes as described in the passage?

A. Scientist 1's Theory = Scientist 2's Theory < Earth's
B. Scientist 1's Theory < Scientist 2's Theory = Earth's
C. Scientist 1's Theory > Scientist 2's Theory > Earth's
D. Scientist 1's Theory > Scientist 2's Theory = Earth's

24. Which of the scientists claimed that the active volcanoes of Io most likely contain sulfur, which liquefies at a lower temperature than silica rock?

F. Scientist 1 only
G. Scientist 2 only
H. Both Scientist 1 and Scientist 2
J. Neither Scientist 1 nor Scientist 2

25. Scientist 2's explanation would be most strongly weakened relative to Scientist 1's if which of the following observations were made?

A. That silica rock melts at a much lower point than previously thought.
B. That sulfur has the ability to build upon itself in such a way that it does not break or crack under significant pressure.
C. That Jupiter's mass is significantly larger than previously thought.
D. That Jupiter's mass is significantly smaller than previously thought.

26. If sulfur is yellow, and magma is red, then what color plume would each scientist expect to see in a high definition image of one of Io's volcanic eruptions?

F. Scientist 1 = yellow, Scientist 2 = orange
G. Scientist 1 = yellow, Scientist 2 = red
H. Scientist 1 = orange, Scientist 2 = red
J. Scientist 1 = red, Scientist 2 = yellow

Passage V

A *voltage divider* is a series of resistors that can be tapped at intermediate points to produce a specific fraction of the voltage applied between its ends. A *voltage tap* allows an observer to measure the voltage at the specified junction between resistors.

Voltage dividers follow the principle of *Kirchoff's Law*, which states that the sum of all voltages in a circuit must equal zero. In an ideal circuit, the output of each voltage tap is directly proportional to the resistance of the circuit at the point of measurement. Each resistor reduces the voltage by an amount proportional to their resistance, known as a resistor's *voltage drop*.

Figure 1 is a diagram of a voltage divider in a circuit that is powered by a 12 volt supply. The circuit contains three resistors in series: R1, R2, and R3. The circuit in Figure 1 also contains 3 voltage taps which measure the currents V_1, V_2, and V_3. These voltage taps are located between R1 and R2, between R2 and R3, and after R3, respectively.

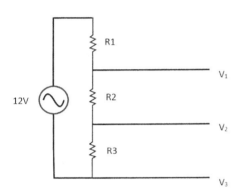

*Note: since Vin is 12V, then $V_1 = \dfrac{R2 + R3}{R1 + R2 + R3} \times 12V$

Figure 1

An electrical engineering student conducted four trials in which he altered the resistance (measured in *ohms*) of resistors R1, R2, and R3 and measured the voltage drop at each voltage tap. The results of the four trials are recorded in Tables 1–4.

Table 1			
Resistance (ohms)		Voltage Drop	
R1	100	V1	4.0
R2	100	V2	4.0
R3	100	V3	4.0

Table 2			
Resistance (ohms)		Voltage Drop	
R1	100	V1	2.0
R2	200	V2	4.0
R3	300	V3	6.0

Table 3			
Resistance (ohms)		Voltage Drop	
R1	300	V1	2.25
R2	900	V2	6.75
R3	400	V3	3

Table 4			
Resistance (ohms)		Voltage Drop	
R1	10	V1	0.108
R2	100	V2	1.081
R3	1000	V3	10.81

27. According to the results of Trials 2–4, from which of the following resistors was the greatest percent of voltage drop observed following R1, R2, and R3, respectively?

	Trial 2	Trial 3	Trial 4
A.	R2	R3	R2
B.	R1	R1	R1
C.	R3	R2	R3
D.	R3	R3	R3

28. According to the results of Trial 4, the percent of voltage drop recorded by the second resistor in the series is closest to which of the following?

F. 9%
G. 33%
H. 91%
J. 100%

29. Is the statement, "When the resistance of a resistor is doubled, the recorded voltage drop is doubled" supported by the results of Trials 1-4?

    A. No; the voltage drop will also depend upon the resistance of the other resistors in the voltage divider.
    B. No; there is no direct relationship between the resistance and the voltage drop.
    C. Yes; Trials 1 and 2 provide evidence enough to prove this claim.
    D. Yes; Trials 2 and 3 provide evidence enough to prove this claim.

30. What were the independent (manipulated) and dependent variables in each of the 4 trials?

Independent	Dependent
F. Voltage drop	Resistance
G. 12V power supply	Voltage drop
H. Resistance	Voltage drop
J. Resistance	12V power supply

31. According to the results of the trials, which of the 3 resistors, if any, reduced the voltage proportional to their resistance by more than 50% of the entire circuit?

    A. R3 of Trial 2 and R3 of Trial 4
    B. R2 of Trial 3 and R3 of Trial 4
    C. R3 of Trial 2 and R2 of Trial 4
    D. None of the resistors

32. Is it possible to manipulate the voltage divider in such a way as to produce an exception to *Kirchoff's Law*?

    F. Yes; the user can alter the voltage current to do so.
    G. Yes; the user can change the number of resistors to do so.
    H. No; without voltage taps, the circuit can not be considered a voltage divider.
    J. No; no matter the voltage or number of resistors, the voltage divider will always follow *Kirchoff's Law*.

33. Imagine that a fourth resistor (R4) were to be added to the voltage divider after R3, which was then followed by a corresponding voltage tap (V4). If the resistance of each resistor were set at 100 ohms, the expected reading at V4 would be:

    A. 1.5 volts
    B. 2.0 volts
    C. 3.0 volts
    D. 4.0 volts

Passage VI

Caffeine is a central nervous system stimulant found in coffee that is commonly used by individuals to increase alertness and focus. Because of this, a group of scientists wanted to test if caffeine administration could increase brain function in rats. To do so, rats were given an assessment called the Morris Water Maze test in which rats are placed one at a time in a pool of opaque water and must search for a hidden platform by swimming. The faster a rat can reach the platform, the better the brain function is thought to be. Once a rat has reached the platform, it is removed from the maze, the timer is reset, and the next rat is placed in the water.

In Trial 1, 8 rats (Rats 1-8) were administered a dose of caffeine before being subject to the Morris Water Maze test. The results are recorded in Figure 1 below.

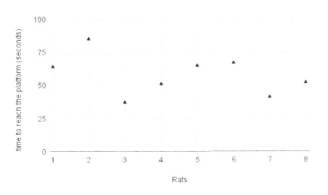

Figure 1

In Trial 2, 8 new rats (Rats 9-16), which were *not* given caffeine, were subject to the Morris Water Maze test. The results are recorded in Figure 2 below.

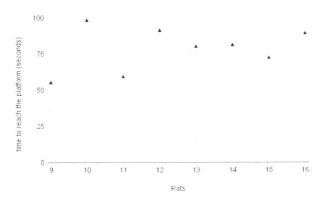

Figure 2

In Trial 3, the same 8 rats from Trial 1 (Rats 1-8) were again administered the Morris Water Maze test (with the platform in a new location) exactly 1 hour after Trial 1. The results are recorded in Figure 3 below.

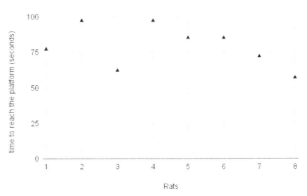

Figure 3

34. Which of the following factors did *not* directly contribute to the amount of time it took rats to complete the Morris Water Maze test, thus accounting for discrepancy among the 24 results?

   F. Whether or not a rat was administered caffeine
   G. The platform's new location in Trial 3
   H. That rats are better swimmers than mice
   J. The opaque nature of the water itself

35. Given that rats are not worn to significant exhaustion of energy by a swim of less than 100 seconds, which of the following conclusions can be reached by the scientists based on the results of the three trials?

   A. That, once caffeine wears off, there is a withdrawal in the user that inhibits performance
   B. That, once caffeine wears off, there is an improvement in the user in terms of performance
   C. That, once caffeine is administered, there will be an immediate, negative effect on performance
   D. That, despite the administration of caffeine, performance is impacted neither negatively nor positively

36. According to the study, which of the following rats exhibited the greatest drop in performance after an hour of rest following the administration of caffeine?

   F. Rat 4
   G. Rat 5
   H. Rat 6
   J. Rat 8

37. Suppose scientists repeated Trial 3, but retested the rats after a rest of 15 minutes as opposed to 1 hour. Assuming that 15 minutes rest is enough time for a rat to recover from physical activity, it would be expected that Rat 3 would perform the Morris Water Maze test in a time:

   A. Between 40 and 60 seconds
   B. Between 60 and 70 seconds
   C. Between 70 and 90 seconds
   D. Between 90 and 100 seconds

38. The average time it takes a rat that has not been administered caffeine to complete the Morris Water Maze test is roughly:

   F. 0.50 minutes
   G. 0.75 minutes
   H. 1 minute
   J. 1.25 minutes

39. Suppose Rat 1 and Rat 9 were placed in the Morris Water Maze test at the same time and the winner recorded. Suppose then that this was repeated for Rat 2 and Rat 10, and so on 8 times until Rat 8 and Rat 16 also competed. How many of the competitions would have been won by rats who did not consume caffeine?

   A. 1 of 8
   B. 2 of 8
   C. 7 of 8
   D. 8 of 8

40. Based on the results of the 3 trials, which of the following rats finished with the fastest average time to complete the Morris Water Maze test?

   F. Rat 11
   G. Rat 9
   H. Rat 4
   J. Rat 2

Step 6 Correct Answers

Practice Test 1

Passage I	Passage II	Passage III	Passage IV	Passage V	Passage VI
1: D	8: F	14: G	21: D	28: G	34: G
2: H	9: C	15: A	22: G	29: C	35: D
3: B	10: J	16: H	23: A	30: G	36: H
4: F	11: C	17: B	24: H	31: B	37: A
5: D	12: H	18: F	25: B	32: J	38: J
6: J	13: B	19: C	26: F	33: A	39: C
7: A		20: F	27: D		40: J

Practice Test 2

Passage I	Passage II	Passage III	Passage IV	Passage V	Passage VI
1: B	7: D	14: H	20: H	27: C	34: H
2: F	8: J	15: D	21: B	28: F	35: A
3: B	9: C	16: F	22: F	29: A	36: F
4: G	10: G	17: C	23: C	30: H	37: A
5: D	11: D	18: J	24: H	31: B	38: J
6: G	12: J	19: B	25: B	32: J	39: A
	13: A		26: F	33: C	40: G

Stumped on any? You will find the explanations for each answer beginning on page 365 (Practice Test 1) and 370 (Practice Test 2).

In Conclusion

Congratulations! If you have completed this entire workbook, I must say, I am impressed. Rest assured that you have not wasted your time with out of order prep. You have systematized your preparation, and in doing so you've put first-things-first, and I hope you have seen which areas of practice and skill need more work.

If you are still in need of practice, I recommend doing an internet search for the terms "Preparing for the ACT" followed by the current year (like: "Preparing for the ACT 2023"). This will bring up a PDF document of an authentic, recent, and publicly available ACT test that you are free to use and practice with. There are, of course, also dozens of ACT prep books of all kinds.

The ACT also has a program called **Test Information Release** (or TIR). If you take the ACT exam in December, April, or June, you are eligible. Essentially, you can pay an extra fee to get back from the ACT your original answers to the test, the correct answers, and the questions themselves. This can help you see what is actually bringing your score down or up from the ACT's point of view.

What follows is the explanations to every practice question in this book. Thanks for using The ACT Math and Science System!

ACT Math

Explanations

Answer Explanations - Step 2

Correct answers:

Backsolving:	**Picking Numbers:**	**Drawn to Scale:**	**The Calculator:**
1: D	4: G	8: H	9: D
2: F	5: E		10: G
3: D	6: J		
	7: A		

1. Correct answer: **D**. The typical way to solve this problem would be to set up an equation and solve for your missing variable. Since this question is looking for an average, then we need to add up all relevant terms, divide by the number of terms, and set it equal to the average that is desired. In this case, such an equation would look like this:

$$\frac{(19 + 27 + 34 + 27 + x)}{5} = 30$$

After multiplying both sides by 5 so that the 5's cancel on the left hand side, we are left with this:

$$(19 + 27 + 34 + 27 + x) = 150 \, .$$

Then, of course, subtracting 19, 27, 34, and 27 from both sides, we are left with this:

$$x = 150 - 19 - 27 - 34 - 27 = 43$$

However, there is a reason that this example is under the *Backsolving* section; we can also solve by trying out answers one at a time and seeing if it is correct. Let's start in the middle with C: 34. When we do the math to determine the average, it looks like this:

$$\frac{(19 + 27 + 34 + 27 + 34)}{5} = \frac{141}{5} = 28.2$$

Thus, we see by *Backsolving* that answer choice C (34) is too low, and when we go higher to answer choice D (43), we do the math to find that it is the correct answer:

$$\frac{(19 + 27 + 34 + 27 + 43)}{5} = \frac{150}{5} = 30$$

2. Correct answer: **F**. Of course, this early into our book, we haven't yet discussed lines, the formula of a line, what it means for a line to have solutions, or for two lines to have a solution, etc. For our purposes here, we simply need to understand this: each of these five answer choices is an (x, y) coordinate, thus an x and a y value. When we plug in the answers one at a time (aka *Backsolving*), which of them satisfies the equation we've been given? Let's try them one at a time until we find the correct answer. Start with F:

$$5 + \frac{1}{2}(-4) = 5 - 2 = 3$$

…that's it! In other words, when we plug in $x = -4$ and $y = 5$ into the given equation, it *satisfies*, or also equals 3.

3. Correct answer: **D**. Here, to solve this problem without *Backsolving*, we need to begin with the number we know and work backwards. We know that 3,150 baseball bats are permanently damaged. We know also that these permanently damaged bats are 3 out of 4 damaged bats, and that then 1 out of 60 bats produced. First, let's figure out how many bats per year are are damaged. If 3,150 bats are permanently damaged, and this is 3 out of 4 damaged bats, then we can set up an equation like this to determine the number of damaged bats:

$$3,150 = (\frac{3}{4})(x)$$

In this equation, x represents the number of damaged bats, When solved, we get that there are 4,200 damaged bats every year. This isn't yet the correct answer. We also know that the 4,200 damaged bats are only $\frac{1}{60}$ of all bats produced. Thus, if we multiply the number of damaged bats by 60, we will learn the number of bats produced in the manufacturing facility each week:

$$4,200 \times 60 = 252,000$$

However, of course *Backsolving* is another means to solve the problem. If you're stuck and can't quite figure out the forwards math one step at a time, why not simply try out the answer choices one at a time? Let's start with answer choice C (141,750) and pretend that this is how many bats are produced each week. First, we reduce it to $\frac{1}{60}$ of its size to find how many damaged bats there are, then multiply this new number by 0.75 (or multiply by $\frac{3}{4}$) to find the permanently damaged ones:

$$141,750 \times \frac{1}{60} = 2362.5, \text{ then}\dots 2362.5 \times \frac{3}{4} = 1771.875$$

This number is far lower than our given 3,150 permanently damaged bats. Thus, going higher to answer choice D (252,000) will yield the correct answer.

4. Correct answer: **G**. This problem would normally require us to simplify, add like terms, and simplify some more. However, let's use the *Picking Numbers* strategy first to solve, then we'll look at a more traditional way. Because the correct answer choice is equivalent to the polynomial in the question stem (that just means the question itself), and because both have the variable x, then let's choose a number for x, plug it into the question to get a value, then see which answer choice also gives us the same value when we plug in the same number for x. When choosing a value for x, you want to avoid numbers like -1, 0, and 1; go a little bit bigger. Let's pretend that $x = 4$. Plugging that into the question looks like this:

$$\frac{(4^2 - (5 \times 4) - 6)}{(4 + 1)} + 4 + 1 = \frac{(16 - 20 - 6)}{5} + 5 = \frac{-10}{5} + 5 = -2 + 5 = 3$$

So, if the polynomial in the question itself $= 3$ when $x = 4$, then all we have to do is plug $x = 4$ into each answer choice one at a time until we get a value of 4. Starting with F, we get $4 - 5 = -1$, not 3. Try again. Moving onto G, we get $2(4) - 5 = 8 - 5 = 3$. That's it!

The more traditional way to solve this problem involves simplifying, which would require us to factor first. I say that because in the numerator of the question, we have a trinomial: $x^2 - 5x - 6$. A trinomial will factor into two binomials, to look something like this (I'm making up these numbers): $(x - 4)(x + 7)$. Does that look familiar? That is the kind of form we have to get this trinomial into. So that we can (more than likely) cancel out the term in the denominator (the $x + 1$).

To factor a trinomial into two binomials, we need to find two numbers that *multiply* to give us the last number in the trinomial (in our case, -6) that also *add together* to give us our middle number (in our case, -5). There are four pairs of numbers that multiply to give us -6: -3×2, -2×3, 6×-1, and -6×1. But, which pair of them also add up together to equal -5? That would be the last pair in the sequence: -6×1. These two numbers are going to be added to an x term in each of our two binomials that result from the factoring of a trinomial.

Thus, here is how our trinomial breaks down when factored: $x^2 - 5x - 6 = (x - 6)(x + 1)$. Having accomplished this step, we can now write out our entire equation, replacing the trinomial with the two resulting binomials so as to cancel them out. Once they are canceled, we can then simplify and add like terms, like so:

$$\left(\frac{x^2 - 5x - 6}{x + 1}\right) + x + 1 = \frac{(x - 6)(x + 1)}{x + 1} + x + 1 = (x - 6) + x + 1 = 2x - 5.$$

5. Correct answer: **E**. Because this problem, again, is in the *Picking Numbers* section, let's use that strategy first to solve. Then, we will solve it in the more traditional way. If we're looking for an average, that means adding all terms together and then dividing by the number of terms. Here, we have 4 terms, all of which contain the variable a. Let's pick a number for a, then find the average, then apply that same value for a into the answer choices until we find the same average.

When utilizing *Picking Numbers*, avoid really small numbers for variables, like -1, 0, and 1. Let's pretend in this case that $a = 5$ and go from there. If $a = 5$, then our four terms become actual values, like this:

First: $\qquad\qquad 3a^2 - 7 = 3(5)^2 - 7 = 75 - 7 = 68$

Second:	$2a^2 + 1 = 2(5)^2 + 1 = 50 + 1 = 51$
Third:	$-4a^2 + 12 = -4(5)^2 + 12 = -100 + 12 = -88$
Fourth:	$3a^2 - 2 = 3(5)^2 - 2 = 75 - 2 = 73$

So, when $a = 5$, our terms become 68, 51, -88, and 73. Let's add them together and divide by 4 to find the average:

$$\frac{68 + 51 - 88 + 73}{4} = \frac{104}{4} = 26$$

Now, we need to simply plug in $a = 5$ into our answer choices one at a time and see which of them is equal to 26. Starting with A, we get the following: $-a^2 + 1 = -25 + 1 = -24$, so this choice is incorrect. Now move on to B: $\frac{1}{2}a^2 + 1 = 12.5 + 1 = 13.5$, also incorrect. Now let's try C: $a^2 + \frac{1}{2} = 25 + \frac{1}{2} = 25.5$, also wrong. Now try D: $-a^2 + \frac{1}{2} = -25 + \frac{1}{2} = -24.5$, still wrong! That leaves us with only one choice, E: $a^2 + 1 = 25 + 1 = 26$, that's it!

Hopefully, you'll be able to do some of this math in your head and see more quickly than it took you to read this paragraph that the correct answer is E!

Now for a more traditional solving. If you don't want to pick numbers in this particular problem, then don't worry, you don't have to. All you have to do is treat these four terms just like numbers, meaning: add the four terms together and divide by 4, like this:

$$\frac{(3a^2 - 7) + (2a^2 + 1) + (-4a^2 + 12) + (3a^2 - 2)}{4}$$

You must be careful now to add like terms without making a simple mistake. Start with the a^2 terms, then the whole numbers:

$$\frac{(3a^2 - 7) + (2a^2 + 1) + (-4a^2 + 12) + (3a^2 - 2)}{4} = \frac{(3a^2 + 2a^2 - 4a^2 + 3a^2) + (-7 + 1 + 12 - 2)}{4} = \frac{4a^2 + 4}{4} = a^2 + 1$$

6. Correct answer: **J**. The absolute best way to solve this particular problem is to invent a certain number of people in line to buy ice cream (aka, *Picking Numbers*), apply the percentage changes to this number of people one day at a time, and then figure out the percent increase at the end. Many students on a problem like this simply attempt to add the percentages together (in this case, 35% + 40% = 75%), but that will be incorrect since the 40% "step" in this problem is applied *after* an initial 35% change has happened.

Step 1: Let's assume that the number of people in line to buy ice cream is initially 100. Why 100? Not only is it easy to apply percent changes to 100 (since, after all, 100 is the baseline for all percentages), but it is also easy to see a percent change when compared to an initial number of 100 in the very end of the problem.

Step 2: Increase our starting point by 35%. To increase a number by 35%, we must multiply it by 1.35. Thus, a 35% increase of our initial 100 people in line looks like this: $100(1.35) = 135$.

Step 3: Increase this new number of people in line by another 40%. Using the same math as the previous step, this increase looks like this: $135(1.4) = 189$.

Step 4: We began with 100 people in line, then after our two subsequent percent increases, went up to 189 people in line. Thus, it is easy to see that the combined percent increase over the two increases is 89%.

7. Correct answer: **A**. This question requires some logical thinking, some *Picking Numbers*, and some math skill as well. Before we do any of that, let's wrap our minds around what is actually being asked: which variable, *a, b, c,* or *d* is the smallest; not the variable manipulated or changed in any way, but the actual variable itself. First, let's put the math skill to the test by rewriting the inequality in a form that makes more sense; in other words, we need to get rid of the negative exponents. To do so, the exponents need to be moved (if they're in the numerator they go to the denominator, or vice versa) as they are made positive. Like this:

$$a^{-2} > b^{-2} > c^{-2} > d^{-2} = \frac{1}{a^2} > \frac{1}{b^2} > \frac{1}{c^2} > \frac{1}{d^2}$$

Some with excellent thinking skills may be able to solve the problem by clear and concise thinking at this point, and if that is you, then that is good. However, most of us need to turn this into something more concrete, something more real, and to do that, we should pick numbers. In other words, let's choose values for a, b, c, and d that make the above inequality real. Let's just start with b and c and go from there. Let's choose that $b = 4$ and $c = 5$ and see if the inequality holds true. If not, we can reverse the terms.

$$\frac{1}{b^2} > \frac{1}{c^2} = \frac{1}{4^2} > \frac{1}{5^2} = \frac{1}{16} > \frac{1}{25}$$

Now the question is this: is it true that $\frac{1}{16}$ is greater than $\frac{1}{25}$? Yes, it is true. We chose correctly the first time for b and c. Now, let's pick numbers for a and d that also make the inequality true. How about $a = 3$ and $b = 6$. When we do that, our inequality now looks like this:

$$\frac{1}{a^2} > \frac{1}{b^2} > \frac{1}{c^2} > \frac{1}{d^2} = \frac{1}{3^2} > \frac{1}{4^2} > \frac{1}{5^2} > \frac{1}{6^2} = \frac{1}{9} > \frac{1}{16} > \frac{1}{25} > \frac{1}{36}$$

Now, let's recall the actual question: "which of the following numbers has the least value"? A lot of students here will see, and correctly, that $\frac{1}{36}$ is the smallest of the values in our hypothetical inequality, and because $\frac{1}{36} = \frac{1}{d^2}$, students will then say that the correct answer to the question is d. However, that would be wrong. The question asks for which *variable* is the smallest of the four, not which manipulated variable is the smallest. Remember the numbers we picked to make the inequality true: $a = 3$, $b = 4$, $c = 5$, $d = 6$. Thus, d is actually the largest variable, and a is the smallest. This is why a is the correct answer. To make the inequality true, it must be the smallest of the 4 options.

8. Correct answer: **H**. Before we use any kind of knowledge of angles to accurately solve this problem, let's use the strategy that is being taught here: the *Drawn to Scale* strategy. The angle that is being asked about is $\angle ACB$. Tilt your paper so that segment CB is flat, or the bottom of a triangle. Now…what angle does it simply *look like*? It should look pretty close to a 90° angle, maybe slightly smaller. There is only one angle that is close to 90°, which is H: 85°. That is all you need to get this particular question correct.

Mathematically speaking, what is at play here is a law called the Law of Transversals; more information about this law is found in the lesson Math *Have to Know* #10 on angles. Simply put, because this shape is a parallelogram, that means that segments AD and BC are parallel, as are segments AB and DC. Because we know that $\angle FDA$ is 115°, we also know that $\angle DAB$ is 115°. If $\angle DAB$ is 115°, and $\angle CAB$ is 30°, then we also know that $\angle DAC$ is $(115° - 30°) = 85°$. Without getting into every detail of how the Law of Transversals works (again, see Math *Have to Know* Strategy #10), $\angle DAC$, which we have just learned is 85°, is the exact same as $\angle ACB$. Thus, $\angle ACB$ must also equal 85°.

9. Correct answer: **D**. Again, you may have been taught to find a common denominator between these three fractions, then edit the fraction so that it is equivalent to the original, then add the fractions, then simplify the new fraction to find your answer. There's nothing wrong with that at all, except that it is time consuming. And guess what you don't have a lot of on the ACT Math test? Time. Instead, use the calculator to your advantage and save yourself precious seconds. When I type these terms into the calculator and add them, here's what I get:

$$\frac{4}{17} + \frac{1}{2} + \frac{1}{68} = 0.2353 + 0.5 + 0.0147 = 0.75$$

Of course, converting 0.75 into a fraction isn't too terribly difficult. If you were given a difficult decimal, say something like 0.4358, then work your way through the answer choices one at a time, dividing the fractions in your calculator until you find a match.

10. Correct answer: **G**. In the correct ordering of this inequality, the danger is in students attempting to do the work all in the head and making a simple mistake. Here, we are given a fraction (⅓) to put in correct order with decimals. Simply type the fraction, whatever it is, into the calculator to also make it a decimal before comparing. Of course, this fraction is the equivalent of 0.33, so now we have 3 fractions that we simply need to order correctly: 0.33, 0.3, and 0.04. Because the inequalities in the answers start with the largest and move to the smallest, let's identify them from greatest to least. Well, it just so happens that I just did that when I listed them a moment ago: 0.33 is the largest, then 0.3, then 0.04. So, our inequality needs to begin with (⅓) as the largest. Only G does this, and double checking, it lists the others in proper order as well.

Answer Explanations - Step 3

Correct answers:

1: B	11: C	21: D	31: E	41: A	51: B
2: G	12: K	22: K	32: K	42: K	52: K
3: B	13: B	23: C	33: C	43: D	53: C
4: K	14: H	24: J	34: G	44: H	54: F
5: A	15: E	25: B	35: A	45: B	55: B
6: K	16: F	26: K	36: J	46: K	56: F
7: A	17: B	27: E	37: A	47: A	57: C
8: H	18: H	28: G	38: J	48: H	58: H
9: E	19: D	29: D	39: C	49: B	59: E
10: K	20: F	30: J	40: G	50: F	60: G

1. Correct answer: **B**. The estimate for the total job was $1,950, which includes the fee that is charged no matter how much fence is installed. Thus, ($1,950 − $600) = $1,350 represents the amount of money that is actually spent on fence installation. Because Cliff wants 150 feet of fence, then determining the cost per foot of fence for the installation is now a simple division problem: ($1,350 ÷ 150) = 9. Thus, Baldwin Fence, Inc. charges $9 per foot of fence.

2. Correct answer: **G**. A significant-enough number of ACT Math questions describe a shape or a diagram; sometimes it's a triangle, other times a sphere, etc. The rule is this: if a shape is being described, then *draw it out*. This prevents simple mistakes and ensures that you get the answer correct (or at least maximizes your chances). Here, you simply need to draw a small rectangle and a larger rectangle around it, labeling it with the appropriate sizes.

Because this question is asking for the part of the wall *not* covered by the white board, we need to find the area of the larger board and subtract the area of the smaller white board from that. The area of the wall as a whole is this: (10ft × 9ft) = 90ft^2 . The area of the white board is (4ft × 7ft) = 28ft^2 . Thus, 90ft^2 − 28ft^2 = 62ft^2.

3. Correct answer: **B**. This question is a good example of a *ratio* question (more on that in *Have to Know* Lesson #8). A ratio or rate consists of two values that are in a relationship, like miles-per-hour, as in driving, or cups-of-flour-per-cups-of-sugar, as in a recipe. Although the question itself, especially in a modeling situation as we have here, is extremely unlikely to frame it this way, it is necessary for you to rewrite the ratios as fractions, which will set up a cross-multiplying situation that is much easier to solve. Here, we are working with water-per-tablespoons-of-coffee to make a strong coffee. Here is the recipe he reads about online, rewritten as water-per-tablespoons-of-coffee (water in the numerator, tablespoons of coffee in the denominator:

$$\frac{\frac{2}{3}}{1\frac{1}{4}} \text{ cups of water/tablespoons of coffee grounds}$$

As a reminder, the question is asking us to find how many coffee grounds would be needed if he has $2\frac{1}{2}$ cups of water. Thus, we can set up a cross-multiplying equation to solve for our missing amount of coffee grounds (let's call it x) that looks like this:

$$\frac{\frac{2}{3}}{1\frac{1}{4}} = \frac{2\frac{1}{2}}{x}$$

Cross multiplying, as a reminder, means multiplying the numerator of one term by the denominator of the other, then vice versa, and setting them equal to each other. For us, that would result in this:

$$\frac{2}{3}x = (2\frac{1}{2})(1\frac{1}{4})$$

Personally, whenever I'm dealing with multiplying or dividing fractions on the ACT, I almost always convert them to decimals. Otherwise, we have to change the values of the two terms on the right to get rid of the leading coefficients of 2 and 1. Solve from here however you like, but I'm going to change to decimals, like this, and solve for x:

$$0.667x = (2.5)(1.25)\dots x = \frac{(2.5)(1.25)}{0.667}\dots x = 4.685 \text{ tablespoons of coffee needed.}$$

Because the answer choices are in fractions, I simply need to go one at a time and determine which is equivalent to 4.685. It must be B or C since the two of them begin with a 4. When I type $4\frac{11}{16}$ into the calculator, I get something very close to 4.685 (there's bound to be fractional error since I rounded $\frac{2}{3}$ to 0.667). Thus, B is correct.

4. Correct answer: **K.** In this example, the starting values of the two stocks is irrelevant; what is relevant is the difference between them, which is $30. The question can be simplified perhaps by first realizing this: how long, then, will it take for Stock A to gain $30 on Stock B? If Stock A is going to increase by $1 a day, and Stock B is going to increase by $0.50 a day, then that means that Stock A is going to gain $0.50 a day on Stock B. So, if Stock A, relatively speaking, increases by $0.50 a day, then how long will it then take it to gain the $30 necessary? The result of this simple division will be our answer:

$$\frac{\$30}{\$0.50} = 60,$$ thus, 60 total days for the two stocks to reach the same value.

5. Correct answer: **A.** The biggest danger in this problem is making a simple mistake (as in many ACT Math problems). The mistake to be made is this: see that minus sign straight in the middle, between the two terms? That minus sign means that *everything* to the right of it must be subtracted, one term at a time. Let's take this one step at a time:

Step 1: Distribute each y term to look like this:

$$y(6 - y) - y(y + 9) = (6y - y^2) - (y^2 + 9y)$$

Step 2: Add like terms. Again, the two terms in the rightmost parentheses (y^2 and $9y$) must *both* be subtracted, like this:

$$(6y - y^2) - (y^2 + 9y) = (6y - 9y) + (-y^2 - y^2) = -3y - 2y^2$$

This corresponds, meaning is the same thing as, choice A: $-2y^2 - 3y$.

If you're scared of making a simple mistake, recognize that this question is a strong candidate for the *Picking Numbers* strategy, since the question and answer both have a variable. Choose a value for y, something like $y = 3$, plug it into the question and answers, and look for a match!

6. Correct answer: **K.** There are two ways to solve this problem. First, you can use *Picking Numbers*, choose a value for both x and y, then plug those values into the question and answers and find a match. Another way is to simply simplify the complicated expression one step at a time. This is what we'll do here. The first thing to do is to work on the term in the numerator, since you have multiple terms being raised together to the 4th power, like this: $(3x^{-2}\sqrt{y})^4$. To get rid of that 4th power, it must be applied to each term one at a time, like this:

$$(3x^{-2}\sqrt{y})^4 = 3^4(x^{-2})^4(\sqrt{y})^4 = 3^4(x^{-2})^4(y^{\frac{1}{2}})^4$$

Notice that I changed the last term, the $\sqrt{y}$ to a y raised to the power of $\frac{1}{2}$. These two terms are equivalent, and for our purposes it will be easier to work with. Now, the first term is simple enough. $3^4 = 81$. This is enough for us to go ahead and eliminate answer options G and J, since there are no numbers in the denominator and the two of them do not have the number 81 in them. It is the next two terms where students make mistakes. If you have a value with an exponent being raised to *another* exponent, you multiply the exponents together, like this:

$$3^4(x^{-2})^4(y^{\frac{1}{2}})^4 = 81(x^{-2 \cdot 4})(y^{\frac{1}{2} \cdot 4}) = 81x^{-8}y^2$$

Because the term in the numerator in the original question was already in this kind of form, let's put the two together now: our newer, simplified numerator over the original denominator:

$$\frac{81x^{-8}y^2}{x^2y^{-5}}$$

From here, you next need to know what to do with negative exponents. It is simple enough: make the exponent positive and reciprocate it (if it's in the numerator, move it to the denominator, and vice versa). Thus, our expression gets simplified to this:

$$\frac{81x^{-8}y^2}{x^2y^{-5}} = \frac{81y^5y^2}{x^2x^8}$$

Lastly, you need to know what to do with like terms with exponents that are multiplied together. Here, you *add* the exponents together, like this:

$$\frac{81y^5y^2}{x^2x^8} = \frac{81y^{5+2}}{x^{2+8}} = \frac{81y^7}{x^{10}}, \text{ which is choice K.}$$

7. Correct answer: **A.** There are two ways to solve this problem. The first is to use *Picking Numbers* and choose a value for a, then plug that into both the question and the answers. The second way is to find common denominators for the fractions in both the numerator and denominator, then properly divide. Let's solve it both ways.

First, *Picking Numbers*. Let's pretend that $a = 4$ so that the fraction of which is a part will simply equal 1. Now, I'm also going to convert all of these fractions to decimals, that way I can solve the entire thing in my calculator, like this:

$$\frac{\frac{a}{4} + \frac{1}{3}}{\frac{1}{2} - \frac{1}{3}} = \frac{1 + 0.333}{0.5 - 0.333} = \frac{1.333}{0.167} = 7.982$$

Now the question is this: which of the five answer choices equals approximately 7.982 when a has a value of 4? You can tell that when I say "approximately 7.982" that that really is probably going to mean 8; there is a bit off error when you round off fractions to the nearest decimal (which we did twice in the equation above). When you plug in $a = 4$ into answer choice A, you get $\frac{3(4) + 4}{2} = \frac{16}{2} = 8$…that's it!

Second, we can solve the "proper" way. The first step here is to find common denominators and rewrite the fractions equivalently with their new denominators, like this:

$$\frac{\frac{a}{4} + \frac{1}{3}}{\frac{1}{2} - \frac{1}{3}} = \frac{\frac{3a}{12} + \frac{4}{12}}{\frac{3}{6} - \frac{2}{6}} = \frac{\frac{3a+4}{12}}{\frac{1}{6}}$$

The second step is to divide the fraction in the numerator by the fraction in the denominator. This is one of those tricky little steps that many students forget how to do, but it is fairly simple. Take the fraction in the denominator, reciprocate it (aka flip it), and then multiply it by the fraction in the numerator, like this:

$$\frac{\frac{3a+4}{12}}{\frac{1}{6}} = (\frac{3a+4}{12})(\frac{6}{1})$$

From there, simply multiply, and then simplify:

$$(\frac{3a+4}{12})(\frac{6}{1}) = \frac{18a+24}{12} = \frac{3a+4}{2}$$

8. Correct answer: **H.** Again, there are two ways to solve this problem. You can use *Picking Numbers*, which would mean choosing a value for x and applying it to the question and finding a match in the answers. In fact, unless you are fast at simplifying trinomials (which is a necessary step in solving this problem the "proper" way), then this is what you should do. The second way to solve it, as I said, is to factor the trinomials in the numerator and denominator and then cancel out like terms (you can learn more about factoring trinomials in *Good to Know* Lesson #5: Parabolas). Let's solve it both ways.

First, *Picking Numbers*. Let's assume that $x = 3$ and see what value we get. Plugging in $x = 3$, our expression is reduced like this:

$$\frac{(x^2 + 5x + 4)(x - 8)}{(x^2 - 7x - 8)(x + 2)} = \frac{(3^2 + 5(3) + 4)(3 - 8)}{(3^2 - 7(3) - 8)(3 + 2)} = \frac{(9 + 15 + 4)(-5)}{(9 - 21 - 8)(5)} = \frac{28(-5)}{-20(5)} = \frac{-140}{-100} = \frac{7}{5}$$

Then, we must plug in $x = 3$ into each answer choice until we get an answer that also equals seven fifths. Because the math here is simple enough, I can look ahead and see that H is going to give me what I'm looking for, like this:

$$\frac{x+4}{x+2} = \frac{3+4}{3+2} = \frac{7}{5}$$

Second, we can factor the trinomials in both the numerator and denominator and simplify by canceling out like terms. The trinomials I am talking about are the expressions in the numerator and denominator that feature an x^2 term. Let's simplify each trinomial one at a time, starting with $(x^2 + 5x + 4)$. A simplified trinomial will result in two binomials (x plus or minus some number) times (x plus or minus some number). To figure out those "some number"s, we need to ask ourselves this question about this trinomial in particular: what are two numbers that *multiply* to equal the last term in the trinomial (4), but also *add* to equal the middle number in the trinomial (5)? Well, $(4 \times 1) = 4$, and $(4 + 1) = 5$, so we've found our two "some number"s, which are 4 and 1. Thus, our factored trinomial looks like this:

$$(x^2 + 5x + 4) = (x + 4)(x + 1)$$

We have to do the same thing to the trinomial in the denominator: $(x^2 - 7x - 8)$. We need two numbers that *multiply* to give us -8 and add together to give us -7. There are lots of numbers that multiply to give us -8 (like 4 times -2, and -1 times 8), but only one pair that also adds up to -7: -8 and 1. Thus, our factored trinomial looks like this:

$$(x^2 - 7x - 8) = (x - 8)(x + 1)$$

Let's rewrite the entire expression with our trinomials factored, then cancel out like terms. In other words, if a binomial appears in the numerator and in the denominator (like you're about to see with $(x + 1)$), then they simply cancel out. Our work now looks like this:

$$\frac{(x^2 + 5x + 4)(x - 8)}{(x^2 - 7x - 8)(x + 2)} = \frac{(x + 4)(x + 1))(x - 8)}{(x - 8)(x + 1)(x + 2)} = \frac{(x + 4)}{(x + 2)}, \text{ which is answer choice H.}$$

9. Correct answer: **E.** The easiest way to conceptualize this problem is to invent your own number set (*Picking Numbers*, essentially) and do the math that the question is asking. The question presupposes that we have a number set consisting of 5 numbers, and it doesn't really matter what those five numbers are. How about we use this set for our purposes: {1, 1, 1, 1, 1}. Right now, the mean or average is 1. The question asks us this: if we increase the mean by 5, how much would the sum of the numbers increase? Well, our current mean is 1, and to increase it by 5 would mean we'd have to have a number set with a mean of 6, something that now looks like this: {6, 6, 6, 6, 6}. The sum of our previous number set was $(1+1+1+1+1) = 5$, and now the sum of our new number set is $(6+6+6+6+6) = 30$. Thus, the sum of the 5 numbers in our number set would have to increase by 25.

10. Correct answer: **K.** Here, we are asked for the product of the mean and the median of a number set. Before we get to that, we have to figure out what the number set even is! We are told that the number set is each factor of 12 listed in numerical order.

A factor of a number is simply a number that evenly divides into that bigger number. The easiest way to figure out the factors of a given number is to determine all of the pairs that multiply to equal the bigger number. For 12, there are a few pairs that multiply to give us that number: $(1 \times 12 = 12)$, $(2 \times 6 = 12)$, and $(3 \times 4 = 12)$. Thus, the factors of 12 in numerical order, and our number set, is this: {1, 2, 3, 4, 6, 12}.

Next, the question requires us to determine the mean and the median. First, the mean of course is the average, which can be found as such: Mean = $(1+2+3+4+6+12)/6 = 4.667$. The median is the term in the middle, which falls between 3 and 4 in our number set. Thus we need the average of 3 and 4, which is 3.5.

Lastly, the problem asks for the *product* of the mean and the median. The product of two numbers is simply the result if you multiply them. So, our answer is going to result from multiplying the mean and the median that we just determined: $(4.667 \times 3.5) = 16.3345$, which falls between 16 and 17, which is answer choice K.

11. Correct answer: **C.** The difficulty of this problem really lies in the fact that it is a modeling problem; you have to get through the long story, plucking out the math you need along the way. The question requires us to compare the values of the mean, median, mode, and range of two separate number sets: before Author E arrives, and after Author E arrives, and then find which value is *least* changed.

I think the best way to visualize the changes, and see which changes the least, is to create two columns, one for before and one for after.

	Before	After
Number set:	{1, 1, 2, 3}	{1, 1, 2, 3, 21}

Mean (average):	$\dfrac{1+1+2+3}{4} = 1\dfrac{3}{4}$	$\dfrac{1+1+2+3+21}{5} = 5\dfrac{3}{5}$
Median (middle term):	1.5	2
Mode (appears most):	1	1
Range (difference):	$(3-1) = 2$	$(21-1) = 20$

Thus, the number that is changed the least is the mode, because it does not change at all. This is answer choice C.

12. Correct answer: **K.** This question is difficult because it isn't the first step in an equation, and it isn't the last step either. By that I mean that each answer choice is written in a form that has assumed that step or two has been done in the equation to determine the value of t. Let's do the math from the very beginning one step at a time until we get an equation that looks like the answers (featuring numbers like 77 and/or 96 and/or 16, etc.)

Because t represents an amount of tips, our initial equation can and should be written as such:

$$\frac{14+15+11+22+15+t}{6} = 16$$

The 6 in the denominator represents the number of tips received, or the number of nights in a row he receives tips. Because it is an average, we need the equation on the left (the total tips received divided by the number of tips) to equal the average we want, in this case 16. Now, there's just one step left to do to simplify:

$$\frac{(14+15+11+22+15)+t}{6} = 16 \quad \dots \quad \frac{77+t}{6} = 16, \text{ which is answer choice K.}$$

13. Correct answer: **B.** Working an inequality is almost the same as working any other equation (as a side note, for more on Inequalities, see *Good to Know* Lesson #4). You can add the same term to both sides, you can divide or multiply both sides by the same term, etc. The only exception is when multiplying or dividing both sides by a negative number. In that case, the inequality symbol will switch from facing one side to another.

In this problem, each answer choice features an isolated y on the left side of the inequality. Thus, we need to work the actual given inequality in the same fashion and solve for y. First, let's add $9x$ to both sides to isolate the y term on the left side, like this:

$$-3y - 9x > 3x - 6 \quad \dots \quad -3y > 12x - 6$$

At this point, we need to divide both sides by -3 so that the y is isolated by itself on the left side. However, as I said a moment ago, when an inequality is affected by a negative on both sides (NOT addition or subtraction of a negative number, but multiplication or division) then the inequality will switch from > to < or from < to > (or, for that matter, from ≥ to ≤ and ≤ to ≥). That is what is about to happen here:

$$-3y > 12x - 6 \quad \dots \quad y < -4x + 2$$

14. Correct answer: **H.** This kind of problem is extremely common on the ACT Math test. By "this kind of problem" I mean a problem in which a complicated-looking equation is presented with 3 or more missing variables. The *look* of it is intimidating, but this kind of problem is always (always, always, always) way simpler than it seems. The ACT is counting on many students looking at this equation and saying to themselves, "I have no idea what this means, and it is scary." However, don't be so hasty! The ACT on these kinds of problems will always give you the value of all but 1 of the missing variables and ask you to solve for that one missing variable. In this particular equation, there are 3 missing variables as written: P, b, and e. b is the number of bagels, which they give us in the final line of the question (3). e^{-4} is also given to us (0.075). That means that the only missing variable is P, which fortunately is already isolated on the left side of the equation.

I will admit that there is another math concept in this equation that might throw you off, which is that of *factorial*. This is what the ! means after the 4 (it is pronounced "4 factorial"). When you have a number "factorial" you simply multiply the number by each number as it is decreased by 1. For example, 4! is the same thing as $4 \times 3 \times 2 \times 1$.

All we have to do now is plug in the missing variables and put the entire thing into the calculator to find the missing probability of 3 bagels remaining in the display case. Let's rewrite the equation for P, replacing known variables and the 4! with numbers along the way:

$$P = \frac{4^b e^{-4}}{4!} = \frac{4^3(0.075)}{4(3)(2)(1)} = \frac{64(0.075)}{24} = \frac{4.8}{24} = 0.2$$

Thus, H (0.2) is the correct probability.

15. Correct answer: **E.** You don't need to have any concept of the use of the imaginary number i in higher mathematics to get this question correct, or any other question in ACT Math for that matter. Here, simply FOIL the terms one at a time, and any time you get an i^2, simply change it to a -1. As a reminder, FOIL is an acronym that stands for "first, outside, inside, last," and simply refers to an order in which you could multiply terms when two binomials are being multiplied one by another. This particular problem has you multiplying not 2, but 3 binomials all by each other. Let's simply start with the first 2 binomials, then when we've simplified it as best we can, let's add in the third binomial.

Here's what I mean; let's do this math first (and bring in the final $(i + 3)$ when we've simplified this):

$$(i + 1)(i - 4) = i^2 - 4i + i - 4 = i^2 - 3i - 4$$

This is what we get when we multiply the first two binomials together. However, we can't quite bring back and multiply by that third binomial quite yet. Remember: each i^2 is equivalent to -1, so we need to replace the i^2 term first with -1 and add like terms:

$$i^2 - 3i - 4 = -1 - 3i - 4 = -3i - 5$$

Thus, our first two binomials $((i + 1)(i - 4))$ is equivalent to $(-3i - 5)$. Now, let's bring back that third binomial and multiply it by our new, simplified binomial:

$$(-3i - 5)(i + 3) = -3i^2 - 5i - 9i - 15 = -3i^2 - 14i - 15$$

Now, we need to replace the i^2 term with a -1 as we did before and add any like terms to get our final answer:

$$-3i^2 - 14i - 15 = -3(-1) - 14i - 15 = 3 - 14i - 15 = -14i - 12$$

Thus, our three binomials multiplied by each other can be simplified down to $-14i - 12$, or answer choice E.

16. Correct answer: **F.** In order to find the value of $\frac{a}{b}$, we have to, of course, determine the value of a and b. The difficulty is that a and b are both exponents. The trick here is in realizing that when $a = 1$, we get this: $16^1 = 16$. Because that number is much larger than $\sqrt{2}$, we need to figure out what value of b will raise $\sqrt{2}$ to a value of 16. Well, let's try out some different values (all of which you can simply do in your calculator if not in your head):

$$\sqrt{2}^2 = 2 \text{ , and then } \sqrt{2}^4 = 4 \text{, and then } \sqrt{2}^6 = 8 \text{, and then } \sqrt{2}^8 = 16.$$

Thus, when $a = 1$, then b has to equal 8 for the two sides of the equation to be equal to each other.

$$\text{So, } \frac{a}{b} = \frac{1}{8} \text{ , which is answer choice F.}$$

17. Correct answer: **B.** You might think that this problem really belongs in a lesson exclusively on triangles, and that would be true if there wasn't an equation given and you had to find the lengths of the sides of the triangle independently. However, we are in luck, because the ACT here has given us the Law of Sines to help us quickly identify the missing sides of the triangle. Essentially, if we know an angle and its opposite side, we can set that relationship equal to another angle and its opposite side and solve for whatever variable may be missing (thus, Algebra).

First, let's solve for the side opposite that of $41°$:

$$\frac{sin(a)}{A} = \frac{sin(b)}{B} \quad \cdots \quad \frac{sin(52)}{9} = \frac{sin(41)}{B} \quad \cdots \quad B = \frac{sin(41)(9)}{sin(52)} = 7.49$$

Next, we need to solve for the final side. This can be done in innumerable ways (see ACT Math *Have to Know* #9 on triangles for all of the ways). Let's keep using the Law of Sines, since it has been given to us. Let's call the final missing, bottom side C. However, we need the other, third angle that isn't given. But finding the missing angle is simple since the 3 angles in a triangle always add up to 180°. Thus our missing angle can be found by simple subtraction: $180° - 41° - 52° = 87°$. So, since we know the angle opposite our final missing side, let's do the same math as before using the Law of Sines:

$$\frac{sin(a)}{A} = \frac{sin(b)}{B} \quad ... \quad \frac{sin(52)}{9} = \frac{sin(87)}{C} \quad .... \quad C = \frac{sin(87)(9)}{sin(52)} = 11.41$$

Now that we have found the approximate lengths of the other two sides of the given triangle, we can answer the question, which asks for the perimeter to the nearest mile: $9 + 7.49 + 11.41 = 27.9$, or very near 28 miles.

18. Correct answer: **H.** Although this question is appearing under the *Higher Algebra* section of this ACT book, it would be unnecessary to create an equation to solve this problem. The first step in solving it is in actually understanding what the problem is asking. There are 12 mannequins, and each has at least 1 item on it. How many mannequins can display 4 items if each mannequin has at least one item on it?

I think the more efficient way to answer this question is to do some kind of visual representation of the 12 mannequins. Here, each capital 'M' represents a mannequin. Next to each 'M' you'll notice one lowercase 'i', which represents an item.

M: i	M: i	M: i	M: i
M: i	M: i	M: i	M: i
M: i	M: i	M: i	M: i

Now, I've made sure that each of the 12 mannequins has at least 1 item. Since the question states that I only have 25 items to put on the mannequins in the first place, that means I only have 13 items left to distribute. At this point, I need to distribute the 13 items so that mannequins now get full with 4 items:

M: iiii	M: iiii	M: i	M: i
M: iiii	M: ii	M: i	M: i
M: iiii	M: i	M: i	M: i

Although I was able to add extra items to 5 more mannequins before I ran out, I was only able to fill up 4 of the mannequins with all 4 items. Thus, the answer is H.

19. Correct answer: **D.** We simply need to rewrite this line into slope-intercept form, which would mean isolating the y on the left side of the equation. When this is done, whatever coefficient is in front of the x on the right side of the equation is the slope. As a reminder, slope intercept form looks like this: $y = mx + b$, in which m is the slope and b is the y-intercept (where the line crosses the y-axis, though that isn't relevant for this particular problem). Simplifying the problem into this form looks like this:

$$5x - 2y = 7 \quad ... \quad -2y = -5x + 7 \quad ... \quad y = \frac{5}{2}x - \frac{7}{2}$$

Thus, now in slope-intercept form, we can see that the value of m, or the slope, is $\frac{5}{2}$.

20. Correct answer: **F.** Any point that a line touches is a solution for that line. Thus, for any line, there are an infinite number of solutions. However, if two lines cross one another, there is only going to be 1 solution for the two lines: the point where they cross. There are two ways to solve this particular problem. The more visual way would be to put both of these lines into slope-intercept form, graph them one at a time based on the y-intercept and slope, and try to manually see where they cross one another.

Another way to solve this problem would be to use *Backsolving* (which is what I would do), to simply try out the points one at a time. Plug each point's x and y values into each equation and see if it works or satisfies. Fair warning: to be sure, some of the wrong answer points (if not all of the wrong answers) are going to satisfy or be solutions for one line or another, but not both; only one of them is going to satisfy *both* lines' equations. Let's simply try them out one at a time and see which one satisfies both equations.

F. (1, 2): $x - 2y = -3 \quad ... \quad 1 - 2(2) = -3 \quad ... \quad -3 = -3 \quad ...$ so far so good; now the other

$3x - 4y = -5 \quad ... \quad 3(1) - 4(2) = -5 \quad ... \quad -5 = -5 \quad ...$ that's it!!!

Letter F, or point (1, 2), satisfies both equations, making it the correct answer. If you try any of the other points like we did above, it will satisfy one or neither, but not both. Just to give you an idea of what that looks like, take point G for example:

G. (−1, 1): $x - 2y = -3 \quad ... \quad -1 - 2(1) = -3 \quad ... \quad -3 = -3 \quad ...$ so far so good; now the other

$$3x - 4y = -5 \quad \dots \quad 3(-1) - 4(1) = -5 \quad \dots \quad -7 = -5 \quad \dots \quad \text{no, doesn't satisfy!}$$

21. Correct answer: D. I don't have the Midpoint Formula memorized, and even if I did, I wouldn't be using it to set up equations to answer questions involving midpoints. In this particular question, you are being asked to find the coordinates of E. You can think of the problem like this: the line segment DE starts at D $(-4, -2)$, then goes to the halfway point at the midpoint $(1, 3)$, and then continues on the same distance and direction to point E, which is what we need to find.

Well, let's just think about it. On the x-axis, we go from a point of -4 (the x coordinate of D) to a point of 1 (the x-coordinate of the midpoint), which is an increase of 5. Well, we simply need to go 5 more to find the x-coordinate of E, which takes us up to 6. This is already enough to get the question correct, since there is only one answer that has an x-coordinate of 6.
To be thorough, let's find the y-coordinate of E using the same logic. On the y-axis, we go from a point of -2 (the y coordinate of D) to a point of 3 (the y-coordinate of the midpoint), which is an increase of 5. Well, we simply need to go 5 more to find the y-coordinate of E, which takes us up to 8.

If the x-coordinate of E is 6, and the y-coordinate of E is 8, then that makes our final answer D: $(6, 8)$.

22. Correct answer: K. First, the questions is asking for the slope of line q, which is *perpendicular* to line p; this means that the two lines cross forming four $90°$ angles. Before we get into how to compare the slopes of two lines that are perpendicular, let's start here: we have to find the slope of line p.

Slope can simply be remembered as RISE over RUN; in other words, the change between 2 points on the y-axis over the change between the same 2 points on the x-axis. We are given 2 points for line p, which is enough to find its slope. Let's denote $(-3, 5)$ as point 1 and $(0, 4)$ as point 2.

$$slope = \frac{rise}{run} = \frac{(y2 - y1)}{(x2 - x1)} = \frac{4 - 5}{0 - -3} = \frac{-1}{3} = -\frac{1}{3}$$

You'll notice that the slope of line p, or $-\frac{1}{3}$, is one of the answer choices. However, we have to remember that we're looking for the slope of line q, which is *perpendicular* to line p. This doesn't mean that they have the same slope, but quite the opposite. The slope of line q is going to be the *negative reciprocal* of the slope of line p, which means this: make the slope negative, and flip it upside down (moving the numerator to the denominator and moving the denominator to the numerator). Thus the negative reciprocal of $-\frac{1}{3}$ is $-\frac{3}{1}$, or just 3. This is the answer we are looking for.

23. Correct answer: C. You do NOT need to have memorized the distance formula to get this question correct. I, the man typing out this ACT Math book, don't have the distance formula memorized. You don't need it. There is an easier way (which, mathematically, is what the distance formula is based upon in the first place). The easier way is this: simply draw a graph and plot the two points (as I've done below), then make out of them a triangle (as I've beautifully done below). You will notice that the distance between the two points (what the question is requiring us to find) is simply the hypotenuse of a triangle. Then, because we know the lengths of the other 2 sides of our triangle (labeled below), we can use the Pythagorean Theorem ($a^2 + b^2 = c^2$) to find our missing side.

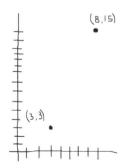
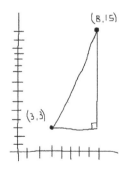
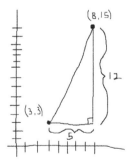

As you see in the last image above, I have labeled the length of the bottom side of the triangle 5. I know this length because it is simply the difference in x values between our two points; aka, $(8 - 3) = 5$. Similarly, I know the length of the right side of the triangle to be 12 because the difference in y values between our two points is $(15 - 3) = 12$.

You may be able to recognize this triangle as a *special triangle* (more on that in ACT Math *Good to Know* Lesson #2: Triangles Part II). This kind of special triangle is called a 5-12-13 triangle, meaning that we can know automatically that the length of the hypotenuse (aka the distance between the two points) is 13. However, let's use the Pythagorean Theorem as well to confirm:

$$a^2 + b^2 = c^2 \quad \ldots \quad (5)^2 + (12)^2 = c^2 \quad \ldots \quad 25 + 144 = c^2 \quad \ldots \quad 169 = c^2 \quad \ldots \quad 13 = c$$

24. Correct answer: J. This question is much easier than it seems. What makes it seem difficult is that there's a *t* variable monitoring time (which ends up being irrelevant) as well as a cloud moving across two-dimensional space (aka, on the (x, y) coordinate plane). Let's draw out what is happening here:

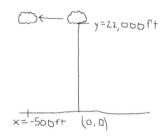

As you can see based on this expert drawing, the cloud is floating at a constant height of 22,000 feet. For our purposes, the path of the cloud floats along a straight line at 22,000 feet. In other words, at $y = 22,000$. If you go into your graphing calculator, hit the Y= button, type in any number (5, for example), then hit GRAPH, you're going to see a horizontal line across the screen from left to right. This is what is happening with this cloud; it is floating along the line $y = 22,000$.

25. Correct answer: B. In this problem, we are looking for values of x that can satisfy the equation $(x - a)(x - b) = 0$. Notice that both of the binomials are being multiplied by one another. This means that if either of them equals 0, then no matter what number the other may equal, the equation as a whole will equal 0. Thus, we simply need to find two values: one that will make the binomial on the left (aka $(x - a)$) equal 0, and another that will make the binomial on the right (aka $(x - b)$) also equal 0.

Well, if $x = a$, then in the binomial on the left, you will end up with this: $(a - a)$, which is equal to 0. In addition, if $x = b$, then in the binomial on the right, you will end up with this: $(b - b)$, which is also equal to 0. Thus, the two values of x that satisfy the equation are a and b, since these two values make the two binomials equal to 0.

26. Correct answer: K. In this question, all we know is that x is positive, y is positive, and z is negative, but we don't know how large or small they are. If we choose numbers for these three variables of all sizes, we will see that it is not possible to know what the sign of their average is. If x and y are small (let's say, 2 and 3), and z is a relatively large negative number (let's say -100), we could end up with an equation like this:

$$\text{Average} = \frac{2 + 3 - 100}{3} = -\frac{95}{3} \text{, which of course has a negative sign.}$$

On the other hand, if we choose relatively large values for x and y (let's say 100 and 200) and a relatively small value for z (say, -2), then we could end up with an equation like this:

$$\text{Average} = \frac{100 + 200 - 2}{3} = \frac{298}{3} \text{, which of course has a positive sign.}$$

Thus, because there are no constraints or limits on the size of x, y, and z, then it is not possible to determine.

27. Correct answer: E. Again, the key to these *Logical Thinking with Variables* problems is to choose values, eliminate possibilities, and repeat if necessary. As for this problem, let's pick numbers for x and y that are equivalent. For example, let's assume that $x = 2$ and $y = -2$. I want to do this because the answer choices set some versions of x and y equal to each other.

Answer choice A puts their absolute values equal to each other. Absolute value simply means the distance a value is from 0, and because 2 and -2 are both 2 spots from 0, it is true that the absolute value of x and y can be the same. As for options B, C, and D, each of them features some variation in which the values of x and y are squared, which is going to make them equal. If $y = -2$, then squaring it will make it $= 4$, which of course is the same as 2 squared. Thus, B, C, and D are all possible.

Answer choice E, on the other hand, is not possible. A negative exponent simply means that the value is flipped from the numerator to the denominator, like this:

$$x^{-1} = y^{-1} \quad \ldots \quad \frac{1}{x} = \frac{1}{y} \quad \ldots \quad \text{(plug in } x = 2 \text{ and } y = -2 \text{)} \quad \ldots \quad \frac{1}{2} = \frac{1}{-2} \quad \ldots \quad \text{can't be equal!}$$

28. Correct answer: G. In this problem, we are given very clear parameters as to the value of three variables: r, q, and p. Let's pick numbers for each of these based on the inequality constraint and see which we can eliminate. Remember: we can eliminate an option if it isn't true or can't be true (since we're looking for the option that *must* be true).

Let's assume that $r = -5$, $q = 60$, and $p = 700$.

F. $p + q < q + r$ ... $700 + 60 < 60 + (-5)$ ... this does not work; on to the next answer.

G. $\dfrac{p}{r} < \dfrac{q}{r}$ ... $\dfrac{700}{-5} < \dfrac{60}{-5}$ ... $-140 < -12$ ... this works! Let's try the rest:

H. $qr < pr$ ... $60(-5) < 700(-5)$ ... $-300 < -3,500$ ... this does not work...next!

J. $p < q - r$ ... $700 < 60 - (-5)$ ... $700 < 65$ ... this does not work...next!

K. $\dfrac{p}{r} < \dfrac{q}{r}$ ... This is the opposite of choice G, which gives us an option that does *not* work.

Thus, we can definitively say that G is the only option that *must* work!

29. Correct answer: **D**. You may think that this is a strange name to decide the name for your baby, and you'd be correct...but don't get distracted! We are looking for the probability that the name does *not* begin with the letter 'R', which means we need two numbers: the total number of names in the hat (which, we are told, is 12) and the number of names that do not begin with 'R', which is 4 (letter 'J') + 3 (letter 'P') + 2 (letter 'C'). Thus, our probability can be determined as follows:

$$\frac{4+3+2}{12} = \frac{9}{12} = \frac{3}{4}$$

30. Correct answer: **J**. The formula for the number of permutations n objects taken r at a time is as follows:

$$_nP_r = \frac{n!}{(n-r)!}$$

Thus, for our purposes here, 12 objects or items taken and arranged 3 at a time is equivalent to:

$$_nP_r = \frac{n!}{(n-r)!} = \frac{12!}{(12-3)!} \text{, or answer choice J.}$$

However, I'm guessing you don't have that formula memorized, and I don't think it will benefit you in the slightest if you do memorize it. What *could* be of great benefit to you, on the other hand, is if you use your noggin to figure out how to solve this problem in an alternative way. Simplify the problem a bit; instead of trying to figure out how to determine the number of ways to take and arrange 3 items from a total of 12 items, let's assume we want to take and arrange 1 item from a total of 5 items. In that case, there are exactly 5 ways to take 1 object out of a group of 5. Thus, plugging in 5 and 1 into the answer choices instead of 12 and 3, we will see that only one of them actually equals 5, which is choice J, like this:

$$\frac{5!}{(5-1)!} = \frac{5 \cdot 4 \cdot 3 \cdot 2 \cdot 1}{4 \cdot 3 \cdot 2 \cdot 1} = 5$$

It's been mentioned elsewhere in this book, but if you are confused about the exclamation point after these numbers, don't be; learning what this means is rather simple. The exclamation point is called "factorial", thus 5! is pronounced "5 factorial." Above you can see what it means; simply multiply 5 by each integer below it down to and including 1. Thus, $5! = 5 \cdot 4 \cdot 3 \cdot 2 \cdot 1 = 120$.

31. Correct answer: **E**. Here, we simply need to do a division problem by forming a fraction to determine the percent likelihood that the answer choices call for. There are 30 electives to choose from, so we know that is the total amount that will go in the denominator. As for the numerator, we are looking for the likelihood that the elective will take place at either the Intramural Fields (11 options) or the Dawson Building (7 options). Thus, our math looks like this:

$$\frac{11+7}{30} = \frac{18}{30} = 0.6 \text{, or } 60\%$$

32. Correct answer: **K**. The table of cars sold represents the number of cars that are likely to be sold on one day, but the question asks for how many cars are remaining on the lot after 5 days. Let's take this problem in steps.

Step 1: We need to find the expected outcome of the number of cars sold in a single day. To do that, we must add the multiplication of the number of cars sold by its probability. Here is how to calculate the expected outcome, aka, how many cars are expected to sell on the lot in a single day:

Expected cars sold in a day = 0(0.2) + 1(0.4) + 2(0.3) + 3(0.1) = 0 + 0.4 + 0.6 + 0.3 = 1.3

Now that we know that it is expected to sell 1.3 cars in a day, we can move on to step 2.

Step 2: We need now to find how many cars are expected to sell across 5 days. This is simple enough; we just need to take our expected outcome and multiply it by 5, like so: (5 · 1.3) = 6.5 . However, the problem asks us for how many cars are expected to be remaining in the lot after 5 working days. This means we need to subtract our 6.5 expected cars sold from the 120 that are in the lot at the beginning of the week, like so: (120 − 6.5) = 113.5, or answer choice K.

33. Correct answer: **C**. First, let's find 75% of 4. That is simply 4(0.75) = 3. Next, let's find 300% of 3. This is simply 3(3.00) = 9. As for their sum, that simply means that we add them together. In this case, the sum of 75% of 4 and 300% of 3 = 3 + 9 = 12, or answer C.

34. Correct answer: **G**. To solve this problem effectively, let's first convert the fraction $\frac{1}{8}$ into a decimal, which is 0.125. Thus, we are now looking for 1% of 0.125. Now, if I wanted to find 100% of 0.125, I would multiply it by 1.00. If I wanted to find 10% of 0.125, I would multiply it by 0.10. However, the question is asking for just 1% of 0.125, which means we need to multiply it by 0.01, like so:

$$0.125(0.01) = 0.00125, \text{ which is answer choice G.}$$

35. Correct answer: **A**. To answer this question correctly, we need to first add up the cost of the items. The total cost (pre-tax) of the items needed to create the ornament is $2.00 + $1.50 + $2.30 + $2.70 = $8.50. Now, this $8.50 is subject to an 8% sales tax, which means that the $8.50 needs to go up by 8%. There are two ways to do the math on this, which are exactly the same. Either:

$$\$8.50 \,(1.08) = \$9.18 \quad \dots \quad \text{or} \quad \dots \quad \$8.50 + \$8.50(0.08) = \$9.18$$

The question asks how much money she will have leftover after spending $10. Thus, the correct answer can be found in this way: $10.00 − $9.18 = $0.82, or 82 cents, option A.

36. Correct answer: **J**. It may seem like the way to solve this problem is to simply add 30% + 40% and get that the answer is 70%, but that isn't how it works. Mathematically speaking, because the number goes up by 30% before being affected by another 40%, the answer has to be *greater* than 70% of the original number, which already narrows down our answer choices.

However, to do the math effectively, let's use some *Picking Numbers*, and assume that there are 100 students who purchase ice cream on Monday. 100 is a good starting point because it will be easy to find the percent increase after the two iterations. If we get an answer in the end that 182 students purchased ice cream on Wednesday (an 82% increase over 100), we know the answer is J. If we get an answer in the end that 191 students purchased ice cream on Wednesday, we know the answer is K.

Monday to Tuesday there is a 30% increase, thus if we start with 100, we get this:

100(1.30) = 130, meaning that 130 students purchased ice cream on Tuesday.

Tuesday to Wednesday, there is a 40% increase, thus if we start with 130, we get this:

130(1.40) = 182, meaning that 182 students purchased ice cream on Wednesday.

As we said before, 182, when compared to our starting point of 100, represents an increase of 82%, or answer choice J.

37. Correct answer: **A**. An added difficulty to this question is that the question gives you a rate of inches, but asks for an answer in terms of feet. Don't let that confuse you; let's find the answer in inches that we're looking for, then simply divide by 12 to find the answer in feet.

Remember, we need to set up our ratio so that a metric will cancel out, leaving the metric we want in the numerator. In this case, we want inches in the numerator in our answer (let's call it x inches), so we need to set up an equation in which seconds cancels, leaving us a value in inches, that looks like this:

$$\frac{45 \text{ inches}}{2.5 \text{ seconds}} \cdot 10 \text{ seconds} = \frac{450 \text{ inches}}{2.5} = 180 \text{ inches}$$

Now, to find our final answer, we simply divide the 180 inches by 12 inches per foot and get a final answer of 15 feet, which is answer choice A.

38. Correct answer: **J.** Just like the above question, we are solving for kilometers, so we want centimeters to cancel. If we multiply our given ratio by the $2\frac{7}{10}$ centimeters, we need to structure the ratio so that kilometers is in the numerator and centimeters in the denominator. Also, don't let the fractions scare you. Simply rewrite them as decimals to make the math easier for the calculator. Our equation to solve will now look like this:

$$\frac{120 \text{ kilometers}}{0.25 \text{ centimeters}} \cdot 2.7 \text{ centimeters} = \frac{324 \text{ kilometers}}{0.25} = 1{,}296 \text{ kilometers}$$

Thus, the answer is J: 1,296 kilometers.

39. Correct answer: **C.** To solve this problem, play with the ratios until the number representing Tree B is the same in both ratios. Like this: if the ratio of Tree A to Tree B is 2:3, then it is also 4:6, 6:9, 8:12, 10:15, 12:18, and 14:21.

I stopped at 14:21 purposefully, since I can see that in the next ratio of Tree B to Tree C, it begins with the number 7, which divides into 21 (which is the value of Tree B where we left off). If the ratio of Tree B to Tree C is 7:5, then it is also 14:10, and then 21:15.

Here is what we now have:

The ratio of Tree A to Tree B is 14:21, and the ratio of Tree B to Tree C is 21:15. Because the Tree B's match, we can see that the ratio of Tree A to Tree C is 14:15, which is answer choice C.

40. Correct answer: **G.** The tangent of any angle, if you remember, is the opposite side over the adjacent side. The angle we are evaluating from is that of F, which just refers to the angle that touches the point F. Opposite point F is a side with length 12, and the adjacent side is the other side that isn't the hypotenuse, which has a length of 16. Thus, our equation looks like this:

$$\tan F = \frac{\text{opposite}}{\text{adjacent}} = \frac{12}{16} = \frac{3}{4}$$

Thus, the answer is G.

41. Correct answer: **A.** The first thing to note about this question is that it is *describing* a triangle, and not giving you a triangle. What that means is that it is important for you to draw it as it is being described in your answer booklet so that you can actually visualize what is happening. Does this mean that you've got to draw an actual tree with leaves and a man named Mr. Wilkins climbing a ladder? No, just a triangle, using the information we've got. I've done this below, and I've marked the missing side of the triangle that the question is asking for (which is the length of the ladder) as x:

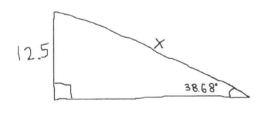

What we need now is an equation that uses the angle we know and the side we know in order to find our missing hypotenuse. Recall our acronym: SOHCAHTOA. Out of the S (sin), the C (cosine), and the T (tangent), one of them is of perfect use to us since it requires the use of the known and the missing sides. This would be sine, since the sine of any angle is defined as the opposite side over the hypotenuse.

Thus we can set up an equation like this, which is how we will solve for x:

$$\sin(38.68) = \frac{12.5}{x}$$

So far so good. Next, we need to solve for x by manipulating the equation so that x is isolated on one side. To do this, we need to first multiply both sides by x to remove it from the denominator, then divide both sides by the sin(38.68) to get the x all by itself, like this:

$$\sin(38.68)(x) = \frac{12.5}{x}(x) \quad \dots \quad \sin(38.68)(x) = 12.5 \quad \dots \quad \frac{\sin(38.68)(x)}{\sin(38.68)} = \frac{12.5}{\sin(38.68)}$$

After canceling out the sin(38.68) on the left side of the equation, we are left with a value for x that can easily be put in the calculator, like this:

$$x = \frac{12.5}{\sin(38.68)} = 20.00 \text{ , meaning that the ladder height (the hypotenuse) is closest to 20 feet.}$$

42. Correct answer: K. You may notice that the length of segment *RM*, which we must find to answer the question, is not actually drawn on this diagram. That means that it is up to you to draw a new diagram or shape to help visualize what you need to do to find this length. Below is such a drawing.

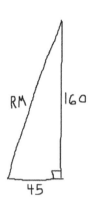

You'll notice, too, that the length of segment *RM* is the hypotenuse of a triangle. Because we know that the length top to bottom of the retail space is 160 meters, we know that the length of the right side of the triangle is also 160 meters. Lastly, because we know that point *R* is the midpoint of segment *LO* at the top, which is 90 meters, we know that half of the segment *MN* at the bottom is 45 meters. Thus, here is our triangle with our one missing side.

Because it is a right triangle, and because there is only 1 missing side, we can of course use the Pythagorean Theorem to find that missing side. As a reminder, the Pythagorean Theorem says that $a^2 + b^2 = c^2$, in which *c* is the hypotenuse and *a* and *b* are the two legs. In the equation below, I'm going to use *c*, but just recognize that *c* and *RM* are the same thing.

$$(45)^2 + (160)^2 = c^2 \quad \dots \quad 27{,}625 = c^2 \quad \dots \quad \sqrt{27{,}625} = \sqrt{c^2} \quad \dots \quad c = 166.21$$

Because the question asks for the length to the nearest meter, we round down to 166, which is answer choice K.

43. Correct answer: D. Fortunately, this question requires the same "triangle" we used in the above question. I'm going to redraw this triangle with information that we know, including the points on the diagram, and simply mark the angle we are looking for as $x°$.

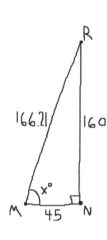

Hopefully, when you first answered this problem, you either drew a brand new triangle like I have done here, or you at least made markings on the original diagram. This is how to avoid simple mistakes. Now, because we know that one angle is 90°, we would be able to easily find our required missing angle (again, called $x°$ on the diagram to the left) if we knew the uppermost angle, or angle *MRN*. But, we don't, so we have to fall back onto another way, which is using the trig functions represented by the acronym SOHCAHTOA.

My default is to use sine if possible, and it is possible here. The difficulty in this problem however is that it isn't a side that is missing, but an *angle*, which means that we are going to have to get into a concept called arcsin (on your calculator it looks like this, $\sin^{-1}$ and is probably a 2nd function above the sin button). This function is used to find a missing angle when the value of sin (aka, the opposite side over the hypotenuse) is known.

Before we actually use arcsin, let's set up what this equation looks like in its original form:

$$\sin(x) = \frac{\text{opposite}}{\text{hypotenuse}} = \frac{160}{166.21} = 0.9626, \text{ or in short, } \sin(x) = 0.9626$$

Now that we have the value of sin, which is 0.9626, the time has come to use arcsin. When done properly, this will give us the missing angle value, and thus our correct answer. To do this, type arcsin (again, you probably on your calculator hit 2nd, then sin), then input the 0.9626 in parentheses following, then hit Enter, like so:

$$\sin(x) = 0.9626 \quad \dots \quad \sin^{-1}(0.9626) = x° \quad \dots \quad x° = 74.28°$$

If you need practice on this, try using arccos and arctan from the exact same angle, and see if you can get the same value for $x°$.

44. Correct answer: H. This problem is similar to the last couple of them in that you are asked to find the distance between two points that ends up being the hypotenuse of a triangle. Here, we are running a point diagonal across a square made up of 4 sides, each with a length of 45 meters. Below I have drawn the triangle we are working with.

Again, the length we are looking for is the hypotenuse of this little triangle. A too-quick student might guess that the correct answer is 45 because this is part of a square. However, this is the diagonal of the square, not a side, which is longer than any of the sides. A simple use of the Pythagorean Theorem is enough to help us find the missing side. Because the Theorem is $a^2 + b^2 = c^2$, I'm going to call the missing side of our triangle here *c*.

$$a^2 + b^2 = c^2 \quad \ldots \quad (45)^2 + (45)^2 = c^2 \quad \ldots \quad 4{,}050 = c^2 \quad \ldots \quad \sqrt{4050} = \sqrt{c^2} \quad \ldots \quad c = 63.64$$

The question asks for the length of the extension cord that runs from L to S to the nearest meter; rounding up, that would be 64 meters, or answer choice H.

45. Correct answer: B. First of all, before we get into the actual mathematics of this particular question, remember our ACT Math mini-strategy #3: *Drawn to Scale*. Every figure on the ACT *is* drawn to scale. In other words, if a line *looks* like it is twice the length of another line, that's because it *is* twice the length of another line, and if an angle *looks* like it is about 135°, that's because it *is* about 135°. If you turn your paper sideways and put line segment *CD* horizontal, doesn't our missing angle *look* like it is about 45° or so? How many answer choices, given the look of the angle, actually *look* like they could be correct answers?

Before definitively answering that question, on to the math. There are two concepts that we need to remember to get this question right. First, that the angles in a line add up to 180°, and second that the angles in a triangle also add up to 180°. With that in mind, let's break this problem down into two steps:

Step 1: If angle *ABC* is 155°, then that means that angle *CBD* (the smallest angle inside the triangle) is 180° − 155° = 25°. Similarly, if angle *CDE* is 80°, then that means that angle *CDB* (the other angle inside the triangle) is 180° − 80° = 100°.

Step 2: We now know two out of three angle values within the triangle *BCD*. This means that we simply need to subtract the two angles that we've figured out from 180° to determine our missing angle, like so: 180° − 25° − 100° = 55°, which is the correct answer.

In closing, back to the *Drawn to Scale* strategy we discussed at the beginning of this answer explanation. Do you see it now? Angle *CDB* is very, very close (just by looks!) to a 45° angle, making the only conceivable answer B: 55°.

46. Correct answer: K. Don't let the look of this figure scare you away. If we use our knowledge of angles from the lesson, we can reason our way to a correct answer. The reason we are given the angle at the bottom of 42° is because once we have the value of the other acute angle in the triangle, we can determine angle *GIH*. Here, I've redrawn the smaller triangle to show you what I mean:

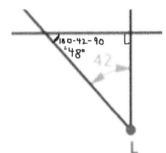

Sorry if that is a little blurry or small, but I've written in there that the value of the angle in the top-left corner is 180° − 42° − 90° = 48°.

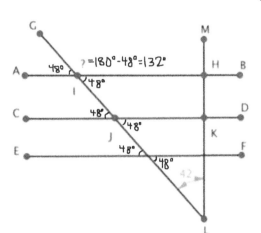

Because of the Law of Transversals, we can be sure that this is the value of many other angles in our figure, as you can see from the image here.

As you can see, we can use the Law of Transversals to determine pairs of opposite angles that also equal 48° (6 in total in our diagram) all the way up to angles *GIA* and *HIJ*. Knowing either one is enough to solve for our missing angle, marked with a question mark.

To find our missing angle (the math of which I've also drawn into the diagram), we simply need to use the fact that the angles in a line add up to 180°.

Thus, 180° − 48° = 132°, which is answer choice K.

Lastly, hopefully you can see by now (with our *Drawn to Scale* strategy in mind) that the angle itself is very obtuse, meaning that the answer must be either J or K. If you can't figure out the math, let this be a bit of a guide in making a smart guess, at the very least!

47. Correct answer: A. The best thing to do here is to draw a crude image of what is being described, two lines crossing each other. Here is what you do know. First, it is impossible that these two lines are perpendicular, which would form four 90° angles.

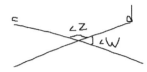

We know this because if all angles were the same, it would be impossible for one of the angles to be bigger than another, let alone 500% bigger. This is also why angles Z and W can't be opposite angles, because that would mean they have the same value. These two angles must, combined, form a line. The lines and angles must look something like the image I've drawn to the left.

Second, we know that two angles in a line add up to 180°. If we call the value of angle W $x°$, then angle Z must be $5x°$, since it is 500% (5 times) bigger. This is enough for us to set up an equation and solve for angle W.

$$x° + 5x° = 180° \quad \dots \quad 6x° = 180 \quad \dots \quad x° = \frac{180}{6} \quad \dots \quad x° = 30°$$

48. Correct answer: **H.** Again, before we get into how to solve this problem mathematically, let's think about the *Drawn to Scale* mini-strategy. Angle *VUW* is a very acute angle. Just by the *look* of it, I would guess it is somewhere around 40°, and there's only one answer choice that's in the ballpark of 40°….on to the math of it!

The fact that there are extra line segments that form a triangle is completely irrelevant to this question. What is relevant is that we have two angles that add up to a line. Let's solve this in two steps:

Step 1: We simply need to set up an equation in which these two angles add up to 180°; this will help us to solve for x, which is necessary in solving this problem. Here is what we need:

$$(16x + 2)° + (4x - 2)° = 180° \quad \dots \quad 20x = 180° \quad \dots \quad x = 9$$

At this point, some students will quickly put that F: 9° is the correct answer. However, at this point all you have done is solve for x, not the angle *VUW*. Again…does that *look* like a 9° angle to you? Hopefully not.

Step 2: Now that we know the value of x, we simply need to plug that in to our missing angle's equation and solve, like this:

$$\angle VUW = (4x - 2)° = (4(9) - 2)° = (36 - 2)° = 34° \text{ , or answer choice H.}$$

49. Correct answer: **B.** Again, it would be helpful if you drew out the four walls: one with a door, one with a window, another with a window, and one with no window or door at all. However, let's now solve it in three steps. First, let's calculate the amount of wall space there is. Second, let's calculate the amount of space is occupied by doors and windows. Third, let's subtract to find how much space is being painted.

Step 1: Each wall is 12 feet by 10 feet. To find the area, simply multiply the two. However, let's remember that there are 4 walls. This is why in the equations below, I am multiplying the area by four:

$$\text{Wall Space} = (10\text{ft} \cdot 12\text{ft}) \cdot 4 = 120\text{ft}^2 \cdot 4 = 480\text{ft}^2$$

Step 2: There are three spaces that are not being painted. In the equations below, I begin with the area of the door, then add in each window:

$$\text{Unpainted Space} = (4\text{ft} \cdot 8\text{ft}) + (3\text{ft} \cdot 5\text{ft}) + (3\text{ft} \cdot 5\text{ft}) = 32\text{ft}^2 + 15\text{ft}^2 + 15\text{ft}^2 = 62\text{ft}^2$$

Step 3: Lastly, simply subtract the unpainted area from the total wall area:

$$\text{Total Painted Area} = 480\text{ft}^2 - 62\text{ft}^2 = 418\text{ft}^2, \text{ which is answer choice B.}$$

50. Correct answer: **F.** What we need to do is to create a rectangle, then create a second one with decreased/increased side lengths, then compare their areas. Just like we saw in previous questions, if we are trying to find percent increases or decreases, it is helpful to begin with the number 100. In our case, 100ft^2 (assuming it is in feet; it doesn't say). Thus, our baseline rectangle is going to be one with a length of 10 and a height of 10 (but, you might object, isn't that a square? Yes, but every square is a rectangle because it has 4 90 degree angles, so it works!).

Second, we need to create a fictional rectangle that meets the decrease/increase requirements. Well, since we chose as a baseline a rectangle with a length of 10 and a width of 10, making percent changes to these sides will not be too difficult.

The length of our new rectangle is 30% smaller than 10, or $(1.00 - 0.30)(10)$, or 7.
The width of our new rectangle is 45% larger than 10, or $(1.00 + 0.45)(10)$, or 14.5.

The area of this new rectangle is (7 x 14.5), or 101.5ft^2 .

If our baseline rectangle had an area of $100ft^2$, and our updated rectangle has an area of $101.5ft^2$, then clearly the area increase is $(101.5ft^2 - 100ft^2)$, or $1.5ft^2$. Well, though the percent increase is obvious based on the numbers that we chose, to find the percent increase we simply need to do a little math:

$$\text{Percent Increase} = \frac{\text{Area Increase}}{\text{Original Area}} = \frac{1.5ft^2}{100ft^2} = 0.015 \text{, or } 1.5\%, \text{ which is answer choice F.}$$

51. Correct answer: **B**. To find the correct answer to this question, we need to solve it in two steps. First, we need to determine the volume of the can of soup. Second, we need to find Frida's daughter's portion, or 40%.

Step 1: The volume of a three dimensional shape that is uniform from top to bottom can be found by calculating first the area of the top or bottom, then multiplying by the height. In this case, since it is a can of soup, it has a circular top. For more on circles, see ACT Math *Have to Know* Lesson #13. For now, let's simply recall that the area of a circle is πr^2, in which r is the radius. However, we aren't given the radius of the can, but the diameter; the radius is simply half of the diameter, or for us (65mm/2), or 32.5mm. For our purposes, the formula for the volume of this can is $\pi r^2 h$, in which h is the height of the can (98mm), r is the radius (32.5mm), and π is a constant with a value of 3.14159 (or just hit the π button on your calculator!).

$$\text{Can Volume} = \pi r^2 h = \pi(32.5)^2(98) = (3.14159)(1056.25)(98) = 325,193.8mm^3$$

Step 2: Now that we have the volume of the can, it is time to determine Frida's daughter's portion, which is 40%. All we need to do is multiply the volume of the can by 0.4, which will give us the 40%:

$$325,193.8mm^3(0.4) = 130,077.5mm^3 \text{, or rounded, } 130,078, \text{ which is answer choice B.}$$

52. Correct answer: **K**. When we are asked for $f(-2)$, that simply means this: what is the value of the function when $x = -2$? So, all we need to do is plug in $x = -2$ into the function wherever there is an x, and that will spit out a value, which is our answer. If $f(x) = 3x^2 - 12x$, then $f(-2)$ can be worked out like this:

$$f(-2) = 3x^2 - 12x = 3(-2)^2 - 12(-2) = 3(4) - (-24) = 12 + 24 = 36 \text{, which is answer choice K.}$$

53. Correct answer: **C**. This question may have the added layer of featuring two variables (a and b), but it works the exact same way as any function problem. The function is defined as $f(a, b)$, and we are asked to find the value of $f(-1, 2)$, so we should plug in $a = -1$ and $b = 2$ into the function and see what value results. If $f(a, b) = 2b^3 + 5a$, then $f(-1, 2)$ can be worked out like this:

$$f(-1,2) = 2b^3 + 5a = 2(2)^3 + 5(-1) = 2(8) + (-5) = 16 - 5 = 11 \text{, which is answer choice C.}$$

54. Correct answer: **F**. This may look complex, like the kind of problem that only someone who is very good at math would be able to get correct, but that is not true at all. The exact same principle applies in this function problem as in any other function problem. If we were looking for $f(2)$, we would plug in 2 anywhere there were an x in the function. Here, we are looking for $f(g(x))$, which means that we will plug in $g(x)$ anywhere there is an x in $f(x)$. Because $g(x) = 2x + 2$, we will have to plug in $(2x + 2)$ anywhere there is an x in $f(x) = x^2 + 3x$, like this:

$$f(g(x)) = x^2 + 3x = (2x + 2)^2 + 3(2x + 2) = (2x + 2)(2x + 2) + 3(2x + 2) =$$

$$(4x^2 + 4x + 4x + 4) + (6x + 6) = 4x^2 + 14x + 10$$

Now, $4x^2 + 14x + 10$ is a fine answer, but it can be factored a bit further (which is how the first three answer choices are presented). Though there's a leading coefficient of 4 in front of that first term, not all terms (4, 14, and 10) are divisible by 4, but they are are divisible by 2. Thus, if we factor out a 2 from each term, we get:

$$f(g(x)) = 4x^2 + 14x + 10 = 2(2x^2 + 7x + 5) \text{, which is answer choice F.}$$

55. Correct answer: **B**. I'm guessing that, if you're reading this explanation, then you're a bit thrown off by the division of one function by another. However, do not be thrown; the problem is as simple as it seems. We are given a value for $f(x)$, which is 21, and we are given a value for $g(x)$, which is 10.5, and we are asked to divide the former by the latter. Like this:

$$\frac{f(x)}{g(x)} = \frac{21}{10.5} = 2 \text{, which is answer choice B.}$$

56. Correct answer: **F.** This problem is the exact same as number 55 above, the difference being that now there are added elements, like variables, trinomials and binomials, and how to divide fractions.

Let's solve this problem in two different ways to help you learn to see these multiple ways as well. The first way we'll solve it is by *Picking Numbers*, and the second is the more traditional way.

Method 1: *Picking Numbers*

We need to choose a value for *x*, plug it in, divide, and see what number we get. Then, we can do the same in the answer choices and match them up. Let's assume that $x = 3$. However, it doesn't matter what you choose. So, when $x = 3$...

$$f(x) = \frac{1}{(x+3)} = \frac{1}{(3+3)} = \frac{1}{6} \quad \text{and} \quad g(x) = \frac{1}{(x^2 + 2x - 3)} = \frac{1}{(3^2 + 2(3) - 3)} = \frac{1}{(9 + 6 - 3)} = \frac{1}{12}$$

Now, I need to divide $f(x)$ by $g(x)$. As a reminder, to divide a fraction into another, take the fraction in the denominator, flip it upside down, and now multiply it by the fraction in the numerator. You'll see that happen here:

$$\frac{f(x)}{g(x)} = \frac{\frac{1}{6}}{\frac{1}{12}} = \frac{1}{6} \cdot \frac{12}{1} = \frac{12}{6} = 2 \text{, so now, which answer} = 2 \text{ when we plug in a value of 3 for } x?$$

F: $x - 1 = 3 - 1 = 2$...that's it!

Method 2: Traditional Simplification of Polynomials

Before we put these terms over one another, we need to factor the trinomial $(x^2 + 2x - 3)$ in the denominator of $g(x)$ into 2 binomials. To do this, we need two numbers that multiply to give us a value of -3, but which add together to give us 2. These two numbers are -1 and 3, which are the two values added to *x* in each binomial, like this:

$$x^2 + 2x - 3 = (x - 1)(x + 3), \quad \text{thus} \quad g(x) = \frac{1}{(x - 1)(x + 3)}$$

Now that we have that simplified, it is time to divide. Again, to divide fraction into another, take the fraction in the denominator, flip it upside down, and now multiply it by the fraction in the numerator. You'll see that happen here:

$$\frac{f(x)}{g(x)} = \frac{\frac{1}{(x+3)}}{\frac{1}{(x-1)(x+3)}} = \frac{1}{(x+3)} \cdot \frac{(x-1)(x+3)}{1} = \frac{(x-1)(x+3)}{(x+3)} = x - 1 \text{, which again, is choice F.}$$

57. Correct answer: **C.** You might think, "Isn't 1 foot a little wide for the diameter of a skinny umbrella?" Well, you'd be right; Carla needs to take it easy.

However, that kind of thinking is a distraction...stay focused!

We need to find the area of the larger circle, then find the area of the smaller circle, then subtract the latter from the former, which will give us the total area of the tablecloth after the (unnecessarily big) hole has been cut. Let's recall that the formula for the area of a circle is this: Area $= \pi r^2$. There is a simple mistake to be made in this problem, however, which needs to be noticed before we get started. We are given the *radius* of the larger circle, which is what we need, but we are given the *diameter* of the smaller circle, which is 1 foot. We need to make sure we're working with the *radius* of the smaller circle, which is 0.5 feet.

$$\text{Larger Circle Area} = \pi r^2 = \pi (4.5)^2 = \pi (20.25) = 63.62 \text{ft}^2$$

$$\text{Smaller Circle Area} = \pi r^2 = \pi (0.5)^2 = \pi (0.25) = 0.79 \text{ft}^2$$

Now, subtracting the area of the smaller from the larger: $63.62 - 0.79 = 62.83$, which is choice C.

58. Correct answer: **H.** This is a two step problem. First, we need to use the circumference given to find the radius of the circle, then second, we need to use that radius to find the area of the circle.

Step 1: recall that the formula for the circumference of a circle is this: $2\pi r$. Thus, to find the radius, we need to set the circumference that we are given equal to this formula, and solve for r, like so:

$$\text{Circumference} = 2\pi r \quad \ldots \quad 22 = 2\pi r \quad \ldots \quad \frac{22}{2\pi} = r \quad \ldots \quad r = 3.50$$

Step 2: now that we know that the radius of this circle is 3.50, we can use that information to find the area. Recall that the formula for the area of a circle is this: Area = πr^2. Now we just need to plug and solve:

$$\text{Area} = \pi r^2 = \pi (3.5)^2 = \pi 12.25 = 38.48, \text{ which rounds to 38.5, or choice H.}$$

59. Correct answer: E. In this problem, we are comparing the areas of two circles. We need to solve it in two steps. The first step will be to find the area of each circle (we will call one "smaller circle" and the other "larger circle"), and then the second step will be to subtract.

Step 1: Let's begin with the smaller circle. We know that the radius of this circle is 5 feet, which is enough for us to find the area. Recall that the formula for the area of a circle is this: πr^2.

$$\text{Smaller Cirlce Area} = \pi r^2 = \pi (5)^2 = \pi (25) = 78.54 \text{ ft}^2$$

As for the second, bigger circle, all we know is that the radius of this circle is 40% longer than that of the smaller circle. To increase the radius of the first circle by 40%, simply multiply it by 1.4, like this: $5(1.4) = 7$. Thus, the radius of the larger circle is 7, which means that we can now find its area:

$$\text{Larger Cirlce Area} = \pi r^2 = \pi (7)^2 = \pi (49) = 153.94 \text{ ft}^2$$

Step 2: We are asked how much larger is the area of the second, larger circle than the first, smaller circle, so now all that's left for us to do is subtract:

$$\text{Larger Circle Area} - \text{Smaller Circle Area} = 153.94 \text{ ft}^2 - 78.54 \text{ ft}^2 = 75.40 \text{ ft}^2$$

Because the answer requires us to round to the nearest square foot, we round down from 75.40 to 75, which is answer choice E.

60. Correct answer: G. Recall that the arc of a circle is simply a piece of the circumference, and that there is a ratio at play here: as the arc of a circle is to the circumference, so too the interior angle of the arc is to all the angles in a circle. Let's lay these 4 things out one at a time and see what we know:

1) The arc of the circle: this is what we're trying to find; let's call it x.

2) The circumference: we don't yet know this, but we can find it. We are told that the pizza has a diameter of 16, which means a radius of 8. If the formula for the circumference of a circle is $2\pi r$,   then the circumference of this pizza is $2\pi r = 2\pi (8) = 50.27$ inches.

3) The interior angle: we are told this: 55°.

4) The total degree of a circle: this is 360°.

Now that we know 3 of the 4 values, we can set up an equation in which we cross multiply. First, let's actually set up the ratio:

$$\frac{\text{arc}}{\text{circumference}} = \frac{\text{interior angle}}{\text{sum of all angles}} \quad \ldots \quad \frac{x}{50.27} = \frac{55}{360}$$

As a reminder, to cross multiply, you set up a new equation in which the numerator of one side is multiplied by the denominator of the other side, and vice versa, and the two values are set equal to each other. Or, similarly, in this equation, you can just multiply both sides by 50.27 to isolate the x. Either way, you will end up with the same thing.

$$\frac{x}{50.27} = \frac{55}{360} \quad \ldots \quad x = \frac{55(50.27)}{360} = 7.68 \text{ inches.}$$

Thus, back to the original question. The length of the outside arc of this crust of pizza is 7.68 inches, or answer choice G.

Answer Explanations - Step 4

Correct answers:

1: C	11: E	21: A	31: C	41: D	51: A
2: H	12: H	22: G	32: H	42: G	52: F
3: D	13: D	23: C	33: A	43: B	53: E
4: F	14: G	24: K	34: K	44: J	54: H
5: D	15: B	25: B	35: E	45: C	55: D
6: K	16: J	26: J	36: G	46: G	56: F
7: B	17: C	27: B	37: A	47: A	57: B
8: F	18: J	28: K	38: H	48: K	58: J
9: A	19: E	29: D	39: E	49: C	59: E
10: G	20: F	30: F	40: J	50: K	60: H

1. Correct answer: C. One by one, multiply like terms. First, we know that $4 \times 3 \times 8 = 96$, eliminating answer choices A and B. Next, multiply the x terms. What needs to be remembered here is that when multiplying variables, you do not *multiply* their exponents, but rather, you *add* their exponents. Thus:

$$x^2 \times x^2 \times x = x^{2+2+1} = x^5$$

This is already enough to get the question correct, since only choice C begins with $96x^5$. To be thorough, we will multiply the y terms. If the y terms multiply to equal y^6, which is also attached to answer C, we can definitively say we've found the correct answer:

$$y^4 \times y^2 = y^{4+2} = y^6$$

Thus, after this very thorough look, the correct answer is C.

2. Correct answer: H. Because the question asks for the mean, there is no need to order the numbers in numerical order. Simply add the lengths of the ribbons and divide by the total number of ribbons:

$$\frac{10 + 12 + 9 + 10 + 11 + 12}{6} = 10.667$$

Because the question asks you to round to the nearest tenth of an inch, we round up to 10.7, which matches with answer choice H.

3. Correct answer: D. This problem requires you to convert the words into an Algebra problem. Before the equal sign, it says, "Three times the sum of x and -4," which looks like this: $3(x - 4)$. After the equal sign, it says, "the addition of 8 and $-x$," which looks like $8 - x$. Thus, our Algebra problem looks like this:

$$3(x - 4) = 8 - x \quad \ldots \quad 3x - 12 = 8 - x \quad \ldots \quad 4x = 20 \quad \ldots \quad x = 5$$

This matches answer choice D.

4. Correct answer: F. First, determine how much money per month Chipper puts away. If he puts away 7% of his \$66,000 salary per year, that means he puts away $66,000(.07) = \$4,620$ each year. Now, divide that by 12 to determine how much is put away per month: $\$4,620/12 = \$385$.

To find how much more Chipper puts away per month than Parker, subtract Parker's monthly savings from Chipper's: $\$385 - \$150 = \$235$, which is answer choice F.

5. Correct answer: D. Because both buses are traveling towards each other, find the distance traveled by each bus in 4 hours, then subtract those distances from the 1,000 miles they start apart from each other. But 1 travels at 60 miles per hour. Over four hours, that's:

$$60 \frac{\text{miles}}{\text{hour}} \times 4 \text{ hours} = 240 \text{ miles}$$

Similarly, Bus 2 travels at 55 miles per hour. Over four hours, that's:

$$55\frac{\text{miles}}{\text{hour}} \times 4 \text{ hours} = 220 \text{ miles}$$

Subtract both distances from the original 1,000 miles they started apart: $1,000 - 240 - 220 = 540$ miles apart after four hours of driving towards each other, which is answer choice D.

6. Correct answer: **K**. This is one of those problems that looks far more complicated than it is. You have 4 binomials (an expression with two terms, like z and 2) that are all being multiplied by one another and set equal to 0. If any of the four binomials actually equals 0, then no matter what the other terms equal, the entire expression will equal 0. For example, let's say that $z = -2$. In that case, the first binomial, $(z + 2)$, would look like this: $(z + 2) = (-2 + 2) = 0$, which would make the entire thing equal to 0. Thus, -2 is one value of z that makes the expression = 0. Move on to the other three binomials and determine what values of z make each one equal 0.

For $(z - 4)$, if $z = 4$, it will be equal to 0. For $(z + 3)$, if $z = -3$, it will be equal to 0. Lastly, for $(z - 6)$, if $z = 6$, it will be equal to 0.

This means our four z values that make the expression equal 0 are: $-2, 4, -3$, and 6. The questions asks for us to find the median of these terms, which is the middle term in an odd number set or the average of the 2 middle terms in an even number set. We do have an even number set (there are 4 numbers to work with), but first we have to order them in numerical order, like this: $\{-3, -2, 4, 6\}$. The median will be the average of the middle terms, which are -2 and 4. Thus, our median is: $(-2 + 4)/2 = 1$, which is answer choice K.

7. Correct answer: **B**. This question requires use of the Pythagorean Theorem (since the two sides and segment BD form a right triangle), which is written as $a^2 + b^2 = c^2$, in which a and b are the two legs of a right triangle and c is the hypotenuse. In this case, the hypotenuse is segment BD with length 10. The reason we can solve it is because the two legs are the same. In essence, we can rewrite the Pythagorean Theorem to look like this: $a^2 + a^2 = c^2$, since a and b in this triangle are identical. This gives us then $2a^2 = c^2$, which we can then solve for a since we know $c = 10$, like this:

$$2a^2 = 10^2 \quad \dots \quad 2a^2 = 100 \quad \dots \quad a^2 = 50 \quad \dots \quad a = \sqrt{50} \quad \dots \quad a = 5\sqrt{2}, \text{ or answer B.}$$

8. Correct answer: **F**. Here, try integers of various kinds (if necessary) to eliminate wrong answers, which is the main strategy for these logical thinking with variables questions. Let's try first $x = 1$ and see what happens:

$$(2(1) - 4)^4 - 1 = (-2)^4 - 1 = 16 - 1 = 15$$

Because the result, 15, is an odd number and a positive number, we can then eliminate G, H, and J as correct answers. Let's choose a number this time that's a little bit different than 1, maybe an even negative number, like $x = -6$, to see if there is a variety of possible outcomes (which is necessary for K to be correct):

$$(2(-6) - 4)^4 - 1 = (-12 - 4)^4 - 1 = (-16)^4 - 1 = 65325$$

Another positive, odd number. Looking closely, the only way for this expression to be negative is if $x = 2$, since then you would have 0 in parentheses being raised to the 4th power, which is 0, then subtracting 1 would make the expression equal -1. Thus, for all $x \neq 2$, the expression will always be positive and odd, which is answer choice F.

9. Correct answer: **A**. Because segment JI is parallel to segment HF, angle $\angle JIF$ will be equal to angle $\angle HFG$; thus, $\angle HFG = 115°$. Similarly, because segment LK is parallel to segment HG, angle $\angle LKG$ will be equal to angle $\angle HGF$; thus, $\angle HGF = 20°$.

At this point, we now have 2 of the 3 angles of triangle $\triangle HFG$, which means we can subtract the 2 angles we know from 180° to find the missing angle $\angle FHG$. Like this: $180° - 20° - 115° = 45°$, which matches answer choice A.

10. Correct answer: **G**. For questions requiring the simplification of an expression involving multiple variables, like this one, simplify like terms one at a time until you settle on the correct answer.

First, there is a -15 term in the numerator, which is being divided by a 3 term in the denominator. The result must be -5, and because there are no other negative terms in the entire expression to make it positive, we can eliminate answers H and J, since they make the expression as a whole positive.

Next, move on to the x term. In the numerator, there is an x, and in the denominator, there is an x^3 term. When variables raised to an exponent are being divided or multiplied, you subtract or add the exponents, respectively. In this particular case, the math with the x variable looks like this:

$$\frac{x}{x^3} = \frac{1}{x^{3-1}} = \frac{1}{x^2}$$

So far, then, we know that the final answer must begin with -5 and must have an x^2 term in the denominator. This is already enough for us to get the question correct! Only answer choice G features this combination. To be thorough, you can follow the same step above with each other variable, but below is the entire expression simplified one step at a time so you can see each point in the process:

$$\frac{-15x\,y^3 z^8}{3x^3 y^2 z} = \frac{-5y^{(3-2)} z^{(8-1)}}{x^{(3-1)}} = \frac{-5yz^7}{x^2}, \text{ which matches answer choice G.}$$

11. Correct answer: **E**. First, put the line in slope-intercept form ($y = mx + b$), like this:

$$6x - 5y = 10 \quad \dots \quad -5y = -6x + 10 \quad \dots \quad y = \frac{6}{5}x - 2$$

Because the question asks for a line parallel to this one, we simply need to identify the slope, which in the original equation is m and right before the x, which above is $\frac{6}{5}$. Thus, the correct answer is E.

12. Correct answer: **H**. Because the pool is contained within the walkway, the area of the walkway will be determined by finding the area of the rectangle made by the walkway, then subtract the area of the pool.

If the pool is 25 feet long, and the walkway extends 3 feet on both sides, then the larger rectangle made by the walkway is $25 + 3 + 3 = 31$ feet long.

If the pool is 20 feet wide, and the walkway extends 3 feet on both sides, then the larger rectangle made by the walkway is $20 + 3 + 3 = 26$ feet wide.

The area of the larger rectangle made by the walkway is $26 \times 31 = 806 \text{ ft}^2$.

The area of the pool within the walkway is $25 \times 20 = 500 \text{ ft}^2$.

Now that we have our measurements, all that is left to do is subtract the area of the pool from the larger rectangle made by the walkway, like this: $806 \text{ ft}^2 - 500 \text{ ft}^2 = 306 \text{ ft}^2$. This is answer choice H.

13. Correct answer: **D**. To find the probability, divide the total number of black dresses by the total number of dresses, like this:

$$\frac{4 + 6}{7 + 4 + 2 + 3 + 6 + 8} = \frac{10}{30} = \frac{1}{3}, \text{ which matches answer choice D.}$$

14. Correct answer: **G**. To solve this function, plug in $x = 2$ into the function and find the resulting value, like this:

$$f(x) = 2x^2 - x + 1 = 2(2)^2 - 2 + 1 = 8 - 2 + 1 = 7, \text{ which matches answer choice G.}$$

15. Correct answer: **B**. Because two lines are crossing, four angles will be formed. If one of them measures $40°$, then the angle opposite of that one will also measure $40°$. We know that $\angle C$ is the one that measures $40°$, but we are told that $\angle C$ does not equal $\angle D$, so the value of $\angle D$ can't be $40°$.

The other two angles, on the other hand, will form a line with the $40°$ angle. That means that the other two angles (one of which is $\angle D$) must have a value of $180° - 40° = 140°$, which is answer choice B.

16. Correct answer: **J**. First, use the circle's area to find the radius. Recall that the formula for the area of a circle is πr^2. So, if the circle has an area of 36π, then $r^2 = 36$, and $r = 6$. The question asks for the diameter of this circle, not the radius. Since the diameter is $2r$, then the diameter of the circle is $2 \times 6 = 12$, which is answer choice J.

17. Correct answer: **C**. First, recognize that the question requires that Timothy hit at least 5 home runs, so trying out options using $r = 4$ or some lower number will not work. However, the *Picking Numbers* strategy is great for this question. He receives $25 for each home run that he hits over 5. So, let's start by pretending that $r = 6$, which would result in him making $25, and try it out one question at a time.

A: If $r = 6$, then $25r - 5 = 25(6) - 5 = 145$, not 25. Try again.

B: If $r = 6$, then $25(r + 5) = 25(6 + 5) = 25(11) = 275$, not 25. Try again.

C: If $r = 6$, then $25(r - 5) = 25(6 - 5) = 25(1) = 25$, that's it! This is why C is correct.

If you wanted to try another value of r to be thorough, or if you wanted to go through D and E quickly to certainly discount them, that would be fine. But, not if it is going to cost you any real time. Be confident and move on!

18. Correct answer: **J.** Notice that this car is not on sale for 13% of the original price, but for 13% *off*. This means that the sale cost of the car is 87% of the original cost. Thus, if we multiply the original cost by 0.87, we will get the 13% off sale price, like this:

$$\$38,000(0.87) = \$33,060, \text{ which matches with answer choice J.}$$

19. Correct answer: **E.** Here, plug in $x = 9$ into the equation, and solve. Before doing so, let's discuss the two strange variables in the question. When x (or any other number for that reason) is raised to the ½ power, this is the same thing as finding the square root of that number. Secondly, in the denominator, the variable is raised to a negative power. To fix this, make it positive and move it to the numerator. With these two things in mind, and to show what I am talking about, we can rewrite the function to look like this:

$$g(x) = \frac{x^{\frac{1}{2}}}{x^{-1}} = \sqrt{x} \cdot x^1$$

Thus, when $x = 9$, we can solve it like so:

$$\sqrt{x} \cdot x^1 = \sqrt{x} \cdot x = \sqrt{9} \cdot 9 = 3 \cdot 9 = 27, \text{ which matches answer choice E.}$$

20. Correct answer: **F.** Remember that the solution of two lines is the point where they cross. The fastest way to solve for this problem is to plug in $(2, -2)$ (in other words, plug in $x = 2$ and $y = -2$) into each equation one at a time and see if it is *satisfied*.

Start with F, plugging in $(2, -2)$ into each of the two lines:

First line: $y = \frac{1}{2}x - 3$ ... $-2 = \frac{1}{2}(2) - 3$ ... $-2 = 1 - 3$ ... $-2 = -2$, which works!

Second line: $y = 5x - 12$ ... $-2 = 5(2) - 12$ ... $-2 = 10 - 12$ ... $-2 = -2$, which works!

Because the point $(2, -2)$ satisfies the equations of both lines, it is the point where they cross. If you try out this point on any of the other answer choices, it is very likely that $(2, -2)$ will satisfy 1 but not both lines. This is why the answer is F.

21. Correct answer: **A.** To find the percent of his throws that were discus, simply add the discus throws and divide it by the total number of throws. To make the addition simpler, let's first add up the amount of throws he took across the week with each:

Javelin throws = $12 + 23 + 11 + 2 + 19 = 67$
Shot put throws = $18 + 11 + 0 + 15 + 18 = 62$
Discus throws = $0 + 0 + 18 + 15 + 3 = 36$

Now, to find the percent, divide the discus throws by all throws, and then multiply by 100:

$$\frac{36}{67 + 62 + 36} = \frac{36}{165} = 0.218$$

When multiplied by 100, we get 21.8%, which rounds to 22%, which matches answer choice A.

22. Correct answer: **G.** Expected outcome, remember, is not the same thing as *most likely*. Expected outcome relies on knowing the probabilities of all outcomes, and multiplying all of the outcomes by those probabilities. First, let's determine the probability of each throw on Thursday:

$$\text{Javelin} = \frac{2}{2 + 15 + 15} = \frac{2}{32} \approx 0.0625$$

$$\text{Shot Put} = \frac{15}{2+15+15} = \frac{15}{32} = 0.46875$$

$$\text{Discus} = \frac{15}{2+15+15} = \frac{15}{32} = 0.46875$$

Now, we have to determine the most likely distance for each throw. Remember that on Thursday, Drew only throws at 70% of his strength. Thus, we have to multiply each "full strength" throw by 0.7. Let's do that by each throw type:

Javelin = 201(0.7) = 140.7 feet
Shot put = 52(0.7) = 36.4 feet
Discus = 179(0.7) = 125.3 feet

This is all of the data that we need to solve the problem. To find the expected outcome, we need to multiply each throw distance by each probability, and add them together:

Expected outcome = 0.0625(140.7) + 0.46875(36.4) + 0.46875(125.3) = 8.79 + 17.06 + 58.73 = 84.58

This rounds up to 85 feet, which matches with answer choice G.

23. Correct answer: **C**. Because shot put throws do not travel very far at all relative to javelin and discus, they can be easily eliminated; even a shot put throw at full strength isn't going to match either of the other throws, even with arm soreness playing a role. In addition, Friday's throws are weaker than any other day of the week, which is a way to know that E will also be impossible (since letter C is about the same throw, discus, on an earlier day in the week).

That leaves C and D. Finding these distances was part of the analysis needed in the last problem, so just do the same thing: simply find the distance of each throw and compare. To find the distance, take the "full strength" distance and multiply by either 0.9 (a Wednesday throw of 90%), 0.7 (a Thursday throw of 70%), or 0.6 (a Friday throw of 60%).

C: A discus throw on Thursday = 179(0.7) = 125.3 feet
D: A javelin throw on a Friday = 201(0.6) = 120.6 feet

Thus, a discus throw on Thursday will travel the farthest out of the five options, which is why answer C is correct.

24. Correct answer: **K**. To answer this question correctly, simply plug the correct values in for the proper variables, and solve. She works 40 regular time hours, so $h = 40$; she works 3 overtime hours, so $e = 3$; she makes $3,234 in sales, so $s = 3,234$. Plugging them in and solving looks like this:

$$\$(11h + 16.5e + 0.21s) = \$(11(40) + 16.5(3) + 0.21(3234)) = \$(440 + 49.5 + 679.14) = \$1,168.64$$

Thus, the answer is K.

25. Correct answer: **B**. Obviously, there is no formula for the area of a weird shaped figure with two rectangles attached to a triangle; simply divide the figure into as many shapes as necessary, find the areas of the smaller shapes, and add them together. Below I have drawn on the figure some to show how I divided up the figure, which is into two rectangles and a triangle:

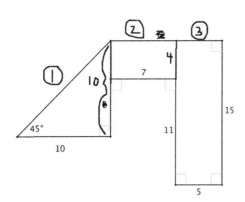

Start with what I've called shape number one. Of course, the area of a triangle is $\frac{1}{2}bh$, where b is the base and h is the height. The tricky thing is that the height is not given to us. However, we know it is 10. Because the angle in the lower left hand corner is 45 degrees, and it is a 90 degree triangle, the other angle must also be 45. Because its opposite side is 10, then the opposite side of the 45 degree angle that is given is 10. With that in mind, $\frac{1}{2}bh = \frac{1}{2}(10)(10) = 50$. So, the area of shape 1 is 50.

Shape 2 is a simple rectangle; multiply the length by the width to get the area, which in this case is $7 \times 4 = 28$.

Shape 3 is also a simple rectangle; multiply the length by the width to get the area, which in this case is $5 \times 15 = 75$.

Now, add the areas together: $50 + 28 + 75 = 153$, or answer choice B.

26. Correct answer: **J.** Again, there is no need to memorize the distance formula. Instead, draw out the two points (as I've done below), then treat the distance between the two as the hypotenuse in a right triangle.

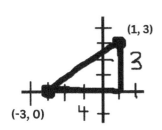

Sorry for the poor drawing, but it gives you the right idea. The distance between the two points is a hypotenuse, and because we know the lengths of the other two sides (just simply counting by tick marks on the coordinate plane, or by finding the difference between each x point and each y point), we can use the Pythagorean Theorem to find the hypotenuse.

The Pythagorean Theorem is $a^2 + b^2 = c^2$, in which a and b are the two legs of the triangle and c is the hypotenuse. Let's plug in our values and solve for c:

$$a^2 + b^2 = c^2 \quad \ldots \quad 3^2 + 4^2 = c^2 \quad \ldots \quad 9 + 16 = c^2 \quad \ldots \quad \sqrt{25} = \sqrt{c^2} \quad \ldots$$
$$5 = c$$

Thus, the distance between the two points is J: 5.

Another method for solving this triangle more quickly is realizing that it is what is called a *special triangle*; we'll learn more about that in *Good to Know* Lesson #2.

27. Correct answer: **B.** Because this problem describes a triangle, but doesn't actually draw it out for you, be sure to actually draw the triangle being described as you solve it. I have done that below:

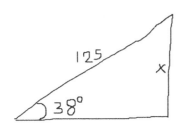

Drawing this triangle allows me to solve the problem without making a simple mistake, because guaranteed the most likely simple mistakes will result in a wrong answer choice. We are looking for the *opposite* side of the 38°, which I have marked with an x. So, we need a trig function (sin, cos, or tan) that uses what we know (the angle and the hypotenuse) and what we need to know (the opposite); this is sin, which is the opposite side over the hypotenuse. Our original equation will look like this:

$$\sin(38) = \frac{x}{125}$$

When I multiply both sides by 125, the x is isolated, then we can solve for x:

$$\sin(38) = \frac{x}{125} \quad \ldots \quad (125)\sin(38) = x \quad \ldots \quad 125(0.616) = x \quad \ldots \quad x = 76.96$$

Because the question asks us to round to the nearest tenth of a foot, we round up to 77.0, which is answer choice B.

28. Correct answer: **K.** Because x must be a negative number by definition (somewhere between, yet including, -3 and -5), then the value of y that would result in the greatest value of the product of x and y would also be negative, since multiplying two negative numbers results in a positive number. Looking at y, there are only two possible values for y: either 2 or -2, since the absolute value of either of those numbers is 2. Thus, the greatest possible product of x and y is $xy = (-5)(-2) = 10$, which is answer choice K.

29. Correct answer: **D.** To find $f(g(5))$, first find $g(5)$; this will result in a number that can then be plugged into $f(x)$. According to the chart, $g(5) = -2$. In other words, when $x = 5$ (bottom of the chart), $g(x) = -2$.

Now, plug -2 into $f(x)$. If we begin in the column on the left that features various values of x, the top line uses the value of $x = -2$. Look over from there to the middle column, the $f(x)$ column, and see that when $x = -2$, the function $f(x) = 3$, which is answer choice D.

30. Correct answer: **F.** Using i is one of the ACT Math test's favorite tricks. I think that the ACT is hoping that some of the students will be familiar with its usage in some sort of math class, but maybe they themselves have never covered it. However, you don't have to have any knowledge of the origin, usage, or purpose of the variable i. The process for solving this ACT Math problem is simple: FOIL (meaning, properly multiply) the two binomials; then, wherever there is an i^2 term, just replace it with a -1 and simplify/solve from there. First, let's multiply the two binomials together without changing the i^2 terms:

$$(i - 1)(i - 1) = i^2 - i - i + 1 = i^2 - 2i + 1$$

Next, replace any i^2 term with a -1 and simplify, like this:

$$i^2 - 2i + 1 = -1 - 2i + 1 = -2i, \text{ which matches answer choice F.}$$

31. Correct answer: **C**. The first expression, $(12x - 41)$, represents the money spent at Grocery Stop. The second expression, $(5x + 30)$, represents the money spent at Fancy Foods. Because we know that she spent $278 total, we can simply add the two expressions together and set them equal to $278. This will allow us to solve for x, then we can plug that number back into Grocery Stop's expression.

Step 1: Solve for x:

$$(12x - 41) + (5x + 30) = 278 \quad \ldots \quad 17x - 11 = 278 \quad \ldots \quad 17x = 289 \quad \ldots \quad x = 17$$

Now that we know the value of x, we can plug it in to Grocery Stop's expression.

Step 2: Plug $x = 17$ into Grocery Stop's expression:

$$12x - 41 = 12(17) - 41 = 204 - 41 = 163$$

Thus, Missy spent $163 at Grocery Stop, which matches answer choice C.

32. Correct answer: **H**. Though you technically do not need to order a set of numbers to find the mode or the mean, it will help avoid simple mistakes to do so. Written in ascending order, the home runs Jeff has in his first 10 games looks like this:

$$\{0, 0, 0, 0, 1, 2, 2, 2, 3, 4\}$$

The mode, remember, is the number that occurs the most, which at the moment is 0.

The mean is the average, which is $\dfrac{(0 + 0 + 0 + 0 + 1 + 2 + 2 + 2 + 3 + 4)}{10} = \dfrac{16}{10} = 1.6$

Now, the question asks how many home runs Jeff needs to hit so that the *mode* of the home runs will then exceed the mean. So, the mode must then either be 2, 3, or 4. However, notice that even if he hits 4 home runs in both games, the mode will still be 0, since then there would still be less games with 4 home runs than 0. The same thing can be said if he hits 3 home runs in these back to back games.

Because there are already 3 games in which Jeff hit 2 home runs, adding 2 more games with 2 home runs brings the mode up to 2. This is because with back to back games of 2 home runs, the number of 2 home run games goes from 3 up to 5, which is more than the 4 games that have 0 home runs.

Now that the mode is 2, test the mean. When you add 2 more games of 2 home runs, the mean does increase, but only slightly, up to 1.67 from 1.6.

Thus, if Jeff hits 2 home runs in Game 11 and then 2 home runs in Game 12, the mode (2) will then exceed the mean (1.67). This is why H is the right answer.

33. Correct answer: **A**. Remember the acronym SOHCAHTOA to remember the values of the functions sin, cos, and tan. The last three letters (the TOA) refers to the tangent of an angle, which is equal to the opposite side over the adjacent side. From the point of view of angle A, the opposite side is side CB, which has a length of 15. The adjacent side is the AB side (not the AC side; that's the hypotenuse), which has a length of 36. Thus:

$$\text{The value of the } \tan A = \frac{15}{36},$$

which can be simplified when the numerator and denominator are divided by 3, like this:

$$\frac{15}{36} = \frac{5}{12}, \text{ which matches answer choice A.}$$

34. Correct answer: **K**. First, if a line is perpendicular to another line that means they have opposite slopes. The opposite of a slope is its negative inverse (meaning make it negative, then move the numerator to the denominator and the denominator to the numerator). The line in the question has a form of $y = -\dfrac{2}{5}x + 3$, in which $-\dfrac{2}{5}$ is the slope. The negative inverse or opposite of this slope is $\dfrac{5}{2}$.

This eliminates answer choices F, G, and H, since those three options do not have the correct slope. However, now it seems like there is a problem: how to choose which of the remaining two lines? Well, according to the question, the line that is correct must pass through point (2, 3). By definition, any point on a line will satisfy the equation if plugged in. So, we must plug in $x = 2$ and $y = 3$ into each line and see which satisfies.

Start with J: $\quad y = \dfrac{5}{2}x + 3 \quad ... \quad 3 = \dfrac{5}{2}(2) + 3 \quad ... \quad 3 = \dfrac{15}{2} + 3 \quad ... \quad 3 = \dfrac{21}{2}$? No, doesn't satisfy!

Now try K: $\quad y = \dfrac{5}{2}x - 2 \quad ... \quad 3 = \dfrac{5}{2}(2) - 2 \quad ... \quad 3 = \dfrac{10}{2} - 2 \quad ... \quad 3 = 5 - 2 \quad ... \quad 3 = 3$, that's it!

35. Correct answer: E. If you remember, the Law of Transversals, in layman's terms, basically means that if two parallel lines are transversed or cut through by another line, then 4 of the 8 angles will have the same value, and so will the other 4; if you know even 1 of 8 angles, you can find them all. Because we are told that the value of $\angle HNO$ is 35°, we now have enough information to find all 8 angles formed by these three lines.

Because $\angle HNO$ is 35°, we also know (according to the Law of Transversals) that $\angle JOL$ also has a measure of 35°. The angle we are looking for, angle $\angle LOK$, shares a line (segment JK) with angle $\angle JOL$; in other words, these two angles must add up to equal 180°. Thus, we can find our missing angle like this:

$$\angle JOL + \angle LOK = 180° \quad ... \quad \angle LOK = 180° - \angle JOL \quad ... \quad \angle LOK = 180° - 35° \quad ... \quad \angle LOK = 145°$$

This is why the answer is E: 145°.

36. Correct answer: G. Begin with Circle Z. We are told that Circle Z's area is 225π; recall that the formula for the area of a circle is πr^2. If $225\pi = \pi r^2$, then $r^2 = 225$. So, the square root of 225 is the radius of Circle Z: $r = \sqrt{225} = 15$.

Now that we know that the radius of Circle Z is 15, we can use that to figure out the radius of Circle Y. We are told that the diameter of Circle Y is the radius of Circle Z, which means that the diameter of Circle Y is 15, meaning the radius of Circle Y is half of 15, or 7.5

Lastly, we are told that the diameter of Circle X is equal to the radius of Circle Y. Because we now know that the radius of Circle Y is 7.5, this means we now know that the diameter of Circle X is 7.5, and thus that the radius of Circle X is 3.75.

Recall that the formula for the circumference of a circle is $2\pi r$. Because we are looking for the circumference of Circle X, plug in the r of Circle X into this equation to solve, like this:

Circumference of Circle $X = 2\pi r = 2\pi(3.75) = 7.5\pi$, which matches answer choice G.

37. Correct answer: A. Because we are asked for $f(g(x))$, we must plug $g(x)$ into the function $f(x)$ anywhere that there is an x. In $f(x)$, there is one x right after the $\dfrac{2}{3}$, so this is where we must put the entire expression $g(x)$, like this:

$$f(x) = \dfrac{2}{3}x - 14 = \dfrac{2}{3}(6x^2 + 18x + 18) - 14 = 4x^2 + 12x + 12 - 14 = 4x^2 + 12x - 2$$

So far, this is good, but it can be simplified further (which is necessary; if you look at the answer choices none of them match $4x^2 + 12x - 2$). The terms are all divisible by 2, which we can factor to the outside of the parentheses, like this:

$$4x^2 + 12x - 2 = 2(2x^2 + 6x - 1), \text{ which matches answer choice A.}$$

38. Correct answer: H. There are two ways of solving this problem, and it doesn't matter which of them you choose. Let's solve it both ways so you can learn both:

<u>First method: factoring the trinomials and simplifying</u>

A trinomial is a polynomial with three terms. In both the numerator and the denominator of this particular problem, there is a trinomial, but also a binomial (a polynomial with two terms). Each of the trinomials can be factored into two binomials being multiplied by one another. One way to do this is to use the Quadratic Formula, but here's the thing: I don't even know the Quadratic Formula, and you don't need it on the ACT (contrary to popular belief). If you know it, and can do it quickly, then yes it could help you during a problem like this one, but I have never encountered an ACT Math problem in which it is necessary.

To factor a trinomial into two binomials, you have to find a special pair of numbers. These numbers are these: what are the two numbers that can be multiplied to result in the last term in the trinomial, but add together to equal the term/coefficient in the middle term? That may sound complicated, but let's follow this process with the trinomial in the numerator, then the one in the denominator.

The trinomial in the numerator is $(x^2 + x - 6)$. We need two numbers that multiply to give us -6, but add together to give us 1 (which is the number, though hidden, in front of the middle x term). If you multiply 3 and -2, you get -6, and if you add 3 and -2, you get 1. Our two binomials, then, will be $x +$ each of these two numbers. Thus, this trinomial can be factored into two binomials that look like this:

$$(x^2 + x - 6) = (x + 3)(x - 2)$$

The trinomial in the denominator is $(x^2 - 5x - 24)$. We need two numbers that multiply to give us -24, but add together to give us -5. If you multiply -8 and 3, you get -24, and if you add -8 and 3, you get -5. Our two binomials, then, will be $x +$ each of these two numbers. Thus, this trinomial can be factored into two binomials that look like this:

$$(x^2 - 5x - 24) = (x - 8)(x + 3)$$

Now that we have done that, we can rewrite the original equation and replace the trinomials with binomials, and then cancel out any binomials that are the same:

$$\frac{(x + 1)(x^2 + x - 6)}{(x - 2)(x^2 - 5x - 24)} = \frac{(x + 1)(x + 3)(x - 2)}{(x - 2)(x - 8)(x + 3)} = \frac{(x + 1)}{(x - 8)}, \text{ which matches answer choice H.}$$

Second method: *Picking Numbers*

A second strategy for solving this problem is by using the strategy *Picking Numbers*, which means pretending that x equals a certain number, then plugging that into the equation and answer choices to find a match. The question says that we can't use $x = 2$, so let's use $x = 3$. Below, I rewrite the problem, putting a 3 anywhere there is an x:

$$\frac{(x + 1)(x^2 + x - 6)}{(x - 2)(x^2 - 5x - 24)} = \frac{(3 + 1)(3^2 + 3 - 6)}{(3 - 2)(3^2 - 5(3) - 24)} = \frac{(4)(9 + 3 - 6)}{(1)(9 - 15 - 24)} = \frac{(4)(6)}{(1)(-30)} = \frac{24}{-30} = -\frac{4}{5}$$

Next, plug in $x = 3$ into each of the answer choices to determine which also equals $-\dfrac{4}{5}$.

Answer F: $\quad \dfrac{(x - 1)(x + 2)}{(x + 8)(x - 2)} = \dfrac{(3 - 1)(3 + 2)}{(3 + 8)(3 - 2)} = \dfrac{(2)(5)}{(11)(1)} = \dfrac{10}{11}$, which is not correct.

Answer G: $\quad \dfrac{(x - 1)}{(x + 8)} = \dfrac{(3 - 1)}{(3 + 8)} = \dfrac{2}{11}$, which is not correct.

Answer H: $\quad \dfrac{(x + 1)}{(x - 8)} = \dfrac{(3 + 1)}{(3 - 8)} = \dfrac{4}{-5} = -\dfrac{4}{5}$, that's it!

39. Correct answer: **E**. There is a midpoint formula that you may have used in math class. I hesitate pulling it out and using it here because it is not necessary to know this formula to solve the little midpoint questions you are likely to find on the ACT. Let's simply think this through first.

A line segment starts at point $(2, -1)$, then moves on to a midpoint at $(0, 3)$. To find the other endpoint, what the question calls (a, b), find the change that was made in the x and y values between these two points, then make the same changes starting from the midpoint.

The line segment starts with an x value of 2, then moves to a midpoint with an x value of 0. That is a change of -2. So, this same change needs to be made starting with the midpoint to find the x value of the other endpoint. So, starting with an x value of 0 (the midpoint), make a change of -2. The result is that the other endpoint, or (a, b), has an x value of -2. Since E is the only answer choice with an x value of -2, this would already be enough to get the question correct.

However, we can apply the same reasoning to the y values of the points. The first endpoint has a y value of -1, then moved to an endpoint with a y value of 3. This is a change in y value of $+4$. So, starting at the midpoint, make the same change to find the y value of (a, b). If the midpoint has a y value of 3, we add 4 to find that the missing endpoint has a y value of $3 + 4 = 7$.

Thus, $(a, b) = (-2, 7)$, which matches answer choice E.

40. Correct answer: **J**. You don't need to have any knowledge about temperatures or the relationship between Celsius and Fahrenheit to get this question correct. The equation given has two variables (F and C), and you are given 1 of the 2 (that $C = 31$), leaving just 1 that you need to find using Algebra, like this:

$$F = \frac{9}{5}C + 32 \quad \ldots \quad F = \frac{9}{5}(31) + 32 \quad \ldots \quad F = 55.8 + 32 \quad \ldots \quad F = 87.8$$

The question requires that you round up to the nearest degree, which is up to 88, which matches answer choice J.

41. Correct answer: **D**. If a line never crosses the y-axis, that means it goes straight up and down. This question asks for the slope of such a line. Remember, the slope of a line can be described as "rise over run," or $\frac{\text{rise}}{\text{run}}$, or can be thought of as the change on the y-axis divided by the change on the x-axis.

If you think about a line that goes straight up and down, but never goes side to side at all along the x axis, then the "rise" will be infinite, and the "run" will be 0. Such a slope would look like this: $\frac{\infty}{0}$, or infinity divided by 0. It isn't possible to divide any number, let alone infinity, by 0; any such attempt or number is undefined, which is why the correct answer is D: undefined.

42. Correct answer: **G**. First, draw the triangle being described so that it can be visualized and to avoid simple mistakes (which I have done below). The question asks for the *area* of this triangle; recall that the formula for the area of a triangle is $\frac{1}{2}bh$, in

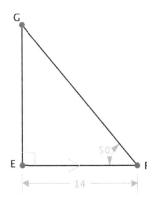

which b is the base and h is the height. Fortunately, we know the base (though you could have drawn this triangle with side GE on the bottom, in which case you'd know the height), which is 14, which means that we need to find the height, which is side GE. To do so, we will need one of or trig functions (sin, cos, or tan). We know the angle to go from (angle F, which is 50), but we need one that uses what we know (side EF) and what we don't (side GE). This needed function is tangent, which is equivalent to the opposite side (GE, which we'll call x in the equation below) over the adjacent side (EF, or 14).

$$\tan(50) = \frac{\text{opposite}}{\text{adjacent}} \quad \ldots \quad \tan(50) = \frac{x}{14} \quad \ldots \quad (14)\tan(50) = x \quad \ldots \quad x = 16.68$$

Side GE, which we called x above, is the height of the triangle. Now, we can plug the base (14) and the height (16.68) into the formula for the area of a triangle, like this:

$$\frac{1}{2}bh = \frac{1}{2}(14)(16.68) = 116.79, \text{ which is answer choice G.}$$

43. Correct answer: **B**. First, let's simplify the exponents on the left side of the equation. When an exponent is raised to an exponent, you *multiply* the exponents. Take this smaller example: x^{3^3}. Some would try to *add* these exponents, but that would be what you would do if the same variables, each raised to an exponent, were being multiplied by one another. Here, we multiply these exponents, like this:

$$x^{3^3} = x^{3 \cdot 3} = x^9$$

If you try out a number for x, like $x = 3$, you will see that this is the case. Now, let's apply the same way of thinking to simplify the term on the left side of the equation in the original problem:

$$(x^{3z+4})^3 = x^{(3z+4) \cdot 3} = x^{9z+12}$$

Now that we have simplified, let's rewrite the original equation: $x^{9z+12} = x^3$.

The key to getting this question correct from here is to recognize that if the base is the same (which is what we have here; both sides of the equation feature a base of x), the exponents can be set equal to each other in a new equation. Then, we can solve for z to get the question correct:

$$x^{9z+12} = x^3 \quad \dots \quad 9z + 12 = 3 \quad \dots \quad 9z = -9 \quad \dots \quad z = -1, \text{ which matches answer choice B.}$$

44. Correct answer: **J**. Because the swimming pools have the same depth, it is unnecessary to know the volume of these pools (which would be the volume of a cylinder). Instead, find the area of both Pool C (which has a diameter of 60) and Pool E (which has a diameter of 100), then make the correct comparison. Recall that the formula for the area of a circle is πr^2.

$$\text{Area of Pool C} = \pi r^2 = \pi (30)^2 = 2,827.43$$

$$\text{Area of Pool E} = \pi r^2 = \pi (50)^2 = 7,853.98$$

To find how much more water Pool E needs compared to Pool C, divide the area of Pool E by the area of Pool C, then multiply by 100 (because the answers are in percents), like this:

$$\frac{\text{Area of Pool E}}{\text{Area of Pool C}} \times 100 = \frac{7,853.98}{2,827.43} \times 100 = 277.78\%, \text{ which rounds up to answer choice J: 278\%}$$

45. Correct answer: **C**. First, create a number set of the first 8 pools (before the addition of Pluto), then find the mean, median, mode, and range:

Number set: {30, 40, 60, 60, 75, 80, 90, 100}

$$\text{Mean (average)} = \frac{(30 + 40 + 60 + 60 + 75 + 80 + 90 + 100)}{8} = \frac{535}{8} = 66.875$$

$$\text{Median (middle term)} = \frac{(60 + 75)}{2} = \frac{135}{2} = 67.5$$

Mode (number that occurs the most) $= 60$

Range (difference between greatest and smallest) $= 100 - 30 = 70$

Now, what you *could* do is spend the time finding all of these values for the same number set, but with the addition of a pool with a diameter of 15 feet. *However*, that is completely unnecessary. The only way that the mode can change is if Pluto's pool had the same diameter as one of the other pools, but it does not. As every other value (mean, median, range) changes, the mode will stay the same. Because the question asks for which value changes the *least*, we can be confident that the correct answer is C: the mode.

46. Correct answer: **G**. To find the measure of the arc of a circle, find the ratio or percent the section occupies by dividing the interior angle (120) by the total angle measures in a circle (360), then set that equal to the arc itself (which we'll call x) divided by the circumference of the entire circle. From there, you can cross multiply to solve for x. As a reminder, the formula for the circumference of a circle is $2\pi r$, or πd, in which d is the diameter; the circumference we need, which is the circumference of Pool H, is $\pi d = 75\pi$.

$$\frac{120}{360} = \frac{x}{75\pi} \quad \dots \quad 360x = 120(75\pi) \quad \dots \quad x = \frac{(120)(75\pi)}{360} = 25\pi, \text{ which matches answer choice G.}$$

47. Correct answer: **A**. The simplest way to solve this problem is to use *Backsolving*, the mini-strategy in which you plug in the answer choices one at a time to determine if it fits in the inequality.

Let's go through the answer choices one at a time to determine if they fit the inequality.

Choice A: $\dfrac{1}{x^2} = \dfrac{1}{(\frac{5}{12})^2} = \dfrac{1}{(.4167)^2} = \dfrac{1}{0.174} = 5.74$

Fortunately, this is as far as we need to go! 5.74 is between 4 and 9. I doubt on the real ACT that you'd have time to go through and check every single answer; that's the kind of step you might need to take if you have spare time at the end (which hardly ever happens, if ever, on ACT Math!). Be confident and move on: the correct answer is A.

48. Correct answer: **K**. Usually, two lines have only 1 solution (the point where they cross). Sometimes, two lines have 0 solutions (they are parallel). For two lines to have an infinite number of solutions, they have to be *the same line*, stacked one on top of another.

Before we get to that, notice how these two lines are separated off from the question, literally stacked one on top of another? That is because there is a way in Algebra to add lines and subtract lines, which is done by adding or subtracting each similar term one at a time; this trick can also be combined with the fact that lines or entire equations can be changed (for example, multiplied by 10 or divided by -7) so long as each term is equally affected. As far as this particular question is concerned, if you can subtract one line from another, and you are left with all 0's, then you know that they are the same line.

As they are written, the $2x$ term from one line sits directly above the $6x$ term in the other line. Because $6x$ is $3 \times 2x$, and these terms are unchangeable, then for these two lines to be the same, each other term in the second line must also be $3 \times$ as large as the first line. If you look at the final term, the number in the top line is 4, and wouldn't you know it, the number in the bottom line is $3 \times 4 = 12$.

That brings us to the middle term. In the top line, we have 7. Sticking with the pattern of multiplying the bottom term by 3 to make it the same line as the one in the top, we need $3 \times 7 = 21$ where there is a z in that second line. This is why the answer is K: 21.

If you still do not understand, think of it like this: Making the z a 21 would mean that if the top line were multiplied by 3 throughout, it would be identical to the bottom line, which simply shows that they are the same; you could then subtract the bottom line from the top line to get all 0's.

49. Correct answer: **C**. First, of course, draw the triangle to get an idea of what it looks like before trying to find the area. I have done that below. Recall of course that the area of a triangle is $\dfrac{1}{2}bh$, in which b is the base and h is the height.

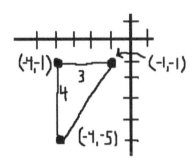

As you can see, I have plotted the three points, drawn lines between them to make a triangle, and labeled the lengths of the two sides that are necessary to find the area (3 and 4, respectively). It may throw some students off that the triangle is "upside down," but that doesn't affect the math at all; the height is still 4 and the "base" is still 3.

Now for the math:

$\dfrac{1}{2}bh = \dfrac{1}{2}(3)(4) = 6$, which matches answer choice C.

50. Correct answer: **K**. To answer this question, which is a kind of *Logical Thinking with Variables* question, use a combination of the *Picking Numbers* and *Backsolving* strategies in which you go one by one down the answer choices, eliminating wrong answers one at a time.

Just looking at the inequality, which again says that $7x^3y^4 < 0$, I can see a couple of things about it. First, no matter what y equals (whether a negative number like -3 or a positive number like 5), the y^4 term will *always be positive*. This means that, for the expression $7x^3y^4$ to be negative, the x^3 term must always be negative. The only way for a cubed number to be negative is if the original number, in this case x, is negative.

Lastly, you are not looking for something that is true. The question asks for an answer that can't possibly be true.

Answer F ($x < 7$): because we already determined that x must be a negative number, then this inequality *can* be true, which means it is not correct.

Answer G ($x > -7$): again, we determined that x has to be a negative number, which means it could possibly be any value greater than -7, like -5 for example. This answer therefore is not correct.

Answer H ($y < 0$): we also determined that y could be any value and that, no matter what, the result would be positive. Thus, it *is* possible for y to be less than 0, making this answer choice also incorrect.

Answer J ($y > 7$): we already determined that y can equal any number negative or positive, including anything greater than 7. Because this choice *is* possible, it is also incorrect.

Answer K ($x = 0$): finally, we've found it! When x is equal to 0, the entire equation is now equal to 0. The inequality is $<$ (less than), not $\leq$ (less than or equal to). For that reason, it is *not possible* for x to equal 0, making choice K the correct answer.

51. Correct answer: **A**. This question is pure *Backsolving*. Simply plug in the values for x into the functions in the answer choices and find which of them results in the numbers stated by the question.

Let's start with A. First, we'll plug in an x value of -3 and see if the result of the function is -14:

$$f(x) = -2x^2 + 4 = -2(-3^2) + 4 = -18 + 4 = -14$$

So far so good. Try at least one more, if not both, to determine if A is truly the correct answer. You know that some of these functions are going to work for some of the values for x, maybe even two out of three. Below, I'll try $x = -1$ and $x = 4$ back to back to determine if they also result in values of 2 and -28, respectively:

$$f(x) = -2x^2 + 4 = -2(-1^2) + 4 = -2 + 4 = 2$$

$$f(x) = -2x^2 + 4 = -2(4^2) + 4 = -32 + 4 = -28$$

Thus, the correct answer is A; the function $f(x) = -2x^2 + 4$ is the function with the values stated in the question.

52. Correct answer: **F**. First, recognize that there are a total of $8 \times 8 = 64$ marbles in the hat. Because there are 8 green marbles, the odds that the first player (Joseph) draws a green is $\dfrac{8}{64}$. Next, we are told that Maximilian draws a green marble. Because there are now only 63 marbles in the hat (Joseph drew one already) and only 7 green marbles in the hat (again, because Joseph drew one), the odds of him also drawing a green marble is $\dfrac{(8-1)}{(64-1)} = \dfrac{7}{63}$. Now, Jude is going to draw a marble, and the question asks for the probability that he also draws a green marble. To find this probability, use the same thinking: when Jude draws, there are now only 6 green marbles left (because the previous 2 boys drew green marbles) and only 62 total marbles. Thus, Jude's probability of drawing a green marble is this:

$$\dfrac{(7-1)}{(63-1)} = \dfrac{6}{62} = \dfrac{3}{31}, \text{ which is answer choice F.}$$

53. Correct answer: **E**. First, you have to know that the legs of a triangle are the two sides that are *not* the hypotenuse; in other words, the two legs are the two sides that meet at a 90° angle. That means that we can use the Pythagorean Theorem to find the missing side (the hypotenuse) and add the three together to find the perimeter of the triangle.

If you look at the answer choices, you will see that many of them are in a form that adds or multiplies a number by a square root of some kind. If you do the work on your calculator and come up with a decimal, simply try out the answer choices in your calculator to match them.

First, find the missing hypotenuse. The Pythagorean Theorem, as a reminder, says that $a^2 + b^2 = c^2$ in which c is the length of the hypotenuse:

$$a^2 + b^2 = c^2 \quad \ldots \quad 10^2 + 15^2 = c^2 \quad \ldots \quad 100 + 225 = c^2 \quad \ldots \quad \sqrt{325} = \sqrt{c^2} \quad \ldots \quad c = \sqrt{325}$$

To simplify $\sqrt{325}$, "square out" any factors of 325 that are also perfect squares. For example, $325 \div 25 = 13$, thus $\sqrt{325} = \sqrt{25 \cdot 13} = 5\sqrt{13}$. This means that the perimeter is equal to $10 + 15 + 5\sqrt{13} = 25 + 5\sqrt{13}$, which matches answer choice E.

Another option is to put $\sqrt{325}$ in your calculator and get that the length of c is 18.03. Add that to 10 and 15, and get that the perimeter of the triangle is $18.03 + 10 + 15 = 43.03$. When you put the answer choices in your calculator, you will get only one of them that equals approximately 43.03, which is answer choice E.

54. Correct answer: **H**. One way to solve this problem is to carefully add the fractions in the numerator and denominator (after carefully multiplying) by finding common denominators. Then, properly divide whatever fraction over fraction you end up with. However, I have some advice in that department:

DO NOT DO THAT ON AN ACTUAL ACT!

Put *all of this in your calculator*! This is the ACT Math mini-strategy we simply called *The Calculator*, stressing the use of your calculator to your advantage. Your pre-Algebra or Algebra teacher would have expected you to perfectly solve this kind of thing, but this isn't math class: it's the ACT. Start with the numerator, then everything in the denominator. Take steps, writing down what you've solved for thus far on occasion so that you don't make a simple mistake. Lastly, you'll probably be rounding sometimes because of the fractions, so don't expect the final answer you come up with to perfectly match to the hundredth's place the correct answer. Here's an example of what that might look like:

$$\frac{\frac{1}{6} + \left(\frac{5}{2} \cdot \frac{2}{3}\right)}{\left(-\frac{11}{12} + \frac{11}{4}\right) - \left(\frac{-3+14}{-3+15}\right)} = \frac{1.83}{1.83 - 0.92} = \frac{1.83}{0.91} = 2.00, \text{ which matches answer choice H.}$$

On a side note, if you want to solve this by finding common denominators, etc., it's not *bad* to do that, just time-consuming. That process would take me, personally, a couple of minutes. Putting it all in the calculator, on the other hand, takes me about 30 seconds.

55. Correct answer: **D**. The two expressions being described need to first be properly written out by you into a mathematical form.

First, "When x is squared and added to 4 times y, the result is 13" =

$$x^2 + 4y = 13$$

Second, "when the product of 2 and y is added to the product of negative 2 and x, the result is negative 16" =

$$2y - 2x = -16$$

Next, you are asked which of the following values of x and y is a solution for this system of equations. The only thing to do is to plug in each answer choice's x and y values and see if the equation is satisfied.

A: $x = 8$; $y = 0$

$$x^2 + 4y = 13 \quad \ldots \quad 8^2 + 4(0) = 13 \quad \ldots \quad 64 + 0 = 13 \quad \ldots \quad \text{No, it doesn't satisfy; try B.}$$

B: $x = 0$; $y = -8$

$$x^2 + 4y = 13 \quad \ldots \quad 0^2 + 4(-8) = 13 \quad \ldots \quad -32 = 13 \quad \ldots \quad \text{No, it doesn't satisfy; try C.}$$

C: $x = 10$; $y = 2$

$$x^2 + 4y = 13 \quad \ldots \quad 10^2 + 4(2) = 13 \quad \ldots \quad 116 = 13 \quad \ldots \quad \text{No, it doesn't satisfy; try D.}$$

D: $x = 5$; $y = -3$

$$x^2 + 4y = 13 \quad \ldots \quad 5^2 + 4(-3) = 13 \quad \ldots \quad 25 - 12 = 13 \quad \ldots \quad \text{Yes, it satisfies!}$$

$$2y - 2x = -16 \quad \ldots \quad 2(-3) - 2(5) = -16 \quad \ldots \quad -6 - 10 = -16 \quad \ldots \quad \text{Yes, it satisfies!}$$

Thus, the correct answer is D.

56. Correct answer: **F**. MC starts writing at 2:00 at a pace of 17 words per minute. She writes for 3 minutes until Clare starts writing, meaning she has already written $3 \times 17 = 51$ words.

The easiest way to conceptualize how many minutes it will take for Clare to catch MC is by thinking this: if Clare writes at 22 words per minute, and MC at 17 words per minute, then that means that every minute Clare will gain $22 - 17 = 5$ words on MC. After 10 minutes (in other words, at 2:13), Clare will have gained 50 words. Though that is *close* to the 51 words that she has to gain, it isn't quite there, since we are asked to *round up* after Clare catches MC.

This means that sometime between 2:13 and 2:14 Clare will catch MC, which then rounds up to 2:14, which is answer choice F.

57. Correct answer: **B**. Triangle *ECF* is a right triangle, which means that we will need to use one of our trig functions (sin, cos, or tan) to find the length of *EC*. We know that the length of *FC* is 4, so what we need is either another side of the triangle, which isn't possible to find in this case, or another of the missing angles. Well, if $\angle AGD$ is 150°, then $\angle DGE$ must be $180° - 150° = 30°$.

Because *GD* is parallel to *EF*, this means that $\angle FEC$ is also 30°. Now we have enough to solve for *EC*, but we need a trig function that uses what we know (4, the opposite angle) and what we don't know (*EC*, the adjacent angle), which would be tangent. For simplicity's sake, let's call the length of *EC* just x:

$$\tan(30) = \frac{4}{x} \quad \dots \quad x\tan(30) = 4 \quad \dots \quad x = \frac{4}{\tan(30)} \quad \dots \quad x = \frac{4}{0.577} \quad \dots \quad x = 6.93$$

Because the question asks us to round to the nearest tenth of a meter, we round down to 6.9, which is answer choice B.

58. Correct answer: **J**. There are two ways to solve this problem.

The first way is to carefully simplify. Before dealing with the fact that the expression is raised to the ½, let's treat each term within the parentheses one by one and simplify as we go:

$$\sqrt{x^4} = x^2$$

$$\sqrt[4]{x^8} = x^2$$

$$\frac{1}{x^{-2}} = x^2$$

Now, replace each term with its equivalent simplification:

$$\left(\sqrt{x^4} - \sqrt[4]{x^8} + \frac{1}{x^{-2}}\right)^{\frac{1}{2}} = \left(x^2 - x^2 + x^2\right)^{\frac{1}{2}} = (x^2)^{\frac{1}{2}}$$

When a number is raised to the ½, that is the same thing as finding the square root of that number. Thus:

$$(x^2)^{\frac{1}{2}} = \sqrt{x^2} = x, \text{ which is answer choice J.}$$

A second way to solve the problem would be to use the ACT Math mini-strategy *Picking Numbers*. This isn't a "backup" method for those who can't simplify well: *it is a strategy that the best ACT Math test takers are routinely using.* Choose a number for x, then use your calculator to help you solve. Then, apply that same x value to the answer choices to find a match. Let's pretend for this situation that $x = 2$ and see what we get when we do the math:

$$\left(\sqrt{x^4} - \sqrt[4]{x^8} + \frac{1}{x^{-2}}\right)^{\frac{1}{2}} = \left(\sqrt{2^4} - \sqrt[4]{2^8} + \frac{1}{2^{-2}}\right)^{\frac{1}{2}} = \left(\sqrt{16} - \sqrt[4]{256} + 2^2\right)^{\frac{1}{2}} = (4 - 4 + 4)^{\frac{1}{2}} = \sqrt{4} = 2$$

It turns out, that when $x = 2$, the entire expression also equals 2. Looking through the answer choices, J is then clearly correct since it is simply x.

59. Correct answer: **E**. This is one of those "sticker shock" problems, meaning just the look of it is scary. However, the mathematics within are not as scary as it may first seem. Each circle's radius is used in the perimeter twice. Thus, finding the radius of each circle is the hardest step in solving.

You are given the circumference of each circle. Recall then that the formula for the circumference of a circle is $2\pi r$. Set this formula equal to each circle to find each circle's radius:

Circle L: $\qquad 2\pi r = 8\pi \quad \ldots \quad r = 4$

Circle M: $\qquad 2\pi r = 12\pi \quad \ldots \quad r = 6$

Circle N: $\qquad 2\pi r = 14\pi \quad \ldots \quad r = 7$

Again, each circle's radius is used twice in the perimeter of the triangle. Thus:

$$\triangle LMN \text{ perimeter } = 2(4) + 2(6) + 2(7) = 8 + 12 + 14 = 34 \text{ mm, which is answer choice E.}$$

60. Correct answer: **H.** Because the odds of landing on heads or tails is the same, it is irrelevant that the coin should land on heads the first three tosses then on tails the final two. The question might as well ask for the odds of the coin landing on heads all five tosses or on tails for the first four tosses and heads for the fifth.

To determine the probability of any number of events in a row, multiply their probabilities. The odds of landing a coin on heads is $\frac{1}{2}$. Because this is the probability of each coin flip five times in a row, multiply this probability five times, like this:

$$\frac{1}{2} \cdot \frac{1}{2} \cdot \frac{1}{2} \cdot \frac{1}{2} \cdot \frac{1}{2} = \frac{1}{32}, \text{ which matches answer choice H.}$$

Answer Explanations - Step 5

Correct answers:

1: C	7: C	13: A	19: A	25: C	31: C
2: K	8: H	14: J	20: H	26: F	32: K
3: E	9: C	15: A	21: B	27: C	33: A
4: J	10: K	16: H	22: J	28: J	
5: D	11: D	17: D	23: D	29: C	
6: F	12: G	18: G	24: H	30: F	

1. Correct answer: **C**. Here, the *Fundamental Counting Principle* is being wrapped up in the midst of a modeling problem. Here is the best way to think about this problem: if there are 5 different children that can be put in the first position, then that leaves only 4 children for the second position, which leaves 3 children for the third position, which leaves 2 children for the fourth position, which leaves one child for the fifth position. In other words, the number of ways in which this couple can line up their 5 children is:

$$5 \times 4 \times 3 \times 2 \times 1 = 120, \text{ or answer choice C.}$$

2. Correct answer: **K**. If this question is hard to conceptualize with a variable, start out with a number (aka *Picking Numbers*). If she has $x = 3$ movies to choose from, and wants to watch 3 in a row, then how many combinations of movies are possible? Well, if $x = 3$, then there are 3 x 2 x 1 = 6 possibilities. So, which answer = 6 when $x = 3$? Try them out one at a time:

F. $3x = 3(3) = 9$, not 6.

G. $x^3 = (3)^3 = 27$, not 6

H. $x(x+1)^2 = 3(4)^2 = 48$, not 6

J. $x^3 x^2 x = (3)^3(3)^2(3) = 729$, not 6

K. $x(x-1)(x-2) = 3(2)(1) = 6$, that's it!

3. Correct answer: **E**. This is classic, and basic, fundamental counting principle. First of all, before we do the math, if there are 80 police officers and 50 firefighters, and the mayor is choosing one of each, I think you should recognize naturally that that's a *lot* of possible combinations. But, looking at the answer choices, only one of them is greater than 131. This tells me that answer choices A, B, C, and D are designed to throw you off from the real answer.

If there are 80, from which one will be chosen, and 50, from which one will be chosen, the number of possibilities is $80 \times 50 = 4,000$, or answer choice E.

4. Correct answer: **J**. These license plates, we are told, feature 7 spaces for either numbers or letters. However, we also learn that the first three spaces are fixed. This leaves 4 spaces that can feature either one of the 10 numbers (0 through 9) or one of 26 letters. The fact that they *can* be repeated is important, because it makes the math easier.

If there are 10 numbers and 26 letters to choose from, that means there are 36 total characters for each space. In choosing 1 of them 4 times, we need to multiply 36 by itself 4 times in a row, thus:

$$36 \times 36 \times 36 \times 36 = 1,679,616 \text{ possibilities for license plates, or answer choice J.}$$

5. Correct answer: **D**. We have seen these problems before. We discussed then that when the ACT asks you for the distance between two points, if you have the distance formula memorized, then that's great; you should use it. However, most of us don't, but that's OK; I think there's an easier way to find the distance between 2 points, which is to make a triangle in which the hypotenuse is the distance between two points, then use the Pythagorean Theorem (or your new knowledge of special triangles…) to find the distance between them.

Below is an expert drawing of our graphed points, made into a triangle, with the lengths of the legs of the triangles labeled:

Now, because this is a right triangle, and because we know the lengths of the two legs, we could use the Pythagorean Theorem $(a^2 + b^2 = c^2)$ to find the missing length between the two points. However, this problem is occurring in a lesson on triangles that featured special triangles, and one of those special triangles was the 5-12-13 triangle, meaning this: if you have a right

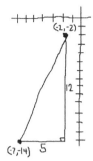

triangle with a leg of 5 and a hypotenuse of 13, you know the other leg to be 12; if you have a right triangle with a leg of 12 and a hypotenuse of 13, you know the other leg to be 5, or (most importantly for us now!) if you have a right triangle with a leg of length 5 and another leg with a length of 12, you *know* that the hypotenuse is 13.

Thus, the answer is D: 13.

6. Correct answer: **F**. This question purely tests your knowledge of the various types of triangles. First, we are told that triangle $\triangle LMN$ is an equilateral triangle, which means that all three of its sides are the same length. We are then told that angle $\angle L$ has a measure of 60 degrees. However, each angle of an equilateral triangle is the exact same (60 degrees; there is no other kind of equilateral triangle), so this measure is true of all 3 of this triangle's angles. Lastly, one of the sides, MN, has a length of 12mm. Again, all three sides of this triangle are the same, so every side is going to have a length of 12mm. With all of that in mind, let's get to the three statements to see which are true and which are false:

> I. The first statement says that triangle LMN is acute, which is true; every equilateral triangle is acute, which simply means that all 3 of its angles are less than 90 degrees. TRUE

> II. The second statement makes the claim that one of the triangles angles, angle N, is greater than 90 degrees, but this isn't possible in an equilateral triangle. FALSE

> III. The third statement makes the claim that another of the triangle's sides, side LM, has a length less than 12 mm. Again, all three sides are going to be of equal length. FALSE

Thus, the correct answer is F; only statement I is true.

7. Correct answer: **C**. The key to this question is remembering what it means for two triangles to be *similar*; it means that their angles are all the same, and that their sides are *relative*. As you can see, side PQ is half the length of side MN; side PR is half the size of side MO; thus, it must be the case that side RQ is half the length of side NO. Because that's true, we know the three sides of triangle PQR, and thus we can find the perimeter (which is what the question is asking for).

$$\text{Perimeter of PQR} = (\text{Side } PQ) + (\text{Side } PR) + (\text{Side } QR) = 3.5 + 4.5 + 3.5 = 11.5$$

8. Correct answer: **H**. First, let's plug in $m = 7$ into the absolute value, and get something like this:

$$|m - 11| = |7 - 11| = |-4|$$

Remember that absolute value simply means the distance a value is away from 0 (in other words, just make it positive if it is a negative value). In this case of course, -4 is a total of 4 away from 0, which is answer choice H.

9. Correct answer: **C**. This question falls mostly into a category that we have discussed before: ACT Math *Have to Know* #6: Logical Thinking With Variables. Here, those variables are sometimes within absolute value signs, which makes them relevant for the current lesson on absolute value, of course.

We are looking for an expression that is *always* negative. Even though j and k can be any value at all (except for 0), any time that either of them is within the absolute value symbols, the result will be positive. This is going to eliminate answer choice A, since it features a positive number over a positive number. Letters B and D share a problem in that it is possible for either of them to be positive; B because if j is a positive value of any kind, the entire fraction will be made positive, and D because if k is a negative number the negatives will cancel and you will be left with a positive value.

That leaves C and E. We can eliminate E because if j and k are both negative (or if they're both positive), the fraction will be positive. Thus, by process of elimination, C is the correct answer. However, we can also see why: the absolute values of j in the numerator and k in the denominator will both be positive, but the fraction as a whole has a negative sign in front, making the expression always negative.

10. Correct answer: **K**. Just like number 9, this question falls mostly into a category that we have discussed before: ACT Math *Have to Know* #6: Logical Thinking With Variables. Here, those variables are sometimes within absolute value signs, which makes them relevant for the current lesson on absolute value.

Immediately, we can see that $|-x|$ is equivalent to x. That will probably help us as we go through the five answer choices. Let's do so one at a time.

F. This expression, if we remove the absolute value signs, is equivalent to $\dfrac{|x|}{|x|^2} = \dfrac{x}{x^2} = \dfrac{1}{x}$, not x.

G. This expression can be reduced like this: $-\dfrac{|x|^2}{|x|} = -\dfrac{x^2}{x} = -x$, not x.

H. This is the same as G, $-x$, not x.

J. This expression is almost 100% identical to letter F: $\dfrac{|-x|}{|-x|^2} = \dfrac{x}{x^2} = \dfrac{1}{x}$, not x.

K. Again, by process of elimination, we've arrived at the correct answer. However, let's work it out and reduce it down:

$$\sqrt{(-x)^2} = \sqrt{x^2} = x$$

because the square root of anything squared is simply the value itself. If you're unsure, choose a number for x and plug the above expression in your calculator and see if they're a match.

11. Correct answer: **D.** The first thing you ought to do is to convert the fraction $\dfrac{3}{8}$ to a decimal so that it matches up with the other two numbers; this will make it much easier to order them properly. Thus, $\dfrac{3}{8} = 0.375$. Now, we have our three decimals: 0.375, 0.35, and 0.04. The other little thing that might trip up some students is that, if they're not careful, they'll think that 0.04 is the largest of the 3 numbers because it starts with the number 4. However, this number has a 0 in the tens place, while the other two have the number 3 in the tens place; that makes it the smallest. Clearly, 0.375 is the largest, 0.35 is in the middle, and 0.04 is the smallest. This makes option D the correct answer in that it orders the inequalities properly.

12. Correct answer: **G.** Because all of the answer choices have solved the inequality in terms of x, we must do the same. Let's simply treat the inequality like an equation by, first, adding $4y$ to both sides:

$$-2x - 4y \le 6y + 2 \quad \ldots \quad -2x \le 10y + 2$$

Now is where there could be a simple mistake made. Remember: if you divide or multiply both sides of an inequality by a negative number, the sign must switch. Notice how that happens when we divide every term by -2:

$$-2x \le 10y + 2 \quad \ldots \quad x \ge -5y - 1 \text{, which is answer choice G.}$$

13. Correct answer: **A.** The variable, the absolute value, and the modeling story all make this problem seem much more difficult than it is (the ACT is expert at making many problems seem more difficult than they really are). All we have to do is use *Backsolving* to go one at a time through the answer choices, plug them in for c, and see which of them is *NOT* within range of the inequality.

$$A: -40 \quad \ldots \quad |-40 - 30| \le 45 \quad \ldots \quad |-70| \le 45 \quad \ldots \quad 70 \le 45 \text{, which does NOT make sense!}$$

Thus, the answer is A, -40, which is a value for c that falls outside the range of the inequality. If you plug in all of the other answer in for c, you will see that they all satisfy the inequality.

14. Correct answer: **J.** The first and most crucial step in this problem, of course, is actually finding the two solutions to this trinomial. Again, DON'T PANIC that you don't have the Quadratic Formula memorized; neither do I. It is very, very, very unlikely (if not impossible) that the ACT will ask you a question that requires your knowledge of the Quadratic Formula. There are easier ways to find the solutions.

The first way would be by graphing; if you don't know how, follow the steps for graphing these in the ACT Math *Good to Know* Lesson #5 on Parabolas; anywhere the parabola crosses the x-axis is a solution.

However, what I'm more likely to do is to simply factor the trinomial into two binomials and set both binomials equal to 0 to find my two solutions. This skill is important for the ACT (and has come up a lot in this book as a result). Let's do that here. Our trinomial, as a reminder, is this: $x^2 - 10x - 24$.

We need two numbers that multiply to give us -24, but add together to give us -10. These two values are -12 and 2. Thus,

$$x^2 - 10x - 24 = (x - 12)(x + 2)$$

Now, set each binomial equal to 0 to find our two solutions:

$$(x - 12) = 0 \quad \ldots \quad x = 12 \qquad \text{and,} \qquad (x + 2) = 0 \quad \ldots \quad x = -2$$

Now that we have found our two solutions (which, again, is where this parabola crosses the x-axis), we can find their mean, which just means the average:

$$\frac{12 + (-2)}{2} = \frac{10}{2} = 5 \text{ , which is answer choice J.}$$

15. Correct answer: **A.** It is impossible to find the solution set (which just means the solutions) for this polynomial without first simplifying. So, this question will take three steps. Step 1, simplify and set equal to 0; Step 2, factor the resulting trinomial; Step 3, set each binomial equal to 0 (or graph it) and find our solutions.

Step 1: Simplify

$$x(x - 1) = 2x^2 + 9x + 25 \quad \ldots \quad x^2 - x = 2x^2 + 9x + 25 \quad \ldots \quad 0 = x^2 + 10x + 25$$

Step 2: Factor

Again, in factoring a trinomial (for us here, $x^2 + 10x + 25$), we need two numbers that multiply to give us the third term in the trinomial (in our case here, 25) that add together to equal the coefficient of the middle term (in our case here, 10). Those two numbers are clearly 5. Thus, we add 5 to x in our two binomials, like this:

$$x^2 + 10x + 25 = 0 \quad \ldots \quad (x + 5)(x + 5) = 0$$

Step 3: Set Equal to Zero

$$(x + 5) = 0 \quad \ldots \quad x = -5 \qquad \text{and,} \qquad (x + 5) = 0 \quad \ldots \quad x = -5$$

Because we get the same value for x, that simply means that this parabola only has 1 solution, which means that the parabola's tip touches the x-axis at $x = -5$, which makes A our correct answer.

16. Correct answer: **H.** You may notice that the shape of these three parabolas is identical; what sets them apart is simply their "height" off of the x-axis. This is determined by the final term in a quadratic, which is the y-intercept of the parabola itself. This is why the answer is H, which puts the changing z variable in the y-intercept slot.

However, if you're not fast enough conceptually to see why this question's solution is what it is, then there is a roundabout way to solve this problem. In real time, perhaps this is the type of question that you circle and come back to, but remember: there is almost always more than 1 way to solve ACT Math problems, including this one. Another way to solve it is *Backsolving*.

As a reminder, *Backsolving* simply means trying out answer choices one at a time. If you know how to graph parabolas on your graphing calculator, why not try out answer choice F with $z = 2$ and see if the resulting parabola is any of the above 3? Then move on to G, then H? This kind of flexibility and quick calculations could earn you another correct answer on the ACT Math test, but only if you have the time to do so.

17. Correct answer: **D.** To get this question correct, we must first be able to remember what the period of a wave is. The period of a wave (which is the same length as the wavelength) is the length of a wave from crest to crest or trough to trough. In other words, from the top of one wave to the top of another or the bottom of one wave to the to bottom of another. Here, we are given the data for these crests and troughs. Let's make a visual kind of chart that lists the crests and troughs, and see if we can go from there to determine the average period:

	Day 1	Day 2	Day 3	Day 4
High Tide	1:15 PM	12:30 PM	11:45 AM	11:00 AM
Low Tide	11:45 PM	11:00 PM	10:15 PM	9:30 PM

The first thing that I notice is that each tide decreases by 45 minutes each and every day, without exception. That might be enough for you to determine the answer, but let's keep going.

Remember; the period is the average distance from crest to crest or trough to trough. Crest to crest will be the time from high tide to high tide, and trough to trough will be from low tide to low tide. Let's make another little chart, this time calculating the time between each high and low tide, like this:

	Day 1 to 2	Day 2 to 3	Day 3 to 4
High Tide	23 hours, 15 min.	23 hours, 15 min.	23 hours, 15 min.
Low Tide:	23 hours, 15 min.	23 hours, 15 min.	23 hours, 15 min.

In this case, they have made the math side of things easy for us; the time between each high and low tide from one day to the next is the exact same, meaning that calculating the average period is not difficult. The average period, or the average length from high tide to high tide or low tide to low tide is 23 hours and 15 minutes, or answer choice D.

18. Correct answer: **G.** The best and fastest way to solve this problem is to conceptualize it. If sin (x), no matter what value of x you can think of, has a value up to 1 and as low as -1, and then I multiply that value by a number (in the case of our problem, c), then that value is only going to increase. For example, if $c = 3$, then the value of sin (x) is going to triple, up to a value of 3 or as far down as -3. Thus, if the "height" of the wave and the "depth" of the wave are increasing up and down as c increases, that affects the amplitude, making it "bigger."

There are only two answer choices that say that the amplitude increases, which are G and K. We can thus eliminate answers F, H, and J.

Conceptually, then, what happens to the period of the wave? Well, the period of a sin wave is simply the angles that sin is using to calculate; if the angles aren't affected, then the period will not be affected. If we were given a function of $f(x) = sin(cx)$, then the period would be stretched or narrowed as the angles change. This is why the answer is G: the period will stay the same as the amplitude increases.

19. Correct answer: **A.** As was said in the lesson accompanying this question, don't be afraid to use the *Drawn to Scale* mini-strategy on this problem if you are stuck. As was alluded to, you can even use the edge of your bubble sheet as a ruler, marking the lengths that you know to compare to the segment *BC*. Clearly, *BC* is not as long as 18 or 19; just by the looks of it, you can tell it is probably about one-third the length of AC, which is 27; that leads me to believe it is likely A or B.

However, there is an algebraic way to answer this question using the 3 values that we know (*AD, AC,* and *BD*). In words, it goes like this: *AC* + *BD* is equal to the length of *AD*, but a little bit longer: the length of *BC* longer to be exact. In algebraic form, it looks like this:

$$AD = AC + BD - BC$$

In the equation above, we have 3 values that we know, and 1 that we don't, which is *BC*, which just so happens to be the value that the question asks for. Let's rewrite and solve for *BC*:

$$AD = AC + BD - BC \quad ... \quad 45 = 27 + 26 - BC \quad ... \quad -8 = -BC \quad ... \quad BC = 8$$

20. Correct answer: **H.** We do not have enough information given to determine in this question the exact number of students who play both a Spring and a Fall sport. However, the question doesn't ask for that. Rather, the question asks for the *minimum* number of students who play both a Spring and Fall sport.

We know there are 25 students in the class; 15 play a Spring sport, and 17 play a Fall sport. If 15 of the 25 students play a Spring sport, then that means that, so far, there are 10 students who do not yet play a sport. If we want to find the minimum number of students who play both, let's assign 10 of these students to a Fall sport. If we do that, now every student in the class plays a sport, but there are still 7 students who play a Fall sport, which means that at an absolute minimum, 7 students have to play both. This is answer choice H.

21. Correct answer: **B.** In the addition or subtraction of matrices, we simply add or subtract one space at a time with its equivalent in the other matrix. The -6 term, for example, in the top left hand corner of the first matrix will subtract from it the 10 in the top left corner of the second matrix. The resulting matrix will be of the same dimensions as the two featured in the question, like this:

$$\begin{bmatrix} -6 & 9 \\ -8 & 4 \end{bmatrix} - \begin{bmatrix} 10 & -4 \\ -1 & 0 \end{bmatrix} = \begin{bmatrix} -16 & 13 \\ -7 & 4 \end{bmatrix} \text{, which is answer choice B.}$$

22. Correct answer: **J.** All we have to do here is multiply the 3 by every term in the matrix one at a time; the resulting matrix will be of the same dimensions after it is affected: 2×2, like this:

$$3 \begin{bmatrix} 0 & -2 \\ 6 & 5 \end{bmatrix} = \begin{bmatrix} 0 & -6 \\ 18 & 15 \end{bmatrix}, \text{ which is answer choice J.}$$

23. Correct answer: **D.** Matrices can be multiplied if the number of columns in the first matrix is the same as the number of rows in the second matrix. The resulting matrix, if this is the case, will be the opposite: it will be the number of rows in the first times the number of columns in the second. I remember as I'm typing this our acronym from the lesson on matrices: **CRRC**, or "Calm Rivers Reveal Crocs."

So, first we have to check if the number of columns in the first matrix matches the number of rows in the second. The first matrix has only 1 column, and the second matrix has only 1 row: so far, so good. This will mean that the resulting matrix will be the number of rows in the first matrix (3) by the number of columns in the second matrix (3).

This analysis is already enough to get the answer correct, and I would bet that if you *can* analyze the problem this well, you will probably be getting the answer fairly easily. There is only one matrix that is 3×3, which is answer choice D.

However, here is the entire thing worked out, just to be thorough:

$$\begin{bmatrix} -4 \\ x \\ 2x \end{bmatrix} \begin{bmatrix} x & 3 & 0 \end{bmatrix} = \begin{bmatrix} -4(x) & -4(3) & -4(0) \\ x(x) & x(3) & x(0) \\ 2x(x) & 2x(3) & 2x(0) \end{bmatrix} = \begin{bmatrix} -4x & -12 & 0 \\ x^2 & 3x & 0 \\ 2x^2 & 6x & 0 \end{bmatrix}, \text{ which is answer choice D.}$$

24. Correct answer: **H.** The simplest way to conceptualize this problem without making a simple mistake (which of course is what can happen if you keep it all in your head) is to convert the entire board's length into inches, get our answer, and then convert it back into feet.

Because there are 12 inches in a foot, we find the total number of inches in the board by doing this: $7(12) + 4 = 88$ inches. Since the board is cut into two equal pieces, the length of each part can be found by dividing the total length of board by two:

$$\text{Part Length} = \frac{88}{2} = 44 \text{ inches}$$

Of course, 44 inches is not an answer choice, so we need to convert it back to feet. Simply divide by 12, and any remainder is the number of inches leftover as well.

$$\frac{44}{12} = 3\frac{8}{12} = 3 \text{ feet } 8 \text{ inches, which is answer choice H.}$$

25. Correct answer: **C.** When you multiply feet by feet, you get square feet; when you multiply yard by yard, you get square yards. That seems obvious, but that means that we need to use the square footage of the floor to find its dimensions in feet, then use that to find the dimensions of the floor in yards, then use that to find the square yardage of the floor. If you simply divide 14,400 by 3 (because there are 3 feet in a yard), you will get 4,800, but that is a mistake and inaccurate.

First, find the dimensions of the floor in feet. We know the square footage is 14,400 ft^2, but that doesn't mean we automatically know the dimensions of the floor. However, it doesn't matter what dimensions we come up with, as long as they are accurate. I can see that 14,400 is a perfect square (it is 120^2), so let's use that and pretend that the dimensions of the floor are 120×120.

Second, we need to convert our dimensions to yards. Since there are 3 feet in 1 yard, we just divide our dimension by 3, so a floor that measures 120 ft $\times$ 120 ft equals 40 yards $\times$ 40 yards.

Lastly, we need to find now the square yardage. Since we now know the dimension in yards (40×40), we just simply multiply one side by the other: 40 yards $\times$ 40 yards = 1,600 square yards, or answer choice C.

26. Correct answer: **F.** The first step to solving this problem is to convert 40 miles per hour into miles per minute. To do this multiply the rate we know (miles per hour) by the number of minutes per hour so that "hours" cancels and we are left with miles per minute.

$$\frac{40 \text{ miles}}{\text{hour}} \cdot \frac{1 \text{ hour}}{60 \text{ minutes}} = \frac{40 \text{ miles}}{60 \text{ minutes}} = \frac{2}{3} \frac{\text{miles}}{\text{minute}}$$

Now that we have the speed Clarence is traveling in miles per minute, we just need to multiply this rate by the 16 minutes he is traveling. This will cause minutes to cancel, leaving us with the number of miles, like this:

$$\frac{2}{3} \frac{\text{miles}}{\text{minute}} \cdot 16 \text{ minutes} = \frac{32}{3} \text{ miles} = 10\frac{2}{3} \text{ miles} \text{ , which is answer choice F.}$$

27. Correct answer: **C.** The subscript following the word *log* in a log function is the base, and the number that a log function is set equal to is the exponent. Let's rewrite this in a form that might be a bit easier to understand and conceptualize:

$$\log_x 343 = 3 \quad ... \quad x^3 = 343$$

Now we can see that there is some number being cubed, and that number is equal to 343. You can solve this from here in couple of ways. Method 1 would be to use *Backsolving* and try out each answer one at a time to see which is the base that, when cubed, equals 343.

Method 2 is to use a calculator. Instead of starting with the *x*, we will start with the 343. In other words, the answer we are looking for is the cubed root of 343. There are a couple of ways to find a cubed root in your calculator. I like to raise numbers to the one-third power, like this:

$$x^3 = 343 \quad ... \quad (x^3)^{\frac{1}{3}} = 343^{\frac{1}{3}} \quad ... \quad x = 343^{\frac{1}{3}} \quad ... \quad x = 7, \text{ which is answer choice C.}$$

28. Correct answer: **J.** The subscript following the word log in a log function is the base, and the number that a log function is set equal to is the exponent; in our question, the variable *x*, represents the solution to a number raised to an exponent. Like before, one helpful step is to rewrite the function so that it makes more conceptual sense.

$$\log_4 x = -3 \quad ... \quad 4^{-3} = x$$

Now we have a much simpler problem to work with; at least, it is simpler if you know what to do with negative exponents! Remember: if an exponent is negative, you make it positive and then flip it (either from the numerator to the denominator or vice versa), like this:

$$4^{-3} = \frac{1}{4^3} = \frac{1}{64} \text{ , which is answer choice J.}$$

29. Correct answer: **C.** First, we must remember that a negative exponent needs to be made positive and then flipped from the numerator to the denominator (or vice versa), which explains what must be done with the 3^{-3} term. However, we must realize that the 3^{-3} might be in the numerator of the larger, greater fraction, but it is in the denominator of the top term; thus, you wouldn't put it in the denominator of the larger term, but the numerator of the upper term, like this:

$$\frac{\frac{1}{3^{-3}}}{3} = \frac{\frac{3^3}{1}}{3} = \frac{3^3}{3}$$

From here, you simply need to simplify, like so:

$$\frac{3^3}{3} = 3^2 = 9 \text{ , which is answer choice C.}$$

30. Correct answer: **F.** We need to take our time on this problem and ensure we don't make any simple mistakes. The first step is to change any variables with negative exponents into those with positive exponents by moving them from either the numerator to the denominator or vice versa. Before combining like terms, let's do this first step first:

$$\frac{a^{-3}b^2c^{-4}}{a^2b^{-2}} = \frac{b^2b^2c^1}{a^2a^3c^4}$$

Now, let's remember a couple of more rules about exponents. First, when two of the same variables raised to exponents are multiplied by one another (like we have with b in the numerator above and a in the denominator above), to combine them, you simply add their exponents together. Second, when you have two of the same variables being divided one by another, you subtract the smaller from the larger, and put the answer in the place of the larger. In the above equation, this is the case with c. You'll see how this happens as we simplify the problem above here:

$$\frac{b^2 b^2 c^1}{a^2 a^3 c^4} = \frac{b^4}{a^5 c^3}, \text{ which is answer choice F.}$$

31. Correct answer: C. If you can remember the formula of a circle, then you can get this question correct. As a reminder, the formula for the area of a circle is $(x - h)^2 + (y - k)^2 = r^2$, in which (h, k) is the center of the circle and r is the radius. Getting this question correct is as simple as plugging in the values given by the question into the equation.

If the circle is centered on $(-1, 3)$, then that means that $h = -1$ and $k = 3$. If the radius is 5, then $r^2 = 25$, thus:

$$(x - h)^2 + (y - k)^2 = r^2 \quad \dots \quad (x + 1)^2 + (y - 3)^2 = 25, \text{ or choice C.}$$

32. Correct answer: K. There is a LOT going on in this problem! But let's start with the ending: we are told that we are looking for circles that have an area of 64π. Recall that the area of a circle is πr^2, thus another way of saying that this circle has an area of 64π is to say that it has a radius of 8. Now, it is time to go through each of the three circles described and determine if it has a radius of 8 (aka an area of 64π).

Circle I. Because we are given the center of the circle $(-2, -2)$ and a point through which the circle passes $(6, -2)$, we have enough information to determine the radius of the circle, which is simply the distance between these two points. We have discussed on multiple occasions in this book that there is no need to memorize the distance formula (though if you have it memorized, that's great). Instead, you can simply draw a line between the two points and treat the line between them like the hypotenuse of a triangle, the length of which can then be found using the Pythagorean Theorem. However, in this case, finding the radius is much simpler.

Look at the points: they share a y value, meaning they are going to be the same "height." The line between them is going to be a straight line across $y = -2$. If you graph the points by hand, you will see what I am talking about. The distance between them, then, is simply the difference in values on the x-axis, or $6 - (-2)$, or 8. Thus, because the distance between these two points is 8, it has a radius of 8. So far, this point checks out, eliminating answer choices F and J.

Circle II. Remember that the formula for the circumference of a circle is $2\pi r$, thus if the circle described here has a circumference of 16π, it has a radius of 8. Thus, this circle also checks out, eliminating answer choice H.

Circle III. There is no need to graph this equation or any such thing; instead, realize that the formula of a circle is $(x - h)^2 + (y - k)^2 = r^2$, so all we need to look at is the last term: the r^2. Here, $r^2 = 64$, so $r = 8$, meaning it has a radius of 8. This circle, too, meets the requirements of the question.

Thus, Circles I, II, and III all have an area of 64π, which is answer choice K.

33. Correct answer: A. When you are given the formula for a line, such as $y = 2x - 4$, you can determine which points from a list of options are on this line by plugging each x and y value into the equation and seeing which of them satisfy. This exact same way of thinking is true of a circle. Each point that the circle goes over, when plugged into the equation of the circle, will satisfy. So, to solve this particular problem, plug in each answer choice's x and y values one at a time into the circle's equation and see which satisfies.

A. $(2, -2)$

$$(x - 2)^2 + (y - 5)^2 = 49 \quad \dots \quad (2 - 2)^2 + (-2 - 5)^2 = 49 \quad \dots \quad 0^2 + (-7)^2 = 49 \quad \dots \quad 49 = 49$$

Yes, it satisfies! This is the correct answer! There is no need to go any further. However, for the sake of showing you an answer that does *not* satisfy, let's move on to answer choice B:

B. $(2, 5)$

$$(x - 2)^2 + (y - 5)^2 = 49 \quad \dots \quad (2 - 2)^2 + (5 - 5)^2 = 49 \quad \dots \quad 0^2 + 0^2 = 49 \quad \dots \quad 0 = 49$$

No, 0 does not equal 49! This answer (and C, D, and E) does not satisfy. Thus, the correct answer is A.

Answer Explanations - Step 6 - Practice Test 1

Correct answers:

1: C	11: B	21: E	31: D	41: B	51: E
2: G	12: J	22: F	32: K	42: F	52: F
3: B	13: E	23: D	33: E	43: B	53: A
4: K	14: H	24: J	34: H	44: K	54: G
5: A	15: B	25: B	35: C	45: D	55: E
6: K	16: H	26: H	36: J	46: F	56: K
7: A	17: D	27: A	37: E	47: C	57: C
8: J	18: F	28: H	38: J	48: H	58: J
9: D	19: C	29: C	39: A	49: D	59: A
10: F	20: G	30: G	40: G	50: G	60: K

1. Correct answer: C. First, we must determine how much money Chip made from the selling of the candy bars, like this: $1.30 × 28 = $36.40. Now, when we subtract how much money Chip had leftover after his purchase of the fishing poles, we will learn how much he actually spent on purchasing them, like this: $36.40 − 13.90 = $22.50 . Lastly, we are looking for the average amount that Chip spent on the three fishing poles that he bought. We simply need to take the money spent, which we just found, and divide it by three, which will give us our final answer, like this: ($22.50 ÷ 3) = $7.50 , which is answer choice C.

2. Correct answer: G. First, we need to determine the amount of hours that it took him to drive. If he left at 6:00 AM, and arrived at 10:00 PM, then that means it took him 16 hours to get to his destination. Now, the question asks for an answer in miles per hour; that's a clue to the kind of math we need to do here. Put the number of miles traveled in the numerator, and the number of hours in the denominator, then the result will be in miles over hours, or miles per hour. Thus, since we are given that he traveled 880 miles, our equation looks like this:

$$\frac{880 \text{ miles}}{16 \text{ hours}} = 55 \text{ miles per hour, which is answer choice G.}$$

3. Correct answer: B. In order to determine how many blocks Sylvia walked her dog today, we need to first determine how much she actually charged her client for block-walking today. What I mean is that we need to subtract the base fee of $12 from the total charge of $29.50, like this: $29.50 − $12.00 = $17.50 charged for the blocks walked. If she charges $1.25 per block, we simply need to divide this per-block charge in to the $17.50 to determine the number of blocks walked, like this: $17.50 ÷ $1.25 = 14 blocks walked, which is answer choice B.

4. Correct answer: K. Don't let the word "translated" scare you; you can use context clues to understand that the point is simply "moved" 5 coordinate units down and then "moved" 9 coordinate units right. A simple mistake to be made would be that the moving down 5 units is mentioned first, but "up and down" on the (x, y) coordinate plane affects the y value, which is second. So, if the original point had a y value of −6, then moving down (in a negative direction) 5 would give the new point a y value of −11. Then, it is mentioned that the point is moved 9 units to the right, or in a positive direction on the right axis. The original point had an x value of 4, thus increasing it by 9 results in an x value of 13. The final answer, then, is $(13, -11)$, or answer choice K.

5. Correct answer: A. Adding matrices with the same dimensions is as easy as adding terms together in the same location in each matrix, the result of which will be a matrix with the same dimensions (in our case here, a $4 × 4$ matrix). For our purposes here, the upper left corner of the first matrix has a value of 4, and the upper left corner of the second matrix has a value of −8, thus the upper left corner of the resulting matrix will have a value of $4 + (−8) = - 4$. Already, we can eliminate choices B, D, and E.

Let's move to the upper right corner. The upper right value of the first matrix is 9, and the upper right value of the second matrix is 3, which means that the resulting upper right value will be $9 + 3 = 12$. Because answer choice A is the only one of our remaining options that has this value, we have done enough to conclude that it is the correct answer.

To be thorough, here is what it looks like when we add these two matrices together more formally:

$$\begin{bmatrix} 4 & 9 \\ -3 & 7 \end{bmatrix} + \begin{bmatrix} -8 & 3 \\ 4 & 0 \end{bmatrix} = \begin{bmatrix} -4 & 12 \\ 1 & 7 \end{bmatrix}, \text{ or answer choice A.}$$

6. Correct answer: K. We are looking in this problem for "a certain number," let's call it x, the square root of which is 7.48921. If the square root of x is 7.48911, then we simply need to square this value to find x. In other words:

$$\sqrt{x} = 7.48921 \quad \ldots \quad (\sqrt{x})^2 = (7.48921)^2 \quad \ldots \quad x = 56.08827$$

The question, however, asks us to place the number between two values, which we can do. 56.09 falls between 49 and 64, which is answer choice K.

7. Correct answer: A. In this problem we are given A and the midpoint of segment AB and asked to find point B. Actually graphing the two points could help you avoid simple mistakes, but if we apply the same changes that are made on the x and y axis between points A and the midpoint to the midpoint itself, we will find point B.

Point A has an x value of 2, and the midpoint has an x value of 4. That is a change of $+2$ on the x-axis, which means that the x value of point B will be $4 + 2 = 6$.

Point A has a y value of -4, and the midpoint has a y value of 1. That is a change of $+5$ on the y-axis, which means that the y value of point B will be $1 + 5 = 6$.

Thus, the coordinates of point B is $(6, 6)$, which is answer choice A.

8. Correct answer: J. To find the probability that the winner is not a green car, we need to put the total number of non-green cars over the total number of cars, and simplify. If there are 20 total cars, and 16 of them are non-green (because the question states that 4 are green), then the probability that the winner of the race is not a green car looks like this:

$$\frac{\text{non-green cars}}{\text{total cars}} = \frac{16}{20} = \frac{4}{5}, \text{ which is answer choice J.}$$

9. Correct answer: D. This is a classic Modeling-to-Algebra ACT Math problem. We have to carefully translate these words into an Algebra problem so that we can find our missing value (the number of books he had on the bookshelves last year), which we'll call x.

One key to answering this question well is realizing that 207 books "is" 30 more than 3 times x. I put quotations around the word "is" because that word is the equivalent of an equal sign in these kinds of problems. Thus, whatever equation we come up with, it will $= 207$.

Now for the equation on the left side of the $=$ sign. It says that 207 is "30 more than 3 times the number." Well, "the number" is x, thus x is going to be multiplied by 3. In addition, since 207 is "30 more", then that means we are going to add 30 to it, thus:

$$3x + 30 = 207$$

Now we have an equation to solve. Subtract 30 from both sides, then divide both sides by 3:

$$3x + 30 = 207 \quad \ldots \quad 3x = 177 \quad \ldots \quad \frac{3x}{3} = \frac{177}{3} \quad \ldots \quad x = 59, \text{ which is answer choice D.}$$

10. Correct answer: F. Most often, function questions feature only one variable, like $f(x)$. However, in this case we have two. However, the mathematics of it is still the same, no matter how many variables we have. If $f(x, y)$ is given, and we need to find $f(2, -1)$, then plug in 2 anywhere in the equation there is an x and plug in -1 anywhere there is a y in the equation, like this:

$$f(x, y) = -(x^3) + 3y = -(2^3) + 3(-1) = -(8) + (-3) = -8 - 3 = -11, \text{ or answer choice F.}$$

11. Correct answer: B. In this problem, we need to set up an equation and solve for our missing variable, segment BC, which is possible based on what we know. The last two data points we are given is that segment AC is 21 units long and that segment BD is 24 units long. When you add those two distances together, you get a distance that is equal to all of segment AD, plus a little bit extra, but that little bit extra is BC. Thus, $AC + BD = AD + BC$. Now, we plug in what we know and solve for what we do not know (which is BC):

$$AC + BD = AD + BC \quad \ldots \quad 21 + 24 = 34 + BC \quad \ldots \quad 11 = BC, \text{ which is answer choice B.}$$

Again, if you are stuck on this problem, it is a good candidate for the *Drawn to Scale* mini-strategy. First of all, just based on the *looks* of it, segment BC seems like it is about one-third of the entire line segment, AD, which is 34 units long, and only 11 is anywhere in that ballpark. You could also use your answer key as a kind of ruler, measuring out the lengths you do know along its edge and comparing it to segment BC.

12. Correct answer: **J.** The variable y in this question is used in both of the binomials that are being multiplied to equal 0, which means that there will be two values of y that make the expression as a whole equal to 0. If either of the binomials (meaning either of the terms within the parentheses) can be made to equal 0, then the expression as a whole will equal 0.

First, let's start with the first binomial: $(y + m)$. Again, if this binomial can be made to equal 0, the expression as a whole will be made to equal 0. Because we are adding m to y, then the only value for y that can make this expression equal 0 is $-m$, since $(-m + m) = 0$. So, $-m$ is one of our two values, which eliminates answer choices F, G, and K.

Second, let's move on to the second binomial: $(y - n) = 0$. Again, if this binomial can be made to equal 0, the expression as a whole will be made to equal 0. Because we are subtracting n from y, then the only value for y that makes this expression equal 0 is n, since $(n - n)$ will always $= 0$. Thus, n is the second of our two values. Given that our two values for y that satisfy the equation are $-m$ and n, the answer is J.

13. Correct answer: **E.** In order to determine the solutions for this expression, it needs to first be simplified by distributing the $7x$ term, adding like terms, and setting everything equal to 0. When all is set equal to 0, finding the solutions means finding the values for x that satisfy the equation, in other words finding the values of x that make the equation as a whole then equal 0. First let's simplify and set the equation equal to 0, like this:

$$x^2 = 7x(x - 0) - 54 \quad \ldots \quad x^2 = 7x^2 - 54 \quad \ldots \quad 0 = 6x^2 - 54 \quad \ldots \quad 0 = 6(x^2 - 9) \quad \ldots \quad 0 = x^2 - 9$$

You might be a little confused by that last step…where did the 6 go that was in front of the $(x^2 - 9)$ term? Well, we divided both sides by 6, and 0 divided by 6 is still 0.

Now we are left with this: $x^2 - 9 = 0$, and we have to determine what the solution set is for this expression. We have discussed elsewhere in this book how to factor a trinomial, which is a polynomial with three expressions, including an x^2 term, an x term, and a number, but here we have a binomial (only two terms in the expression) that begins with an x^2 term. However, we can easily make this into a trinomial, then factor like we are used to. To do this, we need to add a $0x$ term into the middle, like this:

$$x^2 - 9 = x^2 + 0x - 9$$

With that done, we can now factor. To factor this term into two binomials, we need two numbers that multiply to give us a -9 (our last number) and add up to give us a 0 (the middle number). Those two numbers are 3 and -3, since $3 \times -3 = -9$ and $3 + -3 = 0$. Thus:

$$x^2 - 9 = x^2 + 0x - 9 = (x - 3)(x + 3)$$

To find the solutions, set each binomial equal to 0 and solve for x. First, there is $(x - 3) = 0$, which, when solves, yields a result of $x = 3$, which is already enough to get the question correct, since E is the only option that features this as a result. However, we should also solve this for x: $(x + 3) = 0$, which, when solved, yields a result of $x = -3$, which is our second result.

However, there is another way to get this question correct, that might perhaps be even faster than the above method: *Backsolving*. Why not try out each answer choice one at a time to determine if it satisfies the equation? Of course we know that $\{-3, 3\}$ satisfies, but let me show you what it would look like when you come to a number that doesn't satisfy.

Let's begin with A $\{-4\}$ and see if this is the solution for the equation. All we need to do is to plug in -4 anywhere there is an x in the equation (even without simplifying the equation!) and see if it satisfies:

$$x^2 = 7x(x - 0) - 54 \quad \ldots \quad (-4)^2 = 7(-4)(-4 - 0) - 54 \quad \ldots \quad 16 = -28(-4) - 54 \quad \ldots \quad 16 = 58? \quad \text{NOPE}$$

When you enter in -4, or any other value for x that doesn't make sense or satisfy, then you can be sure it is not a solution, which will happen with every answer choice besides E.

14. Correct answer: **H.** Because you are not given any numbers in this question or diagram (we aren't told the lengths of any segments, the measure of any angles, the perimeter/circumference or area of any shape, etc.), this is an eyeball test. In other words, you are being forced to use the *Drawn to Scale* mini-strategy in this question. Before we get to the answer, we need to recall what it means for the arc of a circle to have a degree measure. The measure of any arc of a circle (an arc, again, is a "piece" of the circumference of a circle) is equivalent to its interior angle. For example, arc JG has a degree measure that is equivalent to angle JEG in the center of the circle. To the naked eye, let's approximate the measure of each of these angles one by one and see which has the greatest degree measure.

F: Angle FKJ looks, to me, to measure roughly $45°$.

G: Angle *FGH* looks, to me, to also measure roughly 45°.

H: Arc *FJ* appears to have an interior angle that measures roughly 135°, so the biggest so far.

J: Arc *JG* appears to have an interior angle that measures roughly 45°.

K: Arc *GH* appears to have an interior angle that measures roughly 45° (though there isn't an actual angle there for you to immediately visualize, you could draw it in there if it's helpful).

Thus, clearly, answer H is correct in that it appears to have the largest angle. In this kind of ACT Math question it isn't going to be close; in other words, if you're being forced to eyeball angles and to determine the biggest or smallest, the answer (if you're analyzing them correctly) is going to be obvious, as is the case here.

15. Correct answer: **B**. If two lines are parallel, they have the same slope. If two lines are perpendicular, their slopes are negative reciprocals of one another. Here, we are told that the slope of segment *EJ* is $\frac{3}{2}$, and asked to find the slope of a segment that is perpendicular to segment *EJ*. Thus, we need to find the negative reciprocal of $\frac{3}{2}$; to do so requires two steps. First, make it negative, and second, flip it upside down (take what's in the numerator and flip it to the denominator, and take what's in the denominator and flip it up into the numerator). Thus, the negative reciprocal of $\frac{3}{2}$ is $-\frac{2}{3}$, or choice B.

16. Correct answer: **H**. Because exactly half of the circle is within the triangle, we need to find the area of the circle and cut it in half. We are told that the diameter of the circle is 22, which means a radius of 11. Recall that the formula for the area of a circle is πr^2, and seeing that each answer keeps π without multiplying through, let's work on the radius squared. The area of this circle is:

$$\pi r^2 = (11)^2 \pi = 121\pi$$

So, if half of the circle lies within triangle *KFI*, then dividing 121π by 2 = 60.5π, or answer choice H.

17. Correct answer: **D**. There are multiple ways to solve this problem, but here is an easy way. Step 1, determine how many times $\frac{1}{5}$ can be divided into $3\frac{2}{5}$, and then Step 2, multiply that number by 14 to determine how far apart the mountains are.

Step 1:

$$3\frac{2}{5} \div \frac{1}{5} = 17$$

Step 2:

$$17 \times 14 \text{ kilometers} = 238 \text{ kilometers, or answer choice D.}$$

18. Correct answer: **F**. Don't let the fact that the number 11 is used twice confuse you. The first thing to recognize is that we are given a rate in miles per *hour*, but we want to know how far Candace will run in 11 *minutes*. I think the easiest way to solve this problem is to change the speed or rate from miles per hour to miles per minute. If there are 60 minutes in an hour, then:

$$11 \text{ mph} = \frac{11 \text{ miles}}{1 \text{ hour}} = \frac{11 \text{ miles}}{60 \text{ minutes}} = \frac{\frac{11}{60} \text{ miles}}{1 \text{ minute}} = 0.18333 \frac{\text{miles}}{\text{minute}}$$

Thus, Candace can ride her bike at a rate of 0.18333 miles per minute. If we multiply that rate by the number of minutes she is going to ride (11), the minutes will cancel, and we will be left with the number of miles that Candace can ride in 11 minutes:

$$\frac{0.18333 \text{ miles}}{\text{minute}} \times 11 \text{ minutes} = 2.02 \text{ miles}$$

Because the question asks for the answer rounded to the nearest mile, we round down to 2, which is answer choice F.

19. Correct answer: **C**. This is a simple math problem dressed up in the guise of something more complicated. Simply put, one of the five answer choices will equal 7 when a value of *z* = 3 is entered, and that same answer choice will equal 28 when a value of *z* = 12 is entered. All you have to do is try out the answer choices one at a time using these two values for *z* (3 and 12, respectively) and see if you get the same output (7 and 12, respectively). Let's simply start with choice A and work our way through:

A: $\dfrac{3}{7}z = \dfrac{3}{7}(3) = \dfrac{6}{7}$, which is not 7, so move on.

B: $7z = 7(3) = 21$, which is not 7, so move on.

C: $\dfrac{7}{3}z = \dfrac{7}{3}(3) = \dfrac{21}{3} = 7$, which works! Now try a z value of 12 and see if the result is 28:

$\dfrac{7}{3}z = \dfrac{7}{3}(12) = \dfrac{84}{3} = 28$, which also works! This is why C is the correct answer.

20. Correct answer: **G**. First, realize that $\triangle WXZ$ is a right triangle, so $\angle XZW$ is 90°. That means the steps to solving this problem are as follows: 1) Find the measure of $\angle WXZ$, then 2) Subtract our two known angles from 180° to find our missing angle ($\angle VWY$).

Step 1: The angles in a line add up to 180°, which means that we simply need to subtract 114° from 180° to determine the measure of $\angle WXZ$, thus: $180° - 114° = 66°$.

Step 2: Again, now that we know two of the angles of our triangle, we need to subtract these from 180° to determine the angle measure of $\angle VWY$, like this: $180° - 66° - 90° = 24°$, which is answer choice G.

21. Correct answer: **E**. It is probably very tempting to think that if the stock fell by 5% three times, then went back up to where it started, that it rose 15%. But percentage questions are tricky and always require that you do the math to ensure the correct answer.

First, let's decrease $500 by 5% 3 times. Start with $500, then subtract 5% by subtracting $500(0.05). Here are our three decreases:

> Decrease 1: $500 − $500(0.05) = $475.00
> Decrease 2: $475 − $475(0.05) = $451.25
> Decrease 3: $451.25 − $451.25(0.05) = $428.69

So, after three straight decreases of 5%, the stock is now worth $428.69, which means it has decreased in total by an amount of $71.31.

Now, to find the *increase*. Remember: we have to now determine the percent that the stock rose in the fourth hour when it came back to $500. You might be tempted to find what percent $71.31 is of $500, but that would be inaccurate. When the stock rises in the fourth hour, it rises *from* $428.69, so we need to find what percent $71.31 is of this value, like this:

$$\frac{\$71.31}{\$428.69} \times 100 = 16.63\,\%$$

When rounded as the question asks for, the result is 17%, or choice E.

22. Correct answer: **F**. There are a number of ways to solve this particular problem, but I suspect the difficulty is not necessarily the math, but the *story* that the math is wrapped up in. If you remember, these kinds of math problems are called *modeling* problems and they make up a significant portion of questions on ACT day. If you are having a difficult time with these kinds of problems, try reading the last sentence first, since the last sentence always contains the actual question.

Let's identify which category he is in at the moment. If we add up his first 5 race speeds, then divide by 5, we get this: (42.50 + 45.50 + 45.00 + 51.25 + 47.75)/5 = 46.40 seconds. This means that, at the moment, he is currently outside of the Good range and in the Average range. Let's try scores one at a time and determine if adding in this particular 6th score is good enough to move him up into the Good range with an average that is 46.09 or less.

> F: 44 seconds　　...　(42.50 + 45.50 + 45.00 + 51.25 + 47.75 + 44.00)/6 = 46.00

Thus, answer choice F is correct in that a speed of 46.00 seconds moves his average into the Good range. If you try answer choice G (or any other, since the speeds are all higher), you will get an average speed that falls in the Average category or worse. Answer G, a speed of 45.00 seconds, results in an average of 46.17 seconds, just outside of Good range.

23. Correct answer: **D**. Given that y must always be less than -2, you could start by *Picking Numbers*, inserting -3 in as y, and see what happens to the value of x. Here is what happens when we do that:

$$x = \frac{y}{y-1} = \frac{-3}{-3-1} = \frac{-3}{-4} = \frac{3}{4} = 0.75$$

Even though we are being forced to choose negative numbers for y, the equation as a whole will always end up positive, since we are dividing a negative by a negative in all circumstances. This realization eliminates options A, B, and C, leaving just D and E.

Based on our math when $y = -3$, it is easy to see that values for x that creep closer and closer to 1.00 as y gets more and more negative. For example, if $y = -99$, then we are going to get a value for x of $(-99/-100)$, or 0.99. However, the question never says that the value of y has to be an *integer*, just that it has to be lower than -2. In other words, it is possible that a value of y that equals something like -2.1 or -2.55 could give us a value for x that equals 0.71, which is why D is the correct answer.

24. Correct answer: **J**. This question is asking for the least possible number into which 21 and 49 divide evenly. It sounds more complicated than that, but all you have to do is go through the answer choices (*Backsolving*) from smallest to largest to determine which number is the smallest that both 21 and 49 can go into.

      F: 7   ...   Well, neither 21 nor 49 go into 7. Next.

      G: 49   ...   Though 49 goes into 49, 21 does not divide into 49 evenly.

      H: 70   ...   Neither 21 nor 49 divides into 70 evenly.

      J: 147   ...   (147/21) = 7, and (147/49) = 3

This means that J is the correct answer because both 21 and 49 divide into it evenly.

25. Correct answer: **B**. To determine the likelihood that Richard's ball lands in the sand trap, we have to first determine the total amount of square footage there is that his ball could land in, which is this amount:
198 + 94 + 134 + 124 = 550 square feet.

Next, we simply need to divide the sand trap's area by the total area to determine our percent likelihood:

$$\frac{134 \text{ ft}^2}{550 \text{ ft}^2} \times 100 = 24.4\%$$, which is answer choice B.

26. Correct answer: **H**. A parallelogram is a shape with 4 sides, and each pair of sides is parallel and equal. A square and a rectangle are both examples of a parallelogram because both of their pairs of sides are parallel, but you can also have parallelograms that don't feature right angles.

In this particular problem, there is enough information to determine the lengths of all 4 sides. First, if one side is 22 inches long, then, by definition, this parallelogram features a side parallel to this side with a length of 22 inches. Second, if two sides have lengths of 22 inches each, then that means that the combined length of the other two sides is 102 inches (the perimeter given in the problem) $- 22 - 22 = 58$ inches. If the other two sides are a combined 58 inches long, and because they are the same length because this is a parallelogram, then divide 58 by 2 and learn that each other side is 29 inches long.

Thus, our four sides are of length 22, 22, 29, and 29 inches, which is answer choice H.

27. Correct answer: **A**. There is a lot of information in this question that is unnecessary, which is a common feature of ACT Math problems. The entire question boils down to this: what is the distance between the origin, meaning point $(0, 0)$ in the standard (x, y) coordinate plane, and point $(40, 96)$?

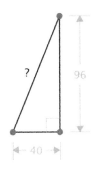

If you know the distance formula, you can certainly use it here. However, as I've discussed elsewhere in this book many times, the simplest way to solve these distance problems is to make a right triangle in which the distance between the two is the hypotenuse, then use the Pythagorean Theorem to solve.

Here is what such a triangle will look like. On the bottom, we know the length to be 40 because the question says that the ball traveled 40 feet down the first base line, and similarly we know the right side of the triangle to have a length of 96 because the question says that the ball traveled 96 feet down the third base line. Now, we can use the Pythagorean Theorem ($a^2 + b^2 = c^2$, in which c is the hypotenuse) to solve:

$$40^2 + 96^2 = c^2 \quad \ldots \quad 1{,}600 + 9{,}216 = c2 \quad \ldots \quad \sqrt{10816} = \sqrt{c^2} \quad \ldots \quad c = 104$$

Thus, answer choice A is correct: the ball traveled 104 feet.

28. Correct answer: **H**. This is a straightforward know-it-or-you-don't triangle concept problem. An isosceles triangle is one with two sides of equal length. In the case of this triangle, side AB and side AC are clearly the same length. If they have the same length, they have the same opposite angle. Because we know the angle opposite side AC (aka, angle B) is $72°$, we can then deduce that the angle opposite side AB (aka angle C) is also $72°$, which is answer choice H.

29. Correct answer: **C**. There are a number of ways that you could go about adding up the total cost of these bicycle orders, but I believe the easiest way to be to figure out the price of each X, Y, and Z bike, then multiply the cost by the number of bikes ordered.

Step 1:   - The cost of each X bike is: $55 + $20(2) + $24 = $119
                     - The cost of each Y bike is: $58 + $24(2) + $24 = $130
                     - The cost of each Z bike is: $70 + $33(2) + $24 = $160

Step 2: There is an order for 2 X bikes, 7 Y bikes, and 5 Z bikes, so if we multiply these three numbers by their respective prices, and add them together, we will get the total cost to the manufacturer:

           2($119) + 7($130) + 5($160) = $238 + $910 + $800 = $1,948, which is answer choice C.

30. Correct answer: **G**. In order to avoid simple mistakes, let's first convert the 7 feet 3 inch board into inches. Then, when we find one-third of it, we will convert it back into feet.

If there are 12 inches in a foot, then the board is $12(7) + 3 = 87$ inches long. Then, finding one-third of this board means dividing it by three, thus: (87 inches/3) = 29 inches.

Lastly, we need to convert 29 inches, which is the length of one-third of the original board, into feet. 12 inches divides into 29 2 times with 5 leftover, meaning the length of one-third of the original board is 2 feet 5 inches, or answer choice G.

31. Correct answer: **D**. Point H, we are told, is at point $(-4, 2)$, but that it is reflected across the x-axis to point H'. Although the point reflects across the x-axis, the x value does not change, but rather the y value. This makes sense if you think about it: for the point to go "down" across the x-axis, the y value must change, and since it is a perfect reflection, the y value will go from 2 to -2. Thus, H' rests at $(-4, -2)$, which is answer choice D.

32. Correct answer: **K**. Because all of the answer choices have our x and 21 terms in the numerator (in other words, they are not in the denominator beneath a 1), then we will have to manipulate our terms to do the same. When you move a value raised to an exponent from either the numerator to the denominator or the denominator to the numerator, you simply make the exponent negative, like this:

$$-\frac{1}{x^z} \times \frac{1}{21^z} = -x^{-z} \times 21^{-z}$$

Now notice that each term (both the x and the 21) share the same exponent: $-z$. This means that we can multiply the x and the 21 together in parentheses, and then raise the entire parentheses to the power of $-z$, like this:

$$-x^{-z} \times 21^{-z} = (-x \times 21)^{-z}, \text{ which is answer choice K.}$$

33. Correct answer: **E**. Begin with a pretend set of 5 numbers, say {1, 1, 1, 1, 1}. Right now, the mean (aka average) is 1 and the sum is $1 + 1 + 1 + 1 + 1 = 5$. The question requires that we increase the mean of the 5 numbers *by* 7, which means we have to increase the mean of our number set *to* 8. This new number set will do the trick: {8, 8, 8, 8, 8}. The sum of our new number set 40, which means that the sum of our number set has increased by $40 - 5 = 35$, which is answer choice E.

34. Correct answer: **H**. We know that on Day 1 Genevieve runs 11 blocks, but the exact distance she runs on the next 3 days is to be determined by increasing the previous day's distance by (⅗), or 60%. Let's take it 1 day at a time, then add up the distances in the end. To find 60% of a number, simply multiply it by 0.6:

Day 1's distance = 11 blocks

Day 2's distance = $11 + 11(0.6) = 17.6$ blocks

Day 3's distance = $17.6 + 17.6(0.6) = 28.16$ blocks

Day 4's distance $= 28.16 + 28.16(0.6) = 45.056$ blocks, which matches answer choice H.

35. Correct answer: C. First, we know that the umpire in training watches 1,000 video clips of pitches and 1,000 video clips of close calls at first base, for a total of 2,000 video clips. Then, we are told that each clip lasts 8 seconds. The problem is, we are told that the umpire will be paid $35 per hour, making this a tricky conversion. You could either determine how many hours 8 seconds is, or you could determine how much money he is paid per second; either one of these methods will work, so let's choose the second one and determine how much money he is paid per second.

If he is paid $35 per hour, then he is paid $35 \div 60 = 0.58333 per minute (since there are 60 minutes in an hour). If he is paid $0.58333 per minute, then he is paid $0.58333 \div 60 = 0.0097222 per second (since there are 60 seconds in a minute).

He watched 2,000 video clips at 8 seconds per video, meaning a total of $2,000(8) = 16,000$ seconds of video clips. To determine how much he was paid, multiply these seconds by the amount he is paid per second to determine how much total he was paid, like this: $0.0097222 \times 16,000 = 155.56, which is answer choice C.

36. Correct answer: J. Because the Retiring Umpire makes perfect calls, it is easy for us to determine how many inaccurate strike calls there were by the New Umpire, which is $393 - 319 = 74$ bad strike calls. To determine what percent were in accurate, divide the number of bad calls (74) by the total number of strike calls (393 for the New Umpire), like this:

$$\frac{74}{393} \times 100 = 18.8\%, \text{ which is answer choice J.}$$

37. Correct answer: E. First, we need to determine how many of each kind of clip the New Umpire incorrectly labeled. First, for the balls and strikes videos, we can compare either balls or strikes. Using strikes, we see that he mislabeled $393 - 319 = 74$ videos. Second, for the safe and out videos, we can compare either safe or out. Using safe, we see that he mislabeled $502 - 421 = 81$ videos. In total, then, he mislabeled $74 + 81 = 155$ out of 2,000 videos. To determine the probability that one chosen clip is mislabeled by the New Umpire, simply divide 155 by 2,000. However, we are being asked for the probability that this same draw happens twice in a row. Well, if it happens once, then there are now only 154 mislabeled videos out of 1,999 that remain. To find the possibility of 2 in a row, we need to multiply these two numbers by one another, like this:

$$\frac{155}{2,000} \times \frac{154}{1,999} = 0.00597, \text{ which rounds up to 0.006, which is answer choice E.}$$

38. Correct answer: J. The fact that David is a scientist in a lab or the fact that there is danger in the pressure of a container exceeding 255 Pascal are both irrelevant to the math of this question. Typically, one question per ACT Math test will feature an equation like the one in this problem, and you will have to solve for one of the variables. Usually the equation will feature variables that you aren't used to seeing, but again, they will give you the values of all of them but one in order to solve. Fortunately, in our case, we are being asked to solve for P, which means that all we have to do is carefully plug in all of the values on the right side of the equation. Before we get to the math below, we know this: $n = 550$, $R = 0.082$, $T = 220$, and $V = 42$.

$$P = \frac{nRT}{V} = \frac{550(0.082)(220)}{42} = \frac{9,922}{42} = 236.2 \text{ Pascal}$$

The question asks for us to round to the nearest Pascal, which is 236, or answer choice J.

39. Correct answer: A. There are a number of ways to solve this problem, and most begin with simplifying the equation. However, it is possible to solve this question without doing so, which would be by using the:

Method #1: *Backsolving* mini-strategy. Where this equation crosses the x axis is a *solution*, and will result in a y value of 0. Thus, if I plug in a value of x from any of the five answer choices and get 0, that will work, then I need to try the next. If I plug in a value of x from any of the five answer choices and get a number that is not 0, then I can abandon that answer choice as incorrect and move on. I see that two of the answer choices have $x = 3$ as a potential solution, so I can evaluate two answer at the same time by trying out $x = 3$ first, like this:

$$y = \frac{-(x+3)(x^2 - x - 6)}{(x+2)} = \frac{-(3+3)(3^2 - 3 - 6)}{(3+2)} = \frac{(-6)(0)}{5} = \frac{0}{5} = 0, \text{ which works!}$$

Now I can be confident that the answer is either A or D, since these two have a solution of $x = 3$. Let's try the other answer choice for D, which is $x = 2$, and see if it also satisfies by resulting in an answer that yields $y = 0$:

$$y = \frac{-(x+3)(x^2 - x - 6)}{(x+2)} = \frac{-(2+3)(2^2 - 2 - 6)}{(2+2)} = \frac{(-5)(-4)}{4} = \frac{20}{4} = 5 \text{ , which is NOT 0, so A is correct.}$$

Any other methods to solve begin with simplifying the equation. Notice that the equation has a trinomial that needs to be factored $(x^2 - x - 6)$; seeing that the equation has a binomial $(x + 2)$ in the denominator, it seems likely that this binomial will be canceled out with a resulting binomial after we factor the top. So, let's factor this trinomial now, then rewrite the equation and cancel what we can. We need two numbers that *multiply* to give our last term (-6), but *add* to give us our middle term (-1); these two numbers are -3 and 2, which means that our trinomial factors like this: $x^2 - x - 6 = (x - 3)(x + 2)$. Let's now rewrite our equation and cancel out what we can:

$$y = \frac{-(x+3)(x^2 - x - 6)}{(x+2)} = \frac{-(x+3)(x-3)(x+2)}{(x+2)} = -(x+3)(x-3), \text{ and now we FOIL or multiply:}$$

$$-(x+3)(x-3) = -(x^2 + 3x - 3x - 9) = -(x^2 - 9)$$

From here, you could also use *Backsolving* to find a solution.

Method #2: Factor and Solve. From here, we can also factor our $-(x^2 - 9)$ term into two binomials, set those binomials equal to 0, and solve for x both times. Some students may immediately recognize that this term is the "difference of squares", but others may notice that we went a little bit too far in our simplification and already can see what our two binomials are! Look at this again:

$$-(x+3)(x-3) = -(x^2 + 3x - 3x - 9) = -(x^2 - 9) \quad \ldots \quad \text{our two binomials are two steps earlier!}$$

Thus, $-(x^2 - 9)$ factors into $-(x + 3)(x - 3)$. Now, split these into two terms, set equal to 0, and get our two solutions for x, like this:

$$-(x+3) = 0 \quad \ldots \quad -x - 3 = 0 \quad \ldots \quad -x = 3 \quad \ldots \quad x = -3 \text{ , and}$$

$$(x - 3) = 0 \quad \ldots \quad x = 3$$

Thus, our two solutions (which is where the equation crosses the x-axis are $x = -3$, and $x = 3$, or answer choice A.

40. Correct answer: **G**. Though this problem looks unbelievably complicated, let's simplify our thought as much as possible. First, recall that the amplitude of a wave is the distance between (in our case) the x-axis and the crest (or top and bottom) of a wave. Second, recall that the graph of sin normally has an amplitude of 1 (since the highest value of sin possible is 1, and the lowest value of sin possible is -1, both of which are a distance of 1 from the x-axis).

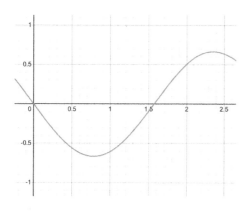

Now, it doesn't matter at all what degree measure is after the "sin" part of the equation. It looks confusing that we are working with $\sin(2x - \pi)$, but no matter what $(2x - \pi)$ is equal to, the resulting value of sin will be somewhere between 1 and -1; thus, the value after sin does not affect, at all, the amplitude of the graph of sin.

However, what is $1 \times \frac{2}{3}$? Well, it's just $\frac{2}{3}$, which means that the amplitude of the wave of sin will be "squished" down or changed so that the highest point of the wave can only reach to $\frac{2}{3}$, and the lowest point of the wave can only reach to $-\frac{2}{3}$. Either way, the resulting amplitude is $\frac{2}{3}$, which is answer choice G. Below, I put a graph of $\frac{2}{3}\sin$ just so you can visualize what we are talking about:

As you can see, the highest the wave gets off of the x-axis is 0.66, or $\frac{2}{3}$, and the lowest is goes down off of the x-axis is $-\frac{2}{3}$, but either way, the amplitude is now $\frac{2}{3}$.

41. Correct answer: **B**. First, plot these three points, and draw this triangle (like I've done below). Second, remember what the altitude of a triangle is; simply put, the altitude of a triangle is its height. Draw a straight line down from the uppermost point to form to 90 degree angles with the base, like the triangle shown here (the altitude is labeled x).

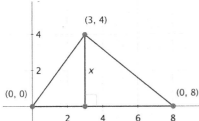

Now, fortunately, there is not any triangular math that you need to do. If all you had been told was the lengths of the three sides, then yes, you'd have some work to do. Here, because the bottom of the triangle sits on the x-axis, the height is simply how "high" the triangle goes on the y-axis, which is 4. This is why the answer is B: 4.

42. Correct answer: **F**. First, because the question asks us for how many cars are expected to be rented on any given day, let's determine how many cars are rented based on each rental rate (which we can find because we are given how many cars are in the lot, 120). To do so, multiply the rental rate by 120.

- Rental rate of 0.25 means 0.25(120) = 30 cars rented.
- Rental rate of 0.50 means 0.50(120) = 60 cars rented.
- Rental rate of 0.75 means 0.75(120) = 90 cars rented.
- Rental rate of 0.90 means 0.90(120) = 108 cars rented.
- Rental rate of 1.00 means 1.00(120) = 120 cars rented.

To find the *expected number* of cars to be rented, multiply the probabilities of each rental rate (0.10, 0.20, 0.40, 0.20, and 0.10, respectively) by the number of cars rented with that rental rate (30, 60, 90, 108, and 120, respectively) and add them together, like so:

$$30(0.10) + 60(0.20) + 90(0.40) + 108(0.20) + 120(0.10) = 3 + 12 + 36 + 21.6 + 12 = 84.6 \text{ expected per day.}$$

The question asks us to find the number of expected cars rented to the nearest whole number, thus we round up 84.6 to 85, which is answer choice F.

43. Correct answer: **B**. The first principle to recall is that two angles in a line add up to equal 180°. Thus, we can set up an equation in which the two equations representing the angles add together to equal 180°, solve for x, then use our knowledge of x to find the value of the smallest angle.

First, adding our angles together, setting them equal to 180°, and solving for x:

$$(4x + 28) + (x + 2) = 180 \quad \dots \quad 5x + 30 = 180 \quad \dots \quad 5x = 150 \quad \dots \quad x = 30$$

Some will be tempted at this point to put that A is the correct answer, but the question asks for the value of the smallest angle, not the value of x; finding x is simply one step towards finding the right answer. The acute angle on the right, represented by the equation $(x + 2)°$, is clearly the smaller angle. Thus, if $x = 30$, then the value of this angle is $(30 + 2)° = 32°$, which is answer choice B.

44. Correct answer: **K**. This problem could conceivably be done in the head. If b decreases by 2, then that would mean the value of a will decrease by 3(2) = 6. Then, if c increases by 1, then that would mean that the value of a will increase by −4(1) = −4; in other words, it would decrease by 4. A decrease of 6 plus a decrease of 4 equals a decrease of 10, which is answer choice K.

However, it might be more fitting to choose values for b and c, find a value, then decrease b by 2 and increase c by 1 and see how much the answer changes.

First, let's assume that $b = 2$ and $c = 2$:

$$a = 3b + 7 - 4c = 3(2) + 7 - 4(2) = 5$$

Second, let's decrease b by 2 (so, $b = 0$) and increase c by 1 (so, $c = 3$):

$$a = 3b + 7 - 4c = 3(0) + 7 - 4(3) = 7 - 12 = -5$$

Thus, because the difference between 5 and −5 is 10, we can know that the changes to b and c cause a to decrease by 10, which is answer choice K.

45. Correct answer: **D.** The best way to solve this problem is to draw something so that you can visualize it. For example, maybe draw 11 circles to represent the 11 rooms, and each dot put into the circle represents a person. Here, each X represents a room, and each * following it represents a person.

First, recognize that each room has to have a minimum of 2 people in it (as shown below with two * after each X).

X**	X**	X**
X**	X**	X**
X**	X**	X**
X**	X**	

Because each room has 2 people already in it, and because there are 11 rooms, then that means that there are now $90 - 2(11) = 78$ people left to distribute between the 11 rooms. Because we are looking for the greatest number of rooms that can be filled with 12 people, distribute the remaining people one room at a time until it is full, then move on to the next room, like this:

X***********	X***********	X**
X***********	X***********	X**
X***********	X*********	X**
X***********	X**	

As you can see, there are 6 rooms that are completely filled, which is answer choice D.

46. Correct answer: **F.** One strategy for answering this question, which I believe is the fastest, begins with converting the recipe to gallons and liters, respectively, using the conversion formulas given below the problem. This would be done because the problem requires an answer using gallons and liters.

According to the conversion metrics, 1 gallon = 128 ounces, so the 400 ounces called for by the recipe equates to $\frac{400}{128} = 3.125$ gallons.

According to conversion metrics, 1 liter = 4.22675 cups, so the 5 cups of flour called for by the recipe equates to $\frac{5}{4.22675} = 1.18294$ liter.

So now we can say that the recipe calls for 3.125 gallons of water for every 1.18294 liters of flour.

The questions itself asks how many gallons are needed for 25 liters of flour. To answer this question, let's set up a cross-multiplication problem; we will let g represent the missing gallons, like this:

$$\frac{3.125 \text{ gallons}}{1.18294 \text{ liters}} = \frac{g}{25 \text{ liters}} \quad \ldots \quad 3.125(25) = g(1.18294) \quad \ldots \quad \frac{3.125(25)}{1.18294} = g \quad \ldots \quad g = 66.04 \text{ gallons}$$

At this point, you know the number of gallons needed for the larger-scale recipe. However, each of the answer choices is written in a way that does the converting that we just went through the trouble to do ourselves. The reason I believe this method is easiest is because it takes the converting out of your head where simple mistakes can be made and puts it into real numbers. Simply go through each answer choice one at a time, and determine which one also equals 66.04. This is easily accomplished with the calculator. First, let's try F:

$$\text{F:} \quad \frac{(400)(25)(4.22675)}{(5)(128)} = \frac{42267.5}{640} = 66.04 \text{, which is correct; thus, F is the correct answer.}$$

47. Correct answer: **C.** First, it must be kept in mind that you are looking for which expression or expressions are NOT equal to x. So, if any of the three does equal x, it is an incorrect answer.

I. In the numerator, x is raised to the -1 power. To change this, the x is moved to the numerator and the exponent is made positive (see below). Then, to combine like terms that are being multiplied, you add their exponents:

$$\frac{x^2}{x^{-1}} = x^2 x^1 = x^{2+1} = x^3 \text{, not } x \text{, which eliminates answer choice D.}$$

II. The absolute value of a number is equal to how far it is away from a value of 0. So, the absolute value of x is going to be x, but the absolute value of $-x$ is also going to be x. This means that II equals x, which makes it an incorrect answer for this particular problem. This eliminates, in total, D, B, and E.

III. If you are stuck on the conceptualization of this problem, then choose a value for x, plug it in here, and find out what number you end up with and see if it is equal to x. In words, when you square a negative number, you get a positive square (for example, -3 squared $= 9$). Then, when you take the square root of that number, you can get two different answers: 3 or -3. However, this problem has a large negative sign out in front of it, which makes these answers (for example) now -3 or 3, respectively. Thus, this expression can equal either x or $-x$. This might be confusing, but this is why the question asks for expressions that are not *always* equal to x, which is the case here: this expression is not always equal to x because it can also equal $-x$.

Thus, the two answer that are NOT always equal to x are I and III, which is answer choice C.

48. Correct answer: **H.** There is no fancy way to get this question correct; you simply need to try out various integers until you determine how many there are that will make the equation lie between 0.480 and 0.205.

Before I start to try any numbers, I see that if a has a value of 6, then the fraction will equal 0.5. Along those same lines, because 0.200 is one-fifth, I can see that if a has a value of 15, the fraction will equal 0.2. That said, I know that I'm working, in general, with integer values between 6 and 15, but *not* 6 and 15 themselves. Let's try $a = 7$ and $a = 14$ and see if they have values that fit the problem's requirements:

$$\text{If } a = 7, \text{ then } \frac{3}{a} = \frac{3}{7} = 0.429, \text{ which lies between 0.480 and 0.205}$$

$$\text{If } a = 14, \text{ then } \frac{3}{a} = \frac{3}{14} = 0.214, \text{ which also lies between 0.480 and 0.205}$$

Thus, if 7 and 14 meet the requirements, but 6 and 15 do not, then I need to count the number of integers between (and including) 7 and 14. These are $a = 7, 8, 9, 10, 11, 12, 13$, and 14, a total of 8 integers, which is answer choice H.

49. Correct answer: **D.** The best and most mistake-free means of answering this question is to use *Picking Numbers*. Let's pretend that the average weight of his first 4 fish is 10 ounces (yes, I know that those are little fish for a bass fishing tournament, but that doesn't matter!). The question requires that we find the weight of a fifth fish that will raise the average to $a + 3$, then find how much bigger that value is than a.

So, if $a = 10$, then we need the average to rise to 13 ounces with a 5th fish. If the average after 5 fish is 13, then that means the total weight of all 5 fish is $5(13) = 65$ ounces. Remember that we already know the total weight of our first 4 fish ($10+10+10+10 = 40$ ounces), which means that the fifth fish must weigh $(65 - 40) = 25$ ounces.

If the fifth fish must weigh 25 ounces, that would mean that it weighs $(25 - a) = (25 - 10) = 15$ ounces more than a, which corresponds with answer choice D.

50. Correct answer: **G.** If two lines are intersecting, then four angles are formed. If $\angle Z$ is bigger than $\angle W$, then we can know that these two angles add up to one line, or $180°$. With that in mind, we need to set up an equation that sets the addition of these two angles equal to $180°$. To do so, let's call the value of $\angle W$ x for the purpose of simplicity. Here is what such an equation would look like (note: since $\angle Z$ is 1100% larger than $\angle W$, we multiply x by 11 to represent $\angle Z$).

$$\angle W + \angle Z = 180 \quad \dots \quad x + 11x = 180 \quad \dots \quad 12x = 180 \quad \dots \quad x = 15°$$

Because x is $\angle W$, we know that $\angle W$ is equal to $15°$, which is answer choice G.

51. Correct answer: **E.** To answer this question correctly will involve working backwards from s_4. This is because to answer the question, to find the value of s_1, you have to have the value of s_2 (because, as you can see on the right side of the equation, you need the value of $s_{(n+1)}$), and to find the value of s_2, you need the value of s_3, which is why you need the value of s_4, which is given. So, let's go one at a time, working our way down and plugging in our new value until we can solve for s_1, like this:

$$s_3 = \frac{1}{2}s_{(n+1)} + |\, n\,| + 4 = \frac{1}{2}(77) + |\, 3\,| + 4 = 38.5 + 3 + 4 = 45.5 \text{ (now use this to solve for } s_2)$$

$$s_2 = \frac{1}{2}s_{(n+1)} + |\, n\,| + 4 = \frac{1}{2}(45.5) + |\, 2\,| + 4 = 22.75 + 2 + 4 = 28.75 \text{ (now use this to solve for } s_1)$$

$$s_1 = \frac{1}{2}s_{(n+1)} + |\, n\,| + 4 = \frac{1}{2}(28.75) + |\, 1\,| + 4 = 14.375 + 1 + 4 = 19.375 \text{ , which is answer choice E.}$$

52. Correct answer: **F.** Use *Picking Numbers* and choose any number less than −2, carefully solve all three expressions for a numerical value, then carefully order them from smallest to largest.

To start, let's pretend that $x = -3$. With that decided, our three expressions become:

$$-x^3 = -(-3)^3 = -(-27) = 27$$

$$-\frac{1}{x^2} = -\frac{1}{(-3)^2} = -\frac{1}{9} = -0.111$$

$$|x| = |-3| = 3$$

Now that we've done so, we can see that −0.111 is the smallest term, 3 is second smallest, and 27 is the largest. These correspond to $-\frac{1}{x^2}$, then $|x|$, then $-x^3$. So, our final inequality looks like this:

$$-\frac{1}{x^2} < |x| < -x^3 \text{, which corresponds to answer choice F.}$$

53. Correct answer: **A.** In reviewing this kind of question with countless students over many years, I have learned that many students think that their graphing calculator must somehow be able to show this many decimals in one way or another, and then they need to count their way there. However, that would be both impossible and a waste of time, especially with a digit as far away from 0 as the 333rd.

Instead, realize that we have a repeating pattern of 6 digits after the decimal. So, the 6th digit will always be a 1, the 12th will always be a 1, the 18th will always be a 1, and so on: every 6th place will be a 1. We need to find a number close, but less than, 333 that is divisible by 6. Since $(330 \div 6) = 55$, we know that the 330th place after the decimal is a 1. That means that the 331st is a 7, the 332nd is a 4, and then the 333rd is a 0, which corresponds to answer choice A.

54. Correct answer: **G.** This question is a two step process. First, we need to take the amount of emails on the list and reduce it to 15% of its total, then take this new number and reduce it down to one-sixth of its total.

Step 1: 15% of 122,000 is $122,000(0.15) = 18,300$ (so, 18,300 on the email list will attend the event)

Step 2: $\frac{1}{6}$ of 18,300 is $18,300(\frac{1}{6}) = \frac{18,300}{6} = 3,050$

So, the amount of shirts that should be printed after properly reducing the email list is 3,050, which corresponds to answer choice G, since it falls within the range of 3,000 and 3,100.

55. Correct answer: **E.** Do not be scared by the presence of the imaginary number i, which you may have either used in math class at some point or heard friends in other math classes talking about. If $i = \sqrt{-1}$, then any time there is an i^2 term that emerges as you solve, simply replace it with a −1. At least, this is how we will solve this problem at first. Then, I will show you a second, faster way.

Let's begin with the term in the numerator. As you would any other time you have two binomials being multiplied, use FOIL to multiply all of the terms, like this:

$$(-3i + 1)(2i + 2) = -6i^2 + 2 + 2i - 6i = -6i^2 - 4i + 2$$

Now that we have done that, let's replace the i^2 term with a −1 and simplify:

$$-6i^2 - 4i + 2 = -6(-1) - 4i + 2 = 6 - 4i + 2 = 8 - 4i$$

Thus, the previously-scary looking numerator has been reduced down to simply $8 - 4i$.

All that remains to do is to divide this now-simplified numerator by the term in the denominator, which is a 4.

$$\frac{8 - 4i}{4} = 2 - i$$

The 4 in the denominator can divide into both terms in the numerator, simplifying this expression all the way down to the correct answer, which is E: $2 - i$.

However, I promised at the beginning of this explanation to solve this problem in a little bit of a simpler way. This requires that you have a graphing calculator. Graphing calculators have the means to type in the term i into a math equation. On the graphing calculator sitting in front of me, that would be done by hitting "2ND" then the period button at the bottom of the calculator. If you simply type in the original equation, term for term, just typing in the i whenever you encounter it, your graphing calculator will spit out the correct answer: $2 - i$.

It could be that this is possible on some scientific calculators. However, the last couple of them that I looked at recently did not have this as an option. If all you have is a scientific calculator, though, just do the math like we did at first above and solve it that way.

56. Correct answer: **K**. First, recognize that the two triangles being described are *similar* triangles. In ACT Math *Good to Know* Lesson #2 on Triangles, we said that similar triangles are triangles with the same angles and equivalent sides. The question says that $\triangle ABC$ has a hypotenuse of 10, and $\triangle XYZ$ has a hypotenuse of 5. This means that each side of $\triangle ABC$ will be double that of each side of $\triangle XYZ$. Thus, this problem can be solved two ways. Either find the perimeter of $\triangle ABC$ and half it, or find the perimeter of $\triangle XYZ$ as the question asks for, which is what we will do here.

We are also told that $\triangle ABC$ has another side that is 8 inches long, which is opposite that of an angle with a measure of $53.13°$. This means that $\triangle XYZ$ has a side that is 4 inches long, also opposite that of an angle with a measure of $53.13°$. We now have all of the information we could possibly need to find the last side of $\triangle XYZ$. Probably the simplest way is to simply use the Pythagorean Theorem, that $a^2 + b^2 = c^2$, on this triangle, since we know that it is a right triangle. When we do that, and calling our missing side b, we get the following:

$$4^2 + b^2 = 5^2 \quad ... \quad 16 + b^2 = 25 \quad ... \quad b^2 = 9 \quad ... \quad b = 3$$

We now know the three sides of the triangle: 3, 4, and 5. Thus, the perimeter is $3 + 4 + 5 = 12$ inches, or answer choice K.

It should be noted that there are a host of other ways to solve this problem. You might recognize right away that if $\triangle XYZ$ is a right triangle, has a hypotenuse of 5, and a side of 4, that it is then a *special* triangle, a 3-4-5 triangle, which can also be learned more about in the same *Good to Know* lesson as *similar* triangles. You can also use your knowledge of sine, cosine, and tangent to figure out any missing sides as well. All roads will lead you to the same perimeter of 12.

57. Correct answer: **C**. The best way to answer this problem is to invent two triangles (akin to the *Picking Numbers* strategy) that fit the criteria and then compare them to determine how much smaller the new triangle is compared to the original.

Let's first pretend that our original triangle has a base of 10 and a height of 10. Thus, our original triangle has an area of $\frac{1}{2}bh = \frac{1}{2}(10)(10) = 50$.

Let's then create a second, smaller triangle based on the parameters in the question. First, we are told that this second triangle has a base that is increased by 10% compared to the original. To increase a number by 10%, multiply it by 1.10, like this: $10(1.10) = 11$, which is the base of the second triangle. Second, we are told that this second triangle has a height that is decreased by 35% compared to the original. To decrease a number by 35%, multiply it by $(1 - 0.35)$, or 0.65, like this: $10(1 - 0.35) = 10(0.65) = 6.5$, which is the height of the second triangle.

Thus, our second triangle has an area of $\frac{1}{2}bh = \frac{1}{2}(11)(6.5) = 35.75$.

The area of the first is 50, the area of the second is 35.75. Since we are looking for what percent smaller the area of the second is compared to the first, we first need how many units smaller it is, which is $50 - 35.75 = 14.25$. This is where many students run into difficulty: what to do with this number? Since we are comparing the decrease *to the first triangle,* we divide the first triangle by this decrease of 14.25 and multiply by 100 to get a resulting percentage, like this:

$$\frac{14.25}{50} \times 100 = 28.5\%$$

Thus the second triangle is 28.5% smaller than the original, which matches C.

58. Correct answer: **J**. To find the probability that these two die add up to a sum of 15, we need to determine the *number* of combinations that result in a 15 and divide it by the number of all possibilities.

First, let's determine the number of combinations that will result in a 15. To do so, let's begin with the 12-sided die, and work our way down one at a time to find combinations:

12-Sided Die		6-Sided Die	
12	+	3	= 15
11	+	4	= 15
10	+	5	= 15
9	+	6	= 15

Thus, there are only 4 combinations of die that will result in a total of 15.

Second, we need to determine the number of possible dice combinations. To do so, simply multiply the number of options from the first die by the number of options from the second. In other words, if there are 12 options on the first die, and 6 on the second, then the total number of pairs is $(12 \times 6) = 72$.

Third, divide the number of combinations that result in a 15 by all possible combinations to get the probability of rolling a 15, like this:

$$\frac{4}{72} = \frac{1}{18}, \text{ which matches answer choice J.}$$

59. Correct answer: **A**. You would think that this problem would be as simple as dividing 5,625 by 3, which is 1,875, but that would be incorrect. You need to use the square footage to find possible dimensions of the floors, convert those dimensions to yards, then multiply to get the square yardage.

First, based on a square footage of 5,625, invent dimensions for the floors. As an example, when you divide 5,625 by 25, the result is 225, which will work for us. In other words, you can now pretend that the floors that Michael is working with have dimensions of 25ft × 225ft.

Second, convert these new dimensions into yards by dividing each dimension by 3, like this:

$$25 \text{ ft} \times 225 \text{ ft} = (25 \div 3) \text{ yards} \times (225 \div 3) \text{ yards} = 8.33 \text{ yards} \times 75 \text{ yards}$$

Third, now that we have new dimensions in yards (8.33×75 yards), we can multiply the two to determine the square footage:

$8.33 \times 75 = 624.75$ square yards. You might think this is *close* to answer choice A, but off by 0.25. That is true, but the deficit can be accounted for because we rounded 8.33333333333333 (and on forever) down to 8.33; whenever you round, results will be inexact.

60. Correct answer: **K**. Before randomly doing some math, understand that this question is saying that four of the answer choices are the exact same, and only one of them is different. With that in mind, there are a few different ways to answer this problem. One way would be this: options J and K feature the exact same base (x) raised to different exponents. This means, right away, that because these are so obviously two different numbers, one of them has to be the correct answer *because* it is the one that is different from the others. Looking up at H, you can see that it results pretty simply in the ninth root of x, which is the same thing as raising x to the one-ninth power, which means that K is different, making it the right answer.

Another way to solve this problem is to use *Picking Numbers*. In this strategy, choose a number for x, plug it into the original, then plug it into the answer choices one at a time to determine the correct answer. For this strategy to work, you need to be able to find the cubed root of a number on your calculator, or even the eighteenth root, or the ninth root, and so on. Many calculators feature secondary functions that can do this, but if you aren't already versed on using the calculator in this way, then try this: to find (for example) the cubed root of a number, raise it to the $\frac{1}{3}$ power; to find (for example) the eighteenth root of a number, raise it to the $\frac{1}{18}$ power. In your calculator, type the number, then $^\wedge$, then $(1 \div 18)$.

Let's assume then that x equals 27. I chose 27 because it is a number that results from another number (3) being cubed. First, I will cube this number, then find the cubed root of it 3 times in a row, like this:

$27^3 = 19,683$

First cubed root: $19,683^{\frac{1}{3}} = 27$

Second cubed root: $27^{\frac{1}{3}} = 3$

Third cubed root: $3^{\frac{1}{3}} = 1.442$

Thus, when $x = 27$, the result of the question's expression is 1.442; if you try out $x = 27$, you will get a result of 1.442 for each answer as you go, except for K, since $x^{\frac{1}{6}} = 27^{\frac{1}{6}} = 1.732$

A final way to solve would be to conceptualize the problem one step at a time. The cubed root of anything cubed is simply the number itself. Cube that number (x), and the result is $x^{\frac{1}{3}}$, then cube it one last time, and the result is $x^{\frac{1}{3} \cdot \frac{1}{3}} = x^{\frac{1}{9}}$. If you've recognized that the answer must be J or K, then this conceptualization will lead you to see that the correct answer is K, since it does *not* match the expression in the question.

Answer Explanations - Step 6 - Practice Test 2

Correct answers:

1: C	11: C	21: A	31: D	41: E	51: D
2: G	12: H	22: K	32: G	42: H	52: J
3: D	13: B	23: E	33: A	43: B	53: C
4: F	14: K	24: G	34: K	44: J	54: F
5: E	15: B	25: B	35: A	45: C	55: E
6: J	16: F	26: F	36: K	46: H	56: F
7: A	17: E	27: C	37: C	47: D	57: B
8: J	18: J	28: F	38: H	48: K	58: G
9: B	19: D	29: E	39: D	49: A	59: A
10: G	20: H	30: H	40: J	50: G	60: K

1. Correct answer: **C**. Because Elisa paid $705 for an internet service that includes not only a monthly fee, but also a onetime fee of $225, let's subtract this onetime fee from the total $705 she paid, like this: ($705 − $225) = $480. The remainder, in other words the $480, is what Elisa paid for internet month by month. Since the internet costs $20 per month, let's divide $480 by $20 to determine the number of weeks she paid for, like this: ($480 ÷ $20) = 24. Thus, Elisa has paid for 24 weeks of internet service, or answer choice C.

2. Correct answer: **G**. Recognize first that the political party has overpaid for signs. They ordered 425 signs, which made them eligible for a discount (only $2.15 per sign), but they paid full price ($2.50 per sign). So first, let's determine how much they paid for the signs, which is this: (425 × $2.50) = $1,062.50. Next determine how much the political party should have paid total, which is this: (425 × $2.15) = $913.75. Lastly, to determine the discount they deserve, subtract what they should have paid by what they did pay, like this: ($1,062.50 − $913.75) = $148.75, which is answer choice G.

3. Correct answer: **D**. First, determine how fast the bus is traveling in miles per hour. How to do so is in the phrase "miles per hour", aka, total miles divided by total hours will result in a speed in miles per hour. So far, the bus has traveled 90 miles in 1.5 hours, so we can find the bus's speed like this:

$$\frac{90 \text{ miles}}{1.5 \text{ hours}} = 60 \text{ mph}.$$

With that done, we simply need to use the speed of the bus and apply it to the four hours that are to be traveled, like this:

$$60\frac{\text{miles}}{\text{hour}} \times 4 \text{ hours} = 240 \text{ miles}, \text{ which is answer choice D.}$$

4. Correct answer: **F**. Because the restaurant only offers 1 dish that is Christopher's favorite, the odds of the waitress choosing his favorite meal is going to be 1 "over" something, or 1 "in" something. What the 1 is going to be over or out of is the total number of meal options that the waitress can choose from. If you read too quickly, you might be tempted to choose an answer choice with 17 in the denominator. But remember: there are 17 meals at the restaurant, but 5 are disqualified because they are spicy, which means that there are a total of (17 − 5) = 12 meals the waitress can choose from. This is why the answer is F: there is only a 1 in 12 or 1 over 12 chance that the restaurant will choose his favorite meal.

5. Correct answer: **E**. We need to first recognize what p is to help figure out where it should go in this particular equation. Because p is a number of students in a class, just like 21, 27, 22, 25, and 21, it is going to be added to those 5 numbers before it is affected to find an average. This narrows down our answer choices to D and E. If you look at D and E, they have the same form in that they both feature the number of students in all 6 classes (including p) being divided by a number, which will result in an average of 24. The reason E is correct as opposed to D is that answer choice E correctly divides the addition of the 6 classes by 6 to find the proper average. If I wanted to find the average of, say, 4 different numbers, I would divide their sum by the number of numbers (in this case, 4).

6. Correct answer: **J**. Let's simply plug in $x = 11$ and simplify as much as we can before we deal with the absolute value:

$$x^2 - |7 - x| - (-x) \quad \ldots \quad (11)^2 - |7 - 11| - (-11) \quad \ldots \quad 121 - |-4| + 11 \quad \ldots \quad 132 - |-4|$$

Now, at this point, we have to determine what to do with the absolute value. Recall that absolute value denotes how far a value is away from 0; in other words, if what is between the bars is positive keep it positive, but if it is negative, make it positive! Thus, we can finish out our solution like this:

$$132 - |-4| \quad ... \quad 132 - 4 \quad ... \quad = 128, \text{ which is answer choice J.}$$

7. Correct answer: **A.** Don't let the phrasing of this question seem tricky. All you need to do is plug in $m = 16$ and solve the equation then for n, which you can do, since you would now have one equation with only one missing variable. You don't need to set the equation equal to m first. Let's plug in $m = 16$ and solve the equation one step at a time.

$$m - n = \frac{9}{4}n + 3 \quad ... \quad 16 - n = \frac{9}{4}n + 3 \quad ... \quad 13 = n + \frac{9}{4}n \quad ... \quad 13 = \frac{13}{4}n$$

At this point, we need to divide both sides by $\frac{13}{4}$ to solve for n. Dividing $\frac{13}{4}$ by $\frac{13}{4}$ is straightforward enough, but what about dividing 13 by $\frac{13}{4}$? To do so, reciprocate (aka flip) the fraction and multiply by 13, like this:

$$13 = \frac{13}{4}n \quad ... \quad \frac{13}{\frac{13}{4}} = \frac{\frac{13}{4}}{\frac{13}{4}}n \quad ... \quad 13 \times \frac{4}{13} = n \quad ... \quad 4 = n \text{ , which is answer choice A.}$$

8. Correct answer: **J.** To answer this question, you have to identify which piece of the pie chart refers to chocolate. It should be enough to look at the pie and see which is the largest piece (which, we are told, is chocolate). However, we can be objective about this as well. The angles in a circle add up to $360°$, so if we subtract the other three angles from this amount, we will determine the missing, chocolate angle, like this: $360° - 115° - 50° - 45° = 150°$, which is larger than any of the angles.

Do not be like many students who quickly select options like "Cannot be determined from the given information." This answer is rarely correct; what it means is that even if the world's greatest mathematicians sat down with this problem, they couldn't solve it.

Now that we know the value of chocolate's angle, finding the percentage of students who prefer chocolate is rather simple. The percent of students who prefer chocolate is the same percentage of the entire circle that the angle $150°$ is. If we divide $360°$ by $150°$ and multiply by 100, we will get the proper percentage, like this:

$$\frac{150°}{360°} \times 100 = 41.67\% \text{ , which can then be rounded to 42\%, or choice J.}$$

9. Correct answer: **B.** Whenever the ACT asks you to find the area of a strange shape, draw lines to break it up into smaller shapes that you know how to find the area of. In this case, you should draw a line and break it up into two smaller rectangles. If you draw a line left to right to make the left to right rectangle at the top longest, you will now have two rectangles: one of them 41 by 6, and the second 16 by 7.

Before I do the math on that, notice what I said about that second rectangle: it *won't be* 22 by 7 after you draw the left to right line creating two rectangles. You can bet that a wrong answer to this problem will be what will happen if you add the areas of two rectangles 41 by 6 and 22 by 7, but doing so will result in you double counting the area where the two rectangles meet in the upper left corner.

OK, back to our math. Like I said, drawing the left to right line results in two rectangles: one of them 41 by 6 and the other 16 by 7. To find their combined area, multiply and add, like this:

$$(41 \times 6) + (16 \times 7) = 246 + 112 = 358 \text{ , which matches up with answer choice B.}$$

10. Correct answer: **G.** We can't find the value of $f(g(2))$ without first finding the value of $g(2)$. To find that, let's plug in $x = 2$ into that equation, like this:

$$g(x) = \frac{x^3}{2} \quad ... \quad g(2) = \frac{2^3}{2} \quad ... \quad g(2) = \frac{8}{2} = 4$$

Now that we have $g(2)$, we can find $f(g(2))$, which is equivalent to finding $f(4)$. So, we'll plug in $x = 4$ into the f function, like this:

$$f(x) = 4x - 2 \quad ... \quad f(4) = 4(4) - 2 \quad ... \quad f(4) = 16 - 2 = 14, \text{ which is answer choice G.}$$

11. Correct answer: **C**. There are two ways to solve this particular problem (at least, two simple ways). The first would be to

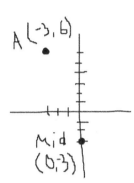

graph what you know to visualize the missing point, like you see I've done (not so beautifully) here. Though I haven't drawn a line between A and its midpoint, you can probably get a pretty good idea where point B must be. If the line continues down and to the right, we will end up with a point in quadrant IV (the bottom right quadrant of the (x, y) coordinate plane). The points in this quadrant have a positive x value and a negative y value. Only two answer choices have these values or fall into this quadrant, which are C and E. At least C *looks* like it could be correct; E on the other hand would make our line be no longer a line. This is one way to determine that the answer is C, or $(3, -12)$.

Another way to solve this problem would be to determine the x and y changes from A to the midpoint, then make the same changes from the midpoint itself, which will result in point B. On the x-axis, we move from a value of -3 to 0 from A to the midpoint, or a $+3$ shift on the x-axis. This means that from the midpoint to point B, there will be another $+3$ shift. So the x-coordinate for the correct answer will be $0 + 3 = 3$. Knowing this is already enough to determine the correct answer, since only one answer features an x-coordinate of 3. On the y-axis, we move from a value of 6 to -3 from A to the midpoint, or a -9 shift on the y-axis. This means that from the midpoint to point B, there will be another -9 shift. So the y-coordinate for the correct answer will be $-3 - 9$ $= -12$. Thus, our final answer after this shifting will be that the coordinates of point B are $(3, -12)$, which is answer choice C.

12. Correct answer: **H**. This is a question that requires caution. One of our ACT *Good to Know* math lessons was on tricky conversions. Here, we begin with how Aaron can type a certain number of words *per minute*, but we need to know how many *hours* it takes him to type a certain number of words.

Thus, let's begin by converting the number of words he can type per minute into the number of words he can type per hour. If he can type 112 words per minute, and there are 60 minutes in an hour, then he can type $(112 \times 60) = 6{,}720$ words per hour.

Now that we know the number of words per hour that Aaron can type, we need to determine how many hours it takes him to type 8,400 words. Simply divide 8,400 words by 6,720 words per hour to be left with the number of hours, like this:

$$(8{,}400 \text{ words} \div 6{,}720 \text{ words per hour}) = 1.25 \text{ hours}$$

Don't worry that the answer choices are all in fractions. Fortunately, an answer like 1.25 is easy to convert into a fraction, but that is what your calculator is for. If the answer had been a decimal that wasn't that easy to convert to a fraction, then you would simply go one answer at a time, converting the fractions into decimals in your calculator until you found a match. However, in this case, our decimal to fraction conversion isn't too difficult: $1.25 = 1\frac{1}{4}$, which matches answer choice H.

13. Correct answer: **B**. There is a technical, more difficult, algebraic way to solve this problem, which would be to create two equations with two missing variables, then solve using either substitution or elimination. If you're interested in that (which could come in handy on more difficult problems), I'll go through it after showing you the simplest way, which would simply be *Backsolving*, or going through all of the answers one at a time.

Let's start with A, and pretend that Carlos made 7 of the 2 point shots. That would mean he scored 14 points this way, leaving $(37 - 14) = 23$ points remaining for 3 point shots. Well, 23 isn't evenly divisible by 3, so it's not possible that this is the answer. Move on to B and pretend that Carlos made 8 of the 2 point shots. That would mean he scored 16 points in this way, leaving $(37 - 16) = 21$ points remaining for 3 point shots. If he took 15 shots total, and we are pretending he took 8 of the 2 point shots, that would mean he had to take 7 of the 3 point shots, which would mean 21 points. That works! Thus, the answer is B.

I promised to take you through a more technical way, which would be creating two equations with two missing variables. The missing variables would represent how many 2 and 3 point shots. Let's call 2 point shots x and 3 point shots y. We know two things about these shots, which will make up our two equations. First, we know that the total number of shots is 15, which means that $x + y = 15$. That is our first equation. Second, we know that the total number of points is 37. Because 2 point shots count for 2, and 3 point shots count for 3, our second equation is this: $2x + 3y = 37$.

There are two ways to find the missing variables from two equations. The first is **substitution**, which means solving one equation for x or y and plugging it into the other equation. For example: we know that $x + y = 15$, but we can subtract x from both sides to solve for y, like this: $y = 15 - x$. Now, I can plug in $(15 - x)$ for y in the other equation, which would leave us with only x variables, like this:

$$2x + 3y = 37 \quad \ldots \quad 2x + 3(15 - x) = 37 \quad \ldots \quad 2x + 45 - 3x = 37 \quad \ldots \quad -x = -8 \quad \ldots \quad x = 8$$

Thus, the number of 2 point shots is 8.

The second way to find the missing variables from two equations is using **elimination**. This method requires manipulating one of the equations in such a way so that when the equations are added to each other or one is subtracted from another one of the variables cancels out to 0. Because we are solving for x, we will do this to make y disappear, leaving one equation with one variable.

Because one of our equations features a $3y$ term, and the other a singular y term, let's multiply the entire second term by 3 so that the y term there becomes $3y$. Like this:

$$3(x + y = 15) \quad \dots \quad 3x + 3y = 45$$

Now, let's subtract one equation from another, which consists in adding or subtracting like terms that are put into the same columns, canceling the y terms out to 0, like this:

$$\begin{array}{r} 3x + 3y = 45 \\ - \ 2x + 3y = 37 \\ \hline x + 0y = 8 \end{array}$$

$x + 0y = 8$, or $x = 8$, which is answer choice B.

14. Correct answer: **K**. This is the second problem in a row in which *Backsolving* is going to be the most effective method. At first, there are 30 poker chips in the hat, 6 of which are black. This means that the current odds of drawing a black poker chip is $\dfrac{6}{30} = \dfrac{1}{5}$.

Let's go one answer at a time, starting with H: 5. If we add in 5 black chips, the odds of drawing a black go up to $\dfrac{6+5}{30+5} = \dfrac{11}{35}$, which can't be simplified further. This comes out to a little less than a third, and because we need the odds to rise all the way up to near 50%, we need more black chips.

Try J: 13. If we add in 13 black chips, the odds of drawing a black go up to $\dfrac{6+13}{30+13} = \dfrac{19}{43}$, which can't be simplified further, but we are getting closer.

Move on to K: 14. If we add in 14 black chips, the odds of drawing a black go up to:

$$\dfrac{6+14}{30+14} = \dfrac{20}{44} = \dfrac{10}{22} = \dfrac{5}{11},$$ which is the answer we're looking for. Thus, the answer is K.

15. Correct answer: **B**. This is the kind of question that you want to answer by using your calculator, of course. Before we enter any numbers into the calculator, however, let's work on converting 6.71×10^{-3} to a different number. The 10^{-3} simply means that the decimal point is to be moved three places to the left, or in the smaller or negative direction. Moving it once to the left will put it to the left side of the 6, as in 0.671. Moving it a second time will move it in front of the 0 that I added there, like this: 0.0671. Finally, moving it a third time will move it in front of the next 0, resulting in this: 0.00671. Thus, $6.71 \times 10^{-3} = 0.00671$.

Now, to find 4% of this number, we don't multiply it by 4; that would be finding 400% of the number. We also don't divide by 4, which would be reducing it to 25% of what it is now. We also don't multiply by 0.4, which would be to find 40% of the number. Instead, to find 4% of a number, multiply that number by 0.04, like this:

$$4\% \text{ of } 6.71 \times 10^{-3} = (0.04)0.00671 = 0.0002684, \text{ or answer choice B.}$$

16. Correct answer: **F**. First, this kind of question is very common in ACT Math. By "this kind of question" I mean a question in which a multi-variable equation is given, and then you are given all of the variables you need to solve the problem. Here, it is a simple case of plugging in the correct variables and doing the math correctly. The only other tricky thing about this problem is that you are given the *diameter* of the sphere, but the equation calls for the radius. Of course, the radius of a circle is half the diameter; so, if the diameter is 12, then the $r = 6$. We are also told that $h = 1$, which gives us all we need to solve:

$$\pi r^2 \dfrac{h}{3} = \pi (6)^2 \dfrac{1}{3} = \pi (36)(\dfrac{1}{3}) = 12\pi, \text{ which is answer choice F.}$$

17. Correct answer: **E**. Before we can talk about finding the *product* of the two solutions for this expression, we have to figure out how to actually find the solutions in the first place. For more detail on doing this, see *Good to Know* Lesson #5: Parabolas.

To find the two solutions for a parabola (which is what this expression is), first we need to factor the trinomial into its two binomials. As a reminder, the expression we're working with is $x^2 - 10x + 21$. To factor, we need two numbers that multiply to give us our last term (21), but add together to give us our middle term (-10). Those two numbers are -3 and -7. Thus:

$$x^2 - 10x + 21 = (x - 3)(x - 7) = 0$$

Some students will be too quick and assume that the two *solutions* will be -7 and -3. That might result in the correct answer for this particular problem, but that would be a happy accident. Technically, we have to set each binomial equal to 0, then solve for x both times, which will result in our two solutions, like this:

$(x - 3) = 0$ $\qquad\qquad\qquad\qquad\qquad\qquad (x - 7) = 0$
$x = 3$ $\qquad\qquad\qquad\qquad\qquad\qquad\qquad x = 7$

Thus, our two solutions are 3 and 7. The problem however asks for the *product* of these two solutions, which means you multiply them together. Because $(3 \times 7) = 21$, the answer is E: 21.

18. Correct answer: **J**. Recall that the formula for the area of a circle is πr^2, in which r is the radius. Thus, our first step is to find the radius of this circle. Unfortunately we aren't told what the radius is, but instead we are given two equations. First, we are told that the radius is $3x - 2$, then that the diameter is $5x + 1$. Because we know that two times the radius of a circle equals its diameter, we can set up an equation in which we multiply what we know the radius to be by 2, then set it equal to the diameter. This will set up one equation with one missing variable, like this:

$$2r = d \quad \ldots \quad 2(3x - 2) = 5x + 1 \quad \ldots \quad 6x - 4 = 5x + 1 \quad \ldots \quad x = 5$$

However, the radius isn't 5; that's just the value of x. If the radius is $3x - 2$, then the radius is $3(5) - 2 = 13$.

Since all of the answers already feature π, then we just need to find r^2, which is $13^2 = 169$. Thus, the area of the circle is 169π, or answer choice J.

19. Correct answer: **D**. The scientific, technical jargon of this question is only a distraction; let's boil it down. If 3.20 ml is recommended for dogs weighing 70 pounds, and if the dosage decreases 0.04 ml every pound, what is the dosage recommendation for a dog weighing 42 pounds?

First, determine how many pounds fewer the 42 pound dog is: $(70 - 42) = 28$ pounds less. Next, multiply the 28 pounds by 0.04 ml, since that is the amount decreased per pound: $28(0.04) = 1.12$. Lastly, subtract 1.12 from the 3.20 baseline to get the recommended dose for a 42 pound dog, like this: $3.20 - 1.12 = 2.08$ ml, which is answer choice D.

20. Correct answer: **H**. The area of the shaded region is the width times the length, of course, but the width is y and the length is x. So, we simply have to figure those out, starting with y. The right side of the larger figure is 7, which means that the left side must also be 7. So, $y + y + 3 = 7$, or $2y = 4$, or $y = 2$. The bottom of the larger figure is also 7, which means that the top of the larger figure must also be 7. So that means that $x + x + 1 = 7$, or $2x = 6$, or $x = 3$.

So, back to our original problem. The area of the shaded portion is xy, or $(2)(3)$, or 6, which is answer choice H.

21. Correct answer: **A**. We learned a lot about logs (aka logarithms) in *Good to Know* Lesson #10, so if you want a lot of detailed information, look there. Let's remember that logs are used to find missing exponents, and they take this form:

$$\log_{base} amount = exponent$$

So, in this problem we have the expression $\log_x 125 = 3$. Thus, what is missing is the *base* that satisfies this equation (in other words, can be rewritten as): $x^3 = 125$. Now we have an easier way to determine x: what is the cubed root of 125? In other words, what number, when cubed, equals 125?

One way to answer this question from here, of course, is to use *Backsolving*, cubing each answer to determine if it equals 125. Another easy way to find the cubed root of a number is to raise the number to the $(1 \div 3)$ power, like this:

$$x^3 = 125 \quad \ldots \quad 125^{\frac{1}{3}} = x \quad \ldots \quad x = 5, \text{which matches answer choice A.}$$

22. Correct answer: **K**. A *greatest common factor* is a number that can equally divide into two or more numbers. For example: the greatest common factor of 10 and 100 is 10, since $(10 \div 10)$ and $(100 \div 10)$ both equal whole numbers (1 and 10, respectively).

Here, the variable a can go into both terms, and so can a b^2 term as well. This means that the greatest common factor of a^3b^2 and ab^3 is ab^2, which as the question states, also equals 24. Thus, $(a \times b \times b) = 24$.

Now that we know that, we need to use the rest of the clues to determine what b could equal. The easiest way to determine that is perhaps to use *Backsolving*. Let's start with H: 8…could b possibly equal 8 if we have to square it and then make it divisible into 24? Since $8 \times 8 = 64$, this is impossible. This is also impossible if you go one smaller and try out answer choice J: 6, since $6 \times 6 = 36$. That brings us down to K: 2. Since $2 \times 2 = 4$, which is divisible into 24, it is therefore possible for b to equal 2, making K the correct answer.

23. Correct answer: **E**. First and foremost, draw a line with fixed points and values. This will show you what can and can't be changed. In a question like this, the answer will be definitive; you don't have to worry that the correct answer is up for interpretation. Most likely, some segment will be always smaller or larger no matter what than one of our defined segments (the ones that are 8 and 10 units long).

Now that the segment has been drawn, all that's left to do is to go through the answer choices one at a time to determine which of the answers/inequalities *must* be true. Start with A, that $GJ < 8$. There is no way to know if this is true or false, since the segment GJ is undefined. On the little segment I drew above, it looks a little smaller, but that's just a drawing; in reality, GJ could be 100 units long. Move on to B, that $8 > FG$. Since FG is 10 and JH is only 8, this isn't true. Move on to C, that $GH < 10$. It is possible that GH could be less than 10, but that would only be true if GJ were defined as less than 2, but because GJ is undefined, we can't be sure. Move on to D, that GJ is < 10. Again, GJ is undefined, and we have no idea how long it is. Lastly, try E, that $8 < GH$. Since GH includes JH, but also includes GJ, it always must be the case that GH is larger than JH, which makes E the correct answer.

24. Correct answer: **G**. A simplistic (I don't mean that word in a bad or negative sense!) way to solve this problem would be to draw a number line with marks one second apart. Then, you could put a dot for each bird call until you get them falling at the same number.

However, this question is essentially asking for the *least common multiple* of these two numbers, which just means the smallest whole number that they both divide into equally. With 3 and 7, it is relatively simple to find; it just so happens that when you multiply the two of them together, you get the least common multiple, which is 21, or answer choice G. With more complicated numbers, you may need to make a list of each number's multiples and find the same number, like this:

3:     3, 6, 9, **21**, 15, 21, 24, 27…
7:     7, 14, **21**, 28, 35…

Such a list makes it clear that the earliest time the two birds will call at the same time is at the 21 second mark; again, that is answer choice G.

25. Correct answer: **B**. Though the painting being described is a rectangle, this is in reality a triangle problem. We are given two sides of a right triangle, and asked to find the missing side. First, draw the triangle being described to avoid simple mistakes, as I've done below.

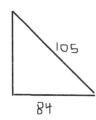

As you can see, we are simply missing the left side of the triangle, and because it is a right triangle, this means that we can use the Pythagorean Theorem to solve for the missing side. As a reminder, the Pythagorean Theorem is $a^2 + b^2 = c^2$, in which a and b are the two legs of the triangle and c is the hypotenuse. Plugging in our one leg and the hypotenuse that we know, and solving for the leg we do not know, looks like this:

$$(84)^2 + b^2 = (105)^2 \quad … \quad 7{,}056 + b^2 = 11{,}025 \quad … \quad b^2 = 3{,}969 \quad … \quad \sqrt{b^2} = \sqrt{3{,}969} \quad … \quad b = 63$$

Thus, answer choice B is correct; the height of the painting is 63 inches.

26. Correct answer: **F**. First, write the inequality as described in the question; getting it from words into a form that is more mathematically understandable will help. If 3 times n is added to -12, there is a positive result, like this: $3n + (-12) > 0$, or more simply, $3n - 12 > 0$.

Second, consider a number for n, any number, that will satisfy this inequality. The first number for n that comes into my mind to satisfy the inequality is $n = 5$, which results in this:

$$3(5) - 12 > 0 \quad … \quad 15 - 12 > 0 \quad … \quad 3 > 0, \text{ which satisfies.}$$

From here it is plain to see that if we chose $n = 4$, we would end up with, after doing the math, an inequality that said $0 > 0$, which doesn't make any sense. Thus, any number greater than $n = 4$ would satisfy the inequality, which is answer choice F.

27. Correct answer: **C**. Most of the time, I would begin an answer explanation to this kind of question involving parabolas by explaining how to factor then simplify. This time, however, let's use this as an opportunity to first review the *Picking Numbers* strategy, then we'll solve in the traditional way.

To use the *Picking Numbers* strategy, choose a number for x that is greater than 8 (since it says "For all $x > 8$..."), so let's go with $x = 10$, which will make our math more simple. We will now plug in $x = 10$ into the original equation and see what we get:

$$\frac{(x^2 - 10x + 16)(x + 3)}{(x^2 - 5x - 24)(x - 2)} = \frac{(100 - 100 + 16)(10 + 3)}{(100 - 50 - 24)(10 - 2)} = \frac{(16)(13)}{(26)(8)} = \frac{208}{208} = 1 \text{ , which is answer choice C.}$$

The more traditional route, of course and as I said, involves factoring each trinomial and then simplifying by canceling out whatever binomials may be in both the numerator and the denominator. First, let's factor the trinomial in the numerator, which is this: $(x^2 - 10x + 16)$. To factor a trinomial, look for two numbers that multiply together to give us our last term (16) which add together to give us our middle terms (-10). In this case, I see that $(8 \times 2) = 16$, but adding those terms gives me positive 10. However, $(-8 \times -2) = 16$ and add together to give me -10. Thus, this trinomial factors into these two binomials: $(x - 8)(x - 2)$.

Now, on to the binomial in the denominator, which is this: $(x^2 - 5x - 24)$. Again, we need two terms that multiply to give us the third term (-24) but which add up to the middle term (-5). These two numbers are -8 and 3. Thus, this trinomial factors into these two binomials: $(x - 8)(x + 3)$. Now, rewrite the entire equation with all known binomials:

$$\frac{(x^2 - 10x + 16)(x + 3)}{(x^2 - 5x - 24)(x - 2)} = \frac{(x - 8)(x - 2))(x + 3)}{(x - 8)(x + 3)(x - 2)}$$

As you can see, each binomial has a twin. The $(x - 8)$ term in the numerator will cancel with the $(x - 8)$ term in the denominator, and the same will happen with the $(x + 3)$ and $(x - 2)$ terms. After canceling everything, you will be left with 1, which is answer choice C.

28. Correct answer: **F**. Try out each answer choice one at a time to determine if it satisfies the inequality, taking special care to correctly use the absolute value bars; as a reminder, absolute value bars make whatever number is between them positive. With a question like this, and because ACT Math answers are almost (if not) always in numerical order from largest to smallest or smallest to largest, it is increasingly likely that the answer here will be either F or K. For no particular reason, let's try K.

Answer K has a value of \$150; let's plug in this number for m and see if it satisfies:

$$|m + \$25| \le \$175 \quad ... \quad |\$150 + \$25| \le \$175 \quad ... \quad |\$175| \le \$175 \quad ... \quad \$175 \le \$175$$

Yes, K satisfies the equation, which means it is not the correct answer, since we are looking for a number that is *not* in the range.

Now, let's try F, which gives m a value of $-\$205$:

$$|m + \$25| \le \$175 \quad ... \quad |-\$205 + \$25| \le \$175 \quad ... \quad |-\$180| \le \$175 \quad ... \quad \$180 \le \$175$$

This does not satisfy, since \$180 is greater than \$175. Thus, the answer is F: m can't equal $-\$205$.

29. Correct answer: **E**. One deceptive thing about this question is the answer choices. Only one of them is a huge number, whereas 4 of them are relatively small. However, don't let this be a problem; don't let this fool you. Let's consider a smaller situation first. If he was comfortable cooking 2 meat dishes, 2 vegetable dishes, and 2 desserts, then he'd be comfortable cooking $(2 \times 2 \times 2) = 8$ different meals. Similarly, if he can cook 80 meat dishes, 55 vegetable dishes, and 22 desserts, he is comfortable cooking $(80 \times 55 \times 22) = 96,800$ different meal combinations, which is answer choice E.

30. Correct answer: **H**. The simplest way to solve this problem is also a laborious one: plot the points, then consider the general slope of the line that generally passes through the points, then (if necessary) consider the y-axis of the line.

First, I have graphed the points below. You can see already that there is a kind of line that unites them all. However, the question says that there will be a line that *approximates* them, which means that it will, in general, fit the points; in other words, the line that is the answer to the question won't perfectly pass through each and every point.

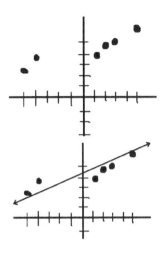

Next, consider a possible slope. On the next drawing down on the left, I've drawn in a possible line that approximates the data points. Let's recall the slope-intercept formula of a line: $y = mx + b$, in which m is the slope and b is the y-intercept (where the line crosses the y-axis). The first thing to notice is that the line has a positive slope (it has a "rise" on the positive y-axis as it "runs" left to right on the positive x-axis). This eliminates answer choices F and K, since they both have negative slopes.

The other options for slope are 3, 4, and $\frac{1}{3}$. If a slope is 3 or 4, that means it will "rise" or go up the y-axis 3 or 4 points, then "run" over 1 on the x-axis. This is NOT what our slope looks like here; it looks like the opposite (in other words, the slope is not very steep); it looks like it "runs" 3 or 4 before going up ("rise") by 1. This kind of shallow slope is fractional, which fits well with the remaining answer that has a slope of $\frac{1}{3}$. This answer choice, H, also has a y-intercept of +4, which fits fairly well with the line that I drew on top of my plotted points. For all of these reasons, H best approximates the plotted points.

31. Correct answer: D. This was mentioned in *Good to Know* Lesson #10, but any time a number of any kind is raised to the power of 0, the answer is 1. The only exception is 0, which, when raised to the power of 0, equals 0. Thus, this expression, as complicated as it is, is always going to equal 1 since it is raised to the power of 0; the answer then is D: 1.

32. Correct answer: G. Sin and cos are two trigonometric functions that rely on knowing the three sides of a right triangle. Since we are told that the $cos\ \theta = \frac{12}{13}$, and because the cos of an angle is equal to the adjacent side of an angle over the hypotenuse of the triangle, we can assume then that the adjacent side of this triangle relative to θ is 12, and that the hypotenuse of the triangle is 13.

That would leave the "opposite" side of θ, the third side of our triangle, as undefined. You may be able to quickly recognize that this is a special, 5-12-13 triangle, and thus that the third, opposite side must be 5. If you used the Pythagorean Theorem, that $a^2 + b^2 = c^2$, you would find the same.

Since the sin θ is going to equal the opposite side over the hypotenuse, we then know that the sin $\theta = \frac{5}{13}$, which is choice G.

33. Correct answer: A. What we know about the original picture is that it has a length of 8 and a width of 10, and thus an area of 80. Hold that thought for now.

After she cuts it, we know that the new length will be 87.5% the length of the original. To find this length, multiply the original length by 0.875. Since the original length is 8, the new length will be 8(0.875) = 7.

We now have all that we need to set up an equation to solve for the missing width, which we can call x. We are told that the new area will be 70% of the original area, which recall was 80. This means that the area of the new picture will be 80(0.7) = 56. Since we know now that the length of the new side is 7, and the area is 56, then the width can be found by solving this equation: $7x = 56$. Divide both sides by 7 and find that x, or the missing width, = 8, which is answer choice A.

34. Correct answer: K. Recall the formula for a circle, which is $(x - h)^2 + (y - k)^2 = r^2$, in which (h, k) is the center of the circle and r is the radius. Since the center of the circle is the origin, that means $(h, k) = (0, 0)$. This eliminates F, G, and H as answer options, since $(x - 0)^2 + (y - 0)^2$ is equivalent to $x^2 + y^2$. Lastly, the radius of the Chocolate Pie is 5.5, meaning $r^2 = 30.25$. Thus, the entire correct equation of the circle that fits this pie shape when centered at the origin is $x^2 + y^2 = 30.25$, which corresponds with answer choice K.

35. Correct answer: A. Since we are dealing with the area of the Chocolate Pie when compared to the area of both other pies, let's go ahead and find all three areas, recalling that the area of a circle $= \pi r^2$.

Chocolate Pie Area $= \pi r^2 = \pi (5.5)^2 = \pi\ 30.25 = 95.03$
Apple Pie Area $= \pi r^2 = \pi (6)^2 = \pi\ 36 = 113.10$
Key Lime Pie Area $= \pi r^2 = \pi (5)^2 = \pi\ 25 = 78.54$

Let's use *Backsolving* and try out each answer one at a time. Because we know that A is the correct answer, let's try out a wrong answer first, like B. B says that the Chocolate Pie is 121% of the Apple Pie. That would mean that when you multiply the Apple

Pie's area by 1.21, you would get the area of the Chocolate Pie. However, the area of the Apple Pie is already *larger* than that of the Chocolate Pie; multiplying it by 1.21 will only make it bigger. B can't be correct.

Now let's try A, which says that the Chocolate Pie is 84.03% of the Apple Pie. To test if this is true, multiply the Apple Pie's area (113.10) by 0.8403, and see if the result is the area of the Chocolate Pie, like this: $113.10(0.8403) = 95.04$. Sure enough, that's within one hundredth of the area of the Chocolate Pie, which can be expected when decimals are being rounded (which they are here, and which is why the question requires that areas and percentages be rounded to the nearest hundredth of a percent). Thus, the answer is A; the Chocolate Pie's area is 84.03% of the Apple Pie's.

36. Correct answer: **K.** Fortunately, if you properly found the area of all three pies in the previous problem, you are one step closer to solving this problem. As the interior angles of these three pieces are to 360°, so too the area of the piece will be to the area of the pie as a whole.

Two of our pie's pieces (Piece 1 and Piece 3) are cut with interior angles of 25°. This means that these pieces are $\frac{25}{360} \times 100 = 6.94\%$ of the pie. Piece 2 is $\frac{20}{360} \times 100 = 5.56\%$ of the pie.

Now that we know what percentage of their respective pies these pieces occupy, we can determine their areas by multiplying the areas by the percentages. Recall the area of the entire Chocolate Pie is 95.03, the area of the Apple Pie is 113.10, and the area of the Key Lime Pie is 78.54 (these areas were just calculated in the previous question's answer explanation).

> Piece 1 is 6.94% of Key Lime Pie's area, or 6.94% of 78.54 = $78.54(0.0694) = 5.45$
> Piece 2 is 5.56% of Chocolate Pie's area, or 5.56% of 95.03 = $95.03(0.0556) = 5.28$
> Piece 3 is 6.94% of Apple Pie's area, or 6.94% of 113.10 = $113.10(0.0694) = 7.85$

Thus, Piece 3 is larger than Piece 1 is larger than Piece 2, which corresponds with choice K.

37. Correct answer: **C.** This question is testing your ability to recognize and properly use the Law of Transversals and other knowledge about angles. The first thing to note is that the segment BD is almost irrelevant; the only reason it is relevant is because we are told that angle $\angle ABD$ is 118° and is bisected by segment CB; 'bisected' means that it perfectly cuts the angle in half. This is important for us because it tells us that angle $\angle ABC$ is half of 118°, or is 59°.

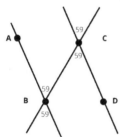

With that in mind, I've redrawn the three segments as a little bit longer. Remember what the Law of Transversals means: if two parallel lines are transversed ("cut through") with another line, then each pair of alternate interior angles are equal. Additionally, if you know even 1 of the 8 angles formed when a line passes through two others, you can determine the value of all 8 angles. Four of them will be the same, and the other four will be the same as well. Here, $\angle ABC$ is 59° as we've already determined, but that means by definition that angle $\angle BCD$ is also 59°, which is answer choice C.

38. Correct answer: **H.** Because the grass that needs replacing is in square feet, but the grass patches are sold in dimensions of inches, one or the other needs converting before we divide one by the other and determine how many grass patches are needed. It would be easier if the grass patches of 25 inches by 25 inches were converted to feet. Since there are 12 inches in a foot, then each side of each patch of grass is:

$$\frac{25 \text{ inches}}{12 \text{ inches per foot}} = 2\frac{1}{12} \text{ feet} = 2.083 \text{ feet}$$

Now, this means that each patch of grass is 2.083 by 2.083 feet. Next, we must find the square footage of each patch of grass so that we can divide them into the total square footage of the dead grass.

$$2.083 \text{ ft} \times 2.083 \text{ ft} = 4.34 \text{ ft}^2$$

Now, because we know the total square footage of the grass that needs replacing (1,350) and the square footage of each patch of grass (4.34), we simply need to divide the latter into the former to determine how many patches are needed:

$$\frac{1,350}{4.34} = 311.06 \text{ patches of grass needed}$$

However, the question does NOT ask for you to round the patches to the nearest integer or whole number. Instead, it asks what is the minimum number of patches needed to replace all of the dead grass. In other words, 311 is not quite enough, because there will be a small amount of grass yet uncovered (.06 patches worth). This means that you must round *up* to ensure there is enough grass purchased to cover all of the dead grass. This, of course, is 312, or answer choice H.

39. Correct answer: **D**. To answer this question, you need a proper number set, of which you can find the mean, median, mode, and range. When I say "proper number set", I mean that the numbers given need to be listed in numerical order. Below I list them in numerical order, then do the proper math to find the four values needed.

Numerical order number set: $\{0.05, 0.05, 0.05, 0.05, 0.06, 0.06, 0.09, 0.10, 0.11, 0.11\}$

Mean (average): $\dfrac{(.05 + .05 + .05 + .05 + .06 + .06 + .09 + .10 + .11 + .11)}{10} = \dfrac{0.73}{10} = 0.073$

Median (middle term, or average of 2 middle terms if even number of terms in set): 0.06

Mode (occurs the most): 0.05

Range (difference between largest and smallest term): $(0.11 - 0.05) = 0.06$

Thus, as you can see, it is the median and the range that are the same. This corresponds with answer choice D.

40. Correct answer: **J**. For numbers 40, 41, and 42, the absolute first thing that you should do is draw an image of the tower. Like I have done here:

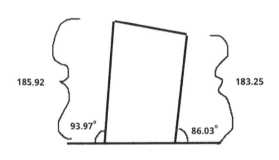

Question number 40 asks us to find the height of the tower if it were to stand upright. In other words, question 40 is asking for the length of either side of the tower. If you look at the answer choices, you will see that each of them features the angle 86.03 degrees, which means we need to solve this from this particular angle.

Your first thought might be this: isn't the length of that side simply 183.25? Well, no. That is the *height* of the tower on that side; we want the length of the actual wall, which is the hypotenuse of a very tall right triangle. From the point of view of the 86.03 degree angle, we know the opposite side (which is 183.25), but again, the length of the wall is the hypotenuse of this triangle. We need to identify one of our three functions (sin, cos, tan) that uses the opposite side and the hypotenuse, which is sin. Sin, if you remember, is the opposite side over the hypotenuse. Thus, we can set up an initial equation that looks like this (let's call the length of the wall, thus the length of the hypotenuse, x):

$$\sin(86.03) = \frac{183.25}{x}$$

Now, we have to rearrange the equation to solve for x. To do so, multiply both sides by x, then divide both sides by $\sin(86.03)$, like this:

$$(x)\sin(86.03) = \frac{183.25}{x}(x) \quad \dots \quad \sin(86.03)(x) = 183.25 \quad \dots \quad x = \frac{183.25}{\sin(86.03)}$$

This corresponds with answer choice J.

41. Correct answer: **E**. This question has nothing to to with the actual tower, of course, but rather with Chandra's reading speed. The absolute easiest way to solve this problem is by using the *Picking Numbers* strategy from earlier in the book. Let's pretend that $x = 700$. This is simple because if she can read at 700 words per minute, and there are 350 words per page, then she can read 2 pages per minute. If she can read two pages per minute, it will take her 7.5 minutes to read 15 pages.

With that in mind, plug in $x = 700$ into the five answer choices to see which one will result in an answer of 7.5 minutes. Start with:

A: $\dfrac{350x}{15} = \dfrac{350(700)}{15} = 16{,}333\dots$not 7.5!

B: $\dfrac{x}{350(15)} = \dfrac{700}{350(15)} = \dfrac{1}{7.5}\dots$not 7.5!

C: $\dfrac{15x}{350} = \dfrac{15(700)}{350} = 30...$, not 7.5!

D: $\dfrac{350}{15x} = \dfrac{350}{15(700)} = 0.03...$not 7.5!

E: $\dfrac{350(15)}{x} = \dfrac{350(15)}{700} = 7.5...$that's it!

Thus, the answer is E.

42. Correct answer: **H**. First, determine the volume of this new tower. The volume of a cylinder is the area of the circle of one side times the height of the cylinder. The area of a circle is πr^2, and because we know the diameter of this new tower is 50, that means the radius is 25. Thus, the area of the circle of this cylinder is $\pi r^2 = 625(3.14159) = 1,963.49$. Multiply this area by the height, which is 185 ft, and the result is this: $1,963.49(185) = 363,246.34$ cubic feet.

The original tower has a weight of 16,000 (2,000) pounds (since we know it weights 16,000 tons, and there are 2,000 pounds per ton). Thus, the weight of the tower is 16,000 (2,000) = 32,000,000 pounds.

Lastly, the question asks for pounds per cubic foot. Divide the pounds (32,000,000) by the cubic feet (363,246.34) to get pounds per cubic foot, like this:

$$\dfrac{32,000,000}{363,246.34} = 88.09,$$ which when rounded to the nearest whole number, is 88, or answer choice H.

43. Correct answer: **B**. There are three ways to solve this particular problem. Let's go through all three ways, not because you need all three to solve one problem, but so you can find the easiest for you. I'll start with what I believe to be the easiest, then move on from there.

Method 1: Elimination - this method relies on the strange idea in Algebra that you can add equations to one another or subtract one equation from another. When you do this properly, you will be left with only one equation with only one variable. To do so, you have to manipulate at least one of the equations so that there will be canceling out. In the two equations in this problem, I see that if I multiply the second equation by 2, that the second term will be $-2y$, which, when added to the first, will result in the y terms canceling.

First, multiply the second equation by 2, like this: $2(4x - y = -29) = 8x - 2y = -58$

Second add the two equations together, like this:

$$\begin{array}{r} 3x + 2y = 14 \\ + \ \underline{8x - 2y = -58} \\ 11x + 0y = -44 \end{array}$$

Now, we have just one equation with one variable; only x remains. Divide both sides by 11, and learn that $x = -4$. Since only answer B says $x = -4$, we have our answer. If you needed to find y, then simply plug in $x = -4$ into either of the original equations and solve for y.

Method 2: _Backsolving_ - I hope by this point that this is one of the tools in your ACT Math toolbox that you've grown accustomed to using! Try out the values of x and y one answer at a time to see if they work on BOTH equations. You can bet that at least one of the wrong answers will work for one equation, but not both.

Start with A, that $x = 2$ and $y = 4$. Plug that into the first equation: $3(2) + 2(4) = 14$ ... $6 + 8 = 14$, which works! Like I just said though, you have to now try this on the second equation, like this:
$4(2) - 4 = -29$ ... $8 - 4 = -29$ ... ??? Not quite! It doesn't satisfy.

Move on to B, that $x = -4$ and $y = 13$. Plug that into the first equation: $3(-4) + 2(13) = 14$ ... $-12 + 26 = 14$, which works! Try plugging in those two values into the second equation to see if it also works; if so, we have found our answer. If not, it's on to the next answer choice. So, plugging $x = -4$ and $y = 13$ into the second equation looks like this: $4(-4) - 13 = -29$ ... $-16 - 13 = -29$, which also works! There you have it; by _Backsolving_, we are able to show that B satisfies both equations.

Method 3: Substitution - substitution involves solving one of our equations for a variable, replacing this variable with whatever is on the other side of the equation in the other equation, then solving for the one missing variable. That sounds much more confusing than it is, so follow along to see how substitution works.

Step 1 is to choose an equation to solve for x or y. I see that there is a $-y$ term in the second equation, which will be simple enough to solve for y. Let's rearrange and manipulate it to do so:

$$4x - y = -29 \quad \dots \quad -y = -4x - 29 \quad \dots \quad y = 4x + 29$$

Now, we can take this value of y (which is $4x + 29$) and plug it in where there is a y in the other, first equation. This will eliminate any y's, leaving us with an equation with only x's, which can then be solved. Like this:

$$3x + 2y = 14 \quad \dots \quad 3x + 2(4x + 29) = 14 \quad \dots \quad 3x + 8x + 58 = 14 \quad \dots \quad 11x = -44 \quad \dots \quad x = -4$$

Now that we know that $x = -4$, we have enough information to solve the answer. If you need to find y, simply plug in $x = -4$ into any equation and solve for y.

44. Correct answer: **J**. First, and before we figure out what to do with the y^5 term, let's simply solve the equation in a way that isolates y^5 on one side, like this:

$$15x = 5y^5 - 25 \quad \dots \quad -5y^5 = -15x - 25 \quad \dots \quad y^5 = 3x + 5$$

So far, so good. To isolate the y by itself, we will need to find the fifth root of both sides. Just like the square root of anything squared is just the thing itself (the square root of 3^2 is just 3, for example), the fifth root of anything "fifthed" or raised to the power of 5 is just the thing itself. Finding the fifth root of something, though, is the same thing as raising it to the $\frac{1}{5}$ power, like this:

$$y^5 = 3x + 5 \quad \dots \quad (y^5)^{\frac{1}{5}} = (3x + 5)^{\frac{1}{5}} \quad \dots \quad y = (3x + 5)^{\frac{1}{5}}, \text{ which matches answer choice J.}$$

45. Correct answer: **C**. First, recall that an equilateral triangle is the special type that has 3 sides of equal length, which means it also has 3 angles that are identical: all 3 angles are 60°. With this knowledge, we can "slice" an equilateral triangle in half down the height to create a new triangle that we can evaluate using sin/cos/tan. In such a case, we would know the length of one of the sides and the value of two of the angles. Below, I have created this equilateral triangle; notice that both the right and left hand sides are right triangles.

Because the area of a triangle is $\frac{1}{2}bh$ in which h is the height and b is the length of the base, we have to find what is missing which, in our case, is b. But because this is an equilateral triangle, it doesn't matter which side you rest the triangle on; it will look like this triangle here.

Now for the actual math. Notice that I have labeled the right side of the triangle with an x. This is what we need to find out that we can find the base and then the area. We need a trig function (sin, cos, or tan) that uses the side we know (that $h = 20$) and the side we need to know (the x). You could use cos from the 30° at the top, or sin from the 60° in the bottom right. Let's go with sin, like this:

$$\sin(60) = \frac{20}{x} \quad \dots \quad x\sin(60) = 20 \quad \dots \quad x = \frac{20}{\sin(60)} \quad \dots \quad x = \frac{20}{0.866} \quad \dots \quad 23.09$$

Now that we know one side is 23.09, we know that all three sides are 23.09, which means we know the base is 23.09.

Thus, the area of our triangle is $\frac{1}{2}bh = \frac{1}{2}(23.09)(20) = 230.95$. The question asks us to round to the nearest square inch, which is up to 231. This is our answer, which corresponds with answer choice C.

46. Correct answer: **H**. First, identify the first six prime numbers; as a reminder, a prime number is a number that is divisibly by only itself and the number 1. Thus, the first 6 prime numbers are 1, 2, 3, 5, 7, and 11.

The mean of these numbers is $\dfrac{1 + 2 + 3 + 5 + 7 + 11}{6} = \dfrac{29}{6}$

Second, identify the factors of 10. A numbers factors are all of the numbers that can evenly divide into it. The numbers that all evenly divide into 10, and thus 10's factors, are 1, 2, 5, and 10.

The mean of these numbers is $\dfrac{1 + 2 + 5 + 10}{4} = \dfrac{18}{4}$

Lastly, multiply the two together and simplify: $\dfrac{29}{6} \times \dfrac{18}{4} = \dfrac{522}{24} = \dfrac{87}{4} = 21\dfrac{3}{4}$, which is answer choice H.

47. Correct answer: **D**. If two matrices can not be multiplied together, it is undefined. Thus, four of these options *can* be multiplied together, and we have to figure out which ones. Fortunately, you don't have to do all of the math; if you can remember the rule about which matrices can and can't be multiplied, you can answer this question rather quickly.

The rule is this: two matrices can be multiplied together if the number of columns in the first matrix equals the number of rows in the second matrix (the columns are up and down; rows are left and right). Sometimes, just reversing the order of the two matrices makes them go from able to be multiplied to undefined. Let's go through the answer options one at a time.

Answer choice A says *AB*. Matrix *A* has 2 columns; matrix *B* has 2 rows. These can be multiplied, so this is an incorrect answer.

Answer choice B says *BA*. Matrix *B* has 1 column; matrix *A* has 1 row. These can be multiplied, so this is an incorrect answer.

Answer choice C says *DB*. Matrix *D* has 2 columns; matrix *B* has 2 rows. These can be multiplied, so this is an incorrect answer.

Answer choice D says *BD*. Matrix *B* has 1 column; matrix *D* has 3 rows. These are different, thus it can't be multiplied and is undefined and the correct answer.

48. Correct answer: **K**. First, cancel out like terms between those in the numerator and the term in the denominator. All three terms are divisible by both 2 and a^2, which will eliminate the term in the denominator entirely. It should be noted that when exponents are being divided, the exponents themselves are subtracted, not divided. For example, if I divide a^{16} by a^2, which is necessary in this step for this problem's simplification, the result is not a^8, but rather $a^{16-2} = a^{14}$. Here is the first step:

$$\frac{8a^{16} - 6a^4}{2a^2} = 4a^{14} - 3a^2$$

Now, the question becomes whether or not this term can be further simplified. There is no common factor between 4 and 3, so those will stay the same. However, there is a common factor between a^{14} and a^2, which is a^2. So, we can divide both terms by a^2 (but remember: exponents get subtracted when one is divided by another) and put it in front of parentheses, like this:

$$4a^{14} - 3a^2 = a^2(4a^{12} - 3), \text{ which is answer choice K.}$$

49. Correct answer: **A**. To answer this question correctly, properly identify the ratios involved and cross multiply. Before I do that, it is worth noting that it is perfectly acceptable if you want to leave these numbers as fractions, then simplify at the end. However, I'm going to convert each of these fractions into a decimal number first. This keeps me from making a simple error that can come from working these kinds of problems as fractions. This will be my first step:

$$1\frac{3}{4} = 1.75 \qquad 2\frac{1}{8} = 2.125 \qquad 2\frac{1}{3} = 2.333$$

Next, I want to set up my ratios and cross multiply. One way to think about this ratio is in terms of chocolate chips per butter. So, I'll put chocolate chips in the numerator, butter in the denominator, and set that equal to the same ratio with the missing butter that we need to find as *x*. Our recipe calls for a certain amount of both ingredients which (using my decimal conversions) looks like this:

$$\frac{1.75 \text{ chocolate chips}}{2.125 \text{ butter}}$$

Now, I set the ingredient amounts that Molly will use equal to this with the amount of butter we need to find labeled as *x*:

$$\frac{1.75 \text{ chocolate chips}}{2.125 \text{ butter}} = \frac{2.333 \text{ chocolate chips}}{x \text{ butter}}$$

After cross multiplying, we this equation, which we can solve for *x*:

$$1.75x = 2.125(2.333) \quad \dots \quad x = \frac{4.958}{1.75} = 2.833$$

Lastly, we have to figure out which answer choice corresponds to 2.833. Only one answer choice falls between 2 and 3, which is answer choice A. Sure enough, if you put $2\frac{5}{6}$ in your calculator, you will see it is equal to 2.833.

50. Correct answer: G. It's important to recognize that this question is asking for the *minimum* number of athletes who play both a winter and a spring sport. There are 55 total, so let's subtract the 29 who play a winter sport. That leaves 26 football players. What's left is that 31 of them now play a spring sport. We can assume that the 26 leftover play a spring sport, but that still leaves 5 who also play a spring sport. Thus, at a minimum, at least 5 football players play both a spring and winter sport, which is answer choice G.

51. Correct answer: D. Though wrapped up in a very long modeling/story problem, this is really a simple probability problem. Add the number of laptops that had 0, 1, or 2 defects and divide it from the total number of laptops, like this:

$$\frac{(193 + 111 + 152)}{(193 + 111 + 152 + 105 + 53)} = \frac{456}{614} = 0.74$$

The question and answers require that we find the fraction that best approximates our probability of 0.74. Although $\frac{2}{3}$ might seem pretty close at first, letter D is spot on, since $\frac{74}{100} = \frac{37}{50}$, thus D is correct

52. Correct answer: J. Notice that the bottom side has a length of 5. Because every line meets at 90°, we know then that the two lines that are parallel to the bottom side also add up to 5. So far, that is 10. We also know that the two vertical sides on the right of the figure have a length of $4 + 1 = 5$, so that means that each other vertical side on the left, those perpendicular to those on the right, also add up to 5. So far then, that's a total perimeter of 20. There are two sides yet to be taken into account, which are the two horizontal sides that cut into the figure from the left, each with a length of 3. Thus, the total perimeter is 26, which is answer choice J.

53. Correct answer: C. Simply add each day's steps without making a mistake. If you add 50 steps each day 10 times in a row, you get this list of numbers: 1000, 1050, 1100, 1150, 1200, 1250, 1300, 1350, 1400, and 1450. Add them up carefully for a total of 12,250, which is answer choice C.

54. Correct answer: F. The formula for the area of a parallelogram has not been discussed in this book until now since it does not fall into either the *Good to Know* or *Have to Know* categories. The formula for the area of a parallelogram is simply bh, in which b equals the length of the base and h equals the height from the base. This works for every parallelogram, even squares and rectangles.

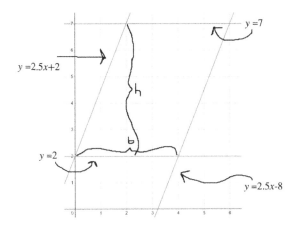

The first thing to do is to draw out the parallelogram by making a quick graph of the four lines. Two of the lines ($y = 2$ and $y = 7$) are parallel to the x-axis and stretch left to right. For the other two lines, start at their y-intercepts ($+2$ and -8) and plot points by the slope (they both have a slope of $2\frac{1}{2}$, which means go up on the y-axis $2\frac{1}{2}$ before going over 1 on the x-axis).

In this diagram, I've labeled the four lines. You'll notice the y-axis on the left and the x-axis on the bottom (in other words, this parallelogram is in Quadrant I of the coordinate plane), and that I've labeled the base and the height with b and h, respectively.

Now for the mathematics of it. The base, b, goes across the line $y = 2$ from an x value of 0 to an x value of 4. Thus, the base is $(4 - 0) = 4$. The height stretches from a y value of 2 to a y value of 7. Thus the height is $(7 - 2) = 5$. Since the area of a parallelogram is bh, then the area is $bh = 4(5) = 20$ square units, which is answer choice F.

55. Correct answer: E. There are two ways to solve this problem, but the first (factoring trinomials, canceling binomials, etc.) is tricky. Instead, use *Picking Numbers*, choose a value for y, and then plug it into both the expression in the question and the answers and find a match. The added difficulty is that many of the y terms are underneath a radical (in other words, you have to find the square root of y routinely), which means you'd have to choose a value of y that is a perfect square. Let's go with $y = 4$, plug it in, and see what we end up with:

$$\frac{(-\sqrt{y} - 3)(y + 5\sqrt{y} + 4)}{(\sqrt{y} + 1)(y - 4\sqrt{y} - 21)}) = \frac{(-\sqrt{4} - 3)(4 + 5\sqrt{4} + 4)}{(\sqrt{4} + 1)(4 - 4\sqrt{4} - 21)}) = \frac{(-2 - 3)(4 + 5(2) + 4)}{(2 + 1)(4 - 4(2) - 21)})$$

Now that the radicals have been eliminated, it is simple math (taking care to avoid those simple mistakes) that simplifies from here:

$$\frac{(-2 - 3)(4 + 5(2) + 4)}{(2 + 1)(4 - 4(2) - 21)}) = \frac{(-5)(18)}{(3)(-25)} = \frac{-90}{-75} = \frac{18}{15} = \frac{6}{5} = 1.2$$

Now, plug in $y = 4$ into the answer choices to properly determine which $= \frac{6}{5}$ or 1.2. Start with A and B, which plainly equal 2 and -2, respectively, after finding the square root of $y = 4$. Move on to C:

C: $\dfrac{\sqrt{y}}{\sqrt{y} + 7} = \dfrac{\sqrt{4}}{\sqrt{4} + 7} = \dfrac{2}{9}$, so not correct.

D: $\dfrac{\sqrt{y} + 4}{\sqrt{y} - 7} = \dfrac{\sqrt{4} + 4}{\sqrt{4} - 7} = \dfrac{6}{-5} = -\dfrac{6}{5}$, so not correct.

E: $\dfrac{-\sqrt{y} - 4}{\sqrt{y} - 7} = \dfrac{-\sqrt{4} - 4}{\sqrt{4} - 7} = \dfrac{-6}{-5} = \dfrac{6}{5} = 1.2$, which is correct!

56. Correct answer: **F**. First, remember that the graph of cos(x) has an amplitude of 1. This is because the value of cosine can only go as high as 1 or as low as -1, and either way, the wave will have a distance of 1 from the x-axis (which is the definition of amplitude). When the graph of cosine is multiplied by 3, the amplitude triples because the final output of cosine is tripling. This is enough for us to determine that the correct answer must either be G or K.

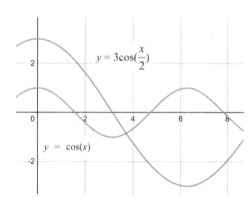

However, the question now becomes this: what happens when the value of x, which is the angle that cosine is measuring, is divided by 2? Even though the graph of cosine features a wave that relies on the value of cosine in radians (π, 2π, etc.), we can conceptualize the problem enough for us to get the correct answer if we think about it in terms of degrees.

Think about this: the x-axis of the graph of cosine is the angle that cosine is measuring, but if we cut that angle in half by dividing it by 2, then it will take *twice as long* for the wave to make a full rotation. In the graph of cos(x), the wave makes a full rotation after 360°, but if we are dividing the angles by 2, it will take twice as long; the wave will have to stretch along the x-axis to 720° before a full rotation is made. This is why the answer is F, which not only account for the new graph having 3 times the amplitude, but correctly says that the new graph will also have twice the period.

57. Correct answer: **B**. An expected outcome is NOT the same thing as the most likely outcome. The most likely outcome is that she would draw one of 36 number cards and end up winning $10. However, the expected outcome is the result of multiplying the possible results by their individual probabilities and adding them together.

There are 4 aces out of 52 cards. The odds of drawing an ace is $\dfrac{4}{52} = \dfrac{1}{13} = 0.077$

There are 12 face cards out of 52 cards. The odds of drawing a face card is $\dfrac{12}{52} = \dfrac{3}{13} = 0.231$

There are 36 number cards out of 52 cards. The odds of drawing a number card is $\dfrac{36}{52} = \dfrac{9}{13} = 0.692$.

Now that we have determined the probabilities, we multiply each probability by each respective prize (ace=$150, face card = $100, number card = $10) and add up the three. Let's do that in one big step to find the final answer:

$$\$150(0.077) + \$100(0.231) + \$10(0.692) = \$11.55 + \$23.10 + \$6.92 = \$41.57$$

Since the question requires that we round to the nearest whole dollar, we round up to $42, which is answer choice B.

58. Correct answer: **G**. There is an extremely fast way to get this question correct. It is impossible for a rectangle to have a perimeter that is an odd number. Try any combination of numbers for a rectangle's width and length, and you'll never come up with an odd numbered perimeter. That's enough to choose choice G.

However, let's work out the mathematics of this problem as well. Essentially, we are going to have to factor out 240 in pairs and find the respective perimeters.

$240 = 240 \times 1 =$ a perimeter of $(240 + 240 + 1 + 1) = 482$, which is answer choice F (so F is incorrect).

Now, I notice that the final three answers are all relatively close, so I will try to find the dimensions of this rectangle that get me in that range.

$240 = 20 \times 12 =$ a perimeter of $(20 + 20 + 12 + 12) = 64$, which is answer choice J (so J is incorrect).

This guess has put me squarely between two other options, so I will try to play with the perimeter to see if these final two answer choices are possible.

$240 = 15 \times 16 =$ a perimeter of $(15 + 15 + 16 + 16) = 62$, which is answer choice K (so K is incorrect).

$240 = 24 \times 10 =$ a perimeter of $(24 + 24 + 10 + 10) = 68$, which is answer choice H (so H is incorrect).

By process of trial and error, we have eliminated four of the answer choices, leaving only G.

59. Correct answer: **A**. Before reading through the answer choices, think about what you know about three lines with different slopes. Each of them will cross over the other at some point; it's also possible that the three intersect at the same point. None of the three can be parallel, though two of them can be perpendicular. That said, let's go through the choices.

Choice A says that two of the lines never cross the x-axis. Well, for a line not to cross the x-axis, that means it is parallel to the x-axis with a slope of 0. If *two* lines were to never cross the x-axis, that would mean they both are parallel to the x-axis and both have slopes of 0. Because the question says that the lines have different slopes, the correct answer has already been found. A is correct because it is impossible for two of these three lines to never cross the x-axis.

60. Correct answer: **K**. First, find the volume of the original ball room. The ball room has a length of 300 ft, a width of 150 ft, and a height of 20 ft. Thus, the volume $= 300 \times 150 \times 20 = 900,000$ ft^2.

Now, find the volume of the proposed, larger space. The owner wants the length to increase by 25%, thus the new length $= 300(1.25) = 375$ feet and the new width $= 150(1.25) = 187.5$ feet. Since the height of the ceiling will remain at 20 feet, the volume of the new space $= 375 \times 187.5 \times 20 = 1,406,250$ ft^2.

Lastly, find the percent growth to the nearest 1%. To do so, first find the actual growth in square feet, which is this: $1,406,250$ ft$^2 - 900,000$ ft$^2 = 506,250$ ft^2. Second, find what percent the of the original 900,000 this increase represents by division, like this:

$$\frac{506,250 \text{ ft}^2}{900,000 \text{ ft}^2} = 0.5625, \text{ or } 56.25\,\%, \text{ which, when rounded to the nearest 1\%, is 56\%, or answer K.}$$

ACT Science

Explanations

Answer Explanations - Step 1

Correct Answers:

Passage I:	Passage II:	Passage III:	Passage IV:	Passage V:	Passage VI:
1: B	5: C	9: C	13: C	17: C	21: C
2: J	6: F	10: G	14: F	18: G	22: J
3: D	7: A	11: A	15: B	19: D	23: B
4: F	8: H	12: J	16: J	20: J	24: J

Passage I:

1. Correct answer: **B**. Be careful because this question asks you to refer to *Figures* 1 and 2, not *Tables* 1 and 2. There are a couple of varieties of fruit that clearly show a pretty large difference: Bloody Butcher and Juane Flamme. If you look down at Figure 2, on the other hand, there is not much difference (though there is a difference, of course) between the control and experimental groups of both Thai Hot and Ancho: this eliminates answer choices C and D as incorrect. Now, back to A and B. Both options show a pretty large difference as has been said, but it is clear from the graph that the difference is greater in Juane Flamme (with a much lower measurement in the control column), which is why B is the correct answer.

2. Correct answer: **J**. Here, you are asked to refer to Tables 1 and 2, which compare the control's fruit yield to the experimental's fruit yield. Where this question gets tricky is in the final few words: *relative to the control*. In other words, we're not looking necessarily for the *greatest* experimental yield; if we were, the answer would be California Wonder (which is why H is incorrect). Instead, as you can see, the control column yields more fruit than the experimental 100% of the time. Thus, the phrase "relative to the control" just means something like this: which experimental yield is closest to the total control yield? If you look at the second-to-last row, you'll see that Thai Hot's experimental yield (291) is *almost* the same as the control (295). Thus, answer choice J (Thai Hot) is correct.

3. Correct answer: **D**. First of all, this question is referring to *sodium concentration*, a value that is measured in Figures 1 and 2 (the graphs on the right). Second of all, the question makes it clear that there is *only 1* fruit's control yield that will result in a saltier taste (aka, the control has a higher salt concentration than the experimental yield). If you look at the figures, there is only 1 of the 6 fruits that has the white column (the control column) stretching higher than the experimental, which is Ancho. This is why the correct answer is D: Ancho. The other options (A, B, and C) all feature fruits with an experimental yield that has a higher salt concentration than the control.

4. Correct answer: **F**. This question is simple in that it simply asks you to find the fruit with the greatest sodium concentration. The difficulty is this: Figure 2's three varieties of pepper *all* have a very low sodium concentration. It may look like Thai Hot has a sodium concentration through the roof, but if you look over on the y axis, you'll see that the tall black bar equates to a sodium concentration of only 15. The three tomatoes in Figure 1, however, have sodium concentrations of roughly 320, 315, and 160, respectively: way higher than 15. Thus, answers H and J, because they are both peppers with low sodium concentrations, can be eliminated as incorrect. Letters F and G are both varieties of tomato as measured in Figure 1, but Bloody Butcher's black bar is slightly higher than Juane Flamme's, and the white bar is clearly higher. This is why the correct answer is F: Bloody Butcher.

Passage II:

5. Correct answer: **C**. Figure 2 displays the calculated momentum of each cart as it crosses the finish line. The question asks about Cart B, which is denoted with triangle data points in the figure. Of course, there is no data on what the momentum would be if Cart B were dropped from a height of 4.5 meters. Instead, we have to make a best guess (infer) based on the data that we do have. According to Figure 2, when Cart B was dropped from a height of 4 meters it had a momentum of something like 170 kg·m/s. When released from a height of 5 meters, it had a momentum of something like 190 kg·m/s. Thus, we need to choose an answer between these two choices. There is only one option between the two, which is C: 180 kg·m/s.

6. Correct answer: **F**. If you look at Figure 1, you'll see that as the height increases, the difference in velocity between the three cars widens. The closest that the three are (aka, the "smallest difference in velocity" occurs at the very beginning, when the three cars are dropped from a height of 1 meter. This is why the answer is F: 1 meter.

7. Correct answer: **A**. Figure 1 gives the recorded velocities for the three cars. This question is dealing however with only Cart C, which is denoted with circle data points on the figure. If you look at the trajectory of Cart C, you see a steady increase in velocity as height increases. At 5 meters, the circle is *really close* to 7.5 m/s already, so if it were released from a height of 8 meters, it seems extremely likely that it will cross the finish line at a speed higher than that. This eliminates answer choices C and D, which both say "No." Choice B states that the cart has already reached these speeds, which isn't true. This is why the correct answer is A: an increase of 1 or more m/s is expected.

8. Correct answer: **H**. This question requires you to compare the calculated velocities of carts released at various heights. To answer correctly, either circle the various data points on Figure 1 as you go or jot the rough values next to the four answer choices and simply pick the biggest. Cart A released at a height of 1 meter (choice F) has a velocity of roughly 4 m/s. Cart A released at a height of 2 meters (choice G) has a velocity of roughly 6.5 m/s. Cart B released at a height of 3 meters (choice H) has a velocity of roughly 7 m/s. Cart C released at a height of 4 meters (choice J) has a velocity of roughly 6 m/s. This is why the correct answer is H: Cart B released at 3 meters has the highest velocity of the 4 choices.

Passage III:

9. Correct answer: **C**. To get this question correct, simply look at each table and see which beakers had reached a temperature of 0 degrees after 70 minutes had elapsed. Table 1 (Beaker A)? Yes. Table 2 (Beaker B)? Yes. Table 3 (Beaker C)? Yes. Table 4 (Beaker D)? No. Three of four have reached the temperature. Because the question says what percent *had* reached a temperature of 70 degrees, the correct answer is C: 75%.

10. Correct answer: **G**. First, ensure that you are looking for data in the correct table. In this case, we are dealing with Beaker C, which is measured in Table 3. Of course, we don't have data on what the temperature was after 37 minutes had elapsed. However, we can *infer* to the correct answer by finding data points around the 37 minute mark. After 35 minutes, the temperature was 17 degrees. After 40 minutes, the temperature was 14 degrees. Thus, the correct answer must be between 17 and 14 degrees. This is why the correct answer is G: 16 degrees; it is the only answer between these two values.

11. Correct answer: **A**. Let's go through each Table one by one and see each drop in temperature over the time span between 10 and 45 minutes having elapsed. Table 1 (Beaker A) records 36 degrees at 10 minutes and 8 degrees at 45 minutes (a drop of 28 degrees). Table 2 (Beaker B) records 23 degrees at 10 minutes and 8 degrees at 45 minutes (a drop of 15 degrees). Table 3 (Beaker C) records 38 degrees at 10 minutes and 11 degrees at 45 minutes (a drop of 27 degrees). Table 4 (Beaker D) records 22 degrees at 10 minutes and 10 degrees at 45 minutes (a drop of 12 degrees). This is why the correct answer is A: Beaker A; it records the greatest drop in temperature (28 degrees) over the time span specified in the question.

12. Correct answer: **J**. This question is very similar to number 11 above. Simply go table by table and see how long it took each beaker to make the drop from 20 to 0 degrees. Beaker A (Table 1) made that drop in roughly 36 minutes. Beaker B (Table 2) made that drop in roughly 52 minutes. Beaker C (Table 3) made that drop in roughly 35 minutes. Beaker D (Table 4) made that drop in roughly 61 minutes. Thus, it clearly took Beaker D the longest to make that temperature drop, which is why J, or Beaker D, is the correct answer.

Passage IV:

13. Correct answer: **C**. According to Table 2, only foods with CT values less than 35 have a high/moderate likelihood of causing a severe peanut allergic reaction. Thus, the answer is "No," the manufacturer doesn't need this label, which eliminates answers A and B. Letter D mentions CT values "less than 50", but that scale doesn't exist at all. This is why the correct answer is C, which states correctly that a CT value between 36 and 40 means a very low possibility of causing a severe peanut allergic reaction.

14. Correct answer: **F**. According to Table 2, only foods that have a CT value of less than or equal to 29 have a high likelihood of triggering an allergic reaction. Looking at Table 1, there is only 1 food on the scale (the first one, Cereal bar I) that has a CT value that low. This is why the correct answer is F: 1.

15. Correct answer: **B**. First, determine how many foods fall in the high to moderate range. According to Table 2, only foods with a CT value of 30-35 are in this range. Looking at Table 1, there are only 3 foods that fall into this range (Cereal bar II, Cereal bar III, and Cookes with fiber). Out of these three, only 1 of them (Cereal bar III) mention peanuts on their packaging. This makes B, 33%, the correct answer, as only 1 of 3 mention peanuts on their packaging.

16. Correct answer: **J**. If you look over Table 1, there are 4 food products (Cereal bar II, Cereal bar IV, Chocolate with pistachio, and Sausage with walnut) that contain tree nuts and/or walnuts. These have CT values of 32.40, 35.90, 36.80, and ND (nonexistent), respectively. Because the ND food only contains walnuts and the other three contain tree nuts, it seems likely that anything with tree nuts will result in a CT value between 32 and 37. Only 1 of the 4 answer choices appropriately approximates such a CT value, which is answer choice J. The other answer choices simply give CT values that are much too high and not supported by the food choices in Table 1.

Passage V:

17. Correct answer: **C**. First, realize that we need to be referencing Experiment 1, and thus Table 1, which was conducted under a pH of 8 with 1mM of Trypsin. Then, it's a matter of finding the right row (left-to-right) and column (up-and-down) on the table. We are told to look at the row giving data about a substrate level of 0.09. This already eliminates answer choices A and B, both of which give absorbance values not in this row. We are also told that there has been 2 minutes of interaction. Looking across from 0.09 and down from 2 minutes, we see an absorbance value of 0.154, which makes C the correct answer. Answer choice D, 0.184, is the data point for 2.5 minutes of interaction, which is why it is incorrect.

18. Correct answer: **G**. First, realize that we need to be referencing Experiment 2, and thus Table 2, which was conducted under a pH of 6 with 1mM of Trypsin. Second, look across the row (left-to-right) for 0.15mM of substrate. The question asks for the time it would take to see an absorbance level of 0.040. However, there is no absorbance level of 0.040 in this row of the table. This means that we are going to have to approximate a time that is not actually in the table itself. After 0.5 minutes of interaction, we see an absorbance value of 0.027. After 1 minute of interaction, we see an absorbance level of 0.053. Thus, the 0.040 number is between these two, which means that our time will be between these two. If you look at the answer choices, they are all given in seconds. 0.5 minutes of course is 30 seconds, and 1 minute is 60 seconds. Thus, if our correct answer falls between these two, the correct answer must be G: 45 seconds of interaction.

19. Correct answer: **D**. The question asks for the "highest average" absorbance levels, but this is the same thing as saying, "Which substrate level results in the highest absorbance values?" The reason I say that is to remind you that the ACT Science test is not going to ask a question that requires the use of a calculator. Instead, for this question, you can simply look at the values and see which conditions are giving the highest values. First of all, the higher values are certainly coming from Table 1, which comes from Experiment 1, which was conducted under a pH of 8. This eliminates answer choices A and B, both of which propose certain conditions under a pH of 6. Answer choice C proposes a substrate level of 0.15 and D proposes a substrate level of 0.24. However, any comparison of the two reveals that there is a higher absorbance value across the board when the substrate level is 0.24. This is why the correct answer is D.

20. Correct answer: **J**. Let's begin with letter F and see if it will result in an absorbance value of 0.062. After 1 minute of a substrate of 0.04 interacting with the Trypsin under a pH of 8, the absorbance value was 0.035, but after 1.5 minutes it was 0.053; this means that after 1.25 minutes, the value would be closer to 0.043, not 0.062. This is why F is incorrect. Second, let's try G. After 1 minute of a substrate of 0.09 interacting with the Trypsin under a pH of 8, the absorbance value was 0.082, and it only gets higher from there (in other words, it isn't going to go back down to 0.062 as another 15 seconds goes by). This is why G is also incorrect. Third, let's try H. After 2 minutes of a substrate of 0.04 interacting with the Trypsin under a pH of 6, the absorbance value was 0.023, but after 2.5 minutes it was 0.027; this means that after 2.25 minutes the absorbance value would be closer to 0.025. This makes H also incorrect. Lastly (as if eliminating all three other choices wasn't enough!) let's try answer choice J. After 2 minutes of a substrate of 0.09 interacting with the Trypsin under a pH of 6, the absorbance value was 0.055, and then after 2.5 minutes, it had risen to 0.068. This means that after 2.25 minutes (between the two), the absorbance value could be expected to measure roughly 0.062, which is why choice J is the correct answer.

Passage VI:

21. Correct answer: **C**. Though the question itself is quite long, there is one student who found the greatest percentage of neutrophils in both Study 1 and Study 2, and that is Student 3. This makes answer choice C the correct answer. The other three students simply did not find a percentage of correct cells as well as Student 3 was able to.

22. Correct answer: **J**. In this question, you will have to use what you know in Tables 1 and 2 to determine how many neutrophils are present in each study. The easiest place to start is actually Study 2, since Student 3 was able to correctly identify 100% of the neutrophils. Well, if Student 3 said there were 17 neutrophils, and that is 100% correct, then there must be 17 neutrophils present in Study 2. This eliminates answer choice F as incorrect since there must be more than 17 between the two studies if there are 17 already in Study 2. Immediately here some students will think that 17 times 2 is 34, so that must be correct. However, there is no 34 option, so we must identify the correct number in Study 1 also to determine the correct amount. If you look up at Study 1, you will see that Student 1 identified 5, which is 33% correct. Well, 33% is equivalent (after rounding, of course) to ⅓. Thus, if 5 is ⅓ of the total, then there must be 15 neutrophils in Study 1. Thus, 15 + 17 = 32, which is why the correct answer is J: there are 32 total neutrophils between the two studies.

23. Correct answer: **B**. Of course, first acknowledge that the optical microscope is used in Study 1. Thus, this is where we need to apply the 47% number. If you did number 22 correctly and identified that there must be 15 neutrophils in the study, then one way to get this question correct would be to see that half of 15 (or 50% of 15) is 7.5, so the most logical whole number of neutrophils to account for 47% of the total is 7 since it is a little less than 7.5. If not, then first see that 47% is between the findings of Student 1 (who identified 5 at 33%) and Student 2 (who identified 8 at 53%). Thus, the correct answer must be either 6 or 7 neutrophils, since it is between these two values as 47% is between the two percentages. This eliminates answer choices C and D. Well, 47% is much closer to 53% than it is to 33%, so we would expect the whole number of neutrophils to also be closer to 8 than to 5. This is another reason why the correct answer is 7, or answer choice B.

24. Correct answer: **J**. The results of the optical microscope are in Table 1, which we need to compare to the results of the fluorescent microscope, the results of which are in Table 2. First, let's start with F, which proposes Student 1. However, Student 1 only found 33% of the neutrophils in Table 1, and found 76% in Table 2. This eliminates F, since Student 1 did *not* do better with the optical microscope. Second, move to G, which proposes Student 3. However, Student 3 only found 67% of the neutrophils in Table 1, and found 100% in Table 2. This eliminates G, since Student 3 did *not* do better with the optical microscope. Third, move on to H, which proposes Student 4. However, Student 4 only found 27% of the neutrophils in Table 1, and found 76% in Table 2. This eliminates H, since Student 4 did *not* do better with the optical microscope. This leaves J, which is the correct answer: each student's percentage is *lower* with the optical microscope as seen in Table 1, not higher; this is why J is the correct answer: none of the students displayed this ability.

Answer Explanations - Step 2

Correct Answers:

Passage I:	Passage II:	Passage III:	Passage IV:	Passage V:	Passage VI:
1: B	4: G	7: D	10: F	13: A	16: G
2: G	5: D	8: H	11: C	14: H	17: B
3: B	6: H	9: C	12: J	15: A	18: H

Passage I:

1. Correct answer: **B**. Answer choice A is incorrect because it states that the fruit with higher salt were watered with "groundwater aquifers," but that's true of the control (less salty) group (this is also why choice D is incorrect). Answer choice C is incorrect because the salt doesn't come from the soil they were grown in, but the water itself. This is why the correct answer is B, because it alone states that the salt comes from the alternative water source.

2. Correct answer: **G**. The word "variant" is defined in the passage as a new variety of crop; it is also stated that different variants were tested in the experiment. The variants themselves are also listed under "Tomato variant" and "Pepper variant" in Table 1 and Table 2, respectively. This is why the answer is G, the California Wonder; the other answers aren't variants of peppers or tomatoes.

3. Correct answer: **B**. The entire purpose of the experiment is to test the control and experimental groups with different water, which is why the second option (II) is false. This means that automatically that answer choices C and D are incorrect, since both include II as true. Since A and B both include I (the variants of crops tested), we only need to worry about III. However, it is stated in the second paragraph that they were grown in the same soil, which means that B is the correct answer: both I and III are true of all plants.

Passage II:

4. Correct answer: **G**. This question of course requires a rereading of the paragraphs to find the order of events. Paragraph 2 says that "velocity was *measured* as each cart crossed the finish line", and paragraph 4 says that Figure 2 shows "the *calculated* momentum." So, whatever answer is correct, it must first state that velocity was found/measured, and then that momentum was calculated. This is why the correct answer is G. Choices H and J are incorrect because, at a minimum, each of these options mentions the students making a hypothesis, but there is nothing like that mentioned in the opening paragraphs. Choice F is incorrect because it states the velocity was calculated *after* the momentum was, which is false.

5. Correct answer: **D**. Essentially, this question is asking for this: what difference is there between the 3 carts? If you think about it, if all 3 carts were the same, then they would all have the same measurements for both velocity and momentum at each of the 5 release points. Paragraph 1 mentions that they have different masses, which is why D is the correct answer; none of the other answer choices are mentioned in the experiment at all.

6. Correct answer: **H**. The question asks, essentially, this question: the acceleration due to gravity has an effect on what? Let's start with I: Mass. The mass of the three carts, however, is predetermined; g or the acceleration due to gravity has no effect on it. Thus, answer choice J is eliminated. That brings us to II: Velocity. In the second paragraph, we learn that the equation for velocity, $v = \sqrt{2gh}$, uses g. In other words, velocity depends upon the value of g (which eliminates choice G). At this point, you might be tempted to stop here and choose answer F: II only. However, look at the equation for momentum: $p = mv$. If velocity depends upon the acceleration due to gravity (as we've said), and momentum depends upon velocity (as you can see by this equation for momentum), then momentum is also dependent upon the acceleration due to gravity. This is why the correct answer is H: II and III (velocity and momentum) only.

Passage III:

7. Correct answer: **D**. This question of course references only the written portion of this passage. If you reread the first paragraph, you will see that that the middle few sentences state that hot water: a) Undergoes rapid evaporation, which results in b) A higher concentration of dissolved solids. Answer choices A and C are incorrect because they suppose that a *lower* concentration of dissolved solids is responsible, which is incorrect. The reason B, then, is incorrect is because it states that this higher presence of dissolved solids occurs *before* undergoing rapid evaporation, but this happens after. This is why D is correct: it puts these two steps in the proper order based on the passage.

8. Correct answer: **H**. Each of the four answer choices references the temperature of water as hot or cold. Remember that the Mpemba Effect means that hot water freezes faster than cold water. In the experiment, the "hot" water was water that had been heated to 50 degrees; the "cold" water was room temperature water (see the last line of paragraph 2). This is why the correct answer is H; the students conducting the experiment assumed or defined room temperature water as "cold"; the room temperature

water was not cooled any further before the experiment began. F is incorrect because there is no mention that 50 degrees (or the "hot" water) is boiling. G is incorrect because 30 degrees was the temperature of the "cold" water. J is incorrect because 50 degrees was the "hot" water.

9. Correct answer: **C**. Each of these four answer choice options refers to water being put into a freezer set to -18° Celsius, so that won't be the difference maker. There are 4 types of water used in the experiment: tap/purified water (2 beakers each) at temperatures of 30/50 degrees (2 beakers each). Answer options A, B, and D each refer to one of these water varieties used in the experiment. Answer choice C, on the other hand, mentions salt water, but salt water was never used in the experiment. This is why the correct answer is C: salt water was not one of the water varieties used in the study.

Passage IV:

10. Correct answer: **F**. An assumption, in this case, is going to be something arbitrarily decided by the scientists or simply assumed to be true. Letter G says that ingesting a small amount of peanut DNA can be harmful to those with an allergy, but that's not an *assumption*, but rather a fact, so G is incorrect. Letter H says that PCR analysis is used to determine the presence of a certain DNA, but that is also established fact (literally the purpose of the technique), so H is also incorrect. Choice J says that some products for sale contain traces of peanut DNA; again, this is simply true, not assumed. This leaves the answer that we skipped, answer choice F. The second paragraph states that most instances of PCR analysis stop at 40, thus, it is assumed that this is "good enough" for finding peanut DNA, which is why F is the correct answer.

11. Correct answer: **C**. Again, the last sentence of paragraph 2 states that PCR analysis stops after 40 cycles. If they can only do one a day, as the question states, then that means 40 days of cycles. However, you're also told that it can only happen on weekdays, of which there are 5 per week. 40 divided by 5 is 8, thus the laboratory would need 8 weeks maximum to determine the CT threshold of a sample, which matches answer choice C.

12. Correct answer: **J**. First, determine if a low or a high CT value is good for those with peanut allergies. You might think that a score closer to 0 is good, but that's not the case in the PCR technique; the second to last sentence in the second paragraph says, "The lower the CT value, the more likely it is that the sample contains the DNA of interest." Thus, a low score is worse for those with a peanut allergy in this case. This eliminates F and G, which both say a low score is better. Letter choice H wrongly defines what a "high" score is by stating it means *few* iterations were necessary to detect the DNA, but that's not true: a high score means lots of iterations were necessary to detect the DNA, which means that answer choice J is correct.

Passage V:

13. Correct answer: **A**. Almost immediately, we can dismiss answer choices B and D as possibilities. As you can see by each table, there are 4 substrates tested in each Experiment (eliminating choice B) and 20 different absorbance values (eliminating D). Answer C proposes the pH was the same, but the pH for Experiment 1 was 8 and the pH for Experiment 2 was 6, thus eliminating answer choice C. this is why the correct answer is A: according to the first line of each experiment, each vial contains 1mM of Trypsin.

14. Correct answer: **H**. First of all, let's look at answer choice G, which says something about "less enzymes" being in the vial. However, Trypsin is the enzyme, and we already know that there is 1mM of Trypsin in each vial, which is under the control of those conducting the experiments; thus, G is incorrect. Answer choices F and J basically say the same thing: that a higher absorbance value means, in more or less words, that the enzyme Trypsin didn't get to make product by interacting with the substrate. If two answers are synonyms, they have to be incorrect by default since there can't be two correct answers at the same time. However, there are other reasons why F and J are incorrect beyond that. Letter choice H says the opposite of this, that more substrates were catalyzed. To sort this out, look at the last line of paragraph 2, which says, "a higher absorbance value…would mean more product was made by the Trypsin." This is why the answer choice that is correct is H, which proposes rightly that more absorbance means more product created by the Trypsin when interacting with the substrate.

15. Correct answer: **A**. In the final sentence of paragraph 1, you are told that "any physical or chemical changes to an enzyme's environment, such as *changes in temperature, pH, and salt concentration*, can alter its ability to function." Plain and simple, what is italicized in this sentence are the changes that could test how Trypsin responds in its environment. Of all of the answer choices, only choice A, temperature, is listed there. The only other probable choice would be "salt concentration," but that isn't an option. This is why the correct answer is A.

Passage VI:

16. Correct answer: **G**. The differences between these two microscopes are laid out in the first two paragraphs. Choice F proposes that one difference is that the optical uses photoluminescence, but that is true of the fluorescent; this is why choice F is incorrect. Answer choice H proposes that molecules are "put into an excited state" under the optical, but again, this is true of the fluorescent; thus, choice H is incorrect. Answer choice J proposes that the fluorescent's eyepiece provides additional magnification; however, this is true of the optical (see the third sentence of the first paragraph), which is why J is incorrect. This

is why the correct answer is G: the fluorescent microscope just doesn't have as many lenses as the optical (which has 3 lenses according to the opening paragraph).

17. Correct answer: **B**. First let's identify "the part of the fluorescent microscope responsible for separating out unnecessary light." If you reread the second paragraph, you will see that this is the purpose of the filter ("The filter then works by separating…"), which comes immediately before or after two other parts of the microscope: the detector and the objective lens. This eliminates answer choices C and D, which propose this part of the microscope to be by the condenser or reflector, respectively. However, the rest of the question says that this piece is placed "relative to the path of light." Well, if you look at Figure 2, you'll see that the light goes from the bottom to the top (from the light source to the reflector to the condenser, etc.). Thus, the filter is immediately *after* the objective lens (making choice A incorrect) and immediately *prior* to the detector; this makes choice B the correct answer.

18. Correct answer: **H**. Let's simply go through these choices one at a time and determine if each one was necessary for obtaining accurate results. First, choice F proposes that it was necessary that "the antibody in Study 1…". However, that's as far as we need to go; Study 1 doesn't require an antibody because it is done under the optical microscope; it's the fluorescent microscope that needs an antibody to excite the cells. Thus, F is incorrect. Second, G proposes that it was necessary that 5 minutes was sufficient time to find the cells. However, there is nothing in the entire passage about a time limit being placed on the students; this is why G is incorrect. Next, H proposes that the antibody in Study 2 would only cause the neutrophil cells to turn green (compared to the other cells present). This is certainly true, since if other cells turned green, then the accuracy of finding neutrophil cells would be compromised (this is why H is the correct answer). Lastly, J proposes something about a prohibition on finding square cells, but square cells of this sort are mentioned nowhere in the passage; this is why J is incorrect. Thus, H is correct, as it is the only answer choice to propose a true predisposition of the studies for the sake of accuracy.

Answer Explanations - Step 3

Correct Answers:

Passage I:	Passage II:	Passage III:	Passage IV:	Passage V:	Passage VI:
1: D	4: H	7: A	10: G	13: B	16: G
2: G	5: D	8: F	11: C	14: J	17: C
3: A	6: J	9: B	12: F	15: A	18: F

Passage I:

1. Correct answer: **D**. The purpose of this experiment was to see if there were any crops that could be grown better with the saltier water than the control water from a groundwater aquifer. There is only 1 crop that shows less salt content when grown with the experimental, non-aquifer water, and that is the Ancho. If you look at Figure 2, you'll see the white bar (representing the control group) as higher than the experimental; this means the control had more salt, and thus that the experimental water didn't have a salty, adverse effect on the Ancho. This makes D the correct answer; all other choices have more salt in the experimental group.

2. Correct answer: **G**. A variety of either fruit is going to have the most "naturally" salty taste if it has the highest salt concentration under the control group (since the experimental group is grown with water that contains salt). Again, the three pepper varieties, according to Figure 2, might *look* like they have higher salt concentrations than the tomatoes, but if you look at what those bars correspond to on the *y*-axis, you'll see that the three pepper plant varieties have salt (sodium) concentrations with values of something like 10, 10.75, and 12, respectively. This is much lower than the tomatoes, which is why F and H are incorrect. Of the three tomato varieties, Bloody Butcher looks to have a sodium concentration of something like 150, while the other tomato option (choice J, Juane Flamme) has a concentration closer to 80 or so. This is why the answer is G: Bloody Butcher, since its control group has the highest sodium concentration.

3. Correct answer: **A**. A "tolerance to salt" would mean that the experimental water with heavy salt concentration did not affect the growth (aka the yield). Though some varieties still yielded a lot of fruit from the experimental column (this is true of options B, C, and D, which each had an experimental yield in the thousands), when that total is compared to the control group, it is clear that there is a significant drop off for each of these three in terms of yield from the control to the experimental. The reason the correct answer is A or Thai Hot is not because the amount of yield was the highest, but rather that because the experimental yield was fairly close to the control yield; this means that it was least affected by the salt, demonstrating the "greatest tolerance to salt in its water supply."

Passage II:

4. Correct answer: **H**. First, notice that a cart with a mass of 17 kg would be somewhere between Cart A (12.5 kg) and Cart B (21.8 kg). Thus, to get this question correct, we need to find the answer choice that gives a momentum value (NOT velocity) between Cart A's value and Cart B's value when these carts are released from a height of 4 meters. Looking at Figure 2, we see that Cart A has a momentum of about 210 kg·m/s when released from 4 meters; Cart B has a momentum of about 170 kg·m/s when released from a height of 4 meters. As is expected (and typical of the ACT), only one option is between 170 kg·m/s and 210 kg·m/s, which is answer choice H, making it the correct answer.

5. Correct answer: **D**. First, recognize that *p* means *momentum*, that "a cart weighing 12.5 kg" is Cart A, and that "a cart weighing 34.7 kg" is Cart C. Thus: what is the difference in momentum (Figure 2) between Cart A and Cart C when released from a height of 2 meters? When Cart A is released from this height, it has a momentum of roughly 150 kg·m/s; when Cart C is released from this height, it has a momentum of roughly 80 kg·m/s. That's a difference of roughly 70 kg·m/s. Answer choice D is correct because 75 kg·m/s is certainly the closest estimate out of the answer choices. Choice C, at first, might seem plausible, but a review of the data points will reveal that the real value must be much greater than merely 55 kg·m/s.

6. Correct answer: **J**. This question requires you to make a rough inference of values 4 times in a row, and choose the result that shows the *least* velocity. Typically in these kinds of questions, the correct answer is going to be most obviously correct; it isn't going to come down to a fraction of a difference. First, a cart with a mass of 10 kg is closest to Cart A's mass. Notice that the less a car weighs in this experiment, the higher its velocity (as a side note, increased mass will mean increased friction, or a slower result). Thus, choice F recommends a cart weighing 10kg released from 5 meters; this would be very fast, probably something like 11 m/s. Choice G recommends a cart weighing 10 kg released from a height of 2 meters. This would be something a little faster than Cart A at that same height, something like 7 m/s. Answer H recommends a cart weighing 15 kg (so between Carts A and B) released from a height of 4 meters; this would result in something like 8.5 m/s. Lastly, choice J recommends a cart weighing 35 kg (so almost identical to Cart C) released from a height of 3 meters. Because Cart C at this point hovers barely above the 5 m/s mark, it's safe to say that this hypothetical cart posed by choice J would have a velocity of roughly 5 m/s. Let's

review: choice F = roughly 11m/s; choice G = roughly 7 m/s; choice H = roughly 8.5 m/s; and choice J = roughly 5 m/s. Thus, J is correct because its hypothetical cart would have the slowest velocity.

Passage III:

7. Correct answer: **A**. There are a couple of details present in each of these answer choices that are irrelevant. The first is that it mentions "a gallon" of various types of water; because this amount of water is a constant for all four, it can be ignored. The second ignorable detail is that the water is put into a freezer of -18° Celsius; this is also a constant for all four answers, making it irrelevant. What matters are the other details: the temperature and type of water. It might not be noticeable right away, but the four types of water in the experiment (Beakers A, B, C, and D) are the same as these 4 choices here. Thus, the question becomes this: which type of water froze (reached 0° Celsius) the slowest? Looking back at the tables, it was Beaker D that froze the slowest, and Beaker D is filled with room temperature (30° Celsius) tap water. This is why the correct answer here is A: the gallon of room temperature tap water will freeze slower than the other 3 based on the experiment.

8. Correct answer: **F**. According to the introductory paragraph, "rapid evaporation" is what happens to hot water to make it freeze faster than cold water (thus, the Mpemba Effect). Thus, this question could be reworded to say this: which beaker had hot water and froze the fastest? Beaker A was filled with heated purified water that froze the fastest (only 60 minutes), which makes F the correct answer.

9. Correct answer: **B**. Because the water in this beaker is left at room temperature, we are going to be comparing the data points of Beakers B and D. Because this new beaker features a mixture of purified and tap water, we would expect the correct answer to be somewhere between the time it takes for Beaker B read to read 10° and Beaker D's to read 10°. Well, looking at Table 2, it takes Beaker B 40 minutes to reach a temp of 10°. Looking at Table 4, it takes Beaker D 45 minutes to reach a temp of 10°. Thus, we would expect the correct answer to fall between 40 and 45 minutes. This is why the correct answer is B: 42.5 minutes; no other answer falls within this range.

Passage IV:

10. Correct answer: **G**. Here, you are asked to find the one true statement among four. Simply go one at a time to determine if the statement is true or false about the Cookies with fiber. Answer choice F states that they have a "low to none" likelihood of causing a reaction; for this to be true (according to Figure 2), it would have to have a CT score of 36 to 40, but it doesn't (it's score is 32.25), which makes F incorrect. Answer choice H states that there's a 0% chance of causing an allergic reaction; however, this might be something you could say about a food with a CT score over 40, which this food doesn't have, so H is incorrect. Answer J states that the cycle threshold is not declared, but it is ("CT value" stands for "cycle threshold value"), thus J is incorrect because it is also false. that leave G, which states that it contains traces of peanut DNA; this is true (it just takes 32.25 cycles to find it). That's why the correct answer is G.

11. Correct answer: **C**. The number of "cycles of amplification" needed to find DNA is the same thing as the CT value. Of the foods, there is only 1 that declares that it contains peanuts (Cereal bar I), though others say peanut traces. Thus, finding the "average" of the foods that declare peanuts is easy; it's simply the CT value of Cereal bar I, well, divided by 1. In other words, the answer is 17.97 (or answer choice C).

12. Correct answer: **F**. The food that is least likely to cause a peanut allergic reaction is the food with the highest CT score (remember, the higher a CT score, the more cycles that were needed to detect the peanut DNA). Sausage with walnut, of answer choice F, is the only of the food options that has a score of "N.D.", which means (according to the final sentence of the opening paragraphs) that "there was no detection of the target DNA after 40 cycles." This is why the answer is F. Each of the other foods has a CT value, which means that the DNA was detected after a certain number of cycles of amplification.

Passage V:

13. Correct answer: **B**. First, take a look at the rows of the substrate level 0.15 at a pH of 6 (Table 2) and a pH of 8 (Table 1). What you'll notice straightaway is that the absorbance values in Table 1 are higher. Now, the answer choices state there is more or less "instances of the breaking down of amino acids into proteins" or "proteins into amino acids." If you reread paragraph 1, it doesn't speak of amino acids being broken down into proteins, but the opposite (proteins into amino acids). This eliminates answer choices A and C. The question is whether or not high absorbance values (compared to lower values) means this is happening *more* (answer choice B) or *less* (answer choice D). According to the passage, a "higher absorbance value...would mean more product was made by the Trypsin." This is why the correct answer is B: higher absorbance values means more catalyzing of proteins into amino acids by the Trypsin.

14. Correct answer: **J**. The question asks for the "best conditions for maximizing the amount of product catalyzed." Again, according to the passage, a "higher absorbance value...would mean more product was made by the Trypsin." So, we are simply looking here for the highest absorbance values possible. Straightaway, Table 1 (a pH of 8) has higher values than Table 2 (a pH of 6). This eliminates answer choices F and G. However, though both H and J propose a pH of 8, choice J is correct because it proposes a longer time period (2.5 minutes). For each substrate value, the absorbance value increases as time goes on.

15. Correct answer: **A**. This question is, perhaps, bordering on the more difficult kinds of questions you will see in Step 5 in that there are a lot of little layers to think through. First of all, the word "spectrophotometer" is just a distraction, a big word that sounds scary and more complicated; this is simply the instrument that does the measuring. To get this question correct, first compare the 1 minute values of the substrate level 0.24 at a pH of 6 and a pH of 8. At a pH of 6, we get an absorbance value of 0.090; at a pH of 8, we get an absorbance value of 0.239. Thus, a higher pH means a higher absorbance value, and a lower pH means a lower absorbance value. Because we are looking for the pH level of a vial that results in a value of 0.011 (lower than the pH of 6), we are looking for a pH level *less than 6*. This is why the correct answer is A: it gives the only pH value that is less than 6.

Passage VI:

16. Correct answer: **G**. Firstly, this question references "one of the studies," but this can only be Study 1, since this study asked students to identify "round" cell bodies. Thus, this question is essentially saying this: "In Study 1, Student 4 didn't count 4 cells that were actually neutrophils; what would her percent be if she had counted these 4?" Well, her current percentage is 27% (having identified 4 correctly), and if she had 4 more, she'd be up to 8 total. This essentially doubles her percentage. Only one answer choice is anywhere near a doubling of 27%, which is G: 53% (you might be nervous that 27% doubled should be 54%, not 53%, but the 1% difference can be accounted for because of rounding to the nearest whole number). The other three answer choices are simply incorrect percentages of what her total would be if Student 4 had 4 more correct neutrophils identified.

17. Correct answer: **C**. The question asks for the effect of photoluminescence on the two studies. Since photoluminescence is necessary for the function of the fluorescent microscope, the question is essentially asking for a comparison between how students did with the optical microscope vs fluorescent microscope. Well, it clearly had a positive increase in the sense that all 4 students were able to identify a much higher percentage of neutrophils with the fluorescent microscope in Study 2. This eliminates answer choices A and B, which indicate that photoluminescence caused the numbers to go down. Answer choice D proposes that it quadrupled some students' numbers, but even Student 4's poor percentage (27% in Study 1), when quadrupled, soars to over 100%, which is impossible. this is why D is an incorrect answer. The reason the correct answer is C is that it is true that some students' numbers were more than doubled between Study 1 and Study 2 (this is true of Student 1 and Student 4).

18. Correct answer: **F**. Between the two microscopes, it is clear that it is the fluorescent microscope (both from the descriptions of the microscopes in the written portion of the passage and Figures 1 and 2) that alters or affects light with additional steps compared to the optical microscope. However, the student's guess was that this kind of a microscope would perform more poorly, but the opposite was true. This eliminates answer choices H and J because the student was *not* correct in her guess. Answer choice G correctly says that "No," the student was not correct, but gives the wrong reason: it isn't the optical microscope that alters light more, nor does the optical microscope yield better results. This is why the correct answer is F: No, the student didn't make a correct guess, and the reason is because the microscope that alters and affects light more (the fluorescent microscope) performed better.

Answer Explanations - Step 4

Passage I:
1: C
2: F
3: D
4: G
5: D
6: J
7: A

Passage II:
8: J
9: A
10: H
11: C
12: H
13: B
14: H

Passage I

1. Correct answer: **C**. FRB 181906 is an example of a Fast Radio Burst discussed by Scientist 2. Answer choice A is tempting, but Scientist 2 says that there is another FRB (121102) that also repeats, so A can't be correct. Answer choice B is incorrect because Scientist 2 never discusses how far away any FRB is. Answer choice D is incorrect because the sentence that FRB 181906 is mentioned in contradicts this idea, saying, "…containing the energy output of hundreds of millions of stars." This is why C is correct; choice C rightly restates the position of Scientist 2 (found in the first three sentences of Scientist 2's paragraph) that all FRB's, including 181906 then, are caused by the violent merger of cosmic objects.

2. Correct answer: **F**. If you thought well through number 1 above, you should know that Scientist 2 does *not* rely on "internal disruptions of neutron stars," but rather only on merger of cosmic objects. This eliminates answer choices G and J, since both state that Scientist 2 relies on this idea. Since F and H both refer to Scientist 1, it can be taken for granted that he does believe this. Thus, the question is this: does Scientist 3 "rely on the existence of internal disruptions of neutron stars"? Well, rely means *depend*, or stated in another way, if Scientist 3 were to rely on it, it would be necessary for his argument; the question also says that this scientist relies on it to explain *all* stars. This is not the case for Scientist 3, who outright says that there are multiple origins of neutron stars. This is why the correct answer is F: only Scientist 1 is in this position.

3. Correct answer: **D**. Because Scientist 1 believes that every FRB comes from neutron stars, this discovery would not support his position. As a result, we now know that A and C are incorrect. Scientist 2, on the other hand, says that FRBs are caused by mergers of large celestial objects, thus, yes, such a discovery would support his position. Lastly, Scientist 3 says that there are all sorts of explanations for FRBs, thus such a discovery would also support his position. This is why the answer is D: the discovery of an FRB coming from the merger of two black holes would support the positions of Scientists 2 and 3.

4. Correct answer: **G**. Remember, first, what Scientist 1's main idea is, which is that FRBs come from highly magnetized and unstable neutron stars. Scientist 2, on the other hand, believes that FRB's come from celestial object mergers. Whether or not magnetars *also* release gamma rays, an FRB lasts more than a few milliseconds, or an FRB repeats once every few years is irrelevant to this particular question. This is why the answer is G: if celestial object mergers could not produce radio waves, this would crush the position of Scientist 2.

5. Correct answer: **D**. For this fact to be inconsistent with the positions of any of the scientists, it would have to disprove or run counter to one of their major premises, pieces of evidence, or overall thesis. Because it is Scientist 2 who believes that FRBs come from the merger of objects, that seems the most tempting answer (thus, I've just eliminated Scientists 1 and 3 as possibilities). However, Scientist 2 doesn't depend upon FRBs coming from within the Milky Way. In fact, the only mention of the source of an FRB puts it well outside the Milky Way itself. Although answer choice B is the most tempting wrong answer, the correct answer is D: this discovery would hurt none of the three scientists' positions.

6. Correct answer: **J**. Scientist 1 defines a neutron star as "dense remnants of massive stars that have undergone a supernova." However, it isn't only Scientist 1 that proposes neutron stars as being involved in the origins of FRBs. Scientist 2 says that their collisions with one another or black holes are FRB sources, and Scientist 3 says (essentially) that both Scientist 1 and 2 are correct about FRB origins. Thus, the correct answer is J. The other answer choices either help the position of one or two of the three scientists or none of them at all.

7. Correct answer: **A**. Scientist 1 relies on starquakes as necessary for FRBs, thus the answer must include this scientist (this eliminates answer choice C). However, Scientist 2 doesn't ever use the word "gravity," but it is pretty obvious that it is gravity that is causing these massive mergers of neutron stars and black holes. Thus, Scientist 2 also relies on gravity. Only one of the four answers includes both Scientist 1 and 2, which is A. This makes sense, since Scientist 3 agrees with both of them and their theories about the origins of FRBs.

Passage II

8. Correct answer: **J**. If you were to quickly skim the three paragraphs beneath Scientists 1, 2, and 3, you will see the letters 'DNA' in all three. Scientist 1 speaks of aging as being coded into DNA. Scientist 2 speaks of DNA mutations affecting aging. Scientist 3 speaks of the incomplete replication of the ends of DNA. Thus, all 3 of them recognize that DNA plays some kind of role in the aging process, which is why the answer is J.

9. Correct answer: **A**. Though the question may mention a new word ("thyroiditis"), this question essentially boils down to this: which scientist believes that hormonal output or hormones generally plays a role in the aging process? Scientist 1 says "hormonal changes" help to regulate the aging process, so this statement is definitely true of him. However, only 1 of the 4 answer choices proposes Scientist 1, which is answer choice A, making A the correct answer.

10. Correct answer: **H**. It is Scientist 3 who discusses the shortening of telomeres as most responsible in the aging process (see the first sentence of Scientist 3's paragraph), thus any correct answer must include this scientist. That eliminates letter F. The question now is which other scientist (or scientists) believes that "cellular damage" plays a role in aging. Well, let's look through Scientist 1 first. Upon doing so, I see nothing about "cellular damage." Scientist 1 *does* mention "decline of repair mechanisms," but there's no reason to suspect that that is the same thing as cellular damage, and it certainly isn't stated as much by the scientist. Since each answer but 1 contains Scientist 1 as an option, we now have enough information to get the question correct: the correct answer must be H. If you want to be sure, all it takes is a read of the first sentence of Scientist 2 to see that it is "the gradual accumulation of *cellular damage*" that is responsible for aging. Thus, both Scientist 2 and Scientist 3 are correct, which matches answer choice H.

11. Correct answer: **C**. Scientist 2's main idea is that cellular damage accumulates over time, which causes aging (thus, we can already see why choice D is incorrect; increasing cellular damage would cause a person, then, to age faster!). The correct answer then is going to be a medicine that slows cellular aging. Before rereading Scientist 2's paragraph with all of this information in mind, I see right away that answer choice B can also be eliminated; this idea (the shortening of telomeres) is essential to the argument of Scientist 3, not Scientist 2. That leaves A and C. Upon rereading Scientist 2's paragraph, we see in the second sentence that one cause of cellular damage is "the accumulation of cellular waste products." Thus, a medicine that would help "cells to dispose of waste more permanently" (answer choice C) would slow aging in his view. This is why C is the correct answer. As for answer choice A, the idea of hormonal production being effective would be more in line with the position of Scientist 1.

12. Correct answer: **H**. Cellular senescence is only mentioned by one of the three scientists: Scientist 3. He says, "As telomeres become critically short, cells can no longer divide and function properly, known as cellular senescence." We can eliminate answer choices F and G immediately since they both propose that cellular senescence "is necessary to slow aging," but the opposite is true: cellular senescence furthers aging. Letter choice J proposes that cellular senescence "relies on the proper functioning of telomeres," but that's not true, since cellular senescence is caused by the shortening of telomeres, not the proper functioning of them. This is why the correct answer is H: cellular senescence, according to Scientist 3, is rooted in the gradual shortening of telomeres and furthers the aging process.

13. Correct answer: **B**. There's a lot in this question to confuse you, things like CRS and other scientific jargon. However, essentially this question is asking this: which scientist thinks that the damaging of "the structure and function of molecules" has an effect on the aging process? Scientist 2 mentions a number of factors that cause damage "at the molecular level." Thus, Scientist 2 would be a correct answer, which eliminates answer choices A and C. The question now is whether or not Scientist 3 believes this. However, a rereading of the position of Scientist 3 mentions nothing about breakdowns at a "molecular" level. This is why the answer is B: Scientist 2.

14. Correct answer: **H**. Let's begin with Scientist 1. Scientist 1's claim, in essence, is that aging is genetically predetermined or coded into DNA. Thus, Scientist 1 would *not* agree with this fourth scientist's claim that aging is not genetically predetermined. That eliminates answer choices G and J, both of which refer to Scientist 1. Because both F and H say Scientist 2 agrees with the claim, there is no need to investigate it (it would be a waste of time). Thus, the only remaining question is this: does Scientist 3 agree with this claim? Well, Scientist 3 says that aging is caused, in more or less words, by the shortening of telomeres on the cellular level (aka, not genetically predetermined or coded into DNA). Thus, like Scientist 2, Scientist 3 would agree with this fourth scientist's claim. That is why the answer is H: Scientists 2 and 3.

Answer Explanations - Step 5

Correct Answers:

Passage I:	Passage II:	Passage III:	Passage IV:	Passage V:	Passage VI:
1: C	4: F	7: A	10: G	13: A	16: H
2: G	5: C	8: J	11: B	14: F	17: A
3: B	6: J	9: C	12: J	15: C	18: B

Passage I:

1. Correct answer: **C**. If you look at the various tomato variants as featured in Figure 1, the sodium concentration in the experimental group (watered with water with a high salt concentration) is always somewhere between 2 to 4 times as much as the control group. Only one answer choice falls within this range, which is answer choice C: 75 mmol is roughly 3 times larger than the 27.5 mmol when Better Boy is watered with low content salt water.

2. Correct answer: **G**. Immediately we can eliminate answer choice F, since it only shows the yield of two plants, not 3. Letters H and J either look to split the three variants evenly or to be really close to doing so. However, if you look at the three tomato plants under the control column in Table 1, there is one that is a little bigger than a second that is a little bigger than a third. This is why the answer is G: it most accurately represents the total control yield as seen in Table 1.

3. Correct answer: **B**. Bloody Butcher, when watered with a groundwater aquifer (aka the control group) yields 2,785 grams. Juane Flamme, when watered with a groundwater aquifer (aka the control group) yields 2,317 grams. So, if we have a new tomato with 50% of both, you would expect the yield to be somewhere between the two. There is only one option between the two, which is option B: 2,525 grams.

Passage II:

4. Correct answer: **F**. You may be thinking to yourself, "How am I supposed to answer this question without a calculator??? Unfair!" However, the ACT Science test will never give you a question that requires a calculator; any question that uses a mathematical step will require only a *simple* mathematical step. Here, all you need to realize to get the answer correct is that the recorded velocity on the moon will be *much lower* than the velocity on earth. If you look at Cart B's velocity in Figure 1 when released from a height of 3, you will see that it measures something near 7 m/s. There are only 2 answer choices that are even lower than 7 m/s; this eliminates right away answer choices H and J. However, answer choice G (5.05 m/s) is only *a little bit lower* than 7 m/s. If acceleration due to gravity on earth is 9.8, and on the moon it is 1.625, we need a value much lower than 7 m/s! This is why the correct answer is F: 1.15 m/s.

5. Correct answer: **C**. This is one of those rare ACT Science questions that requires you to have a previous understanding of science. Here, what is required is that you convert an answer from m/s to cm/s by first remembering that there are 100 centimeters in a meter. First, recognize that Cart B has a velocity of roughly 5.5 m/s (if you look at the answer choices, it's clear that it's velocity is 5.48 m/s). In order to calculate this same metric in centimeters per second, simply multiply the answer by 100 by moving the decimal point *to the right* twice. This results in 548 centimeters per second, which aligns with answer choice C.

6. Correct answer: **J**. Here, you are being asked to do some simple math. Again, the ACT Science test is never going to ask you a question that requires a calculator, and they are never going to give you two answer choices that are a mere fraction of a decimal apart, and one of those two is the right answer. With basic reasoning or rounding skills, the right answer will be clear. Here, you are asked to find the acceleration of Cart A as it crossed the finish line when released from a height of 5 meters, which is the velocity over the time. The velocity of Cart A when released from a height of 5 meters is roughly 10 m/s. When you divide that by 1.5 seconds, you get 6.67 m/s^2. This is why the correct answer is J.

Passage III:

7. Correct answer: **A**. The Mpemba Effect says that hot water will freeze faster than cold water. If you look at the tables to see the results of the experiment, the beaker of water that froze the fastest was Beaker A, which contained heated purified water. This *confirms* the Mpemba Effect, and thus *falsifies* the hypothesis that the Mpemba Effect would not work in purified water. This eliminates answer choices C and D, which both lead with "No." Answer choice B, however, falsely states that the water that was the first to freeze was the room temperature water. Thus, A is correct: the hypothesis was falsified because the heated and purified water was the first to freeze.

8. Correct answer: **J**. A fifth beaker, Beaker E, is put into the freezer and takes 85 minutes to freeze. This is much slower than any of the beakers in the actual experiment. Let's go through each answer choice one at a time and see if it rings true about the mysterious Beaker E. First, letter F says that it came from a "freshwater spring" (aka, pure fresh water) and was heated to 50°;

this, unfortunately, is much more like Beaker A (heated purified water) that froze quickly, so F is incorrect. Second, answer choice G says that it came from a "freshwater spring" (aka, pure fresh water) and kept at room temperature; however, this water is akin to that of Beaker B, which froze after 70 minutes, so G is incorrect. Third, answer choice H says that it came from the ocean and heated. This seems much more likely, since ocean water (like tap water in the experiment) contains minerals (like salt) that make freezing go more slowly. However, answer choice J also references salt water, but mentions that the water is "kept at room temperature." This seems much more likely to be true than H because H was heated, and heated water freezes more quickly. This is why the correct answer is J: ocean (mineral rich) water at room temperature would more than likely freeze more slowly than the others.

9. Correct answer: **C**. I have said this before: any math required on the ACT will not be difficult, but simple. By that I mean that "ballparking" your answers is always going to be good enough; the correct answer is not going to differ from wrong answers by mere decimals as they might on the ACT Math test. Now, the first step is to find the temperature of the water referenced by the question in Celsius. The beaker that contains "purified water" put in the freezer at "50°" is Beaker A. After 30 minutes had elapsed, Beaker A recorded a temperature of 17°. Now, the time has come to use the conversion formula to "calculate" this same temperature in Fahrenheit. You might now be thinking, "I can't multiply 17×1.8 in my head!" Me neither. Instead, I'm going to just multiply it by 2 and add 32 and approximate the correct answer. So, $17 \times 2 = 34$. $34 + 32 = 66°$. Only one answer choice is anywhere close to this value (as expected), which is answer choice C, making it correct.

Passage IV:

10. Correct answer: **G**. Before you look at the graphs, think about the answer for yourself, then identify the graph that best fits. What do you know about the relationship between the CT value of a food and the likelihood that it will cause a reaction? Well, the higher a CT value is, the lower the likelihood. Or, to put it another way, as the CT value goes up (on the x axis of these graphs), the likelihood (the y axis) goes down. Choices H and J do not reflect this linear relationship, so they are out. Letter F is incorrect because it gets the relationship backwards; it makes it look like as CT goes up, the likelihood goes up. This is why the correct answer is G: as you move left to right on the x axis (CT value going up), the y value (likelihood of allergic reaction) goes down.

11. Correct answer: **B**. This question looks extremely complicated because it is lengthy, but the basics of it are rather simple. Essentially, this question is asking this: how many food products in Table 1 have a high to moderate likelihood of causing a reaction (a CT value of 30-35) but do NOT declare peanuts or peanut traces on the packaging. Well, there are three food products that have a CT value between 30 and 35: Cereal bar II, Cereal bar III, and Cookies with fiber. Cereal bar I does NOT declare peanuts on the packaging (that's $100,000); Cereal bar III DOES declare peanuts on the packaging (no fine); and Cookes with fiber does NOT declare peanuts on the packaging (another $100,000). That's why the answer is B: the company would owe $200,000 in fines.

12. Correct answer: **J**. This question, like the previous question, looks more difficult than it really is. It confuses you (or attempts to) with talk of half life, etc. The question is essentially this: in 1,042 years a lot of the DNA in these foods will die, so what will the CT value look like then? A CT value means how many cycles of amplification were needed to detect peanut DNA. If it took 40 cycles in the first place, then you try again 1,042 years later when the DNA is much lower, then the CT value is only going to go *higher*; in other words, it will be *way* bigger than 40 now because you will need more and more cycles of amplification to find the DNA since it has become more difficult over time. This is why the answer is J; it is the only answer that has the number of cycles increasing over 40.

Passage V:

13. Correct answer: **A**. This question requires that you have a prior understanding of pH to identify the correct answer. First, let's remember that the Trypsin functioned better in the pH 8 environment compared to the pH 6 environment. Well, the question is, is that a more basic or acidic environment? The way pH works is this: 7 is considered "neutral" (which is the pH of water). Any number lower than 7 is considered "acidic," and the closer the number gets to 0, the more acidic. Any number higher than 7 is considered "basic," and the closer a number gets to 14, the more basic. Thus, the Trypsin enzyme functioned better in a more basic environment (because pH of 8 is higher than 7, it is basic). This eliminates answer choices C and D. However, B is incorrect because it wrongly says that the absorbance levels of the more basic vials are *lower* than the more acidic, but that's not true. Answer choice A is the correct answer because it rightly states that the absorbance levels in the more basic vials (pH of 8) are *higher* than the more acidic vials (pH of 6).

14. Correct answer: **F**. As was stated in the previous explanation, this question (like #13 above) requires you have an understanding of pH on a basic level. See the previous explanation above for more detail, but essentially, a pH of over 7 is basic and a pH of under 7 is acidic. What we find in this experiment is that the more acidic vials (pH of 6 in Experiment 2) have lower absorbance values, thus lower substrates being catalyzed into product by the enzyme Trypsin. This means that the scientist's hypothesis that acidic drinks may cause lesser amino acids in the blood stream (which is what Trypsin does) *could be true*. In other words, the hypothesis is not "rejected". This eliminates answer choices H and J. Answer choice G though falsely states that the acidic vials (pH of 6 in Experiment 2) had *more substrate* catalyzed than the basic vials (pH of 8 in Experiment 1). However, that is not true. This is why the correct answer is F: the more basic vials in Experiment 1 perform better than the acidic vials in

Experiment 2; thus, the idea that acidic drinks could lower the work of Trypsin (amino acids in the bloodstream) is still possible and not rejected.

15. Correct answer: **C**. This is the third question in a row that requires that you have some kind of previous science knowledge. In science experiments, the *independent* variable is the variable that the scientists control. Here, the scientists control the substrate level, for example…and the pH of the vials…and the amount of Trypsin in each vial. This means that A, B, and D are all wrong answers. The *dependent* variable is what is being measured; it is *dependent* upon the independent variables. This is the absorbance value, which is why the correct answer is C.

Passage VI:

16. Correct answer: **H**. First, this student who is coming in late identifies 45 neutrophils when looking through the optical microscope, which means he is identifying 45 cells in Study 1 (thus Table 1). This is obviously *way more* than the actual number of neutrophils in the sample. Answer choice F proposes that he perhaps messed with the reflector, but that is only present on the fluorescent microscope (see Figure 2), which makes this answer choice incorrect. Answer choice G speaks of cells fluorescing green, but again, that is the fluorescent microscope that uses this technology, not the optical, which is why choice G is also incorrect. Answer choice J proposes that he may have "undercounted" cells, but we already know that he way *overcounted* the cells, making choice J also incorrect. That leaves H, which says that he possibly mistook each cell that he saw no matter what for a neutrophil; this is of course plausible, especially compared to the other answers, which means that H is the correct answer.

17. Correct answer: **A**. Here, what is needed is some way to differentiate "other" blood cells from the neutrophils. If they are all blue, the question is, how could a student tell the difference? Well, it has nothing to do with the color of the light, though some students will get confused with the original green light in Study 2 and choose C. But, neither C nor D is correct because they both speak of looking for a certain color light. That leaves answer choices A and B, which at first glance seem identical. There is one word of difference between them, however; A speaks of a *diameter* of 12-14 μm, and B speaks of a *radius* of 12-14 μm. If you look back at the description of what to look for in a neutrophil in the third paragraph, you'll see that in Study 1 students were supposed to look for neutrophils with a *diameter* of 12-14 μm. This makes A the correct answer and B incorrect.

18. Correct answer: **B**. Fortunately, you are told the size comparison between a meter and a μm (aka a micrometer). It is one millionth the size. To get this question correct, start with the number in micrometers. As you can see, the answer choices all feature the number 13 (which is between 12 and 14 μm, as defined by the passage as the diameter of a neutrophil nucleus). Second, move the decimal point to the left one space for every 0 that follows the number 1,000,000 (because it is one millionth of a meter). There are 6 zeros after 1,000,000, which means we need to move the decimal point to the left 6 times, adding in a 0 for every blank space. Let's do it one step at a time: 1 (13 to 1.3), 2 (1.3 to 0.13), 3 (0.13 to 0.013), 4 (0.013 to 0.0013), 5 (0.0013 to 0.00013), and lastly 6 (0.00013 to 0.000013). This is why the correct answer is 0.000013, which corresponds with answer choice B.

Answer Explanations - Step 6 - Practice Test 1

Passage I	Passage II	Passage III	Passage IV	Passage V	Passage VI
1: D	8: F	14: G	21: D	28: G	34: G
2: H	9: C	15: A	22: G	29: C	35: D
3: B	10: J	16: H	23: A	30: G	36: H
4: F	11: C	17: B	24: H	31: B	37: A
5: D	12: H	18: F	25: B	32: J	38: J
6: J	13: B	19: C	26: F	33: A	39: C
7: A		20: F	27: D		40: J

Passage I

1. Correct answer: **D**. The data for Experiment 2 is listed in Table 2. Clearly, the amount of time the ground beef is exposed to the acidic solution in the experiment is 15 minutes. Thus, it is up to you to infer what is likely to happen after an additional 5 minutes. This just means following the pattern that is being established by the data. Initially, according to Table 2, the E. coli count begins to go down to 10,000 at the 10 minute mark. However, at 15 minutes, it has begun to go up again. This trend suggests that this growth will continue, which is why the correct answer is D: greater than 15,000. None of the other three answers is supported by the actual data trends.

2. Correct answer: **H**. It is being proposed here that the ground beef samples of Experiment 3 be exposed to the vinegar solution for 10 minutes as opposed to 5, then put in the storage. Well, according to Experiment 2, after 5 minutes just in a vinegar acid reduces the E. coli count (to 15,000), but after 10 minutes the amount of E. coli is reduced even farther (to 10,000). Thus, if the beef was put in vinegar for 10 minutes before storage, it would "start" in storage with less E. coli than what really took place in Experiment 3. This means that after a day of sitting at 50 degrees, the E. coli count would have to be lower. This eliminates answers F and G. Choice J correctly says "Less," but it falsely says that this would be because the E. coli at the beginning of storage would be increased. This is why the correct answer is H: it says the count will be less and correctly identifies why this is the case.

3. Correct answer: **B**. This question simply requires that you count how many of the experiments' results had an E. coli count of 60,000 or greater. There are none of these in Table 1, there are none of these in Table 2, but there is 1 of them in Table 3 (next to 50°F). This is why the correct answer is B: 1. You may think to yourself, "but wait a second! Next to 40°F it says there is an E. coli count of 60,000!" However, the question says that a beef item would be critical if it is *over* 60,000, not 60,000 or higher.

4. Correct answer: **F**. Experiment 1 exposed the ground beef samples to radiation only. If you reread through Experiments 2 and 3 though, you will find no mention of the word "radiation," nor anything that suggests it (like, "Experiment 1 was repeated with…"). This is why the correct answer is F: only Experiment 1 used radiation.

5. Correct answer: **D**. First of all, recognize that Experiment 1 is the one that tested the E. coli count in ground beef by using radiation exposure. However, to get this question right, you need to have a previous knowledge of what direct and an indirect relationships are. A *direct* relationship means this: as one thing increases, another thing increases (like the more miles you drive, the more gas you use). An *indirect* relationship means this: as one thing increases, another thing decreases (like as the temperature increases the ice in your glass decreases). If you look back at the data in Table 1, you will see that as the time of exposure to radiation goes up (0, 5, 10, then 15 minutes) the E. coli count goes down. One goes up, one goes down: that's an inverse relationship. This eliminates A and B, which both say the relationship is direct. C though is incorrect because it states that the E. coli count *increases*, which is false. That is why the answer is D: it states that the relationship is inverse, and gives the correct reason why.

6. Correct answer: **J**. A first thing to notice would be that the final step for each answer choice is exactly the same: "then store it at 4°F for 24 hours." Because that's the same for each question, it can be ignored (which also means that Experiment 3's data can be ignored). Thus, the correct answer is going to be the combination of steps from Experiment 1 (radiation) and Experiment 2 (vinegar) that lowers the E. coli count. First, we know that the longer the beef is exposed to radiation, the lower the E. coli count. This would seem to eliminate F and G, which only propose 10 minutes of radiation compared to 15 minutes for H and J. As for H, it proposes soaking the beef then in vinegar for 15 minutes. That seems better than 10 minutes of soaking (which is what J proposes), but if you look at the data of Table 2, at the 15 minute mark the E. coli count started to increase again. This is why the answer is J: longer radiation exposure, but the perfect amount of soaking in vinegar.

7. Correct answer: **A**. This question is asking you first to find how many of the results (out of a total of 12) have been exposed to vinegar for *more than* (not equal to) 5 minutes. In Experiment 1, this was true of 0 of the samples. In Experiment 2, this was true of only 2 samples (the ones exposed to 10 and 15 minutes), and in Experiment 3 this is true of 0 samples (they had all been soaked for exactly 5 minutes). Thus, only 2 of 12 have been exposed to vinegar for greater than 5 minutes. Now, you might not be able to figure out to the proper decimal what 2 divided by 12 is equal to, but you don't have to. Remember: basic math ACT questions will never require math that needs a calculator. Instead, look at the answer choices. Choice B says 25%. However, 25%

of 12 is 3, so the actual number must be less than 3. Seeing as there is only one such answer choice, the correct answer must be A: 16.67%.

Passage II

8. Correct answer: **F**. If you look at Figure 1, you'll see that the group with the lowest amount of plants that produced beans is Group 3, the self-pollinating column. The other two, which are both larger, both include bees. Thus, it doesn't matter what type of bees you introduce to the beans (whether wild bees or honey bees); either way, the percent of plants producing beans will increase. This is why the correct answer is F: increases.

9. Correct answer: **C**. This question requires that you go through the three options one by one and see which are true. Let's start with I. "Self-pollination" literally means that no pollinators are allowed to interact with the plants, so this is true. That eliminates answer choice D, since it does not include I as a true option. Move on to II. According to Figure 1, the number of plants produced with self-pollination is certainly *not* "maximized" with self-pollination, but the opposite. This means that II is false, which eliminates answer choice B. So, either A is true (because only I is true) or C is true (because I and III are both true). To figure that out, move on to option III. If you look back at the opening paragraph, you'll see that "self-pollination" is defined as "both the egg and pollen are from the same *G. max* plant." Thus, III is also true, which means that the correct answer is C: I and III only.

10. Correct answer: **J**. This question is a bit deceiving. It asks you for the *number* of bean-producing plants from cross-pollination using honey bees (which is Group 2). You might think right away that the answer is H: 38. However, 38 is roughly the *percent* of plants that produced beans, not the number. If you look into the passage's second paragraph, you will see that 240 plants were used in each group. Thus, the correct answer is going to be way bigger than 38. Mathematically speaking, one way to reason through this question would be like this: 38% is a bit bigger than 33%; so, if 80 is 33% or one-third of 240, then the right answer will be a little bigger than that. There is only one answer choice that meets these requirements, which is answer choice J: 91.

11. Correct answer: **C**. Because it has been determined from the experiment that pollinators increase soybean yield and mass, the presence of honey bees (A), the presence of wild bees (B) and an increase in pollinators (D) would all *increase* soybean yield and mass. This is why the correct answer is C: a decrease in bees for whatever reason would lessen the percent of plants producing beans and the average mass per bean.

12. Correct answer: **H**. At first, letter choice G is the most easily dismissed, mostly because it doesn't make logical sense that a small plant would produce a bigger bean (plus, there's nothing in the passage that would help us infer to such an idea). You might be tempted, first, by answer choice F. However, there is no data on the relationship between plant size and bean size (or plant size at all), thus there's no logical way to infer to this as a reasonable conclusion. As for J, which might also be tempting, there is no information in the passage about the economics of soybeans vs other plant species, so it's impossible to infer whether or not it is a bad investment. That is why the correct answer is H: because the passage says that both wild and honey bees are good for the plants, it is reasonable to conclude that the presence of bees would be good for farmers.

13. Correct answer: **B**. Figure 2 gives the various average masses of the soybeans from different plants. Thus, it is possible that this bean weighing 179 mg could come from any of the 3 groups. However, the question asks which group is *most likely*, and because Group 2's beans average roughly 177 mg, it is definitely *most likely* that this bean comes from Group 2. This eliminates answer choices A and D. The only difference between answer choices B and C is that choice B says that Group 2 is from honey bees, and choice C says that Group 2 is from self-pollinating plants. However, Table 1 clearly states that Group 2 is from plants pollinated with honey bees, which is why B is the correct answer.

Passage III

14. Correct answer: **G**. Remember that Scientist 2's basic idea is that *Homo sapiens* evolved in one place, then moved to other places over time. It is Scientist 1 who holds beliefs more consistent with answer choice J; this is why J is incorrect. Answer choice F is incorrect because Scientist 2 makes no mention of the migration of Neanderthals or Denisovans. Answer choice H is incorrect because the answer presupposed *Homo sapiens* being there…but how can the presence of *Homo sapiens* be the cause of *Homo sapiens* living there? This is why the correct answer is G: Scientist 2 believes that *Homo sapiens* evolved in and migrated from a single point.

15. Correct answer: **A**. Scientist 1 relies on the idea that populations of *Homo sapiens* popped up independent of one another in various places from pre-human species (like *Homo erectus*, mentioned in the question). His main evidence for this is that there are strict similarities between modern humans' anatomies and the most ancient pre-human bones in the same areas. Thus, if a scientist discovers a femur bone basically identical to those in the area in modern times, this supports Scientist 1's idea. This eliminates answer choices B and D. The question then is whether or not this same discovery would help Scientist 2, but the answer there is no: Scientist 2 would need the femur bone to be more similar to the femur bones of modern Africans than modern East Asians. Thus, the correct answer is A: this femur bone would help only Scientist 1.

16. Correct answer: **H**. If a bone fragment from an early *Homo sapiens* individual in Africa was similar to that of modern Europeans, then that would support the idea that *Homo sapiens* came "out of Africa," which is the position of Scientist 2. The

question though asks if this discovery supports Scientist 1, but the answer there is "No." This eliminates answer choices F and G. Answer choice J says that Scientist 1 doesn't rely on anatomical similarities, but that is exactly what he relies on (see the second half of his paragraph). This is why the correct answer is H: Scientist 1 needs those anatomical similarities to tie *Homo sapiens* in modern times to the same locations in the past.

17. Correct answer: **B**. Scientist 2 states that *Homo sapiens* came into existence about 200,000 years ago in Africa. Thus, if a *Homo sapiens* individual were discovered in Europe even longer ago than that, then that would certainly weaken the position of Scientist 2. This eliminates answer choices A and D, since neither weakens the position of Scientist 2. Well, what about Scientist 1? However, Scientist 1 doesn't believe in the "out of Africa" hypothesis and thinks it is true that *Homo sapiens* populations popped up all throughout Africa, Asia, and Europe independently of one another. This is why the correct answer is B: this discovery would weaken only the position of Scientist 2.

18. Correct answer: **F**. Let's go through the options here backwards to see if they are something each scientist would agree with. Answer choice J, factually speaking, makes no sense: if pre-modern humanoid species' bones are indistinguishable from *Homo sapiens*, then how do you know they are from humanoid species? Answer choice H is something that Scientist 1 proposes, but not Scientist 2, so it is false. Answer choice G says that humanoid species were killed off by *Homo sapiens*, but only Scientist 1 says that outright, and it is not OK to infer that Scientist 2 believes that. Thus, answer choice F must be correct. Scientist 1 says *Homo sapiens* killed off these humanoid species, and Scientist 2 says that *Homo sapiens* "displaced and replaced" them. Either way, they lived together, which is why F is correct.

19. Correct answer: **C**. This question is really similar to the previous one, number 18. The question is about a new humanoid species, and each answer choice mentions the relationship between this species and *Homo sapiens* in one way or another. While Scientist 1 states that *Homo sapiens* killed off humanoid species and Scientist 2 states that *Homo sapiens* "displaced and replaced" them, either way, *Homo sapiens* is likely responsible for their deaths. This is why the correct answer is C. None of the other statements is something both scientists would agree with.

20. Correct answer: **F**. The main difference between Scientist 1 and 2 is not *what Homo sapiens* evolved *from*, but where that happened. This is why answers H and J are both incorrect: both of these answers rely on what *Homo sapiens* evolved from. Answer choice G states that Scientist 1 relies on DNA and Scientist 2 relies on anatomy, but that is flipped. Scientist 1 relies on anatomical comparisons between modern humans and ancient humanoid species. Scientist 2, on the other hand, relies on DNA analysis (if you quickly scan Scientist 2's paragraph, you'll see "DNA" over and over). This is why the correct answer is F: it rightly states that Scientist 1 relies on anatomical data and Scientist 2 on DNA analysis.

Passage IV

21. Correct answer: **D**. First, if you look at Figures 2 and 3, you will see that Experiments 2 and 3 more or less resulted in healthy population levels of both *P. aurelia* and *P. caudatum*. Thus, there's really not any evidence there at all to conclude that there's consuming of one another. You might be tempted to think that Experiment 1, on the other hand, shows this, since the experiment results in the precipitous decline of *P. aurelia's* population. However, just because one population declines and the other does well doesn't mean that one of them is consuming the other; there could be a whole host of reasons for this population decline, like a lack of food. This is why the answer is D: there is no direct evidence that these paramecium are willing to consume other paramecium.

22. Correct answer: **G**. If you look at the population levels for each paramecium between Experiment 2 and Experiment 3, you will see this: in both Experiments 2 and 3, *P. caudatum* (the squares on the graph) has a general increase in population. *P. aurelia* (the triangles on the graph), on the other hand, does increase in population in Experiment 2, but keeps a more-or-less steady population throughout Experiment 3. That is why the correct answer is G: *D. nasutum* (present only in Experiment 3) affects the population of *P. aurelia* more than *P. caudatum*.

23. Correct answer: **A**. This question depends on a proper analysis of Experiment 3. Clearly, because the only difference between Experiment 2 (in which both paramecium species thrived) and Experiment 3 (in which *P. aurelia* did not thrive as well) is the addition of *D. nasutum*. So, if you introduce a species that eats *D. nasutum*, then you would have to expect that the population of *P. aurelia* would increase as a result. That is why the answer is A. It certainly isn't B (which says that the population of *P. aurelia* would go down). Choices C and D are *possible*, but neither can be "reasonably expected", which is required by the question.

24. Correct answer: **H**. Simply compare the population levels at 20 days of both parameciums between Experiments 1 and 2. Start with *P. aurelia*. In Experiment 1, it has a population of roughly 35 at 20 days, and in Experiment 2 a population of roughly 60 at 20 days. So, it's population is "Greater than", which eliminates answers G and J. Now, look at *P. caudatum's* numbers. In Experiment 1, it has a population of roughly 80 at 20 days, and in Experiment 2 a population of roughly 80 at 20 days. So, it's population is "Equal to", which then eliminates answer choice F. This is why the correct answer is H: *P. aurelia's* population went up, but *P. caudatum's* stayed the same.

25. Correct answer: **B**. To answer this question correctly, simply determine the rough population levels of both paramecium combined at each of the four population points and see which is the smallest. Answer A proposes P_{20} of Experiment 1, which

shows populations of the 2 paramecium at roughly 80 and 40 for a total of 120. Answer B proposes P_{30} of Experiment 1, which shows populations of the 2 paramecium at roughly 85 and 0 for a total of 85. Answer C proposes P_{20} of Experiment 2, which shows populations of the 2 paramecium at roughly 60 and 80 for a total of 140. Answer D proposes P_{30} of Experiment 3, which shows populations of the 2 paramecium at roughly 85 and 20 for a total of 105. Thus, population levels of the paramecium is lowest (among the 4 choices) at P_{30} of Experiment 1, which is why B is the correct answer.

26. Correct answer: **F**. First, let's begin with H and J, neither of which requires the kind of inference implied by the question but a straightforward reading of Figure 3. The P_{25} and P_{30} of *P. aurelia* are relatively the same, about 20 or so, which means that neither of these is likely to be the correct answer. Answer choices F and G propose the numbers of *P. aurelia* and *P. caudatum* paralyzed in Experiment 3. Remember that Experiment 3 is essentially the exact same conditions as Experiment 2, the only difference being that a toxicyst is introduced in Experiment 3. However, a comparison of the two experiments shows that the toxicyst really had little to no effect at all on *P. caudatum*, but that the numbers of *P. aurelia* were drastically different, implying that the toxicyst killed a great number of *P. aurelia*. That's why the correct answer is F.

27. Correct answer: **D**. A "nutrient free" green algae means that the algae is no longer feeding or supplying nutrients to the two varieties of paramecium, which is in essence the exact same setup for Experiment 1 in which the two paramecium were simply placed in water. Experiment 2 ends with high population levels of *P. aurelia* and *P. caudatum*, but based on Experiment 1, what is likely to then happen when the nutrients run out? If you look at answer choice D, you'll see that it proposes the eventual sharp decline of *P. caudatum*. However, if you look at Experiment 1, *P. caudatum* did just find in the water with no nutrients. This is why the correct answer is D: this population decline of *P. caudatum* could not be reasonably inferred when comparing Experiments 1 and 2.

Passage V

28. Correct answer: **G**. For a substance to be considered *very soluble*, its m_{sv}/m_{su} value would have to be less than one. The m_{sv}/m_{su} values are found in Table 3, which you would then compare to the descriptive terms in Table 2. Looking down Table 3, there are 0 substances that have a m_{sv}/m_{su} value less than 1. Thus, the answer to the question "Was this hypothesis consistent with the results?" is no, since the hypothesis was that 1 of the substances would be "very soluble." This eliminates answer choice J. Letter F proposes that the answer is "no" because more than 1 of the substances falls into this category, but that isn't true. Letter H says there's not enough data to reach a conclusion about this, but that's not true. This is all why the correct answer is G: the answer is "no" because none of the substances fall into the *very soluble* category.

29. Correct answer: **C**. This question requires a straight reading of Table 1, the chart of the 7 substances. This chart shows the amount of each substance dissolved in 100 grams of water at varying temperatures. Simply find the column for HCl (the third substance out of seven from the left), then go down to the 60 degree row, and you'll see the number 55, which is 55 grams. This is why the correct answer is C.

30. Correct answer: **G**. If you look at Table 2, a substance is "freely soluble" if it has a m_{sv}/m_{su} value between 1 and 10. If you look at Table 3, there are only 2 substances that do not fall into this range; in other words, there are 5 that do. That means 5 of the 7 are "freely soluble," which is why the correct answer is G: 5/7.

31. Correct answer: **B**. Table 1 lists the amount of grams dissolved into 100 grams of water at different temperatures. If you look at the column for $NaNO_3$, you'll notice that at some point the concentration goes from below 100 to above 100. At 20 degrees, $NaNO_3$ has a concentration of 86 in 100 grams of water, and at 40 degrees it has risen to 105. Without looking at the answer choices, it seems most likely that $NaNO_3$ reaches *solubility equipollence* somewhere between 30 and 40 degrees. There is only one answer choice that falls into this range, which is answer choice B: 35 degrees.

32. Correct answer: **J**. "Freely soluble" means that the substance has a m_{sv}/m_{su} value between 1 and 10 (according to Table 2). If you look then at Table 3, you'll see that there are 3 substances that contain sodium. The first one, ($Na_2C_2O_4$) has a m_{sv}/m_{su} value much higher than 10. The other two substances that contain sodium ($NaNO_3$ and $NaCl$) are both freely soluble. This is why the correct answer is J; it rightly says that the answer is "No" (not every substance with Na is freely soluble) and gives the correct reason why (only 2 of the 3 substances have a m_{sv}/m_{su} value between 1 and 10).

33. Correct answer: **A**. If the *x* axis is degrees Celsius, then based on the graph given here we are looking for a substance that has a dissolved concentration of around 85 at 0°C, about 55 at 20°C, about 45 at 40°C, about 20 at 60°C, about 15 at 80°C, and about 10 at 100°C. The reason the correct answer is A is because, if you look at the column of concentrations under NH_3, you'll see a gradual decline in concentration as the temperature rises that roughly mirrors the values that we estimated based on the graph provided by the question. Each of the other three choices has an *increasing* concentration as the temperature goes up; NH_3 is the only of the 4 options that has a decreasing concentration as temperature rises. That is why the answer is A.

Passage VI

34. Correct answer: **G**. The two studies actually feature the same number of generations. In each study, there is a P (parental) generation, then an F_1 generation, then lastly an F_2 generation. Put simply, that is three generations, which is why G is the correct

answer. F proposes 2, which is probably a common wrong answer, but though that might be the difference in the number of generations between P and F$_2$, it isn't the total number of generations. Choice H is incorrect because 82 represents the total number of fruit flies observed in Study 1, not the number of generations. Choice J is incorrect because 197 represents the total number of flies of either type observed in both studies combined.

35. Correct answer: **D**. Let's go through each choice and compare each of the proposed phenotype/genotype observations to the students' expected numbers. Choice A: Table 1 says that the observed Brown eye/bb was 19, and the expectation was 20.5 (a difference of 1.5). Choice B: Table 1 says that the observed Red eye/B__ was 63, and the expectation was 61.5 (a difference of 1.5). Choice C: Table 2 says that the observed Sepia eye/ddB__ was 18, and the expectation was 21.6 (a difference of 3.6). Choice D: Table 2 says that the observed Brown eye/D__bb was 30, and the expectation was 21.6 (a difference of 8.4). Thus, Choice D has the greatest deviation, making it the correct answer.

36. Correct answer: **H**. First, understand that the question refers to the last line in Table 2, the _____ eye (phenotype) or ddbb (genotype) eye color. As you can see there, the students found 0 of them in the third generation of the study. The question is simply asking why this is the case. Letter F proposes that based on Study 1, a doubly homozygous genotype isn't possible. However, Study 1, if anything, proposes that is *is* a possibility (since there are observed bb genotype eye color flies); this is why F is incorrect. Letter G proposes that 115 flies simply wasn't enough based on expectations. However, the students only expected 1/16 of the flies to have this eye color, meaning that you'd need at least 16 flies to find 1. Because the study observes 115 flies, there are plenty to find at least 1 based on expectations; this is why G is incorrect. Let's skip to J, which proposes that there's a relationship with ddbb flies and the number of larvae that die before hatching. Is that *possible?* Sure! It could be the case that flies of this type have other issues that cause them to die before hatching. However, is that *stated* anywhere in the passage? No. This is why J is incorrect. That leaves H, which proposes that ddbb (though *genetically* a different color; a unique genotype) manifests as brown (meaning, has a *phenotype* of brown). This makes a lot of sense, since there are many more observed brown eye flies (30) than was predicted (21.6). This is why H is the correct answer.

37. Correct answer: **A**. The purpose of the studies was to compare expectations of eye color both genetically (genotype) and in terms of looks (phenotype), but the only way to get the genotypes "mixed up" enough with various alleles (B, b, D, d in the study) was to study across three generations. This is why the correct answer is A, to ensure enough allele intermixing for diversification worth studying. Choice B is incorrect because it proposes an idea (about sample sizes helping avoid a certain margin of error) that is not found anywhere in the experiment. Choice C is incorrect because it proposes something about creating a population at F$_2$ that with 100% homozygous alleles, but the purpose of F$_2$ is the opposite. Choice D is incorrect for a couple of reasons, but one of which is that the sepia eye type is only relevant to Study 2, not Study 1, which also utilized flies across 3 generations.

38. Correct answer: **J**. In order for this one sheep to have black wool when all of its parents and grandparents had white wool, it must have a genotype of, first of all, recessive genes; white is clearly the dominant gene in this family tree. This eliminates answer choices G and H, both of which propose that this black sheep inherited a "dominant black wool gene." Secondly, in genetics, if one dominant gene is present in the genotype, the phenotype will manifest as that dominant (or white) gene. This means that what is needed is *not* a "heterozygous" genotype, because that would result (according to the definition given in the passage) in 1 dominant gene and 1 recessive gene, which would result in white wool. This eliminates answer choice F. Thus, what is needed is a "homozygous" genotype, meaning containing nothing but recessive genes. That is what answer choice J proposes, which is why it is correct.

39. Correct answer: **C**. In genetics, and in these two studies, all that is necessary for the manifestation of a dominant genotype is the presence of 1 dominant allele. For example, if you look at Table 1 (which was about the fruit fly, which is what the question is about) in F$_2$ at the Red eye row, you'll see the capital B followed by blanks (__). This is because it doesn't matter what follows this dominant allele (whether dominant or recessive); it will be the determining factor for the eye color. This is why the correct answer is C. More research into the role of the second allele is unnecessary because it will have no effect on the observed numbers.

40. Correct answer: **J**. First of all, notice that there are 4 total observations made in Study 2 (more specifically, 3 observed numbers and 4 expected numbers). This eliminates answer choices F and G as options, since neither shows 4 different colors on its two pie charts. The question now is which pair of pie charts between H and J accurately represents the numbers. However, there is a bit of a shortcut to making these comparisons, and that is this: there are 0 observed ddbb genotype flies in Table 2, which means that they will not have a slice of the pie chart. Under the observed column, you'll clearly see that choice H has 4 slices as if all 4 genotypes have observations, but choice J only has 3. This is why the correct answer is J: it correctly (and accurately, for that matter) gives 3 slices of the pie chart to the observed numbers and 4 slices to the expected numbers.

Answer Explanations - Step 6 - Practice Test 2

Passage I	Passage II	Passage III	Passage IV	Passage V	Passage VI
1: B	7: D	14: H	20: H	27: C	34: H
2: F	8: J	15: D	21: B	28: F	35: A
3: B	9: C	16: F	22: F	29: A	36: F
4: G	10: G	17: C	23: C	30: H	37: A
5: D	11: D	18: J	24: H	31: B	38: J
6: G	12: J	19: B	25: B	32: J	39: A
	13: A		26: F	33: C	40: G

Passage I

1. Correct answer: **B**. Again, you are never going to be asked a mathematics question on the ACT Science test that requires a calculator. This means that general estimations and basic math are going to be enough for you to get the question correct. In this question, notice that Figure 1 shows that 88% of the organisms in the lake are bacteria, but that Figure 2 shows the types of bacteria. As far as bacteroidetes go, they are 33% or ⅓ of the bacteria, or 33% of 88% of all organisms in the lake. Well, what's 88% divided by 3 (aka, ⅓ of 88%)? Well, 3 × 30% = 90%, so the correct answer is going to be a little less than 30%. This is why the correct answer is B: 29%.

2. Correct answer: **F**. The passage states this about hypersaline (really salty) lakes: "This type of environment is not suitable for the majority of living microorganisms, as extremely high salinity levels are often toxic to cells." Thus, as the question states, if salinity or salt levels go *down*, you can expect the presence of other types of organisms to go *up*. Thus, the percent occupied by bacteria overall will go down. This eliminates answer choices H and J, which both state that the percent of bacteria would increase. Answer choice G correctly says that the overall percent of bacteria would decrease, but it wrongly states that this would be due to the fact that other life would fail to survive, but the opposite is true. Thus, choice F is correct because it says that the bacteria levels would decrease because other life would be able to survive and thrive in the lake as the salt levels went down.

3. Correct answer: **B**. Ordering species of organisms from lowest to highest percentage occupation level would be much easier if one of the options was 'bacteria' since, according to Figure 1, they occupy 88% of the lake. However, that isn't the case; instead you are given individual bacteria names. Before we answer the question, let's go ahead and list the 5 named organisms from lowest to highest percentage of occupation levels in the lake: 1) Archea; 2) Eukaryota; 3) Firmicutes; 4) Proteobacteria; 5) Bacteroidetes. Now, because each list has 4 organisms, any list that does *not* begin with either archea or eukaryota as the first is going to be incorrect; this eliminates C and D as potential correct answers. Choice A begins with archea and eukaryota, but then falls apart with it lists proteobacteria ahead of firmicutes. This is why the correct answer is B: although it does not list archea first, the remaining 4 are listed in correct order from lowest to highest percentage occupation levels.

4. Correct answer: **G**. Because the passage makes clear that Mars does *not* presently have any lakes, we can eliminate answer choices H and J, both of which speak of lakes in the present tense. That leaves F and G which both speak of radiation and temperatures. The passage says this in the second sentence: "While current conditions on Mars include freezing temperatures and high radiation levels…" These conditions match up with choice G: low temperatures and high radiation make for a lifeless Mars.

5. Correct answer: **D**. If you look at the pie chart in Figure 1, you'll see that there is a slice of Uncharacterized life that represents 5% of the diversity in the lake. Because the question asks "*At most*"…, we can hold that it is possible that this fungus makes up up to 5% of the total life population of the lake. That is why the correct answer is D: 5%.

6. Correct answer: **G**. Because the hypersaline lake on earth is made up of bacteroidetes more than proteobacterias, it is safe to conclude that it is more likely that an ancient Martian lake contained a bacteriodete (if anything!). This eliminates answer choices H and J. In addition, the passage states of course that if a lake had existed on Mars, it would have been hypersaline. This is why the correct answer is G: unlike answer choice F (which speaks of a lake with little or no salt), answer choice G proposes that if any lake were present on Mars in the past it would have been a hypersaline lake.

Passage II

7. Correct answer: **D**. The "two weeks" referred to in this question is not the condition of any of the three experiments. Rather, this is between the use of some wild caught owls immediately in Experiment 2 and the use of other wild caught owls after being in captivity for one month. In Experiment 1, the owls ate 0.9 yellow geckos (see Figure 1) over 24 hours on average. In Experiment 2, the owls ate 0.7 yellow geckos (see Figure 2) over 24 hours on average. Thus, if the owls had been kept in captivity right between the two lengths of these experiments, it is safe to assume that they would eat 0.8 (right in the middle) yellow geckos on average over a 24 hour period. This is why the correct answer is D.

8. Correct answer: **J**. This question is going to require you to do a little bit of basic math. Add up the number of geckos eaten in Figure 1, then do the same things with Figure 2 and 3, and see what the progress is on the number of geckos eaten over the three

experiments. Figure 1 shows an average of 0.9 + 0.8 + 0.7 + 0.5 + 0.5 = 3.4 geckos eaten. Figure 2 shows an average of 0.7 + 0.5 + 0.6 + 0.4 + 0.4 = 2.6 geckos eaten. So far, that's a decrease, which eliminates answer choices F and H, both of which propose an increase. Then finally, Figure 3 shows 1.0 + 0.4 + 0.7 + 0.6 + 0.6 = 3.3 geckos eaten. Thus, the number of geckos eaten goes back up from Figure 2. This is why the correct answer is J, which properly says that the numbers first go down, then up again.

9. Correct answer: **C**. First, understand this this question asks for which color is *least likely* to be found thriving in the habitat of the owl. In other words: which of the following colors is most likely to be eaten by the owl? Second, recognize that getting this question right will require reference to the correct pool of data. You don't need to reference all three figures (which would actually be bad). Instead, see that Figure 1 is the best data to use because the owls in the experiment were put into the habitat the same day they were caught (in other words, they're more wild than the others). The two color geckos in Experiment 1 that are eaten the most are yellow and white, which is why the correct answer is C; a yellowish-white gecko is most likely to be eaten in the wild, and thus least likely to thrive.

10. Correct answer: **G**. You might be tempted to select "Yellow" because its bar on the bar graph is the tallest. However recall that the bar on the bar graph is in reference to how many geckos are eaten. Thus, it is *least likely* that yellow would be the last remaining gecko since it's the most likely to be eaten. Thus, all we have to do is to look at Figure 3 and find which gecko is eaten the least. This is the white gecko, of which only 0.4 are consumed per 24 hours. This is why the correct answer is G: white.

11. Correct answer: **D**. Let's go through each of these options one at a time and determine if they are true or false. Answer choice A is incorrect because it falsely claims that the owls eat less the longer they're in captivity; this is true for the change from Experiment 1 to 2, but after that (Experiment 3) their appetite starts to pick up. Answer choice B is incorrect because it falsely states that there is no difference in the amount that wild and captive owls eat; while there's not too much difference between the number of geckos eaten between Experiment 1 and Experiment 3, there is a big drop in the middle (which also uses captive owls, though only for a month). Answer choice C is incorrect because it falsely states that captive owls eat more than wild ones; however, the experiment in which the owls ate the most is Experiment 1, which used wild owls. Answer choice D, on the other hand, correctly states that wild owls eat more than captive ones; if you compare the numbers from Experiment 1 to Experiment 2, you'll see that the wild ones definitely eat more, and they even eat slightly more than the owls in Experiment 3.

12. Correct answer: **J**. Let's go through each answer choice one at a time to determine if it contains an assumption that is true. Answer choice F says that the variety of species eaten by the owl is an assumption made by the scientists. However, only one animal species, the gecko, is used in the experiment, and it is not *assumed* that owls eat geckos, but established fact. Answer choice G proposes that is is assumed that the amount eaten by wild/captive owls is the same; however, that's not an assumption of the experiment, but the very *purpose* of the experiment. Answer choice H proposes that it is assumed that the owls hunt less when there's no competition for food. However, again, the amount of geckos eaten is the *purpose* of the experiment, not an assumption. That leaves answer choice J, which proposes that it is assumed that 24 hours is enough time to measure eating habits. This is of course true, since all of the data is based on the owls' eating habits over 24 hours. This is why the correct answer is J.

13. Correct answer: **A**. This question, though it is long, is essentially asking you to see what kind of change is most likely as the owls in Experiment 3 become more like the owls in Experiment 1. The greatest and most obvious difference in the data is that the owls of Experiment 3 do *not* eat very many white geckos compared to Experiment 1 (though the yellow, grey, purple, and brown are all relatively close to Experiment 1's numbers). This is why the correct answer is A: most likely, captive owls would eat more white geckos compared to what happens in Experiment 3.

Passage III

14. Correct answer: **H**. This question is as straightforward as it looks. Sampling site #1 has a depth of 1.30 meters, a temperature of 15.5 degrees, and a pH level of 7.97. There is another site that has these exact same characteristics, which is answer choice H: Sampling site #3.

15. Correct answer: **D**. First, understand that a direct relationship is one in which as one value goes up, another value goes up also (or as one value goes down, another goes down). For example, there is a direct relationship between how much you exercise and how in shape you are: if exercise goes up, how in shape you are goes up. There is only 1 direct relationship among the four options, and that is the relationship between the water depth and the pH levels. As depth goes "up" or gets deeper (such as Sampling site 2 to Sampling site 3 to Sampling site 5 to Sampling site 6), the pH levels also go up. That is why the correct answer is D. As for the others, there might be individual examples of each of these relationships, but none of them are shown to be true across all 6 sampling sites.

16. Correct answer: **F**. Let's go one by one and determine the truth or falsehood of the four answer choices. Letter F proposes that Tables 2 and 3 indicate that EDC's are harder to remove from sediment compared to water. This is true, making F the correct answer. Table 2 gives a much higher concentration range of EDC's in sediment, and Table 3 shows a much higher half-life for EDC's in sediment. Thus, F is the correct answer. Choice G proposes the opposite, that removing EDC's from the water is more difficult, but it was just shown how this was false. Choices H and J propose that there is no overlap of the concentration ranges of EDC's in water and sediment, respectively; however, Table 2 shows that both of these overlaps exist (see BPAF and BPB, for example); thus, H and J are also incorrect.

17. Correct answer: **C**. This question requires you to develop an understanding of the relationship between the concentration ranges in water and sediment of various EDC's as given in Table 2. There are two things to notice: first, the concentration range in water is simply *smaller* (both in its minimum value and range) compared to the concentration range in sediment. For the purposes of the questions, this eliminates answer choices A and B (both of which propose a sediment concentration smaller than the water concentration in the question). The second thing to notice about the patterns in Table 2 is that there is always overlap in the range (like overlapping circles) values. Answer choice D does not have this overlap; its minimum value (4,459) is the uppermost value of the water concentration range in the question (4,459). This is why the correct answer is C: this possible sediment concentration range is bigger than the water range and overlaps with it as well.

18. Correct answer: **J**. The fact that the question proposes removing BADGE from "Sampling site #5" is irrelevant; in other words, the correct answer does not depend on the sampling site at all. Instead, it depends on the half-life of BADGE as presented in Table 3. According to Table 3, BADGE has a half-life of 540 in sediment. Some might get this question incorrect because they use the half-life in water, but that is a mistake. We know that Sampling site #5 has sediment because the second paragraph of the passage says so (and Table 2 gives a minimum BADGE present in any body of water at 4,290, so all sites must have BADGE present). Nevertheless, half-life means the amount of time for half of the EDC to disappear or dissolve. Well, after 540 days then 50% would be gone, then after another 540 days, 50% of what's remaining (25% of the total) would then disappear. Thus, for a total of 75% of BADGE to disappear would take 540 + 540 = 1,080 days. This is why J is the correct answer.

19. Correct answer: **B**. To get this question correct, you have to see the little asterisk (*) under Table 1, which says "note: the deeper the stream, the lower the concentration of EDC's in water." In other words, the *less deep* the stream, the higher the concentration. This hypothetical stream is less deep or shallower than any stream in the study. If you look at the range of BPA concentration in water, you'll see that the range is 298 - 3,620. The 3,620 amount, based on the asterisk, *must* refer to the shallowest sampling site (Sampling site #4). This means that a sampling site that's slightly shallower (in our case, a depth of only -0.15m) must have a BPA concentration a little higher than this. This is why the correct answer is B: 4,200. The other three options are all much to small (choice A) or much too large (choices C and D).

Passage IV

20. Correct answer: **H**. In Scientist 1's paragraph, she states that Io is in a "gravitational tug-of-war", so we know for sure that Scientist 1 believes that gravity plays a role in Io's volcanoes. This eliminates answer choices G and J. Scientist 2 though also believes that gravity plays a role; she speaks of "extreme competitive gravitational pulls", etc. That is why the correct answer is H: both scientists believe the gravitational pull in both directions has an effect on Io.

21. Correct answer: **B**. Scientist 2 is the only of the two scientists who speaks of molten rock being a part of the lava flows or volcanic activity on Io (Scientist 1 believes it is all sulfur). This is why the correct answer here is B: only Scientist 2's position is consistent with the hypothetical finding about friction melting rock proposed by the question itself.

22. Correct answer: **F**. If you reread Scientist 1's position, you will see in the 4th sentence that the gravitational pulls of both Jupiter and the Galilean moons play a role in its volcanic activity; this eliminates answer choices H and J from contention as correct answers. The 5th sentence discusses how sulfur can flow at lower temperatures. Thus, answer choice G is also incorrect as sulfur too plays a role in Io's extreme volcanic activity. Letter F is correct because, although the size of Io compared to Earth is mentioned by Scientist 1, it is never presented as a factor directly related to the volcanic activity. This is why F is the correct answer.

23. Correct answer: **C**. Because Scientist 1 proposes that the lava on Io is entirely sulfur, we would expect those plumes to fly highest. This eliminates answer choices A and B, neither of which get this part of the inequality correct. Scientist 2 proposes in his theory that Io's volcanoes possess not only sulfur, but also molten rock. This would mean that these plumes would be lesser than Scientist 1's plumes of course, but because Earth's plumes contain no sulfur and only rock, we'd expect Earth's to be the smallest. This is where D goes wrong: it proposes that Scientist 2's Theory of Io would generate plumes the same size as Earth's. This is why C is the correct answer: Scientist 1's plumes would be higher than Scientist 2's, which would be higher than Earth's.

24. Correct answer: **H**. Scientist 1 says about ⅔ the way through his paragraph that Io's volcanoes are "characterized by extensive flows of molten sulfur," so this proposition is certainly true of him. That eliminates answer choices G and J. Next, although Scientist 2 believes that Io's lava contains at least some molten rock, she says in the final sentence, "Though sulfur is undeniably present on the planet, both in volcanic flows and plumes…" Thus, it is both scientists who believe that the volcanoes of Io contain sulfur, which is why the correct answer is H: Both Scientist 1 and Scientist 2.

25. Correct answer: **B**. Both Scientist 1 and Scientist 2 believe that Jupiter's gravitational pull (and thus, its size) has an effect on the volcanoes. If something were to change about Jupiter's size, it could perhaps weaken both of their positions simultaneously, but it wouldn't weaken only Scientist 2's position. This means that C and D are both false. Answer choice A proposes that a lower melting point of rock would weaken Scientist 2, but that would actually help her, seeing as she proposes that there is rock in Io's magma and that Io's surface temperatures are low due to its distance from the sun. This means that B is correct, and it is correct

because if sulfur can "build upon itself," then that means that the necessity that Io's volcanoes contain rock goes down, which weakens Scientist 2.

26. Correct answer: **F**. Since Scientist 1 proposes that only sulfur flows from Io's volcanoes, and sulfur is yellow, then we first need an answer consistent with Scientist 1 proposing a yellow flume. This eliminates answer choices H and J. Scientist 2, if you remember, believes that the lava flowing from Io's volcanoes consists of sulfur (yellow) and magma (red), which means that Scientist 2 would expect to see an orange plume in a high definition photo. This is why the correct answer is F: it rightly says that Scientist 1 would expect a yellow plume (sulfur) and that Scientist 2 would expect an orange plume (sulfur and magma).

Passage V

27. Correct answer: **C**. This question asks you to find which resistor caused the greatest voltage drop in the Trials 2-4. The resistor that causes the greatest voltage drop is also, by definition, going to be the resistor with the highest resistance in ohms. If you look at Table 2, the resistor with the highest resistance is R3. This eliminates answer choices A and B, since these two answers give the wrong resistors under Trial 2. If you look at Table 3, you'll notice that it is R2 that has the highest resistance. This is now enough for us to get the question correct, since choice D lists R3 as having the highest resistance for Trial 2. This is why the correct answer is C; only choice C properly notes that R3, R2, and R3 have the highest resistance (caused the highest percent of voltage drop) in Trials 2-4, respectively.

28. Correct answer: **F**. Again, the ACT Science test is never going to ask you to perform math that would require a calculator. If you can do basic or rudimentary math you will end up at or near the correct answer most of the time if not always. Here, you are asked to look for the second resistor (R2) in the series in Trial 4. Specifically, you're looking for its percent of voltage drop. If you look at Table 4, you'll see that R2 is responsible for a voltage drop of 1.081 out of 12 total volts. You may not be able to calculate that this is approximately 9% in your head, but you can certainly see that this percentage is less than 100% (choice J), 91% (choice H) and even 33% (choice G). This is why the correct answer is F: 1.081 out of 12 volts is approximately 9% of the entire voltage drop in Trial 4.

29. Correct answer: **A**. The idea that the voltage drop would necessarily double if resistance is doubled is not supported by Trials 1-4. Why not? Well, look at Trial 1: each resistor has a resistance of 100 ohms, resulting in a voltage drop of 4.0 volts. Then look at R2 in Table 2; its resistance has now doubled to 200 ohms, but the voltage drop is the same (4.0 volts). This is because voltage drop is relative to the value of the other resistors. This means that both C and D, both of which say "Yes", are incorrect. Choice B is incorrect also because although it says "No," it gives a false reason why: there isn't a "direct relationship" between resistance and voltage drop (because it depends on the value of the resistance of the other resistors in the series). This leaves A, which correctly says that the answer is "No" for the proper reason: the effect of a resistor depends on the other resistors' values.

30. Correct answer: **H**. Fortunately, you are given here a little definition of an independent variable as a part of the question itself. To be thorough, an *independent* variable is what scientists (or whoever is doing the experiment) controls or changes. In this case, the student is changing the value of the resistance of each resistor in each trial. This means that F and G are incorrect, and the correct answer must be H or J. The *dependent* variable of an experiment is that which is measured; its value *depends* upon the value of the independent variable. In this case, it is voltage drop that is being measured or is dependent upon the resistance. This means that the correct answer is H: resistance is independent (changed) and voltage drop is dependent (measured). As for the 12V power supply, it is neither changed nor measured, but constant.

31. Correct answer: **B**. This question is asking you to look at Tables 1-4 and identify the resistors that are, basically, really effective or big compared to the other two in the series; so "big" that they account for 50%+ of the voltage drop in their series. Instead of looking through the answer choices one by one, let's look through the 4 trials and tables and find if any resistors are responsible for this kind of voltage drop. In Trial/Table 1, the resistors all had the same value (100 ohms), account for an even voltage drop in all 3. Thus, we can reject that one. In Trial/Table 2, R3 accounts for a voltage drop of 6.0, which is exactly 50% of the voltage drop in the series. However, the question says the we are looking for a voltage drop of *over* or *more than* 50%. Thus, we can also reject Trial 2. In Trial/Table 3, R2 causes a voltage drop of 6.75, which is more than 50% of the series. Thus, this is one correct answer. This is already enough to answer the question correctly, since only one of the four answer choices includes R2 of Trial 3 as an option, which is answer choice B. Just to verify, answer choice B also proposes that R3 of Trial 4 also accounts for a more than 50% drop in voltage. Sure enough, if you investigate Table 4, you will see that R3, being so large, accounts for over 90% of the voltage drop in that series.

32. Correct answer: **J**. *Kirchoff's Law* is just that: a law. There's not going to be such a thing as an "exception" unless stated so by the passage (which it doesn't). Having an exception to a law would be like having an exception to 2 + 2 = 4. Thus, you need to right away realize that the answer is "No." This eliminates answer choices F and G. As for answer choice H, it says something about not having voltage taps means there's no voltage divider, but all the voltage taps do is to measure the voltage drop (or, you might say, measure *Kirchoff's Law* working). Whether or not you measure it, the law is still working. This is why the answer is J, which rightly says "No," but also that the law is independent of the number of resistors or voltage.

33. Correct answer: **C**. By this point you may have noticed that the total voltage drop is equivalent to the voltage of the circuit. Trials 1-4 are all conducted with a 12V circuit, and the total voltage drop by each resistor, when added up, equals 12V. Thus, if

there were four resistors, this idea would still apply. If each resistor has equal resistance, then they will have the same voltage drop (no matter the value of the resistance). In this case, with 4 resistors, each will cause a voltage drop of 3.0 volts (because 3 × 4 = 12), which is why the correct answer is C.

Passage VI

34. Correct answer: **H**. This question is essentially asking you to identify the one factor that didn't affect how long it took the rats to finish the maze. Answer choice F proposes whether or not the rat had caffeine, but that certainly *did* affect the rats' finish times. Answer choice G proposes the new location of the platform in Trial 3, but this also certainly affected finish times; if it wouldn't have affected the times, the scientists wouldn't have moved it. Answer choice J proposes the opaque water, but that of course does affect rat times because they can't see the platform under such water. That leaves answer choice H, which is of course correct; how fast rats swim relative to mice is irrelevant to their finish times.

35. Correct answer: **A**. The opening portion of this question (about rats not being exhausted by a swim under 100 seconds) just means that the rats in Trial 3 did not swim more slowly than in Trial 1 due to being tired (something else was affecting them). Let's work backwards through the answers to identify them as true or false. Answer D proposes that caffeine doesn't make a difference in performance, but that is certainly not true (just look at the differences between Trial 1 and 2). Answer choice C proposes that caffeine has a *negative* impact on performance, but that is also not true; the rats in Trial 1 (with the caffeine) swam faster than those in Trial 2. Answer choice B proposes that a rat gets better after caffeine wears off, but that isn't true; the rats in Trial 3 performed much poorer than the rats in Trial 1. This leaves A, which is correct, since it rightly states that a withdrawal from caffeine must account for the poor performance of the rats as seen in Trial 3 compared to Trial 1.

36. Correct answer: **F**. This question is asking you to compare rats' performance in Trial 3 to Trial 1 (since both trials use the same rats). If you look at the four answer choices, you'll realize that this comparison only needs to be made in regards to four of the rats: Rat 4, Rat 5, Rat 6, and Rat 8. Let's find the difference in performance between trials for all four, then compare to find the greatest drop. Rat 4's Trial 1 time was roughly 52 seconds; its Trial 3 time was roughly 95 seconds (a performance drop of roughly 43 seconds). Rat 5's Trial 1 time was roughly 65 seconds; its Trial 3 time was roughly 85 seconds (a performance drop of roughly 20 seconds). Rat 6's Trial 1 time was roughly 70 seconds; its Trial 3 time was roughly 85 seconds (a performance drop of roughly 15 seconds). Lastly, Rat 8's Trial 1 time was roughly 53 seconds; its Trial 3 time was roughly 55 seconds (a performance drop of roughly 2 seconds). By far the greatest drop is seen in Rat 4 (43 seconds), making F the correct answer.

37. Correct answer: **A**. Trial 3 was performed 1 hour after the caffeine dosage. If the trial were repeated with a 15 minute rest, we would expect the result to be somewhere between the Trial 1 result and the Trial 3 result. Rat 3, according to Figure 1, completed Trial 1 with a time of about 38 seconds. According to Figure 3, Rat 3 completed Trial 3 with a time of about 67 seconds. Thus, we would expect the correct answer to be within this range. This eliminates answer choices C and D right away as they are both outside of this range. Answer choice B looks at first like an option, since it begins with 60 seconds on the low end. However, it ends with 70 seconds on the high end, which would already be outside our range; not only that, after a wait of only 15 minutes we would expect the time to be closer to the 38 second mark. This is why the correct answer is A: between 40 and 60 seconds is the best estimate for Rat 3 to finish the test after a 15 minute wait based on its times as given in Figures 1 and 3.

38. Correct answer: **J**. This question is essentially asking you for the average of the 8 times given to you in Figure 2 (since the rats in Trial 2 were never administered caffeine). As always, a rough estimate is enough. This is especially true when it comes to this question, since it is difficult to tell exact times off of the figures. If you make close guesses, then find an approximate average, you'll be fine. However, another, faster way to answer this question (which is how I would ballpark it) is to draw a line across the *x* axis that approximates the average. This will work because the answer choices are pretty far apart, so just getting it close will be good enough. To me, because there are 5 points above 75 seconds (though 2 of them, Rats 13 and 14, are really close to 75) and 3 points below, it seems that the average will be roughly 75 seconds. However, "75 seconds" isn't an option, but 1.25 minutes and 75 seconds are the same thing. This is why the correct answer is J: 1.25 minutes.

39. Correct answer: **A**. This question requires you to compare Rat 1 in Trial 1 with Rat 9 in Trial 2, and so on 8 times. Let's do this one at a time and determine if any of the rats that did not consume caffeine (aka Trial 2) would have won the race. If a rat from Trial 2 wins (which is the number we're looking for, I'll italicize and underline it. Rat 1 vs Rat 9: *Rat 9* (no caffeine) was faster! Rat 2 vs Rat 10: Rat 2 was faster. Rat 3 vs Rat 11: Rat 3 was faster. Rat 4 vs Rat 12: Rat 4 was faster. Rat 5 vs Rat 13: Rat 5 was faster. Rat 6 vs Rat 14: Rat 6 was faster. Rat 7 vs Rat 15: Rat 7 was faster. Rat 8 vs Rat 16: Rat 8 was faster. Thus, only once (Rat 9) was the rat with no caffeine in Trial 2 faster than its competitor in Trial 1. This is why the correct answer is A: 1 of 8.

40. Correct answer: **G**. Two of these rats (Rat 9 and Rat 11) are from Trial 2, which means they don't really have an "average" in any difficult sense because they only did the maze once; their one time is their average. Rat 11 did the maze in about 60 seconds. Rat 9 did the maze in about 55 seconds (so this eliminates answer choice F: Rat 11). As for Rat 4, it did the maze in Trial 1 in a time of about 50 seconds, then did the maze in Trial 3 in about 95 seconds, which gives him an average of something like 73 seconds. Because this is much slower than Rat 9, answer choice H is thus incorrect. Lastly, as for Rat 2, it ran the maze in Trial 1 in a time of about 85 seconds, then did the maze in Trial 3 in about 95 seconds, which gives him an average of about 90 seconds. Because this is much slower than Rat 9, answer choice J is thus incorrect. This is why answer choice G is the correct answer: Rat 9's average time was faster than any of the other three options.

Score Conversion

Math Raw Score	Science Raw Score	ACT Scaled Score
58-60	**39-40**	**36**
56-57	37-38	35
54-55	**36**	**34**
53	35	33
51-52	**34**	**32**
49-50	—	31
48	**33**	**30**
46-47	32	29
44-45	**31**	**28**
41-43	—	27
39-40	**30**	**26**
37-38	28-29	25
35-36	**26-27**	**24**
33-34	25	23
31-32	**23-24**	**22**
30	22	21
28-29	**20-21**	**20**
26-27	19	19
24-25	**17-18**	**18**
21-23	15-16	17
17-20	**13-14**	**16**
13-16	12	15
10-12	**11**	**14**
8-9	10	13
6-7	**9**	**12**
5	8	11
4	**7**	**10**
—	6	9
3	**5**	**8**
—	4	7
2	**3**	**6**
—	—	5
1	**2**	**4**
—	1	3
—	—	**2**
0	0	1

Here is a chart to give you an idea of how you might score on an actual ACT Math and/or Science exam. To figure this out, first find your "raw score," which is simply how many questions you got correct out of 60 (Math) or 40 (Science), for either or both of the full length practice tests of Step 6. The second step is to convert that into an ACT score on a scale of 1-36, which is what this chart is for. Follow the line from the Raw Score column to the Scale Score column to determine your approximate ACT Math and/or Science grade.

This chart assumes that the environment you created for yourself when you took any of the practice tests was as authentic as possible. Did you take it on a Saturday morning? Did you time yourself with exactly 60 and/or 35 minutes? Did you take it in a quiet room? Did you put your phone away? The more realistic the test experience, the more accurate the outcome.

Remember: this is *approximate;* even the ACT itself uses different charts for different tests! Do not count on this for perfect accuracy.

About the Author

Philip J Martin studied Industrial and Systems Engineering and Philosophy at Auburn University before earning his Master's Degree in Theology from the Franciscan University of Steubenville. He has been a classroom teacher for more than a decade, won a Nappie Award for his teaching in 2022, and has taught thousands of hours of ACT prep in person to hundreds of different students. He is the author of *The ACT English System, The ACT Math System, The ACT Reading System, and The ACT Science System* and the creator of *The ACT System*, a systematic approach to ACT prep that puts first-things-first by teaching content and strategy from most to least important. Along the way, he has earned multiple awards for his short fiction and has published poetry, non fiction, and fiction in print, including a collection of short stories titled *Ephphatha* published by Full Quiver Publishing. Today, he lives and writes from beautiful Daphne, AL with his lovely wife and children.

Made in the USA
Las Vegas, NV
20 December 2024

14863176R00214